Items should be returned on or before the last date
shown below. Items not already requested by other
borrowers may be renewed in person, in writing or by
telephone. To renew, please quote the number on the
barcode label. To renew online a PIN is required.
This can be requested at your local library.
Renew online @ www.dublincitypubliclibraries.ie
Fines charged for overdue items will include postage
incurred in recovery. Damage to or loss of items will
be charged to the borrower.

Leabharlanna Poiblí Chathair Bhaile Átha Cliath
Dublin City Public Libraries

Baile Átha Cliath
Dublin City

Leabharlann na Cabraí
Cabra Library
Tel: 8691414

Date Due	Date Due	Date Due
	8·11·18·	

978-1-906018-88-7

A CIP catalogue for this book is available from the National
Library.

Published by Original Writing Ltd., Dublin, 2009.
Printed by Cahills, Dublin.

DEDICATIONS

For

Seamus McGuiness
Friend, Mentor, and Colleague

And

Patrick Diggins
Advocate and Friend

FOREWORD

Professor Heywood's seminal work on Instructional and Curriculum Leadership sits easily with key objectives of **NAPD**

- To show leadership in the formulation of education policy

- To promote the professional and personal development of principals and deputy principals

- To adopt a proactive and dynamic approach to developing the international and European dimension in schools

- To promote strategies for the development of research.

Professor Heywood's latest work, "Managing and Leading Schools as Learning Organizations" is a welcome addition to the armoury of those who maintain that the key function school leaders is to create an environment conducive to learning. This is a completely revised edition of his 1989 work "Learning, Adaptability and Change; the Challenge for Education and Industry", and this new work focuses solely on education and in particular, the school system. While the principles of management and leadership are universal, Professor Heywood's text showcases Irish experiences. We have a huge amount to learn from other education systems and are influenced by research from abroad but there is something inherently different about the Irish psyche, about the Irish education system as it has evolved (warts and all) that makes us different. By offering us a body of work based on Irish schools, with Irish action researchers exploring Irish examples, Professor Heywood has given us wonderful resource to influence the next generation of prospective school leaders.

Context is everything and how the world has changed economically in the last few months. As a nation we have had to cut our cloth to suit the measure but I can't stress enough the importance of education in Ireland's recovery. As the professional association representing school leaders in Ireland you'll forgive me when I say how vital it is to maintain investment in education and investment in leadership.

Heywood's book emphasises the importance of teamwork and treats of the differing leadership and management styles in an informative and easy to understand way. I particularly like the references to colleagues playing games at meetings for the purpose of being destructive but without seeming to be so. Practioners will readily relate to the fact that staff meetings are often held for the purposes of negotiations but newly appointed or aspiring leaders may benefit from the particular examples listed in the text. The section on role ambiguity and role clarification is particularly helpful.

I am very taken by the assertion that what distinguishes one person from another as a leader is the use to which they put the attributes of leadership in the varying situations in which they find themselves. The ability to recognise motivating and de-motivating factors for staff as well as the ability to make staff aware that they have unrealised potential is a key attribute of an effective leader. Although teaching positions may be fewer over the next while, teacher training providers are noticing that many fine young people are making conscious decisions to enter teaching after a number of years in industry. These colleagues have not yet been tainted by experience and on appointment are seeking more responsibility, not necessarily for financial gain. Those of us already in the system see teaching as a profession but I was very taken by the challenging questions posed by the assertion that teachers are often not allowed to behave in a professional manner towards their clients because of restraints placed on them by government. The whole question of professionalism and accountability is raised in a way which forces us to reflect on where we are and where we want to be. Attracting applicants for school leadership positions is a key challenge and

I was again taken with the notion that the most important goal of selection is to avoid bad leaders rather than to search for good ones, such is the negative effect bad leadership can have on schools. However in raising the issue, the characteristics of effective schools are emphasised along with a section on leadership and management styles to suit the occasion.

NAPD maintains that the primary role of each principal is to be the leader of learning in their school. Managing and leading schools mustn't be seen as crisis management just because the economic bubble has burst or the economic worm has turned. Professor Heywood's continues his realistic and consistent approach to schools as learning organizations and his book is an excellent resource for school leaders in situ, while also providing an excellent insight and template for teachers contemplating applying for leadership positions. It is readable and relevant, all the more so for being based on an Irish educational landscape and is a worthy companion to his work "Instructional and Curriculum Leadership".

Clive Byrne

Director
National Association of Principals and Deputy Principals
(NAPD)
Dublin
February 2009

PREFACE

Twenty-five years ago we began our first course in Continuing Professional Development (in-service education -as it was known then) for experienced teachers in the area of communications, human development and other aspects of management. We found that there was a need for an interdisciplinary text that covered not only the study of behaviour in organizations but incorporated studies of many other aspects of education, industry and society. So the study of wealth creation and the basic principles of accounting were included. Also included was a study of the reasons why nations differ among themselves in their ability to achieve, and through comparative studies of some of them to reflect on the relationships that exist between education, industry and society. The advantages and disadvantages of restrictive practices among the professions were also discussed. We thought that this would provide managers, especially those in education with a basic toolkit. Such interdisciplinary texts were and are extremely difficult to find. This is primarily because there are few interdisciplinary courses. Yet the need for interdisciplinary courses has become all the more pressing because graduates, of what ever kind need a variety of 'soft' skills and knowledge to be able to cope with the problems they have to solve at work and in life. If anything this problem has become more pressing and several investigations support this view.

Paul Chapman the publisher took up the challenge and the text of our course became Learning, Adaptability and Change: The Challenge for Education and Industry. Since then that text has stood us in good stead but inevitably many of the examples have become outdated even though it is evident that the principles remain as important as ever. There is no doubt that the principles and ideas presented triggered considerable debate among the teachers who participated in these courses as is evident from the case studies they returned as part of their coursework. Their reports showed that studies of behaviour in organizations were as relevant to education as they were to industry. So I decided to rewrite the text and take only exemplar material from my students thus focusing on the problems of educators and educational institutions alone. Wherever you look educational policy makers have subjected the education systems for which they are responsible to continuing and remorseless change. Whether or not these changes are desirable or not is a different issue. Equally, whether or not these changes have had the desired effects is another problem. But they do pose the same problem that was proposed by a chairman of Rank-Xerox many years ago 'can we teach ourselves to change?' So in the revised text there is an expanded focus on the problems of implementing change.

In answering this question three principles provided the foundation for the original text and no reason has been found to change them or the general ordering of the text. They are first that the factors that impede innovation in an organization or institution, or prevent a society from adapting to new circumstances, are the same factors that inhibit individuals from learning. From the perspective of change, individuals and institutions may be regarded as learners, or learning systems. Neither individuals or or organizations can adapt if they cannot learn. Thus a key function of those who govern or manage is to create an environment (culture) that is conducive to learning. If intelligence is the ability to select and to shape the real world in which we live, we, too, have a responsibility to help those whom we allow to lead and manage to create that environment.

It follows from this that, if this to come about, a much greater participation in the management of educational institutions by all those who work in them will be required. For one reason alone we are better educated and believe we know as much as anybody else about management. But the consequences and responsibilities of this demand to be involved in management are profound. It will require a communality of understanding and education among management and the workforce, in which the principles to be understood relate to adaptability, and thus to learning how to learn in a changing environment.

In this sense we all we all have to exercise direction and control-that is, manage ourselves and sometimes other people. We are all managers and we are all managed. In a democratic society and in participatory management it is an act of management or leadership to let someone else manage or lead. We all have something to contribute to the task of management, and this is the third principle.

If learning and decision making are held to be the same thing, that is goal seeking behaviours, then the activity of learning is an adaptive response. Since the transfer of learning cannot be accomplished without knowledge, adaptation to change in life, whether in the school, community or family cannot be accommodated without an understanding of the factors that contribute to socio-economic behaviour. It is the aim of this book to foster such an understanding, using in particular the school as the focus. Because it is concerned with the effects of the interaction between individuals, organizations and society, it is interdisciplinary and thematic.

With these issues to the fore the following general questions should be kept in mind while reading the text.

1.*Why are some individuals more able to adapt to changing circumstances in the home and in the school than others, and what are the circumstances that encourage or inhibit adaptation?*

2.*Why do some individuals work well in some systems of organization and not in others, and what are the characteristics of organizations that make for effective work?*

3.Why are some individuals better able to provide management/leadership than others?

4. How do we create learning organizations within the constraints that schools have to function?

5. What knowledge/skills do managers/leaders need to perform their tasks in schools?

Throughout the text I have used illustrations that the teachers who have attended my courses have shared with me either in discussion or report. Their work is acknowledged below.

John Heywood

Dublin, January 6th 2009.

CONTENTS

ACKNOWLEDGEMENTS

Although the framework remains the same as that of Learning Adaptability and Change I have excluded the chapter on wealth creation and accounting, although in present circumstances of the credit crunch this might seem to have been perverse! I have also excluded the chapters on national attitudes to growth, the problems of managing an economy, and the comparative study of educational systems in relation to work. Nevertheless, I remain indebted to Dr Norman Carpenter who encouraged me to develop the interdisciplinary courses in the Department of Industrial Studies in the Faculty of Engineering Science at the University of Liverpool from which this thinking and approach emerged.

The continuation of that work in Dublin was greatly encouraged by Dr Michael Murray of the Christian Brothers to whom I am grateful as well as to Mr Patrick Diggins who established our nation-wide outreach programme. I am also greatly in Dr Murray's debt for asking me to direct the Christian Brothers Professional Development Project for principals and teachers the outcomes of which have contributed to the new chapters 8 and 10. Many of the ideas in chapter 10 were first debated with Dr Richard Culver of Binghamton University and his colleagues in the Educational Research and Methods Division of the American Society for Engineering Education. This enabled me to explore the issue of instructional and curriculum leadership simultaneously within a school system and engineering education. I am grateful to them for their collaboration.

I am indebted to Dr Karen Mayo who I first met at the Association of Teacher Educators in the US for enabling Verity Swan and myself to meet with principals in Texas to discuss their role. To our surprise we found that they saw instructional leadership as their main task.

I am grateful to Dr Seamus McGuinness for his helpful suggestions when reviewing the manuscript. I am also grateful to Mr Richard Geoghan for his help in preparing the illustrations.

Most of all my thanks are due to the experienced teachers who attended my introductory course on Management in Education. Not only did they enliven our discussions with their criticisms and experiences but, they wrote informed reports that related theory to practice within the context of their own work. Many of them incorporated mini-pieces of action research in their study and a number went on to substantive action research in their work for a Masters degree. Some of them had to be declared "confidential." Many of them found that having to prepare papers that showed a wide-ranging knowledge of the literature and required them to relate it to practice was "a revelation." Above all they demonstrate just how messy management and leadership are.

Although the examples have been taken from only a few of the reports I retained ninety-three for the purpose of this study. Looking through them yesterday I am gratified to find that while the problems have changed over the twenty years of the course the principles have not. My gratitude is best expressed by presenting the ninety-one for whom I have names.

They are:-

Mary Ahern, Joseph Bambrick, Joe Behan, Brigid Bennett, Frances Boner, Evelyn Brady, Carol Buckley Dan Buckley, Margaret Buckley, Loraine Butler, Grainne Byrne, Butler, Patricia Byrne, Blathnaid Calhoun, Maura callan, Gabriel Calvey, Carole, M. Carragher, Marie Clonan, Paul Comiskey, Ann Comyn, Fionnuala Níc Conmara, Anne Connaughton, Geraldine Connolly, Alen Craven, Gillian Dawson, Mary Dowling, Mary Downs, Niamh Doyle, Norma Doyle, Martine Duggan, Declan Dunne, Sandra Durkan, Ursula Finnegan, Catherine FitzGerald, Maria Fitzmaurice, Ann Foley Brendan

Forde, Breege Flynn, Harry Freeman, Máire Níc Gairbhe, John Gallagher, Susan Gallagher, Róisin Gaynor, Mary Gibbons, R. Harnedy, Cecilia Hartnett, Catherine Henry, Gerard Hughes, Mary Hughes, Matthias Hynes, Colette Kavanagh, James Kavanagh, Cóilín Kelly, Mark Kelly, James Kirby, Michele, J. Lavin Eddie Liddy, Joseph Lynch, Yvone MacNamara, Orlagh Mahon, Mary McBride, Órla McCarthy, Derek McGarrigle, Mary McKeon, Gerard McLoughlin, Peter Mc Inerney, Margaret Teresa Melia, Aingeal Uí Mhaiein, Martina Mulvey, Geraldine Murphy, Gillian Murphy, Padraig Murphy, Liam Nally, Margaret Naughton, Anne O'Brien, Emer O'Connor, Majella Ffrench O'Connor, Séamus Proinsias Ó Fearghail, Susanne O'Hora, Cynthia O'Reilly, Denis O'Reilly, Betty O'Riordain, Maria O'Rourke, Gretta O'Shea, Maria Gorettit O'Sullivan, Fiona Rushe, Fiona Toolan, George Touhy, Niall Tulley, and Adrienne Whelan.

INTRODUCTION

IT MIGHT BE SUPPOSED that a book on management would begin by attempting to define management and relate it to the cultural context in which it is conducted. This would be a mistake for it would necessarily contribute to the stereotype of a manager as some one 'apart' who directs and controls those for whom he she is responsible. It is a perception that causes society to look for heroes' or Gods among managers who will solve the problems of society and is disappointed when they don't. Governments believe that persons who have led big industrial organisations are particularly able to advise on industrial and commercial performance and more especially on small firms of which they have no experience.[1] This point is no better illustrated than in the management of professional football (soccer). If a team is losing, its supporters will call for the head of the manager, and shout for someone else to manage. Nowhere are there more fallen Gods', than among football managers. The failure of the team to win brings down the manager. Thus effective management depends as much on the team as it does on the manager, and the management task is to build an effective team with the money available. A team can break down if some of its members challenge management. The situation is no different in schools. Schoolteachers' can render management impossible. For that matter, it is no different in university departments. Management (or administration as it is called in school systems in the United States) is a two way process in which everyone is involved in the exercise of management. Sometimes the team can make a good manager impotent, at other times a poor manager can debilitate the team. Each schoolteacher and every school pupil knows this to be the case. A class can choose to work with or against a teacher even those with a high reputation. Within the class all the activities, interchanges, and personal duels are mirrored in later-life performances in organizations. Much learning about behaviour in organizations is accomplished at school, in the family and at play by osmosis, but incoherently so. The schoolroom and the school are microcosms of society and institutions. For example it is now commonly accepted that industrial and commercial organizations have to be learning organizations if they are to survive in the present day world.[2] It follows that the factors that impede or enhance thinking and learning in organizations will be the same as those that impede learning and thinking in the classroom. For this reason the first three chapters of this book focus on factors that enhance and impede thinking and learning.

In the schoolroom the management task is to obtain consent to learning not consensus. Management by consensus can be so safe as to preserve mediocrity. The same is true of any organization. The point is that at some stage the pupil, the teacher or the worker has to consent to direction and control. This consent is an act of management in its own right and has to be freely given. This consent may be regarded as a 'gift', and it may be withdrawn. It implies consultation and negotiation as well as direction and control. In this context the study of management, more generally, may be said to be the study of the conditions in which such consent can be freely given. It is the study of how organizational structure can best be arranged to make the most of the *gifts* that a worker brings to his or her task. For this reason later chapters in this book consider the impact of organisational structure on learning or performance as it is more commonly called in institutions.

Consent allows management to direct and control. Direction implies leadership thus 'consent' enables leadership. The difference, if any, between managing and leading, or where leadership takes off from management is a much debated issue and a source of a vast literature in which discussion of leadership in schooling is no exception. In Holland school principals are called school leaders, and in the literature, more generally, there is a confused debate about school leadership, curriculum and instructional leadership.

Since I published *Learning, Adaptability and Change: The Challenge for Education and Industry* in 1989 I have not seen anything that has led me to change my views on this matter. All leadership involves some management and all management involves some leadership. This view applies as much in industry as it does in education. In today's jargon Leithwood has argued that transformational leadership in vogue with policy makers fails if it is not supported by effective transactional practices. (See chapter 9).[3] To put it in another way an organization has to be maintained before it can be developed, and in that maintenance which is very often 'fire fighting' little acts of leadership are often demonstrated. The models that underpin this text are of servant leadership and management and in this view there is a moral dimension to both roles which is underpinned by the concept of service within inquiry centred organizations. The final chapters of this book consider these issues.

Management and leadership are always about change. Even in organizations where the emphasis is on care and maintenance the work force changes as it ages. Schools are good examples of this point. Teachers age and for some of them this process is accompanied by a falling off in performance. A major problem for school management is the *'renewal'* of teachers whose performance is fading as a function of years' in the job. Of course not everyone fades.

More often than not change is imposed from the outside and teachers have to address new technology, new curricular, new modes of organisation and new pupils. During the last twenty years most education systems in the industrialised world have experienced massive change. In Britain, for example they began in earnest with the 1989 Education Reform Act. Since 1969 in Ireland there has been a procession of changes. As in other Countries some were big and some were small, 1969 was a year of big change when free post-primary education was introduced. During the latter years of the nineteen nineties new curricular were introduced in primary and post-primary schools making possible instructional leadership, and middle-management structures were introduced into schools. In all cases teachers had to adapt. With the advent of free education in secondary schools,[4] teachers had to adapt to a broader spectrum of achievement among the pupils in their classes. Many of them found this difficult to achieve. From the perspective of management the most far-reaching changes arose first from the decline in the number of religious teaching and managing schools, and second from the demographic need to amalgamate (merge) schools.

Whereas the principals' of most secondary schools had always been a member of the religious congregation or denomination that founded the school the congregations now found it impossible to provide principals from among their number with the consequence that these posts became available to lay persons. Very often the persons chosen for these posts came from within the school and some of them found it most difficult to adapt to the new role. They had not anticipated that relationships with their colleagues would have to change.

Amalgamations (mergers) of any set of institutions are threatening and adaptation to the changes that mergers bring with them can be very difficulty. Thus management is about enabling change while at the same time ensuring that those who have to implement change feel relatively secure. Schools do provide a relatively secure working environment and any radical change can be unnerving for those working in them. But life is like that even if schools aren't. Throughout life the continual desire for change is balanced by an equal demand for security. The tensions that teenagers experience when they begin to break away from parental strings testify to this fact. Parents have an equally stressful time in adapting to the new circumstances.

Throughout life we are continually placed in situations where we have to make substantial adjustments to our way of life. Of the major changes that are taking place one is that many of us can no longer expect to have a job for life. We have to anticipate changing jobs at regular intervals, and this has implications for how we plan our lives especially in the provision we make for our pensions. But it also has implications for schooling and higher education for these institutions are charged with the task of preparing us for life. Thus there is a demand that they should teach the skills of enterprise learning and among them *adaptability* and *reflective thinking* [5] It is argued that if the peoples of the nations are to compete in the world economy, they will have to be much more adaptable than previously. No wonder a Chairman of Rank-Xerox titled a lecture, *'Can we teach ourselves to change?'*[6]

One consequence of this is that if workers as well as managers, in this case teachers and principals, are to retain their commitment to the goals of the school in which they work, they need to understand the factors that contribute to or impede the organization achieving its goal. It follows that if the school is a learning organization that the factors that impede innovation in an organization, or prevent a society from adapting to new circumstances, are the same factors that inhibit individuals from learning irrespective of whether they are in a classroom or not. Neither individuals nor organizations can adapt if they cannot learn. Thus a key function of those who govern or manage or lead is to create an environment conducive to learning. Learning involves judgement, and the ability to judge change on it merits involves intelligence. The first chapter seeks to relate adaptation, intelligence and learning and to draw from them a definition of management. If we can teach ourselves to change then irrespective of our position in an organisation we learn skills of management and leadership even if they are only for self-management and leadership. But it is not really a question of 'if' we can teach ourselves to change because in the past we have acquired skill in not only responding to change but in driving change. For this reason it is a salutary exercise to reflect on how we managed our development.

Notes and references

[1] Irwin Stelzer (*The Sunday Times*, 26th September 1990) argues that the Prime Minister's important advisers preside over big businesses that are hardly models of successful enterprise. They are more likely to be ghosts of Britain's past than engines of a bright economic future. *"These estimable gentlemen and their big business colleagues do have one advantage: their still-massive organizations can cope with new regulations. They have lawyers and lobbyists to shape those regulations so that their impact is tolerable. They can spare a few of their thousands of employees for extended parental leave. And they have access to government on all levels should they need a bit of relief from particularly burdensome rules. This is not true of the small, entrepreneurial businesses that will dominate the future"* who are faced with increasing costs and regulation.

[2] The idea of an organisation as a learning system has a long history in management theory beginning with the work of Argyris and his colleagues (e.g. Argyris, C., and D. Schon (1978) *Organizational Learning. A Theory of Action Perspective*. Addison Wellesley, Reading, MA). A somewhat different perspective is given in *Analysing Jobs*, by M.B. Youngman, R. Oxtoby, J.D. Monk and J. Heywood (1978, Gower Press, Aldershot). This was followed up by J. Heywood in *Learning, Adaptability and Change* (1989, Paul Chapman/Sage). The concept was, however popularised by P.M. Senge in *The Fifth Discipline. The Practice of the Learning Organization* (1990) Doubleday, New York. There is a debate about the meaning of and differences between the concepts of 'learning organization' and 'organizational learning.'

[3] Leithwood is cited by Hallinger and Snidvongs (2008) as follows. *"Most models of transformational leadership are flawed by their under representation of transactional practices which we interpret to be 'managerial' in nature. Such practices are fundamental to organizational stability. For this reason we have recently added four management dimensions to out own model based on review of relevant literature."* Traditionally authors in education have related managerialism to the trend for scientific management. Management has been associated with the planing, coordination, organization and control of resources. See Hallinger, P and K. Snidvongs (2008). Educating leaders. Is there anything to learn from business management. *Educational Management, Administration and Leadership*, 36, (1), 9 – 32.

[4] In Ireland there are three types of school in the post-primary sector. Secondary schools are denominational and managed by denominational authorities. They receive their major funding from the state although they pay a very small proportion of the teachers' salaries. They are the largest grouping of schools in this sector. Until 1969 they were selective and depended on the ability of parents to pay small fees. Vocational Schools were established to provide a vocational education for those unable to participate in secondary schools (Act of 1930). Community and Comprehensive schools were established after 1969. The differences between them are essentially in the ways in which they are funded and the Boards of Management controlled. Some of these schools are in the trust of denominational authorities. As all pupils now remain in school until the age of 15 there are few differences in curriculum practice since all pupils seek to obtain the Junior Certificate Examination. Both the Vocational and Community and Comprehensive school groupings

have been able to offer a wider range of practical subjects than the secondary schools, and as in the UK there has been an unfortunate academic v vocational divide. Most of the secondary schools were single sex. However, demographic changes have brought about amalgamations between single sex schools of both types. There have also been amalgamations with vocational schools to create new comprehensive/community schools.

[5] The REAL group of the Employment Department in the UK argued that there are four broad areas of learning that are important for equipping students for their working lives. These are Cognitive skills, Social skills, Managing One's Self, and Learning to Learn. Examples of predominantly cognitive skills are handling information, evaluating evidence, thinking critically, solving problems, arguing rationally, thinking creatively, and thinking in synthesis. Examples of social skills are working with others in varied roles, including as leader and as team members and communicating with others. Managing one's self includes initiative, independence, risk taking, achieving, willingness to change, adaptability, and knowing one's self and one's values (reflective thinking). Learning to Learn includes knowing how one learns in different contexts and being able to deploy a range of appropriate styles of learning. (Cited by Heywood J (1994) *Enterprise Learning and its Assessment in Higher Education*. Technical report No 20. Learning Methods Branch, Employment Department, Sheffield)

[6] Subsequently Rank and Xerox split. The lecture was reported in the *Royal Bank of Scotland Review*.

Chapter 1

Managing from Cradle to Grave: Adaptability and Change

Introduction

Throughout life we are called upon to make decisions and take direction and control over our lives. Since management as defined by the Little Oxford Dictionary is 'direction and control' it is perhaps surprising that that we have allowed the term to apply to specific groups of people when we all manage ourselves throughout the day in whatever role we undertake. To decide to act on a direction is an act of management especially when we may not agree with that direction. One of the most maligned occupational groups, the secretaries, carry out many managerial activities during their working day, but managers don't want to know this otherwise they might not only be forced to pay them more but might also find themselves out of a job. At the same time many secretaries feel they could not manage and do not recognise they are managing when they are, and this may be said of many other jobs. It is only recently that teachers have recognised that they use skills of management in the classroom. Somehow we have come to believe that management requires special skills and high intelligence and most of us don't think we have the 'stuff' that would make us a God. So we continue to believe that management requires some specific skills we do not possess yet that is clearly not the case for without such skills how would we survive. Of course some people are better at survival than others, and without much re-

flection we might draw the conclusion that this is as much due on the one hand to personality and on the other hand to the context in which 'direction and control' have to be activated. Another moments reflection will show that we learn to 'direct and control' our own actions and that sometimes our learning is successful and at other times a failure. We know too that we can learn to overcome our failures. So, if this is the case we ought to be able to reflect on the managerial skills we possess, and examine whether they can be developed so as to help us in the managerial activities of work. For this reason, as teachers, it is useful to reflect on those things we learnt in teacher training about growth and development and the things that we might learn from recent developments in these areas and that of intelligence.

Before we do that, however, it is important to recognise that in democracy as it has developed in institutions we all want a say in the management of the institutions we work in, and in the case of this text schools, and this necessarily makes us managers and leaders. The votes we make in staff meetings are managerial actions since they have the intention of forcing change or maintaining the status quo. They may have the intention of forcing certain individuals to undertake a task. To repeat, a vote is a managerial action. Every person is a manager and in staff meetings or within the context of the school, a decision by an individual to allow the principal to manage and lead, is an act of management or leadership. Thus there is an obligation on each person to accept they are involved in the management of the school and thus to understand the activity of management and the nature of leadership. Finally, it is necessary to appreciate that much management, however reactive it may be, is about the management of change, and enabling one's self and others to adapt. Most of life is the subject of a continuous flow of minor changes and occasionally there are large changes some of them unanticipated. We have to do this in our every day lives and when we direct rather than respond passively to adaptation we demonstrate a high level of practical intelligence.

Beginning at the Beginning

It is now a cliché that the first five years of a child's life are of immense importance to his or her subsequent development. The pathological theory of human development described by Freud and modified and developed by his successors in the psychiatric field is within the very broadest of interpretations accepted by most of us. Many of us would believe with the Jesuits view that given a child of five we will be able to mould them in the direction we require. Because of very high divorce rates in Western society and the development of several modes of alliance other than marriage, there is much interest in the structure of the family. For example questions are asked about whether, (and under what conditions) surrogate parents have an equal and positive effect on the child. At the close of the millenium many were shocked to find that two homosexuals had been granted the custody of a child which had been created from the sperm of one of them by in-vitro fertilisation. Since in Ireland and other countries there have been deliberate attempts through taxation to encourage married women to work, there is an interest in the effects that working women have on the development of their children.[1] Research indicates that parenthood-real or surrogate-is of tremendous significance in the development of the child. [2] Since this book is about management and the skills required to manage we look first at some of the actions parents can take to support the intellectual needs of their children and to prepare them for the changes they will inevitably meet in life.

Learning for life begins at birth as the child perceives the environment and relates it through sight and touch to his or her movements. This process is called perceptual motor skill development. Early[3] and others have suggested that this development takes place in stages. During this process, the infant acquires a knowledge of his or her position in its environment, and so learns to distinguish between left and right, top and bottom, and so on. Early argues that if the sequence of the stages that lead to these discoveries becomes disordered, the child is likely to experience learning difficulties as he or she becomes older.[4]

Of course, other factors influence learning. Erikson has pointed out that while much experience of learning is frustrating, too much frustration or indulgence can be harmful.[5] In such a world infants have to decide whether they can trust their environment and the individuals within it. If the infants continuously perceive a hostile environment, this perception is likely to influence their subsequent development. Mistrust, which, as experience tells us is a common impediment to learning as well as a common experience in employment and sport[6] must influence the drive to adapt negatively.

Although many years old Early provided a theory of perceptual-motor-development with which it is easy to relate. In his theory the movements of the infant who is functioning at stage 1 (motor level) produce internal information that becomes the frames of reference for future activity, in the sense that new actions are checked against this frame of reference- which is called the motor base. This system becomes fully organized when the infant is able to use both visual and aural information.

Both teachers and parents can impede the sequence of development. For example, if a young child is made to draw with a crayon before he or she can differentiate between the hand and wrist, elbow and arm, he or she will force their fingers to draw. But the drawing will be characterised by rigidity because the child has acquired a skill in isolation that is not related to the motor base. Early describes a 9-year old, who when writing at a chalk-board kept his whole arm rigid. He made the writing movements from the shoulder because he could not differentiate the components of his arm. Children need to, and normal children do, develop generalized movement patterns. This provides them with an awareness of their potential for movement at any given time.

Young children have to build an internal structure for position, and this is difficult because all positions in the universe are relative. So children have to use their body as a reference point to define right and left and up and down. Part of the function of this internal structure is the co-ordination of hand and eye. The developmental sequence of this is hand –eye, eye-hand. Observe how the child's eye is attracted to the hand. It is only later that the child learns there are two sources of information.

The child develops its internal structure through interaction with the world in which it lives. And these interactions begin soon after birth. Early describes how a child's internal structure organizes incoming information thus,

As a simple example of how internal organization is used to organize incoming information, consider a child as he looks at a tree some 50 or so feet from himself. He knows the direction to the tree only because he knows the direction in which his head and eyes are pointing. He knows the direction of his head and eyes only from his internal structure. His neck muscles produce information about the location of his eyes with respect to his head. Since he is organized internally, this information from these particular muscles tells him the direction of his gaze. Without this internal organization he will not know with accuracy where is eyes are pointing, and so will lack essential information for learning relationships among objects in space. [7]

One objective that management training can achieve is the provision of cognitive knowledge that will provide an internal structure for managing. It may also through action learning (e.g. role-playing, reflection in action) help polish and develop inter- and intra-personal skills (see below).

To return to the child when it's perception has fully developed, the motor aspect drops and information is organized directly. To illustrate the significance of perception in learning, close your eyes and see if you can locate in your mind all the objects that surround you. The final stage of development is when previously learned concepts condition the perceptual activity (More of this in chapter 2).

It is claimed that children with learning difficulties resulting from the perceptual motor sequence being disturbed, can be helped to overcome them if they can be taken through the correct sequence of development with content and materials more appropriate to their age. Early has described several syllabuses that are intended to achieve this goal. One of them requires the child to construct a large globe, and the sequence of its construction is related to the sequence in perceptual motor development.

There is also a positive side, as recent interest in holistic learning in the classroom has shown. Exercises related to perceptual motor skills can, it seems, help to develop important intellectual skills, For example,

Students are directed to work with their non-dominant hand; right handers with their left hand and vice-versa. They are then led through a series of exercises such as finger, hand, arm, shoulder, hip, leg and foot movements on the non-dominant side. These movements are orchestrated with classical music selections. Once everyone is comfortably engaged in these 'non-dominant side waltzes', the entire procedure is rehearsed mentally. Following this covert rehearsal, physical rehearsal is again repeated from the dominant side followed by another period of mental rehearsal. And ending with physical rehearsal. Once a balance between the two sides is achieved, students are directed to draw and write first with the non-dominant hand and then with the dominant hand.[8]

It is claimed that such exercises not only improve handwriting and drawing skills but also creative thinking, which is to suggest that such thinking is related to spatial awareness. [9]

Several things are happening in these activities. First the teacher gives direction and control, in other words, manages the activity. Second, the child develops direction and control and, therefore, learns to manage itself in respect of such activities. Some children might be lucky enough to be told that they are learning to manage themselves, and others might be even more fortunate if they are told that they are learning skills that can be transferred to other activities. It may be argued with some force that management training should begin early.

Third, as perceptual learning takes place, often on a trial and error basis, so the child learns to adapt. The acquisition of knowledge through experience and the learning of the skills of adaptation go hand-in-hand. As we see in Chapter 2, they can come into conflict in later life, for too much experience can impede adaptation. In any case some experiences must be avoided and there must be some formal learning. [10] For example one does not want children to put their hands in hot water, or screw drivers in electric sockets or touch hot irons and so forth.

We learn from the study of infants that the way we perceive the environment is of tremendous importance to our development. It is our perception of the environment through the senses that enables us to accommodate that environment. We also learn that we often do more than passively adapt to the environment for it is evident that often we also try to adapt and control the environment and this is of course what managers have to do. Sternberg's starting point for his tri-archic theory of intelligence was to define intelligence as *the purposive adaptation to, and selection and shaping of real world environments relevant to one's life (p45)*[11] This differs considerably with traditional definitions and although he placed constraints on it as he developed the theory, for the purpose of this discussion it enables us to argue that effective management may be described as intelligent behaviour. To put it in another way management is intelligent behaviour within the context of direction and control. It is those children who fail to learn to control their environment that have great difficulty in coming to terms with working life.[12]

It is not a wholly passive operation of trial and error that leaves us where we are: all our actions take us forward in little steps. It is well understood that the best way for a manager to create change is to accomplish it in little steps if those who have to undertake the change are to internalise it. So we learn that accommodation and adaptation arise from exchanges with the environment.[13] Neither is it merely a matter of receiving information from the environment, for to adapt we must also provide the environment with information. But there is more to it than that, for we observe that those who look after children can encourage or impede their learning. Finally we see that the behaviour of the child in the cot is not something that is random, but an activity that we can with confidence call intelligent.

It is self-evident that children go through different stages of physical development until they reach adulthood. I do not use the term 'maturity' as physical maturity is too readily associated with mental maturity, yet everyday wisdom tells us that this is not so. I also hesitate to use the term 'mental maturity,' for it is equally a matter of everyday observation that mental maturity, or intellectual development, does not necessarily mean that a person is wise in the ways of the world. In this sense, a person would have high levels of moral and emotional development coupled with the skill of reflection.

Another problem is that a 'poor' environment, say one in which the majority of people are unemployed, severely limits the perceptions of what is possible and worthwhile. Worse these perceptions are brought to school and provide a powerful resistance to education.

Anxiety and Identity

Adaptation is not always accomplished with ease, and sometimes not at all. Moreover, anxiety can lead individuals and groups to resist change totally, and to the extent where strikes continue after an organization has closed down and they are unemployed.

An American psychiatrist H.S. Sullivan argues that anxiety is interpersonal in origin and as such can be used to threaten our feelings of self-esteem. Thus when technology threatens work, many individuals (afraid that they cannot cope with the new technology) resist its introduction, and this has been a characteristic of the history of innovation. But this should not be used in support of an innovation irrespective of the morality of the case for or against it, as for example advances in medical technology. Progress and innovation are not synonymous concepts.

Moreover, at the level of the more mundane, and however we define security, there is no doubt that part of the problem of adaptation is the fear of insecurity. Thus there is a lifelong tension between the demands of the new, and the safe haven of where we are. Thus is Ireland at the present time there is among teachers a fear of whole school evaluation and teacher appraisal. Many middle aged teachers are still accommodating to the attitudes and values that today's pupils bring to their classes. These are radically different to those they brought to their classes twenty or more years ago and such teachers require the support of management if they are to adapt.

Young adolescents as they seek their identity, find, as do their families, the break away from their parents perplexing. The drive to develop new and independent forms of behaviour is counteracted by the security of the structure from which we have to depart. For Erikson *"identity always develops and evolves at the intersection of the person and the social, cultural world. This is the juncture at which one's identity both absorbs and reflects society and its mores, permitting one to function inclusively in the world of the persons era."*[14] This search for identity, with its attendant conflicts continues throughout life and work plays a key role in its development. It happens to managers (school principals) just as it happens to their workers (teachers) and it is a cause of much confusion in the work place. Contrasted with many industrial and commercial environments that are high risk educational environments are relatively low risk and probably more inhibitive of adaptation unless it is imposed. What is clear from a psycho-analytic view of development is that when innovators create an environment that appears hostile to those whom they wish to adapt, adaptation will be all the more difficult. But, *"As a function of work, identity certainty increases, learning (about content, contexts, others and self) shows marked development, self-reliance grows, and career salience deepens."* [15]

So we observe that when we talk about other people, and gossip forms a major part of our daily communication, we rate them on many dimensions. The trouble is that, not only do we simplify and rationalize our observations, but we also tend to give black-and-white evaluations about those whom we judge. Yet, if we were invited to defend similar judgements about ourselves, we would probably argue that such judgements cannot be made because we are complex, and that part of that complexity arises from the way the combined force of intellect and personality reacts with the environment. Thus management is about creating an environment that will yield the full potential of the employed, and as will be shown in later chapters this may mean that the manager has to adopt a different role.

Developing our full Potential

The evidence is that neither schools, or the workplace develop the full potential of their pupils or workers and this applies as much to teachers as it does to any other group. If this were not the case why have primary (elementary) schools in the United

States paid so much attention to Howard Gardner's theory of multiple intelligences in spite of its theoretical and scientific weaknesses.[16] In part it is probably a re-action against traditional views of intelligence and IQ for Gardner is opposed to the view that intelligence is general i.e., that there is a single general factor that can be measured by pencil and paper tests. He argued that intelligence is composed of a number of independent specific abilities, and in his first description of his theories he proposed 7 such abilities (see below). Because of the interaction between heredity and training, we each develop these 'intelligences'-some to a greater extent than others. From the beginning of life these intelligences build upon and interact with each other, and at the core of each intelligence there is some kind of device for information processing that is unique to that particular intelligence. Gardner suggests that the presentation of information to the nervous system causes it to carry out specific operations, which, by repeated use and processing, are eventually generated as intelligent knowledge. These 'raw' intelligences are developed through their involvement with symbol systems. Children demonstrate their various intelligences through their grasp of these symbol areas. Then, with further development, each intelligence and its associated symbol system come to be represented as a notational system. For example, at the symbol-system level there is a response to the sound of a musical instrument: at the second-order level there is a response to music. Finally, these intelligences are expressed in interest and vocational pursuits. The seven competences or intelligences are Linguistic, Musical, Logical Mathematical, Spatial, Bodily-Kinesthetic, Interpersonal and Intra-personal although the distinctions between the latter are not entirely clear.[17]

One of the reasons why this theory has found disciples in schools is that it provides a way for them to recognize the worth of each individual in the group and to avoid labelling and ranking according to academic achievement. We all know people who are highly successful in sport and music who are unlikely to be highly rated by tests of academic intelligence. Whether or not these skills equate with intelligence is a different matter. We all know sports players who while talented seem to lack intelligence both on and off the field. In managerial terms they do not seem to able to manage their behaviour. The value of Gardner's theory seems to be as a reminder that in any group of people (pupils) there is a wide variety of talent which schools and organizations (see Ch's 2 and 4) do not exploit. Indeed as MacFarlane Smith [18] showed many years ago in England the curriculum can be restrictive of development particularly in the secondary school. He argued that the supposed shortage of scientists and engineers in England was due to the fact that the traditional grammar school curriculum neglected those subjects that could develop spatial ability (one of Gardner's intelligences) which is necessary for understanding in science and engineering.

Development in the psycho-motor and inter and intra-personal domains is a reminder that education, at least in its pretensions, is as much concerned with the affective and psychomotor as it is with the cognitive, and it is a reminder that managers in particular require skill in the affective domain. In the UK, for example, it seems to be accepted that this is the case and that the products (graduates) of higher education should possess skills in both domains (see figure 1.1).[19] Yet, it would seem that the teaching methods in some primary and post-primary education systems coupled with the subjects to be learnt (i.e. whole class teaching) prevent the development of skills in the affective domain that would necessarily have to be achieved by other teaching methods (e.g. cooperative learning, role playing).

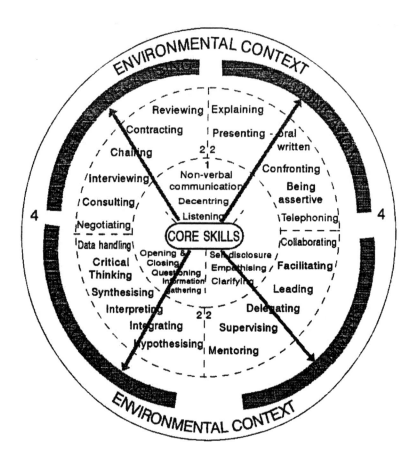

Zone 1. Core skills.

Zone 2 Group skills

Zone 3. Skills in an organizational Context (1st Quadrant Communication then teamwork, problem solving (creativity) and management and organizing),

Zone 4. Environmental Context.

Figure1.1. The Personal Transferable Skills developmental model of the University of Sheffield's Personal Skills Unit (cited in Heywood, 1994 and reproduced with the permission of the Director). Derived from an analysis of 10, 000 job adverts for graduates in Britain by S. Green (1990) *Analysis of Personal Transferable Skills Requested by Employers in Graduate Recruitment Advertisements in June 1989.* Personal Skills Unit, University of Sheffield.

Emotional Intelligence

Developments in thinking about this area were set in motion when Mayer and Salovey published a paper on the intelligence of emotional intelligence.20 This concept of emotional intelligence was popularised a couple of years later by Daniel Goleman. In his thesis he blurred the distinction between Gardner's interpersonal and intrapersonal intelligences.[21] Mackintosh uses the term Social intelligence and points out that it may also be called personal intelligence. In terms of theories of intelligence the concept is controversial since it proposes that there is a social intelligence that is independent of the intelligence measured by IQ tests.[22] However, it is not the purpose of this chapter to become involved in that controversy (except in the notes) but to draw attention to the fact that interpersonal relationships draw on the emotions and can override intelligent cognition to the detriment of the 'situation' being dealt with at the time. Lay people in their everyday observations of people talk about intelligent behaviour, persons being too emotional, and silly (stupid) behaviour.

Robert Sternberg and colleagues found that lay persons think there is a 'social intelligence.' They studied the implicit theories of intelligence held by lay people. They found that the lay persons thought intelligence involved problem solving ability, verbal ability, and social competence (see exhibit 1.1). They also obtained the views of experts in the field. When they compared the two groups they found that the main differences between the groups were (1) that the experts thought motivation was important in 'academic intelligence,' and (2) the social-cultural aspects of intelligence were stressed more by the lay respondents than the experts.

1. Practical Problem Solving Ability
Reasons logically and well, identifies connections among ideas, sizes up situations well, gets to the heart of problems, interprets information accurately, makes good decisions, goes to original sources of basic information, poses problems in an optimal way, is a good source of ideas, perceives implied assumptions, and conclusions, listens to all sides of an argument , and deals with problems resourcefully.

2. Verbal Ability
Speaks clearly, and articulately, is verbally fluent, converses well, is knowledgeable about a particular field, studies hard, reads with high comprehension, reads widely, deals effectively with people, writes without difficulty, sets time aside for reading, displays a good vocabulary, accepts social norms, and tries new things.

3. Social Competence
Accepts others for what they are, admits mistakes, displays interest in the world at large, is on time for appointments, has social conscience, thinks before speaking and doing, displays curiosity, does not make snap judgements, makes fair judgements, assesses well the relevance of information to the problem in hand, is sensitive to other people's needs and desires, is frank and honest with self and others, and displays interest in the immediate environment.

Exhibit 1.1. An implicit theory of intelligence derived by R. J. Sternberg, B.E. Conway, J.L Ketron, and M. Bernstein (1981). People's conception of intelligence. *Journal of Personality and Social Psychology*, 41, 37-55., cited in Sternberg, R.J. (1985). Beyond IQ. A Triarchic Theory of Human Intelligence. Cambridge University Press, Cambridge. P 58.

Dick Culver lists 13 attributes that an academic programme would have to incorporate if it were to focus on the development of emotional intelligence. These are self-awareness, personal decision-making, managing feelings, handling stress, empathy,

Self-awareness: Observing yourself and recognizing your feelings with a view to action or trying to change action in specified circumstances. This can include mode of study, reactions in people etc.

Personal decision-making: Examining one's actions and predicting the consequences. Knowing the basis of the decision i.e. cognition or feeling. This covers the gamut of small and large decisions that relate to everyday actions.

Managing feelings: Requires self-awareness in order to be able to handle anxieties, anger, insults, put-downs, and sadness.

Handling stress: Use of imagery and other methods of evaluation.

Empathy: Understanding how people feel and appreciating that in the learning situation students can become stressed, and that such stress can be reduced by the mode of instruction.

Communications: Becoming a good listener and question-asker; distinguishing between what someone does or says and your own reactions about it; sending "I" messages instead of blame.

Self-disclosure: Building trust in relationships and knowing when one can be open.

Insight: This is different from cognitive insight. It is about understanding one's emotional life and being able to recognise similar patterns in others so as better to handle relationships.

Self acceptance. Being able to acknowledge strengths and weaknesses, and being able to adapt when necessary.

Personal responsibility. Being able to take responsibility for one's own actions. This relates to personal decision making. Learning not to try to pass the buck when the buck really rests with one's self.

Continues over

Assertiveness: The ability to be able to take a controlled stand i.e. with neither anger or meekness. Particularly important in decisions involving moral issues or professional ethics.

Behaviour in groups: Knowing when to participate, lead and follow.

Conflict resolution: using the win/win model to negotiate compromise. This is particularly important in industrial relations, and it applies to both partners in managing conflicts.

Exhibit 1.2 Culver's report of the list of components that make up emotional intelligence from the "Self-Science" curriculum used by Nueva School in California. (Culver, R. S and C. Yokomoto (1999) Optimum academic performance and its relation to emotional intelligence. *Proceedings Frontiers in Education Conference* **13b 7 – 26 to 29, (In the original list behaviour in groups is called group dynamics, but this is somewhat misleading because group dynamics is the study of the interaction between the various members of the group or the study of these interactions)**

communications, self-disclosure, insight, self-acceptance, personal responsibility, assertiveness, group dynamics, and conflict resolution.[23] (See exhibit 1.2). Whatever we think about the concept of emotional intelligence we would probably agree that skills such as those listed by Culver, Goleman and others, are required by managers if they are to manage human relations effectively.

The Management Charter Initiative in Britain demonstrated this point in its personal competence model (see exhibit 1.3). It should be evident that skills in both the domain of cognition and the domain of 'affect' and thus the understanding of and of how one handles one's emotions are required.

Expertise is developed by practice, and we would probably agree that our students ought to be provided with the opportunity to develop such skills in school. But such practice is not given in schools. If this is the case then we are admitting that

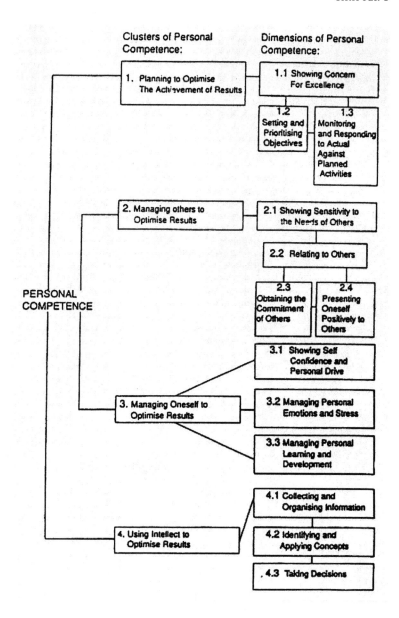

Exhibit 1.3. Personal Competence Model- Management Charter Initiative. Cited in *"Enterprise Learning and its Assessment in Higher Education"*. (1994) Technical Report No 20. Learning Methods Branch. Employment Department. UK

management education in attempting to provide for their development is undertaking a remedial task! Expertise is developed by practice but such practice is not given in schools, at least on a predetermined continuing developmental basis. Surprisingly these dimensions of human behaviour seem to have been little investigated among principals (head teachers) although there is a recognition of their importance.[24] Crawford[25] who conducted an investigation among primary (elementary) heads suggested a working definition of emotion for the purposes of discussing its role in organizations. She distinguished between "feelings" (what we experience), "emotions" (feelings that we show), and "moods" (feelings that persist over time). She argues that we should understand that emotion is inherent in the practice of leadership rather than separate from it, a matter that will be taken up in a later chapter. But there is as O'Connor has pointed out the question of whether it is a competence, a view that derives from the hypothesis that emotional intelligence is more about intelligence than emotions. How we think enables us to control our emotions as well as others. Or is it that emotions are much more than this and that the concept of emotional intelligence is limiting?[26] Reflection suggests there is something in both positions. Whatever else may be said about emotional intelligence it is clearly a concept that resonates with the public at large. Whether or not that is true of the spiritual intelligence that has come into the management literature is another matter.

Spiritual Intelligence

Spiritual is not to be conceived of as religious which is an attribute relating to specific individuals but to a more general condition of human kind relating to the person, the person's interior thoughts, feelings as they are not related to material things. It is concerned with the inner nature of the person and is related to a person's reflective capacity and contributes, therefore to personal growth. It is an intelligence of the kind described by Gardner. It is of interest here because the Church of England has called for head teachers in its schools to exercise spiritual leadership and one of them Tim Luckcock has drawn attention in two articles to the need for attention to spiritual intelligence in leadership programmes for head teachers.[27] In particular he examined the potential of the six leadership styles promoted by the Leadership Programme for Serving Head Teachers (LPSH) in England. He relates the idea of spiritual intelligence to emotional intelligence in particular the later work of Goleman, Boyatzis, and McKee because emotional intelligence is something with which we are now days familiar. In that model going clockwise - the categories of emotional intelligence are- self-awareness, other awareness, relationship management and self-management.[28] He lists a set of principles of emotional intelligence suggested by Zohar and Marshall. They include *"self-awareness, (knowing what I believe in and value), Spontaneity (living in and being responsive to the moment), being vision and value led (acting from principles and deep beliefs), holism (seeing larger patterns, relationships and connections, and a sense of vocation (being called upon to serve a higher purpose)."*[29] One might argue that listing principles is not providing a definition The link with emotional intelligence is evident. They each have cognitive and affective components and a College like Alverno would claim to develop them in its ability-based curriculum.[30] The college lays great stress on self-assessment and what follows from that. The ability to self-assess has become a major goal of higher education in its pursuit of reflective practice.[31] But many, I suggest would say "I follow those principles but am not spiritual." All life is principle driven. What matters is the framework in which it is driven. Luckcock uses a frame-work suggested by Hodgkinson to evaluate whether or not there is scope for such principles in the LPSH course.[32]. The complete list of principles is; First – *Compassion* or, empathy. It has a clear relationship with emotional intelligence. Second – *Celebration of Diversity or valuing other people for their differences, not despite them.* Third - *Field independence- standing against the crowd and having one's own convictions.* That is somewhat different to the learning style of that title. Fourth –*Humility.* That is – *hav-*

ing the sense of being a player in a large drama, of ones true place in the world. Fifth- *Tendency to ask fundamental 'why' questions* Sixth- *ability to reframe.* That is, to stand back from a situation and see it in its wider context. Seventh- *Positive use of adversity,* that is learning from ones mistakes, and finally a *Sense of vocation or being called upon to serve* which fits the servant leader model discussed in chapter 9.[33] Call them what you will, for the most part they are things that we can help to develop, they are personal skills and skills that contribute to intelligent behaviour. Some of course, like humility and compassion are rather more dispositions than skills although it may be argued that reflection on one's dispositions may help them develop. I would not want to deny the importance of the spiritual dimension of life in head teachers. I suspect, if anything that the differences lie in the knowledge which head teachers of differing beliefs bring to their perception of these domains. In any case many would argue that management programmes should help intending managers/leaders acquire those skills they do not already possess. It is important that we should come to an understanding of this domain for most attempts at management training rely on a heavily rationalist model of problem solving and decision when very often rationality is the last thing on display and feelings and intuition dominate. The broad issue remains can we teach intelligence as defined by Sternberg or by those whom he asked about the meaning of intelligence? And if we can does it take the "whole" person into account.

Can we teach Intelligence?

Given the definition of intelligence and management as intelligent behaviour it is of no mean interest to find that Robert Sternberg once asked the question- Can we teach intelligence? In an article in *Educational Leadership,* he answered this question in the affirmative.[34] One of the reasons for his answer was that in his triarchic theory of intelligence he postulates meta-components that are higher order processes that plan, monitor and evaluate an act (or activity). They resemble the components of several decision making and problem solving heuristics. They include: recognition of the problem: recognizing the characteristics of the problem: selecting lower order processes (as defined by Sternberg.[35]): selecting a strategy into which to combine these components: selecting a mental representation upon which the components of the strategy can act: allocating ones mental resources: monitoring the problem solving as it occurs, and evaluating the outcome.

Draw four large squares on a piece of paper and arrange them so that they are adjacent to each other in a single line. Leave a limited space between them. Now ask some friends to describe the process they undergo when they solve a problem or make a decision. The chances are that they will describe some of the processes shown in the boxes in figure 1.2.

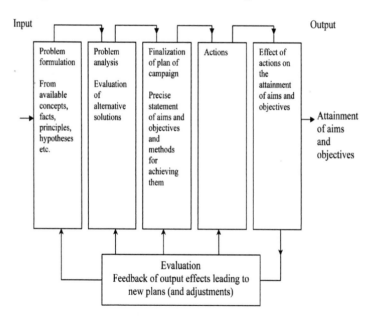

Figure 1.2 A model of decision making process (modified from a schema suggested by F. MacDonald (1969) *Educational Psychology*. Wadsworth. Belmont. CA.)

They may not use the language used in the exhibit but the similarities with the components of the diagram as well as Sternberg's meta components will be clear.

Some respondents may, and some may not, join up the boxes, and the order of the process may vary among them. At least that is my experience of asking several hundred students to do this exercise. Very few put in the feedback line suggesting they do not reinforce what they have learnt. Notice how when the argument is taken in this way that there is no difference between the processes of learning, problem solving and decision making, and some would argue critical thinking. It is in this way that it is possible to consider the organisation as a learning system for the same factors that impede a person from learning skills of problem solving and decision-making are likely to be the same factors that inhibit innovation (problem finding and solving) in an organization.

The model omits an important feature of the decision making/problem solving process that relates in particular to strategic management and that is problem finding. It is a separate and key skill.

When people group together with common goals there is a collective learning. Therefore, it is possible to speak of organisations as learning systems.[36] Learning whether formal or contingent goes on all the time. It is not too strong to suggest that if we don't learn we die. The same applies to organisations. It is possible to draw curves of organisational learning from birth to death, and sometimes incorporate resurrection.

Followed to its logical conclusion then 1. If organisations learn then they also have intelligence[37] and 2, the *enhancers* and *impeders* of learning that are found in classrooms will also be found in organisations.[38] Thus, if we understand how people learn so we can understand how they can be managed. In this sense teaching and management can be regarded as the same thing in the classroom context

Heuristics (or models) that describe learning in this way may be drawn for every occupation as the examples of the engineering design and scientific research process show. Koen defines a heuristic as *"anything that provides a plausible aid or direction of a problem but is in the final analysis unjustified, incapable of justification and potentially fallible."* [39] He gives examples of the concept in terms of synonyms used by engineers such as *"rule of thumb, working basis and guiding principles."*[33] Wales, Nardi and Stager have demonstrated that a heuristic called guided design can help with the development of problem solving and decision -making skills.[40] The stages of the heuristic are *define the situation, state the goal, generate ideas, prepare a plan, take action, look back.* There are many such heuristics of which Polya's for mathematics is perhaps best known.[41] The guided design heuristic has been found by student teachers to work across the subjects of the Irish school curriculum. However, while the results suggested that a large number of students enhanced there learning it is by no means clear that they developed their decision -making skills. The evidence suggests that middle and low achieving students benefited more from the exercise than high achieving students but that this might have been due to the fact that the heuristic provides a structure or scaffold for their learning.[42]

Nevertheless, it is clear that from a very young age children acquire problem solving and decision- making skills that are at a level above that of trial and error and suggest a capability in direction and control that is open to development, and, therefore, to training. The child's acquisition of these higher order skills is very much a function of our perception of the environment and the levels of stress that accompany that perception. Unfortunately much of what is learnt is by osmosis and it remains as tacit knowledge (see below). The opportunity to demonstrate and reinforce the skills is not taken.

Many people including teachers regard the development of critical thinking, problem solving and decision making skills (sometimes grouped within the category of Higher Order Thinking Skills) as an important objective of education. Equally many teachers believe that the system of public examinations circumscribes their development although there is no reason to believe that this is really or should be the case. For this reason management should try to develop whole school policies toward their development (see chapter 7).

Tacit Knowledge

Various authorities have distinguished between academic knowledge and practical Intelligence. The former helps us solve the problems set in school and higher education. For example we can distinguish between school mathematics and the mathematics used by the average person in their daily lives. The latter helps us solve every day problems at work that are very often fuzzy and not tightly defined for which very often there is inadequate information for their solution. Because of our past experience we have built up an informal and implicit bank of knowledge to which we can resort, and this helps us to attempt solutions that are likely to be successful. Mackintosh writes *"tacit knowledge is reflected in your knowing what to do in a given situation (it is procedural knowledge), and getting on and doing it, without necessarily being able to articulate why you are doing it (i.e without declarative knowledge), and without your having been explicitly taught what to do."* [43]

Just as infants learn a large amount of tacit knowledge so the newly appointed principal has to learn a large amount of tacit knowledge. He/she cannot be expected to do this quickly, a fact that needs to be born in mind by his/her staff. Some might call it the acquisition of knowledge by experience, and of course, this is the basis of experiential learning. But there are times when experience can be an impediment to learning as will be explained in Chapter 2.

Conclusions

So far it has been argued from the observation of children's development that given that management is 'direction and control' there is no skill that is peculiarly 'management.' Throughout life we all have to 'direct and control' even it is only ourselves. It seems that some people manage better in some environments than others. Observation would suggest that some managers/leaders are good at promoting innovation and others good at care and maintenance; "reconcilers" as they might be called seem to be short on the ground. This is why debates about management styles are important. This view is consistent with the understanding that societies and institutions require a variety of talents if they are to survive and prosper. In these circumstances it is important that each individual's potential is maximised.

There is continuous pressure on us to change that conflicts with our equally strong desire for security. All organisations change with time some quickly others very slowly. Sometimes it is not every dimension of an organisation that changes. For example the management of schools has changed radically during the last twenty years but the curriculum which is the central activity of a school has changed very little. American writers in particular L. Cuban have pointed out that most substantial attempts at change have not been sustained and that the curriculum (as was) trundles on (as is).[44] Jenkins writing of the changes in the England and Wales curriculum since 1990 said that they simply regularised the curriculum of 1904.[45] Not withstanding, management and leadership in all organisations is involved in managing and leading change.

In this text it is the relationship between the individual and the working environment that is the focus of the study of organizational behaviour. But it is the complexity of the human being that makes behaviour in organizations so difficult For this reason it is important to understand the factors that impede and enhance learning and this is the objective of the next three chapters

Notes and references

[1] For a discussion of the effects of taxation on the family in the UK see Duncan, A and D. Hobson (1990). *Saturn's Children. How the State Devours Liberty, Prosperity and Virtue.* Sinclair-Stevenson, London. Note that there are alternative viewpoints. For example, although only indirectly related to the family see Hutton, W (1996) *The State we're In.* Vintage, London.

[2] see for example Dominian, J (1995. *Marriage.* Heinemann, London. Kaplan, L (1992) (ed). *Education and the Family.* Association of Teacher Educators, Allyn and Bacon, Needham Heights, MA.

[3] Early, G. H. (1969). *Perceptual Training in the Curriculum.* Charles Merrill, Columbus, OH

[4] A slightly longer summary of this work, with details of this curriculum project is to be found in Heywood, J (1982). *Pitfalls and Planning in Student Teaching.* Kogan Page, London.

[5] Erikson, E (1963). *Childhood and Society.* 2nd ed. Norton New York.

[6] See article by Simon Barnes on a cricket Test Match in South Africa in the sports section of *The Times*, December 14th 1999.

[7] Early, G. H. (1975) *Perceptual Training in the Curriculum.* Charles Merrill, Columbus, OH

[8] Jean Huston quoted by Galyean, B. C. (1983) Guided imagery in the curriculum, *Educational Leadership*, 40, (6), 54-58

[9] For example, see Ch. 8 Visual-spatial intelligence in Gardner,H (1983). *Frames of Mind. The Theory of Multiple Intelligences*, Basic Books, New York

[10] One problem is that the naïve understandings of science gained by children often impede their understanding of scientific principles as scientists understand them. Findings such as this led to the development of the constructivist movement in science education.

[11] Sternberg, R.J.(1985). *Beyond IQ. A Triarchic Theory of Human Intelligence*, Cambridge U.P., Cambridge.

[12] This is somewhat of an over simplification since children in all environments learn to manipulate the 'other (s)' with whom they are involved but such manipulations may not help them to be able to more generally cope with life i.e. they require reasonably developed coping skills. An important role for the school is to provide the linguistic data that will help them acquire these skills

[13] In this respect Piaget's concepts of how a child moves from one stage to another are relevant: The basic framework of thought in Piaget's theory is the schema. Beginning with a few elementary schema (frames of reference) the child progresses through the stages, reorganizing old schema and acquiring new and more complex schema. There are three structures that help the child assimilate to changes in the environment when they require a change in existing structures. These are (1) *Assimilation* -- the ability to incorporate new ideas and experiences. (2) *Accommodation* -- the ability to change one's schema in order to introduce new ideas and experiences thereby obtaining congruence between external reality and the child's mental structures. (3)*Equilibration*: -- the adjustive process required for *assimilation and accommodation* -- restoring equilibrium between thought and experience. As the child interacts with the world so it constructs its own knowledge base. The child is an active agent in trying to understand the world

[14] From an evaluation of Erikson's concept by Carol Hoare. Hoare, C (2006). Work as the catalyst of reciprocal adult development and learning: identity and personality in C. Hoare (ed). *Handbook of Adult Development and Learning.* Oxford University Press, New York. P 347

[15] *ibid*. p 353

[16] Campbell, L and B. Campbell (1999). *Multiple Intelligences and Student Achievement: Success Stories from Six Schools.* Association for Supervision and Curriculum Development, Alexandria, VA.
Gardner, H. (1983, 1993). *Frames of Mind.* Basic Books, New York. The comments here are based on the original edition. Gardner believed that there might be many more intelligences.
Critics of his work come from those who work in the field of intelligence as it is related to

what IQ tests measure. Macintosh, N. J. (1998) *IQ and Human Intelligence*. Cambridge U.P., Cambridge) does not say much about social or musical intelligence and nothing about bodily intelligence. He argues that musical intelligence is more normally described as an ability, a talent or creativity. Hans Eysenck (1998, *A New Look at Intelligence*. Transaction Books, New Brunswick, NJ) continues to favour the orthodox hierarchical model. He argues that the 'science' of Gardner's model lacks credibility since it is based on anecdotal evidence only. Moreover, all that Gardner suggests is covered by the hierarchical model, a point which would seem to have been demonstrated by Ian MacFarlane Smith (1964) *Spatial Ability*. University of London Press, London. A more substantial criticism is given by Mike Anderson (1992. *Intelligence and Development*. Blackwell, Oxford. He argues that *"as used by Gardner the term intelligence has no theoretical status. It is sometimes a behaviour, sometimes a cognitive process, and sometimes a structure in the brain. This enables evidence from brains, cognition, and culture to be used as supportive evidence for autonomy, with the only constraint being that the brain structure or cognitive process or the culturally valued behaviour looks like it has something to do with 'language' or 'music' or whatever the intelligence under observation is"* (p67). Hence my view that it is more a theory of talent than anything else, and it is in this sense that it has relevance to education

[17] see Gardner ref. 13

[18] see MacFarlane Smith ref 13

[19] Heywood, J. (1994) *The Assessment of Enterprise Learning in Higher Education*. Technical Report No 20. Employment Department, Sheffield

[20] Mayer, J.D. and P. Salovey (1993) The intelligence of emotional intelligence. *Intelligence*, 17, 433-442.

[21] Goleman, D. (1996) *Emotional Intelligence*. Bloomsbury, London.. Eysenk (see ref.13) argues that the idea that Emotional intelligence could matter more than IQ is unprovable. In the first place there is no way of measuring EQ. If there is such a thing as emotional intelligence then it would be expected that the five abilities that constitute emotional intelligence (knowing one's emotions, managing emotions, motivating one's self, empathy and handling relationships) would be highly correlated. No evidence is presented for this. Eysenck makes a more profound criticism when he notes that Goleman makes no reference to the vast work on personality disorders and that Goleman's abilities relate to personality disorders and coping strategies and that *"what is usually referred to as 'neuroticism' in personality description almost exactly coincides with Goleman's concept."* (pp 109-110). Mackintosh (1998) (see ref.13) suggests there is some limited evidence that supports the view that in so far as some measures of social competence may agree with each other, it may be because they are related to more general aspects of intelligence. (p 370)

[22] Mackintosh. See ref:13

[23] Culver, R.S. (1999) A Review of Emotional Intelligence by Daniel Goleman: Implications for Technical Education. *Proceedings 1999 Frontiers in Education Conference*, San Juan. IEEE, New York.

[24] For a brief review see O'Connor, E (2005). Leadership and emotions: an exploratory study into the emotional dimension of the role of the post-primary principal in Ireland. *Bulletins of the EFEA* No 8, 41 – 58. European Forum on Educational Administration.

[25] Crawford, M (2007) Emotional coherence in primary school headship. *Educational Management, Administration and Leadership*. 35, (4), 521 – 534.

[26] O'Connor cites Fineman, S (2000, Emotional arenas revisited in S. Fineman (ed) *Emotions in Organizations*, Sage, London) in favour of the first. There is support for this going as far back as the sixties from work done by Bernstein from which it is possible to draw the conclusion that the degree of language possessed by individuals influences their emotional behaviour. A Russian study showed how we think through a behaviour before we act it out. See Bernstein B (1966) Elaborated and restricted codes: their social consequences and origins in A. G. Smith (ed) *Communication and Culture*. Holt, Rinehart, Winston, New York. Luria, A. R and I, Yudovitch (1971). Speech: *The Development of Mental Processes in the Child*. Penguin, Harmondsworth. In favour of the second point O'Connor cites Beatty, B

(2002. *Emotion Matters in Educational Leadership. Examining the Unexamined.* Ontario Institute of Education, Ontario, Canada. Doctoral Thesis

[27] The notes in this text are based on Luckcock, T (2008)Spiritual intelligence in leadership development: A practitioner inquiry into ethical orientation of leadership in LPSH. *Educational Management, Administration and Leadership.* 36, (3) 373 -329. See also Personal growth and spirituality in leadership development. A critical analysis of the construction of self in LPSH. *Educational Management, Administration and Leadership*, 35, (4), 535 –554.

[28] Goleman, D., Boyatzis, R and A. McKee (2002). *New Leaders. Transforming the Art of Leadership into the Science of Results.* Little John, London.

[29] Zohar, D and I. Marshall (2004) *Spiritual Capital: using our rational, Emotional and Spiritual Intelligence to transform Ourselves and Corporate Culture,* Bloomsbury, London.

[30] *Self-Assessment At Alverno.* Alverno College Publications, Milwaukee, WI. For a summary see Heywood, J. (2000). *Assessment in Higher Education. Student Learning, Teaching, Programmes and Institutions.* Jessica Kingsley, London.

[31] See for example – Cowan, J (2006). *On Becoming an Innovative University Teacher. Reflection in Action.* SRHE/Open University, McGraw Hill, Maidenhead.

[32] Hodgkinson, C (1996). *Administrative Philosophy. Values and motivations in Professional Life.* Pergamon, Oxford.

[33] as cited by Luckcock ref27.

[34] Sternberg, R.J. (1984). How can we teach intelligence? *Educational Leadership.* 42, (1), 38- 48.

[35] These are not relevant in this context. For a summary see Mackintosh ref 13. For more recent work on learnable intelligence see Perkins, D (1995). *Outsmarting IQ. The Emerging Science of Learnable Intelligence.* Free Press, New York.

[36] The concept of the organization as a learning system is widely discussed in the literature (see also ref 2). It seems to have its origins in the work of Argyris and Schön in the 1960's and 1970's, still much quoted. One aspect of their work was based on the mental health of an organization. Youngman et al (1978) *Analysing Jobs* (Gower Press) attempted to draw the learning curves in terms of innovation of the organization they studied. This work is discussed in ch's 5 and 6. The most quoted book in the field by graduate diploma students in management in education is by. Senge, P. M (1990) *The Fifth Discipline. The Art and Practice of the Learning Organization.* Doubleday Currency. There is a separate field book *(The Fifth Discipline. Field Book)*

[37] The idea of *organizational intelligence* came from Perkins, D (2003). *King Arthur's Round Table. How collaborative Conversations create Smart Organizations*, Wiley, New York. This is a very enjoyable read particularly with those who approach matters from a poetic standpoint. The ideas associated with collective group behaviour and management can be traced back to the work of W. Bion (1960's). There is an excellent paperback by A. Mant in which they are discussed (1970,*The Rise and Fall of the British Manager.* Pan Books)

[38] There has been a recent doctoral study (2006) of factors (*impeders and enhancers*) leading to the implementation of policy strategy in an Iranian University. A list of *impeders* has been drawn up that would be applicable with modification to school systems. Private communication from Professor, J. Sharp, University of Salford, UK.

[39] Koen, B. V. (2003) *Discussion of the Method. Conducting the Engineer's Approach to Problem Solving.* Oxford University Press, New York. P 28

[33] *ibid* p 34

[40] Wales, C.E., Nardi, A.H., and R.A. Stager (1972) Guided Design- A new concept in course design and operation. *Engineering Education*, 62, (6), 539-540. Also among other reports Wales, C.E. Nardi, A.H and R.A. Stager *Professional Decision Making.* Center for Guide Design, West Virginia University, Morganstown, WV, and Teaching Thinking Skills. Research Supports Experience, *Center for Guided Design Newsletter* 9, (1).

[41] Polya, G. (1957) *How to Solve It.* Doubleday-Anchor, Garden City.

[42] Heywood, J (1996) An engineering approach to teaching decision making skills in schools using an engineering heuristic. *Proceedings of the 26th Frontiers in Education Conference*

67 73. IEEE, New York. The remarks in this section do not presuppose that problem solving and decision making are only accomplished by a rigidly linear use of a heuristic. Clearly that's not the case. The heuristic does appear however to help some people learn.

[43] Mackintosh. See ref. 13. p 344. The term tacit knowledge originates with M. Polyani

[44] For example 'democratic schooling.' Cuban, L (1987). *Constancy and Change in Schools (1880s to the Present)*. Paper presented at the Conference on Restructuring Education, Keystone. CO

[45] Jenkins, S (1995). *Accountable to None. The Tory Nationalization of Britain*. Hamish Hamilton, London.

CHAPTER 2

PERCEPTION, LEARNING
AND
MANAGEMENT

Introduction

At the end of the last chapter it was argued that intelligent behaviour was as useful a definition of management as any. Our
starting point is with Sternberg's view of intelligence. He defined intelligence as a mental activity directed toward purposive adaptation to, and selection and shaping of real-world environments relevant to ones life. It is a strategic view in which
we try to take hold of events and direct (plan) the outcomes
even though management is for much of the time reactive, that
is, responding to events as they happen. We might argue that
management in contrast to leadership in the British usage of
the term is concerned rather more with day to day and minute
by minute executive decisions than it is with strategic decisions.
Some might argue that the only time that schools are in a position to take strategic decisions is when the School Plan is prepared.[1] But it is a function of a Board of Managers (governors)
to plan strategically.[2] They will undoubtedly rely on the principal (head teacher) to guide them through the process.

It would seem self-evident that intelligence can be trained
in such a way that the intellectual and emotional traits that
result from heredity and its impact with the persons historical environment are well-disposed to do that to which they are

intelligently directed. Such training requires us to learn about "ourselves" and how we interact with our environment. In its turn it requires an understanding of how we learn and what impedes our learning, and therefore, our potential to adapt. Chapter 1 began this process of reflection by considering the actions of infants as they grow. This chapter continues with this theme.

We saw in the last chapter that the infant learnt by interacting with his/her environment. After the infant has acquired information, he or she can manipulate data in the mind without reference to the environment. Eventually the infant sets him or herself a new task that causes him/herself to experiment again with his or her environment. In this way the infant learns skills in direction and control or self- management.

The activity of sending a signal to objects in the environment and receiving a pulse back, to use an analogy with radar, is called perceptual learning. Thus impediments to perception (seeing, touching and feeling), are impediments to learning. All sorts of 'perceptual' situations face managers and teachers every day. If a 'situation' is misunderstood how may a manager or teacher expect to adapt to the 'situation' without making some error of judgement that may or may not be of consequence. Unfortunately we are all too easily deceived, and one of the greatest deceptions we undergo is the fact that most of us do not believe that we can be easily deceived. If we are to understand the environment, we have to accept as axiomatic, that it is easy to be deceived. By accepting this, we begin to develop sensitivity toward the environment. Even so, we continually lose this sensitivity and this makes adaptability more difficult, particularly as we age. When I began to run in-career courses for teachers, one of my colleagues had to remind me, that during a three-hour session, it is a good thing to provide the participants with a coffee break. This enables them to exchange information about their experiences of school and in particular the management of schools. Later, when they were involved in group-work I made the coffee and much to their amazement brought it to them. In this way I was able to illustrate that dimension of management's role which is facilitation, that is the provision of resources.

Managers and teachers also to have to understand that the way in which knowledge is acquired necessarily prejudices their thinking irrespective of any personality traits that might contribute to particular dispositions. It influences their behaviour, as for example, how they react to body language and dress. Our expectations greatly influence our understanding of events.

Particular sources of learning difficulty arise from ambiguity in language and over- experience. It is argued that many of these difficulties can be overcome if all individuals during their schooling are made aware of these issues and come to view themselves as life long learners. At the same time management has to be prepared to facilitate this learning and release the potential of their organization. In return employees may have to forego some restrictive practices.

Seeing is Believing

To bring home the importance of the need to understand learning in the managerial situation, and to overcome the scepticism of a variety of audiences about the value of the behavioural sciences, I have often resorted to what Peter Hesseling called a 'healthy choc des opinions.' [3]

I have given on many occasions what I called a 'psychological test' to my students. It should be remembered that psychological tests are among other things, used for the selection of people as well as counselling in school, college and work. They are also associated with the measurement of IQ. Depending on the audience I would give a formula which described the reasons why I wanted them to take the test. For example graduate student teachers were told that the purposes of the exercise were (1) to show them the importance of standardisation when setting tests, (2) to illustrate objective items, and (3) to illustrate a test that was culture-free. They were also told I would not look at the scores.

They were required to give one answer to only two or three questions set about each of a number of pictures presented on a screen. They were told that there was only one right answer to each question and that the pictures would be presented at speed since speed is related to intelligence. Several repetitions were made of the point that there was only one right answer.

A typical question is shown in figure 2.1. If you have not seen it before and you look at it quickly you will probably think that line 'b' is longer than line 'a'. However, both lines are, in fact, the same length. It is an optical illusion known as the Muller-Lyot illusion. To their annoyance many of the respondents answered either (a) or (b) depending on where they were sitting in the lecture theatre.

I did the same thing with several other pictures that came from a book by Jane Abercrombie called the *Anatomy of Judgement*.[4] One shows three men in a tube; to most people all the men seem to be of different heights. In fact, they are all the same size. There is also a black-and-white diagram, which the test question suggests could represent snow on a mountain, an inkblot test, or a young child's drawing. When we turn over the page in Abercrombie's book we find that it is picture of a prophet or Christ. Abercrombie writes about the first picture thus

"The face may appear as suddenly as when a light has been switched on. Some people cannot see it with the help of words only, but need some one to trace outline features over the patchwork. The object has not changed, nor has its image on the retina, yet the information received from the object is different- no longer is it seen as a chaotic patchwork, but as the picture of a man, with sharp and clear and characteristics".

It should be evident that how the man is described is a function of past experience. Because I happen to be a Christian I always think of it as the face of Christ. Others without that experience may simply see it as any other man with a beard. Of course when Abercrombie was writing in the nineteen-fifties beards were not popular.

One well-known picture that I use is the picture of the lady in figure 2.2. Is she an old lady or a young lady? There are many other such illusions. Macdonald's once had a paper tray cloth that had a half a dozen illusions on it. So what did I hope would be learnt from this picture show.

First is the ease with which we can be deceived. Second is the generalization that 'beauty is in the eye of the beholder.' Some people see and old lady, others a young lady.The hidden man and lady pictures demonstrate that what is perceived depends not only on what is being looked at but on the state of the perceiver. What the perceiver brings to the problem may 'colour' considerably what is seen. Third the pictures should demonstrate that without some prior frame of reference related to the topic under consideration that it is very difficult to understand new material, and that in these circumstances insight can take a long time and require effort in the search for understanding. When I explain my perception of insight to students I use the rather simplistic anecdote about Archimedes who when he established the principle of displacement in his bath shouted Eureka. We shout or similarly feel when we have established a first-principle to our delight.

However, the most important thing that I wished the student teachers to grasp was that their pupils may not always perceive what the teacher is doing or saying in the same way that the teacher wishes them to do and this may be a reason for misunderstanding. Exhibit 2.1 shows some of the responses that a student teacher obtained when twenty minutes into the period he asked the students to write down on a piece of paper what they had learnt. At the time I was observing the class and as the responses show there was one very astute student.

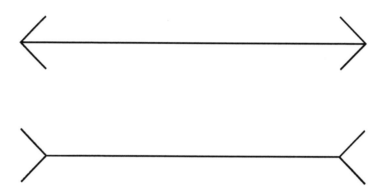

Figure 2.1 Muller-Lyot Illusion.

Figure 2.2 The Old Lady/Young Lady Illusion.

- *I have learnt how a contra entry works*
- *I have learnt to keep my work tidy.*
- *I have learnt how to balance a cash book properly.*
- *I have learnt to look more closely at the question.*
- *I have learnt to be neat and tidy.*
- *I have learnt that if you take your time everything will be correct.*
- *I have learnt that the teacher gets nervous in the class when an inspector is present: and I have learnt a bit more about balancing accounts.*

Exhibit 2. 1

The presentation of material has to be planned very carefully. It is well known for example that the way problems are presented can effect the understanding that individuals have of the problem.[5]

In the case of school management it is a warning that in situations when, for example, a principal is placed in a reactive mode by an unheralded visit from a parent, pupil or teacher and put on the spot, the principal has to remember to keep cool. If he/she does not then they can easily mis-perceive what is happening, particularly if the person is behaving like a grenade in an explosive mood.[6] Action must be slowed down for insight to be gained. It is important to remember that persons who have a complaint, as for example a parent on behalf of his/her child will be highly focused by what the child said to him or her. Time may have to be spent in getting the problem-poser to re-state the problem using different word formulas and in this case to establish what the parent believed the child said.

To summarise,

(1)   'Things' in a classroom, staff room or elsewhere in the
        work situation may not always be what they seem.
(2)   Communication is a two-way affair.
(3)   Communicators do not always perceive each other in
        the same way.

First impressions of pupils can be influenced by remarks
from other teachers in the staff room. It is for this reason that
so much emphasis is put on the need to know what the entering
characteristics of the pupils are in the training of student teachers. There is a case for a general school policy on what entering
data should be collected and this should extend to discussion
of such matters as obtaining the learning styles of the pupils.'[7]
Since our dispositions influence the way we perceive it is argu-
able that trade union negotiations may be more difficult than
they need be because of the different perceptions that the nego-
tiator's have of one another's stance.

Similarly first impressions of a candidate for a teaching post
may not yield the whole truth about a candidate. While the
best-dressed candidate may follow the discipline of convention
he or she may not always be the best candidate for the job. A
candidate who is poorly dressed might be better. It is overall
presentation that matters and a good selection technique for
teachers would allow them to be observed while teaching a class
and not rely on references or interviews alone.

I have always found that persons exposed to this test begin
to search for and recognise the deceptions that continually occur in their own lives. However, I am not sure that they always
grasp the more profound issues relating to perception which
will be discussed in the paragraphs that follow. Our dispositions are not easily changed.

The Problem of Ambiguity

Many situations in life create ambiguities for the observers and they are a powerful influence on human behaviour. They are particularly prevalent in the perceptions we have of the way individuals exercise power and control. Ambiguity is seen in the fact that when power is used *"for a good end or purpose, such as to be generous, it often has the ambiguity of giving a feeling of goodness and of being patronizing to the person who receives."* [8]

It is important to clear up ambiguities because they affect communication, information, interpretation and subsequent action. As Hugh Woodhouse says, *"A consideration of the reality of ambiguity of tension and conflict throughout all aspects of human life can be not just a theoretical exercise but can illuminate the human scene and nerve us to worthwhile efforts in many areas and affairs of daily life."* [9] One of the reasons for stating aims and objectives at both school and classroom levels is to remove ambiguity, hence the need for writing instructions with great care. This applies in particular to official documents.

Whenever there is a conflict in the classroom or school it is essential that the principal or teacher document with clarity what they perceived to have happened as soon after the event as possible so as avoid any ambiguity in any later discussion or inquiry. It may be useful to get all the parties to agree a written summary and sign such a document.

Ambiguities are a fact of life (see p 65). There may be instances where ambiguity enables persons or groups to live relatively harmoniously, as for example, some political agreements. Often the fine details are left for the courts to sort out. But, sometimes it is beneficial not to define roles too tightly (see chapter 3). Ambiguities are not merely inherent in the data presented to our senses but in the way that the data is ordered by our perceptual learning processes. Thus it is that any understanding of human behaviour must begin with an understanding of the factors that influence perception.

The Factors that shape Perception

It will be appreciated that many factors limit our perception. Johnson has listed as many as 37. [10] These relate to prior experience (e.g. recent and frequent events), organizational factors (e.g. conflicts of interest), personality characteristics (e.g. needs, attitudes, and values), and other person characteristics (e.g. ability, age). These same factors influence motivation as will be argued in later chapters. We can see how these function in detail by analyzing the process of perception in more detail. For the purpose of this explanation five interdependent sub-processes will be considered. These are *expecting, attending, receiving, trial and checking, and forming a percept.* They too influence motivation. This model is simplified; perception is not a simple linear process as might be implied from this order.

Before the components of this model are considered in detail it is useful to place them in the more general context of the problem of acquiring information. The reader might on completion of the two sections that follow like to turn to the last but one section on 'consolidation: the effects of experience' which extends this part of the discussion within the framework of a general conclusion.

The acquisition of Information: Learning, categorisation, memory, and the influence of personality.

When we learn, we relate what is happening to us internally (i.e. thinking) or externally (i.e. thinking in response to the stimuli in the environment) and the data is stored in the mind. How that data comes to be stored, that is the way in which it comes to be known is the epistemological problem. For example once learning has begun, one theory holds that we are able to "match" our perception of the environment to what we know, however poor that match might be. It is the nature of the "match" which is the epistemological problem. Aquinas holds that there is no question of there being a correspondence of two disparate things, an object and the thought are just the same form in different subjects and different manners of existing[11], and thought is essentially universal.

According to Aquinas, we are made up of a sense-image *(phantasma)* of what is sensed because sensitive creatures possess an imaging faculty *(phantasia)*, and the intellect acts on the sense image to make it the object of thought. Aquinas uses the analogy of light shining on the sense-image so as to reveal what is intelligible to describe the active intellect. In this way the object of thought is something that is made by the intellect. The likeness is of the *form* not the *material*. So for Aquinas the matching device is the active intellect. From the perspective of learning without a matching device we would not be able to label the objects in the environment. We would not be able to label the cat without information in the mind that contains within it confirmation of the attributes and values that uniquely represent the category cat. The mind does not have to possess all the information about cats for a person to be able to deduce that " *it may be a cat*". But the mind does have to have acquired that information at some previous time for without such internal information we cannot interpret the outer world. This presupposes a memory system and, as is evident from our own experience perceptual experiences leave perceptual traces that never completely disappear. They can be organized into systems and sub-systems.

Neither does the evidence of experience support the view that this "matching" is a passive or perfect activity for our past experience *"directs our searching activity and sets the parameters of the perceptual act."* [12] All of which is to say that our perceptual activities are influenced by our intelligence, personality, interests and values, on the one hand, while on the other hand they are influenced by the environment which informs those parameters. The addition of the information contained in each perceptual act adds to our perceptual 'frames of reference' and therefore, transforms our perceptual world.

Searching and Sampling: Our limited Capacity.

Searching is an activity. It implies that that knowledge is not simply impressed on the mind. Active learning requires that we sample the objects and events in the environment for it is equally self-evident that we cannot deal with all of the information available in the environment.

Much of this information, if not most, must be left as "noise" which hopefully will not interfere with our perceptual focussing. The fact that our perceptual capacity is limited means that we have to select with great care what it is we want to learn, and this applies just as much to a manager as to a learner. Often individuals are asked to do too many things at once with the result that some or all are not learnt (or done effectively).[13] As will be seen in chapter 3 the demands on a principal may cause role conflict.

These constraints apply just as much to listening and touch as they do to visual perception, and even to the perception of rhythm. It seems that where changes of emphasis are intended by spoken or written instructions there is no guarantee that respondents will implement those instructions as desired.[14] Such demands can make decision making difficult. It is for this reason that decision-making strategies have been developed to help individuals and groups make choices. (eg brainstorming).

At a more practical level, I am reminded of situations that are complex, in which perception is made more difficult by the available information; as for example, when driving an automobile at night in a well-lit neighbourhood. In some jobs because of boredom an operative might undertake other activities which could interfere with each other. For example a telephone operator who is also a receptionist who is skim reading a magazine at the same time. The performance of such tasks may be subject to perceptual interference.

Sampling and focussing are as much influenced by ourselves as they are by events. As we shall see, we can be made to attend to events, and this is part of the task that teachers and managers have. The need 'to be', hence the need 'to learn' means that we are always being prepared for perceptual events, and we search at a low level of drive and so continue to anticipate the world.

A model that many teachers have found attractive to explain how we anticipate events is due to George Kelly.[15] It is called Personal Construct Theory. In this model individuals behave as scientists undertaking research. They develop "constructs" and use them to form expectations and to plan their behavioural responses. They compare their new perceptions with their previously formed constructs for validation. It is a theory of expectations.

Kelly believed that persons are organisms in continual activity, and that learning and motivation are built into their system. While this is consistent with the 'necessary and contingent' view of learning taken in this chapter, it does not deny as Kelly does that there are no special inner forces such as drives, instincts and motives required to account for human motivation. Rather it takes the view that at some times *the person will be motivated to behave as a scientist. Individuals use a variety of models of behaviour according to the circumstances appropriate to those in which they find themselves*[16]. But surely they are driven by what Newman calls *"first principles?"*[17]

The essence of *"first principles is that they are conclusions or abstractions from particular experiences"*. They are to quote Miller *"the initial premises of the reasoning process, but they are by themselves the fruits of experience"*. Newman argues that within the objects of knowledge, that is those things which exist externally to ourselves there is a driving force within us which is directed toward the individual phenomena one by one. He calls this driving force in animals 'instinct' and in human beings *'intuition', and this force "spontaneously impels us, not only to bodily movements, but to mental acts"*.[18] The universals (and principles)[19] which we accept arise from the testimony of sense experience which demonstrates that the world with which we are in contact has its own rules *"and that all the phenomena of sense proceed from it"*. (Such universals derive from successive approximations).

The use to which an individual puts first principles makes a person what he or she is. *"By them we form our view of events, of deeds, of persons, of lines of conduct, of aims, of moral qualities, of religions. They constitute the difference between man and man; they characterize them. As determined by his first principles, such is his religion, his creed... they are in short the man."* Newman's view is in the Anglo-Saxon tradition which gives primacy to concrete experience but he differs somewhat in that he argues that the testimony of the mind (i.e. inner moral sensations) is as real as the concrete experience of sight, sound and touch. What is concrete exerts a force and makes an impression on the mind that nothing that is abstract can rival[20]. As Miller[21] explains the mind involves an intellectual act of insight along with the likeness of sense experience in the imagination.

This position has many similarities with those of Bruner and Kelly. For them people actively engage in the construction of their world. Thus they shape their environment and are shaped by it *"Man does not respond to a world that exists for direct touching. Nor is he locked in a prison of his own subjectivity. Rather, he represents the world to himself and acts on behalf of or in reaction to his intentions."*[22]

It is for this reason that training in problem solving and decision making provides for the development of skill in hypothesis formation. I find that even post-graduate teacher trainees have difficulty in formulating hypotheses about their classroom problems without guidance and training. Thus Bruner's theory of perceptual expectancy is very similar to Kelly's.[23] Individuals hypothesize about a likely event, receive confirmation about it from information in the environment, which brings about a confirmatory response from the individual.

Bruner uses the term intuition in a very similar way. It implies the act of grasping the meaning or significance or structure of a problem without explicit reliance on the analytic apparatus of one's craft. It is the intuitive mode that yields hypotheses quickly, that produces interesting combinations before their worth is known. It precedes proof; indeed it is what the techniques of analysis and proof are designed to test and check.[24] Intuition, says Newman, is a force that spontaneously impels us to mental acts.

Our expectations are therefore a major influence on our search mechanism, and it is with these that the simplified model of the perceptual process begins.

Expectancy and Expectations [25]

The expectancy theory of perception suggests that we perceive more readily and more clearly those events that we expect. Our expectations are maps of the future that we have constructed on the basis of past experience. This is also one of the reasons why teachers sometimes tell their students what the objectives of the lesson are. Allport[26] used the term 'set' to describe this stage of expectancy. 'Set' in this sense refers to the way that people receive information in that, generally, information is received more quickly and understood when it has either been brought to their attention or is of interest to them. Formal education becomes difficult for some students and impossible for others because one of its tasks is to bring uninteresting information thought to be of general importance into the perceptual frameworks of the recipients.

Organisational cultures provide their own expectancy maps with a whole range of signals (physical, financial, personal, reward systems, leadership, organisational structure).[27] In schools principals and teachers spend much of their time trying to influence the perceptions of others, that is, apart from their pupils.[28]

According to expectancy theory it is only by developing expectation frameworks that we can effectively sample the available information, and cope with the events with which we are faced. This is how individuals and organisations socialize each other. Both try to shape expectations by creating their own perceptions for us to perceive.

The Pygmalion effect in education has been well described.[29] As in management it has been shown to work both constructively and destructively. In education students have expectations of examinations and tests. They attempt to predict the questions that will be set, and to prepare for examinations by the development of model answers which will meet their expectations.[30] If the questions are set in such a way that they do not perceive their expectations to have been met they are unable to cope with the situation in which they find themselves because they allow their first impressions to dominate their thinking process.

Rist[31] in a study of teacher expectation and achievement found that a kindergarten teacher classified students into slow and fast learners from her initial impressions of physical appearance, forthrightness of behaviour and language usage. She related her impressions to an ideal type which was a social-class based model of the successful child i.e. middle class. The two groups were managed in different ways. Those considered to be "fast" students were encouraged whereas those considered to be "slow" students were controlled. Thus the teacher's expectations came to be fulfilled and at succeeding grade levels. In its turn this fuelled the self-fulfilling prophecy which had arisen from these initial impressions. Other writers explain findings such as these by pointing out that student perceptions of their teachers' expectations could influence their self-image in such a way that it is reflected in one way or another their level of achievement.[32]

Several important studies have been made of teacher attitudes to gender. Thus in a nursery school boys misdemeanours were more likely to be noticed than girls for girls are assumed to be better behaved. Adults expect children to fit in with their gender role expectations and in consequence are more alert to those behaviours. Gender role typing in the very early years has a powerful influence on the attitudes, behaviour and values of children' as they grow older.[33] In high schools in England it was found that teachers were more attached to those students they expect to pass the final public examination (A Level). Even so boys were much more likely to receive this concern than girls from teachers of either sex..[34]

It is clear that teachers have to be very clear about what they are teaching and like medical practitioners need to keep themselves up to date with current thinking. For example oversimplified views of science can have quite adverse effects on learning. A report of a study in Canada published at the time of writing showed that the women performed better in a mathematics test when they were told that female underachievement was due to social factors than when they were told it was due to the genetic predisposition of their sex. Thus the way ideas of nature and nurture are perceived can influence our performance.[35]

Suffice it to say that at this stage our expectations of what and why students achieve and why workers are motivated to work are functions of models or stereotypes which we have created that inform our perceptions.[36] We will pursue this in Chapter 4. In any event principals need to be aware of these problems since they have a bearing on the effectiveness of the school, and this implies careful monitoring of pupil performance.

Chia-Lin Hsieh and Jianping Shen[37] in a small-scale study in the United States investigated the perceptions (expectations) which teachers', principals' and superintendents' had of leadership in American schools. They distinguished between the domains of knowledge, skill and values. They found there were fewer differences between the groups in respect of values than in the other two domains. This suggested that irrespective of task there were common moral values. However, the roles that the different actors played seemed to influence their judgements. Superintendents have to work with different kinds of interest groups in the power structure. Thus leadership is viewed as a process of negotiation, bargaining and exchange. But they also view leadership as identification of values that govern their actions. They consider leadership from practical and moral perspectives. In contrast principals' view leadership from managerial, personality and moral perspectives. For teachers leadership is perceived at the personal level. If they know about the personality of the leader then they can predict what the leader will do in particular circumstances.

Comiskey found similarly[38] in respect of the attitudes of stakeholder organizations to middle management. He interviewed persons (principals) mainly that were representative of seven stakeholder organizations and found that the views of the representatives of the Irish Primary Principals Network (IPPN) and the Irish National Teachers Organization (INTO) differed. He writes- *"while stakeholder organisations support a collegial model of school leadership in which a team ethic is espoused the role of the school principal within such collegial systems is interpreted differently."*

The union representative (INTO) took the role of the principal to be that of primus inter pares whereas the representative of IPPN aligned the role with a Chief Executive Officer model. Of course his sample was very small but it is not unlikely that such views would be distributed among principals. As he put, it the debate revolves around the maintenance of "power". Such orientations influence both the motivation of their holders as well as those for whom they are responsible. We shall return to this topic in chapter 4.

Inevitably such differing perceptions create tensions, and in Ireland it would be interesting to know what perceptions "lay" persons on managerial boards have of leadership and how this conditions their behaviour within those boards.

Further support for the theoretical position proposed in this report is to be found from the fact that the investigators considered that conceptions (expectations) of leadership change when teachers are promoted to principal, and principals are promoted to superintendents. In any case, it is evident that experience within a group influences expectations.

In a later chapter it will be argued that it is axiomatic that a major dimension of the role of a principal (head teacher) is to facilitate teaching and learning in the classroom. Hsieh and Shen found that in the US both principals and superintendents tended to emphasise instructional leadership.[39] It may be argued that this is necessary if 'good' teaching is to be encouraged. But in Ireland Michael Murray and this writer found that principals ignored instructional leadership but this was explained by the history of the culture in which they work where there was a tradition that they should not be involved in instruction.[40] Teachers did not have this expectation of principals and in consequence there were not tensions in this area. At the same time it added to the difficulty that schools had in removing "failing" teachers.

Expectancy and First Impressions

As indicated previously the importance of first impressions cannot be sufficiently emphasised. In the example of the teacher cited above it is clear that first impressions dominated the 'learning' of the teacher. Few of us are free from the prejudice created by first impressions. These first impressions are often conditioned by stereotypical images acquired in our previous experience. As we have seen these are all too easily applied to the roles that we expect girls and boys to adopt in relation not only to behaviour but to the curriculum.

As we have seen objectivity in managing is the ability to stand back from those first impressions because of the dominance they exert over subsequent perceptions.[41] Because these impressions are so often difficult to shift many persons find it difficult to adapt to new circumstances. Clearly part of management development is to get managers to reflect on their practice and to come to realise their own stereotypical behaviour. When we see the power of advertising and the media on our perceptions it is easy to argue that an understanding of the factors which influence our behaviour and in particular our objectivity should be a necessary component of the curriculum at all levels of education.

At the level of personal interaction between principals and teachers, and teachers and pupils, we need constantly to be reminded that appearances do count. For example it seems that the facial expressions that demonstrate our emotions may be culturally influenced[42], and if not understood therefore, a source of misunderstandings in society, and especially in school. Unfortunate though it may be body language (dress, expression, stance) sends powerful and immediate signals which we can and often do misread. How often have you been told that you conveyed the wrong impression? The trouble is that these impressions last and we do not seem to learn from our own experience of the impressions that people have of us.

Expectancy and Cognitive Dissonance

An important characteristic of memory and perception is that we tend to remember our successes and forget our failures.[43] At the same time we tend also to be very consistent in our attitudes and opinions.[44] Apart from the fact that this makes it more difficult to adapt, we try to adapt, by accommodating new perceptions that possess values also contained within our own value maps. We tend to use sets that have served us well in the past. The same is true of problem solving: we tend to use the same heuristic whatever the problem.[45] Bruner has called this persistence forecasting and it can in a new situation prevent us from using more efficient strategies. We tend to believe in the advantages of what we already possess. Dissonance or downshifting arises when we have to accommodate a new value system with which we have no empathy.

For example when a subject that we have to learn is cognitively complex and where values are involved, such as in political studies, a student may be in disagreement with the views held by the teacher. In these circumstances there may be considerable resistance to learning. Apparently this is particularly likely to be the case if the students are only mildly critical of the teacher's standpoint However as Marshall[46] shows, a teacher can cause learning through his teaching style, even if his or her rating with the students deteriorates during the course.

Since we impose meaning on the objects of knowledge it should come as no surprise to find that a pupil can deliberately impose misunderstanding in order to achieve consistency between the message and his feelings. If there is consistency, a pupil can change his attitude to a teacher from like to dislike if the teacher's messages appear to be untenable. This can happen in university when first-year students have to cope with certain value propositions in the social and behavioural sciences: anything that is contrary to the student views can create such dissonance. As a Catholic, I found the study of some aspects of sociology most difficult because of the conflicts created by my own value system. Clifford Longley reported that a similar thing happened to at least one key but conservative figure in the English delegation to the Vatican Council in 1962.[47] *"The ability of people not to hear pronouncements that they are not*

*expecting to hear, or to dismiss the importance of the informa-
tion presented to them because it does not fit into their prevailing mind-set appears to have blocked Derek Worlock's ears
to the message of the Pope's address".* Longley then uses Worlock's[48] diaries to show how this was a function of Worlock's
beliefs reinforced by prior experience. However, as a result of
the Council Worlock was to change his beliefs, a change that
was undoubtedly due to the fact that the Council went on for
several years and helped him develop his thinking.

In management and politics groups often distort their perceptions of the policies of opposing groups the result of which is
a general misunderstanding of the other group's intention, and
in consequence mistrust and suspicion.[49]

Challenges to values may be perceived as threatening. More
generally in situations perceived to be threatening we narrow
our perceptual field and return to our original view.[50] Such behaviour in which we revert to tried and trusted ways can affect
the higher order cognitive functions and thus the ability to solve
new problems. Downshifting of this kind, it is argued is one of
the reasons why students fail to apply the higher levels of the
Bloom Taxonomy.[51]

Cognitive dissonance theory accounts for the behaviour of
institutions, in for example a merger battle and politicians.
For example politicians become so committed to the values
expressed in their slogans that they become unable to enter-
tain reasoned arguments against their points of view even from
some of their own supporters! Of course it is necessary for the
dynamic of political parties although not necessarily for good
government, that their supporters should not deviate from their
beliefs and beliefs are easily entrenched. The same thing can
happen between schools when there are proposals for amalgamation between the teachers in the schools concerned.

It is both a fortunate and worrying aspect of life that we can change our ideas, and learning is possible as a result of reasoning. It is worrying when we change with the crowd and fail to think things through, for in those situations propaganda finds a powerful ally. It is fortunate when we apply reason to our behaviour. These ideas apply as much to the experience of taste and touch as they do to vision.

None of us are free from cognitive dissonance and it needs to be taken into account when planning for change. There are those staff[52] who will not want their value positions changed. Clifford Longley gave one of the best illustrations of a planned approach when he described how Pope John XXIII in his opening address espoused *"standards of doctrinal orthodoxy dear to conservatives"*. However, in so doing he also paved the way for a change of style in approaches to discipline, errors, and heresies within the church, and thus to relationships with other churches.[53]

Intentions to change the curriculum are by no means at this level of debate but they do carry with them challenges to value systems, as for example, when proposals are made for integrated curricula in post-primary education or the introduction of particular forms of secondary education eg democratic schooling. Educational leaders intent on such change will have to ensure that there are links with prevailing values if such changes are to be successful.

The Acquisition of Information: Attribution, Expectancy and Gossip

Related to the idea of a personal construct approach to action and the human desire to investigate is the idea that persons seek to attribute causes to what they see in the actions of others.[54] Once again this is a matter of everyday experience. It derives from the fact that we impose meaning on the objects of knowledge. I would challenge any reader who says that this is not the case, to tell me categorically, that at no time have they ever tried to explain the behaviour of another person as being caused by this or that. And that at some time or another, this has not led to distress or a mistaken action.

"An attribution is an inference about why an event occurred or about a person's dispositions"[55]

Quite clearly the tendency (temptation) to *attribute* is a powerful factor in interpersonal relationships and motivation. Gossip is so often attributive, so is much journalism. Our attributions often result in other persons obtaining erroneous perceptions of other people.

As we have seen one of the purposes of stating aims and objectives at both institutional (school) and classroom levels is to remove ambiguity from the rules required for schools and classrooms to function. If the criteria for discipline are inadequately defined it can create problems throughout the school for teachers by no means agree among themselves as to what constitutes disruptive behaviour.[56] Children too may have their own ideas about what constitutes disruptive behaviour. They may also perceive some teachers to be less fair than others. As we have seen much of the hidden curriculum involves students in learning what behaviours are acceptable. It is for these reasons that some authorities advise teachers to establish learning contracts with their students so that everyone in a class is clear about what is tolerable and what is not.[57] However, these should be the subject of a whole school policy, and there has to be no ambiguity about such policies.

This has implications for the way that rules are written and rubrics set. For example, in England the first Statutory Orders relating to the assessment of the curriculum subject of Technology were interpreted in different ways by the different people involved in schools and Local Education Authorities. This meant that it was very difficult to standardise the assessments as between schools. Among other things teachers had different perceptions of what "designing" is all about and this affected the way in which the assessment task was presented to the students and in consequence the results.[58]

An interesting feature of attribution theory is self-attribution. When things go wrong we tend to blame other people,[59] and because we are confident that something or someone else is to blame we do not evaluate our attributions.[60] We will at once recognize this behaviour in politicians. But it happens in the school among principals, teachers and pupils. The other party is always to blame. Parents always rightly or wrongly believe their child is in the right. Their beliefs' may be a form of cognitive dissonance.

For example, our own failures in examinations, or not to do as well as we expected, rather than outright failure, may be blamed on factors other than ourselves.[61] Similarly teachers may ascribe to students characteristics which they do not possess to account for their failure in tests or to carry out successfully the work set by the teacher. Such students can be described as 'odd', 'disturbed' or 'peculiar.'[62] Some self-attributions can effect our behaviour so that if we believe we are hard working this will stimulate further effort.

Understanding such behaviour is important if we are to develop objectivity, not only in the classroom, but in respect of all activities involving interpersonal relationships, as well as in our understanding of others, and in particular journalists and politicians whose job it is to persuade. As Johnson[63] says attribution research signals *"a need for open communication within faculties, staff rooms, and classrooms and help in understanding educator's and stake holders' explanations for organizational and personal successes, failures and behaviour"*. Attribution and expectations are closely related.

The acquisition of Information: Attention

The importance of attention has already been alluded to in reference to dual task performance. The attention required to drive a motor car is considerable and our perceptions are subject to a whole range of stimuli. Very many objects in the environment are competing for our attention, and in the classroom it is the instructors task to focus attention on that which is to be learnt. The television producer's task is to manipulate our attention to their programmes just as it is the advertisers job to draw a positive response from the material presented. Thus the control of focus is an important area of study in psychology.

Hesseling[62] has made the point that attention is an integrating mechanism. Using the example of the automobile once again, he cites the case of the person who while driving is listening to a friend on a quiet road. So long as the situation is quiet the driver can attend to his friend but as soon as an unfamiliar landmark or vehicle appears (i.e. within the context of the driving situation) the drivers attention has to shift. He or she is only vaguely aware of what has been said. Hesseling uses this example to illustrate the point that anyone who specialises in a functional field learns to give a different kind of attention to detail to those whose occupations are generalists. Then if a person is appointed to a general management function from a job that entailed a high level of focussed detail they not only have to change the focus of their attention but have to attend in quite a different way (e.g. consider generalisations rather than specifies). This applies in particular to the teacher, albeit a post-holder, who becomes a principal. It requires the acquisition of new skills and some find these difficult to obtain.

It will be seen that such a transfer is required of many of those individuals who volunteer to become governors or managers of schools especially if they have no experience of management.

Receiving

Once we have decided to attend we receive. That again is a matter of common sense. It is this that creates the new experience (learning), and it is now that we have to allocate our limited capacities. As we have seen it is often difficult to undertake more than one task at once. Other factors come into play, and it has been shown that perception of task difficulty is a significant factor in task performance. The task must neither be too easy or too difficult.[65]

Our personality contributes to performance and is a partial determinant of our learning capacity. As we have seen one of the major problems is the fact that we are easily wedded to our previous dispositions. These tend to be very stable and contribute to the difficulty we have in the transfer of knowledge and skill to other domains. As Hesseling[66] suggests if a general manager is appointed from among functional specialists it is necessary s/he determine that h/she is able to master more general perceptual strategies. This is a problem for appointing management boards in Ireland. For historical reasons numerous principalships' became available to secondary school teachers. In the past this group of teachers had not been able to obtain principalships because they were the prerogative of the Religious Orders. Some of teachers appointed to these posts found it extremely difficult to adjust to being alone and not part of the 'staff room.' Situations like this create stress, and it is important to be reminded of the obvious fact that some stress either physiological or psychological may effect perception.

One effect of our limited experience that applies to job perception is rather like a societal self-fulfilling prophecy. We come to believe that a person in a job is not capable of doing jobs other than the one defined by her/his job description. We do not believe that he or she either has other skills, or has the skill to be able to transfer to different jobs. This is a serious limitation in societies where there are manpower shortages.[67]

In both attending to and receiving information we can become immune to repeated stimuli. The media and in particular the radio and T.V. have, so some would argue, reduced generally, our time span of attention. We need to be continually stimulated by new things. There are time limits for situation comedies, documentaries and the like and for classroom instruction! If my interpretation of newspaper criticisms of teaching is correct it would seem they would want instruction to be of the highly disciplined chalk and talk variety. That such an approach is to the detriment of learning has been demonstrated elsewhere.[68]

Hesseling draws our attention to the effects on people of repeated stimuli[68] Management can become insensitive to situations such as interpersonal rivalries to the detriment of performance. The same is true of students who continually cause minor disruptions in the classroom. Hesseling suggests that the prior experience of social workers may make them insensitive to the human problems that they daily encounter.

Trial and Check

This component of perception has also been called hypothesis testing by Allport and Bruner.[69] It is part of the matching process to which reference has already been made. *'The trial phase is a tentative reading of a sign, a tentative decipherment of a puzzle, a tentative characterisation of the object; and the check phase is an acceptance or rejection, a positive or negative reinforcement of the tentative perception.'*[70] This process continues until the percept is assimilated into our existing frames of reference or, rejected. We often have to proceed by trial and error because we do not always have the information available to us to make an objective decision. And, as we saw in the activity of receiving it is possible to have a situation where we become unable to decide because of being swamped with an information overload. It is this component of the perceptual process that is related to risk taking. Clearly it is important in the development of the tacit knowledge required for effective performance.

Consolidation: The Problem of Experience

It will be evident that our expectations depend in no small measure on our past experience. We can now begin to summarise. When we learn the experiences of that learning are related and checked with frames of reference that we have in our mind. These have been variously called schema, schemata and categories. They are the basis of concepts and the concept maps that we use to categorize information. Abercrombie,[71] following in the steps of Bartlett, said that schema may *"be regarded as tools, which help us to see, evaluate and respond."* Similarly Allport wrote of categories that *"are accessible clusters of associated ideas in our minds; these serve as frames of reference for fresh perceptual samples of immediate modes of behaviour."*

As I argued earlier, it seems to me that Newman's 'first principles' belong to this category for without first principles there can be no transfer of learning or dynamic of action that is reason. The case for formal education rests on the need to develop a common pattern of first principles. The definitions of Abercrombie, Bartlett and others do not propose anything as simple as a 'memory bite'. Nevertheless it is easy to see how useful this concept would be in information processing models of problem solving and decision making. Each of these concepts, as a function of the context in which they are used, can be persuasive.

The nature of learning is immediately clear. It is that process by which experience develops new and re-organizes old concepts. The concepts are the means we use to describe our schema, categories and frames of reference. These schema contain within them first principles. Concepts are classes of stimuli that have common characteristics. Without them the world is meaningless and communication impossible. How they are learnt and how they are taught are issues of great significance.

As we have seen we approach any situation with preconceptions to which our expectations are related. There is a tendency for these preconceptions to organize our perceptions of the task(s) we propose to undertake. This applies as much to research as it does to taking on a new job, or dealing with a pupil or a colleague of whom we have been given knowledge but have never met.[72] To this extent we give meaning to the objects of knowledge, hence, the adage that no two persons see the same thing alike. Thus what we see, and more significantly what is presented to us (as well as how it is presented) also control that knowledge.

To a large extent knowledge is socially constructed. I say to a large extent because it would seem that if all knowledge is socially constructed then all knowledge is relative. I do not believe this to be the case.[73] I assume that if knowledge is relative then there can be no universals, and this is patently not the case. I also assume that the objectives in the world are 'real' and capable of common understanding even though we may differ slightly in our descriptions of them. It is a matter of observation that perceptions of individuals are sufficiently aligned to make generalizations possible, and that when repeated the same descriptions are possible. It would seem to follow from Newman's view that knowledge is only socially constructed in so far as the sense-experiences to which we are exposed differ. The case for formal education rests on the need to develop a common pattern of first principles.

There are many influences on our perceptions, our peer groups, the family, and by no means least, the people with whom we work. These groups lead us to form similar perceptions.[74] Industrial and commercial organizations create their own culture and it has been shown that working to and within such cultures can breed successful organizations.[75] Such cultures can also be self-defeating.[76] Firms develop their own systems of categories and language associated with those categories. As it passes to individuals, because of the limitations of the jobs they do, this language and the schema with which it is associated also become limited. A perception that has been developed within a narrow range of activities is sometimes called *"deformation professionelle"* It is a characteristic of specialism, and is inhibitive of transfer. Furthermore it causes individuals to overly rely on past experience. When faced with a new problem, individuals who in the past have been highly inventive often look to the past to see if they have done anything like it before. This is their mechanism of trial and check. They do not, contrary to Bruner, necessarily hypothesize about the new problem and bring the "principles" which they learnt in their education to bear on the issue. In these circumstances experience becomes an impediment to innovation.[77]

I would not wish to argue that adult motivation is tied to the past but the way in which we try to meet our needs may well be governed to some extent by this factor. It seems to me that there is an in-built tendency to rely on experience in preference to training. In one enquiry persons below the age of forty valued training where as those over the age of forty thought their experience was more important. Moreover there was some indication that the training might have been valued less for its educational merit than for its contribution to future promotion.[78]

Given that there is an inner consistency in our perceptions, needs and values it is not surprising that experience is highly prized or, that the failures in that experience are forgotten. But as has been indicated this has considerable implications for adaptability. Expert knowledge becomes restricted to the specialist field of work. Intrusions into another field are based on that experience and not on the first principles of the new field of action or enquiry. Similarly specialisms create their own languages and even within organizations specialists can find it difficult to communicate. Burns and Stalker[79] showed how difficult it was for research and development personnel to communicate with manufacturing personnel. Although this must have been compounded by differences in their educational backgrounds.

Hesseling[80] as we have seen believes that specialism can make it difficult for specialists to move into general management. Thus he argues *"that they need also to be confronted with specialists in other fields. in order to get a healthy "choc des opinions."*

Experience is not only valued but it is used as a criterion to categorize individuals. Application forms seek career histories. To obtain these with ease a job title is given. From this title a personnel selector draws information about the potential of an applicant to fill a particular job. If the job falls outside the predicted range of potential then the applicant may be screened out of the selection process even though other parts of the application might suggest that the candidate should be interviewed.

Individuals are prohibited from change because of the unwillingness of management to go beyond over-simplified job descriptions of work actually done and the skills used. In consequence, the mobility of labour is considerably limited. Task analyses show that workers have the skills to undertake a variety of roles. The reason that person's are not adaptable lie as much in the perceptions of the managed and managers as they do in anything else. Thus, while experience is valuable, it can also confirm existing prejudices and acquire new ones associated with the situation in which we find ourselves. Herein lie the foundations of the education for adaptability philosophy and the idea that students should carry with them a *Record of Achievement* that profiles their academic and experience attainments.

To overcome this situation people, whether they are managers or workers, teachers or pupils, have to understand very much more about each other and realise that, in general, most of us have much more to offer than circumstances may allow. We have to view learning as *giving* and management as *service*. We have to view ourselves as learning systems that have to comprehend many worlds of experience.

It was for this very reason that I began some of my classes with the test that I described at the beginning. It was to shock them out of their beliefs about themselves and other people: to show them that things were not always as they seem. It was to show them that there are other worlds of experience.

We have therefore to learn to use our categories less rigidly, and to recognize that we are subject to both bias and prejudice. *The Dictionary of Sociology* (1957) defines bias as *"a conditioned tendency to favour and support a certain point of view or conclusion despite the absence of adequate or even any evidence"*. That we have biases is a matter of everyday reflection. That they are a function of how and what we perceive should by now be self-evident. Some psychologists have related this to personality and distinguished between the authoritarian and democratic personality.[81] The issue is complex as has been shown by Rokeach.[82] Prejudice (as bias is sometimes called) extends to all our problem-solving. But mature individuals, so the argument goes, do have a facility for detachment, and this requires an understanding of one's self and one's biases. For this we need to know how we perceive and the factors which influence the meaning that we impose on the objects and activities of knowledge. The conclusion to which this text has led on several occasions is that the curriculum at all levels of education needs to help us to understand how we learn. However, it should not only be for the improvement of educational learning but to enable us to understand the factors that impede or aid adaptation on the one hand and interpersonal relationships on the other. In this respect the subject of prejudice is sometimes dealt with in moral or religious education classes but is not related generally to the process of learning which it so easily could be.

"At the specific level perceptual skill development can be helped in many subjects of the curriculum as for example art, geography and geometry. That perception involves high level skills is illustrated by environmental perceptions which requires highly complex acts of scanning, observing, defining, redefining, ana-

lysing, categorising, comparing, establishing relationships and creating meaning."[83] We are now in a position to define the curriculum as that mechanism in education that provides for the formal provision of 'new' conceptual frameworks thought to be of value to the individual and society. Curriculum study is therefore the investigation of what these frameworks should be. It depends on an understanding of how we learn, and how we know and the personal and social factors that enhance or inhibit learning.

Perceptual Learning and Reflective Practice

The proposition that all learning is experiential would seem to justify the British view that learning for certain professions and trades is best done through experience. Thus engineering and management should be learnt on the shop floor, and teaching should be learnt in the classroom. As we have seen, this view does not allow either for the inhibitive effect of experience or for the fact of illusion. Unless a practitioner is prompted to reflect on what has happened on the shop floor or, in the classroom during the day the probability of misleading schema being developed which will inform future behaviour is high. All the foregoing analysis testifies to the ease with which stereotypes are formed. Moreover, the evidence demonstrates that misunderstandings in the staff room and classroom can directly or indirectly influence teacher and student behaviours for the worse. There is a danger, not a serious one, that some people might think that the activities of the mind, its imaginations and intuitions are not concrete experiences.

To reflect on experience demands, as both Eisner[84] for teachers, Schön[85] for practitioners and many mystics before them have shown a high level of skill. Reflection has to be informed by theory and this is the relationship of theory to practice. Just as learning is a necessary and contingent activity that requires formalisation so too is reflection. We do take thought: we do cogitate but more often than not it is an occasional if not random activity. But more than this we do hypothesize and we make theories. Attribution theory, personal constructs and the like depend on our ability to hypothesize, that is to theorize, about events now and in the future, Theorising is an outcome of experiential learning which we use to occasion future action. Research is the sophistication of trial and error thinking in particular problem areas.

MacMurray[86] writes *"this does not mean, however, that the reference of theoretical to practical activities is always direct or obvious. Nor does it mean that in our reflection we can or should be aware of the practical reference. [..] All that is contended for is this, that there is a necessary relation between our theory and our practice; that the activities of reflection can never be totally unrelated to practical life; that it is always legitimate to ask of any theory which claims to be true, what practical difference it would make if we believed it"*.

It is my claim that the professional practitioner in education has an obligation to examine the relationship between theory and his or her practice, be it as a manager or a teacher, and that to ignore it is an arrogance that would not be tolerated in any other profession.

Notes and references

[1] In the United States in school systems the term administration is often used for management. The terms executive and strategic do not directly correspond to their usage by Sternberg. Some might prefer administrative instead of executive.

[2] In Britain and Ireland a large amount of the responsibility for running schools is delegated to Boards of Managers (as they are known in Ireland) or Governors (as they are known in England). The Boards in England would have much more responsibility than those in Ireland

[3] Hesseling, P. (1966). *A Strategy of Evaluation Research*. Van Gorcum, Aassen, Netherlands. Most people seem to be sceptics!

[4] Abercrombie, M.L.J. (1960) *The Anatomy of Judgement*. Penguin, Harmondsworth

[5] For example see pp 356 –359 of Mackinstosh, N.J. *IQ and Human Intelligence*. Cambridge UP, Cambridge

[6] Brinckman. R and R.Kirschener (2002) *Dealing with People you Don't Like*. 2nd edition. McGraw Hill, New York.

[7] Heywood, J (1997) An evaluation of Kolb's learning style theory by graduate student teachers during their teaching practice. Association of Teacher Educators Conference.

Washington. ERIC ED 406 333. And (2008) *Instructional and Curriculum Leadership*. Original Writing/National Association of Principals and Deputies, Dublin.

[8] Woodhouse, H.F. (1979). Ambiguity: some implications and consequences. *Studies*, winter pp 265-276

[9] *ibid*

[10] *loc.cit.*

[11] Martin, C (ed) (1988). *The Philosophy of Thomas Aquinas*. Introductory Readings. Routledge, London

[12] *loc.cit* ref 3

[13] Schouten, J. P and J. Kalsbeek (1962)On the evaluation of perceptual and mental load. *Ergonomics*, 5, 251 – 261.

[14] Navon, D. (1985) Attention division or attention sharing? In M. I. Posner and O. S. M Marin (eds) *Attention and Performance*. Erlbaum, Hillsdale, NJ.

[15] Kelly, G (1955). *The Psychology of Personal Constructs*. Vols 1 and 2. Norton, New York. For an introduction see Engler, B (1979) *Personality Theories: An Introduction*. Houghton Mifflin, Boston. For a very brief introduction see Bannister, J in B Foss (ed) *New Horizons in Psychology*. Vol 1. Penguin, Harmondsworth.

[16] *ibid* Engler.

[17] In the *Essay in Aid of a Grammar of Assent* (Longmans Green – 1989 edition) Newman writes *"These so-called first principles, I say, are really conclusions or abstractions from particular experiences; and an assent to their existence is not an assent to things confined to the proposition directly embodying those experiences."*

[18] Miller, E. J (1987). *John Henry Newman on the Idea of Church*. The Patmos Press, Sheperdstown, VA

[19] Cat is the universal. Cats have four legs is the principle

[20] A position that is not inconsistent with Kolb's theory of learning.

[21] *ibid*

[22] Bruner, J .(1962) *On Knowing. Essays for the Left Hand*. Belknap, Press, Cambridge MA. Sometimes the term 'representation' is used instead of perception. See Smith, E. R. (1998). Mental representation and Memory in D. T. Gilbert, S. T. Fiske and G. Lindzey (eds) *The Handbook of Social Psychology*. 4th Edition.. McGraw Hill, New York.

[23] *ibid*

[24] *ibid* Bruner (1962)

[25] See also endnote 1 chapter 4 and associated text for other comments on expectancy theory.

[26] Allport, G. W (1955). *Theories of Perception and the concept of Structure*. Wiley, New York.

[27] Litterer, J. A (1973) *The Analysis of Organizations*. 2nd ed. Wiley, New York.

[30] Schlenker, B. R (1980) *Impression Management. The Self Concept, Social Identity and Interpersonal Relations*. Brooks cole, Moterey, CA

[29] Cooper , H. M and T. L Good (1963) *Pygmalion Grows Up: Studies in the Expectation Communication Process*. Longmans, New York

[30] Heywood, J (1989). *Assessment in Higher Education*. 2nd edition. Wiley, Chichester.

[31] Rist, R. C (1970)Student Social Class and teacher expectations: The self-fulfilling prophecy in ghetto education. *Harvard Educational Review*, 40, (3), 411 – 451.

[32] Good, T. L and J. E. Brophy, (1974) *Looking in Classrooms*. Harper and Row, New York (5th edition 1991).

[33] Davies, D (1984) Sex role stereotyping in children's imaginative writing in H. Cowie (ed). *The Development of Childrens Imaginative Writing*. Croom Helm, London.

[34] Stanworth, M (1982) *Gender and Schooling: A Study of Sexual Divisions in the Classroom*. Hutchinson, London. See also Whyte, J (1983).The hidden curriculum in *Beyond the Wendy House: Sex Role Stereotyping in Primary Schools*. SCDC Publications, London for a summary see Cohen, A and L. Cohen (1988 *Disruptive Behaviour. A Source Book for Teachers* Harper and Row, London).

[35] Henderson, M (2006) Report of a paper in Science in *The Times* p 18. October 20th.

[36] Schein, E. H. (1965) *Organizational Psychology*. Prentice Hall, Engelwood Cliffs, NJ

[37] Chia-Lin Hsieh and Jianping Shen (1998). Teachers', Principals' and Superintendents' conceptions of leadership. *School Leadership and Management*, 18, (1), 107 – 121

[38] Comiskey, P (2007). The interpretation by stakeholder organizations of the in-school management system in Irish primary schools. MSt Thesis, University of Dublin, Division of In-Service Education. Dublin, Ireland.

[39] *loc.cit*. In another small scale study in Texas principals were also found to perceive themselves to be instructional leaders. Swan, V., Heywood, J, and K. E. Mayo (2005). A Comparitive study of the factors influencing the retention of teachers in the Republic of Ireland and Texas in The Motivation and Retention of teachers. *Bulletins of the European Forum on Educational Administration* 2005 No 8. Pp 71 – 116.In any event the principals were fully occupied with administration.

[40] Heywood, J and M. Murray (2005) Curriculum-Led staff development. Towards Curriculum and Instructional Leadership in Ireland. *Bulletins of the European Forum on Educational Administration* 2005 No 4. Publ. Sheffield Hallam University, School of Education for the European Forum on Educational Administration.

[41] Krech, D et al (1982) *Elements of Psychology*. 4th ed. Knopf, New York.

[42] Tagiuri, R (1969). Person perception in G. Lindzey and E. Aronson (eds). *The Handbook of Social Psychology*. Vol 3. 2nd Ed, Addison Wesley, Reading MA.

[43] Bruner, J Goodnow, J. J and G. A.Austin (1956). *A Study of Thinking*. Wiley, New York

[44] Festinger, L (1959) *A Theory of Cognitive Dissonance*. Stanford University Press, Stanford, CA

[45] Luchens, A. S. (1942). Mechanisation in problem solving; the effct of 'einstellung'. *Psychological Monographs* No 248., and Gagne, R. M (1976 ed) *The Conditions of Learning*. Holt, Rinehart Winston, New York.

[46] Marshall, S (1980) Cognitive-affective dissonance in the classroom. *Teaching Political Science*, 8, 111 – 117.

[47] Longley, C (2000) *The Worlock Archive*. Geoffrey Chapman, London

[48] Worlock was secretary to two Cardinals of Westminster and then Bishop of Portsmouth and Archbishop of Liverpool. A Major player in English Catholicism in the second half of the twentieth century.

[49] French, W. L et al, (1985) *Understanding Behaviour in Organizations*. Harper and Row, New York.; Thouless, R. H. (1974). *Straight and Crooked Thinking*. Pan, London.

[50] Combs, A. W and D. Snygg, (1949) *Individual Behaviour. A Perceptual Approach to Behaviour*. Harper and Row, New York.

[51] Caine, R. N. and G. Caine (1991) *Teaching and the Human Brain*. Association for Supervision and Curriculum Development. Alexandria, VA

[52] teachers, secretaries, caretakers, cleaners etc

[53] *ibid* pp 83 – 86.

[54] For a discussion of attribution theory research see Taylor, S. E (1998). The social being in social psychology in D. T. Gilbert, S. T. Fiske and G. Lindzey (eds). *The Handbook of Social Psychology*. 4th edition. McGraw Hill, New York.

[55] Harvey, J. H and G. Weary, (1981) *Perspectives on Attributional Processes*. Brown, Dubuque IA

[56] Galloway, D et al (1982) *Schools and Disruptive Pupils*. Longmans, London

[57] See also Coulby, D and T. Harper, (1985) *Preventing Classroom Disruption: Policy, Practice and Evaluation in Urban Schools*. Croom Helm, London.

[58] Constable, H (1993) A note on the first technology assessment tasks at Key stage 1. *International Journal of Technology and Design Education* 3, (3)

[59] Jones, E. E and R. E. Nesbitt (1971) *The Actor and the Observer. Divergent Perceptions of the causes of Behaviour*. General Learning Press, Moristown, NJ

[60] Olson, J. M and M. Ross (1985) Attribution research. Past contributions, current trends and future prospects in J. H. Harvey and G. Weary (eds). *Attribution. Basic Issues and Applications*. Academic Press, Orlando, FL.

[61] Shaver, K. G (1981) *Principles of Social Psychology*. 2nd ed. Winthrop, Cambridge, MA

[62] Rogers, C. G (1982) The contribution of attribution theory to educational research in C. Anmtaki and C. Brown (eds) *Attributions and Psychological Change*.Academic Press, New York.

[63] Johnson, N. A. (1987) The persuasive power of perceptions. *The Alberta Journal of Educational Research*, 33, (3), 206 –228.

[62] *loc. cit* ref 3

[65] Jaques, E (1970). *Work, Creativity, and Social Justice*. Heinemann, London.

[66] *loc. cit* ref 3

[67] Thomas, B and C. Madigan (1974) Strategy and job choice after redundancy: a case study in the aircraft industry. *Sociological Review*, 22, 83 – 102. and, Youngman, M. B et al (1978) *Analysing Jobs*. Gower Press, Aldershot

[68] Heywood, J. (2008). *Instructional and Curriculum Leadership. Toward Inquiry Oriented Schools*. National Association of Principals and Deputies/Original Writing, Dublin.

[66] *loc.cit* ref 3

[69] Allport, G. W (1961) *Pattern and Growth in Personality*. Holt, Rinehart and Winston, New York.

[70] Solley, C.M and C. Murphy (1960) *Development of the Perceptual World*. Basic Books cited by Hesseling.

[71] *loc. cit* ref 4

[72] Dimen-Schein, M (1977). *The Anthropological Imagination*. McGraw Hill, New York.

[73] The theory of the social construction of knowledge that derives from Piaget is widely quoted and used to advocate certain teaching techniques that others would think good in themselves. It is an epistemological theory that differs from that promoted in this text. *"Rather than viewing truth as the fit between sense impressions and the real world for a constructivist it is the fit of our sense impressions with our conceptions: the authority for truth lies with each of us"* (Driver, R and B. Bell (1986). Student's thinking and the learning of science. A constructivist view. *School Science Review*, 67, 443 – 456). For a commentary in which this philosophy is questioned see Matthews, M. R. (ed) (1998). *Constructivism in Science Education; A Philosophical Examination*. Kluwer, Dordrecht.

[74] *loc. cit* Litterer, (1973).

[75] Peters, T and R. H. Waterman (1984). *In Search of Excellence*, Harper and Row, New York.

[76] Miller, D (1990). *The Icaurus Paradox. How Exceptional Companies bring about their Own Downfall*. Harper and Row, New York.

[77] *loc. cit* Youngman et al (1978)

[78] *ibid*

[79] Burns, T and G. Stalker (1961). *The Management of Innovation*. Tavistock, London

[80] *loc. cit* Ref 3

[81] Adorno, T. W et al (1950) *The Authoritarian Personality*. Harper and Row, New York.

[82] Rokeach, M (1960). *The Open and Closed Mind*. Basic Books, New York

[83] Adams, A (1993). Environmental design in schools. *International Journal of Technology and Design Education*, 3, 2.

[84] Eisner, E (1979). The Educational Imagination. *On the Design and Evaluation of School Programs*. Collier Macmillan, New York.

[85] Schön, D (1983). *The Reflective Practitioner*. Basic Books, New York

[86] MacMurray, J (1956) *The Self as Agent*. Faber and Faber, London.

CHAPTER 3

SELECTING AND SHAPING
THE ENVIRONMENT (ROLES)

Introduction

*Much of the discussion here is about the motivation to work
and is therefore an extension and development of some of the
themes in the previous chapter (chapter 2). When we adapt, we
try to obtain as close a fit as possible between the environment
and ourselves. We do not want to live in an environment in
which we feel uncomfortable. So if our values or our tempera-
ments don't fit, we look for an alternative environment which
is often much easier said than done, or we try to shape the environment better to meet our needs. We do not live in a single
environment but in many- a plurality of social systems as this
has been described. At times in the society in which we live, we
are in the family group, at other times we are in our work group
and sometimes we are in friendship groups. In school there is
a school system, a teaching system, a friendship system, and
a career system. All work involves several systems and these
overlap with other systems like the family and the golf club.
Depending on the particular circumstances, at any one time,
the goals of one system are likely to be more important to us
than those of the other systems in which we are involved. The
goals and their significance continually change, so throughout
life we are required to adapt. None of us can escape the need
to adapt: sometimes we will want to adapt and sometimes we
will want to resist change. As we have seen, how successful
we are will depend on the particular structure of the environ-*

ment and our understanding (perception) of that structure. In so far as schools (and indeed all organizations) are concerned the task of management is the co-ordination and integration of roles. This demands an understanding of human behaviour, and there is no better place to begin this understanding than from a reflection on roles, role behaviour and our responses to the particular situations in which we find ourselves. Effective change often depends on our ability to adapt our role. In this chapter we consider how the role of management in schools has changed over the last decade and continues to change. We consider the need to define roles, some of the situations that may cause stress and conflict, and how the general disposition of our personality relates to our subsequent behaviour in the groups in which we play a role.

Roles, Role Definition, and Orientation to Work

Whoever the individual, whatever his or her personality, they will adapt their behaviour to the situation in which they find themselves. If they can't adapt they may want to leave the organization and if they can't leave then they remain but with a whole lot of problems for them and for the organization. Thus, just as human organizations can be conceived of as systems, so they may also be conceived of as conglomerates of role players, for in any social system the basic unit is the role. Thus an awareness of role theory is essential for any person engaged in the management and leadership of personnel, or the manipulation of people.

A role is, therefore, a pattern of behaviour associated with a particular position. 'It' carries out activities that, if the system is to achieve its goals, have to be co-ordinated. One activity of management is, therefore, the co-ordination and integration of roles. 'It' (the role) does not to have to be a human being; it could be a machine. However, the discussion that follows is confined to human beings.

A contrasting theory of roles comes from the American psychologist George Kelly.[1] He argues that the individual defines the role as they try to understand the behaviour of other people in order to relate to them. In order to understand the world we develop "constructs" that help us interpret the world. From our relationships with other people we develop a self-construct. Our self-interpretation is linked to our role relationships with other people. So a role is *"a process or behaviour that a person plays based on his understanding of the behaviour and constructs of other people. In order to enter into a relationship or a role with another person, we must have some idea of the way in which he or she behaves and construes our behaviour. Interpersonal relationships are predicated on this concept of construct."* Thus Kelly uses role playing to help individuals understand their own interpersonal relationships. It may help a person to see other ways to solve problematic situations. At the more general level the theory is attractive because given the description above it does illustrate how people learn to deal with each other in relationships that are not adequately defined. That is in circumstances of ambiguity (see later).

Ambiguity should be taken into account in the discussion that follows. Although it is based on social-psychological approaches it does not deny that Kelly's approach may be helpful in understanding role behaviour.

As we saw in chapter 2 the performance of role players can be analysed in relation to the roles or *role- orientations* they adopt. For example, in the case of students there are those who have a *social orientation*. They are concerned with the social life that the institution offers, are likely to do less well in college work than those who have either *academic* (pursuit of examinations) or *intellectual* (concerned with knowledge as its own end) orientations to study, irrespective of ability.[2] It has also been argued by Holland (cited by Handy)[3] that students orientations to work cause them to choose different work environments. He distinguishes between those students who have realistic, intellectual, social, conventional, enterprising and artistic orientations. Most of these are obvious but it is worth distinguishing between the realistic, the conventional and the artistic. A realistic person *"seeks objective, concrete goals and tasks and likes to manipulate things [...] they are best suited to agriculture, engineering, outdoor observation work and similar practical jobs."* They are to be contrasted with those who use feelings, intuitions and imagination who are likely to do well in the performing arts, or writing, painting and music. Conventionals *"cope with life by following the rules and selecting goals approved by society and the consumer."* They do well in accountancy. This idea is supported by Kolb's learning style theory. Learning styles predispose students to study in particular areas of knowledge.[4]

The attitudes of large numbers of students in post-primary schools are clearly *instrumental*. They arrange their schoolwork so as to make their dislike of it tolerable. Such attitudes derive from the meaning that life and school has for them. If school performance is related to work success, and they perceive that they will be unemployed because of under achievement, they will undoubtedly develop an instrumental attitude toward schoolwork, and why shouldn't they? The problem for the school is to provide a curriculum that has meaning for them, and this may mean a radical re-appraisal of what is taught, and how it is taught, with all the implications that this may have for the staffing of small groups. One of the problems for educational policy makers is that students may adopt different roles irrespective of their abilities. It is easier for policy makers when they don't because it enables a 'smooth' system to be devised. The more homogenous a population the more easy it is to plan and especially timetable. Not surprisingly, problems arise for those who are expected to manage policies when there is no such homogeneity. But such problems are not confined to the students in their charge for workers have their own orientations to work.[5]

In any educational institution the teaching group comprises a variety of individuals, each with their own value system and idiosyncracies who occupy roles in the organization. Very often personnel come into conflict with each other simply because of personality differences, and this will happen in teams. Sometimes conflict is created because of the perceptions that individuals have of their role. Even in a bureaucracy it is not possible to define a role so exactly that there are no differences in perception about how it should be performed. No two teachers required too teach the same external syllabus in a subject will teach that subject in exactly the same way.

A major problem for employers, and indeed for ourselves, is the fact that at one and the same time we live in a *'plurality of social systems.'* Each of these systems has its' own goals.[6] There is not merely the role system that connects our job to other jobs in the organization for work purposes, but our career system, our peer-group system and, not least the family system. Each of these has a pull on our intentions and may impede the performance required of us to achieve the goals of the institution.

The systems that encompass our everyday lives affect our motivation to work (teach) since they make demands on our energies and there is no way of escape. Typically the unmarried beginning teacher will bring a great deal of motivation to the task. Motivation will be directed toward the effective management of classes in such a way that learning will be enhanced. Much time will be spent in preparation. But when that teacher prepares for and becomes married her/his goals will change and other things may become important. Goals change again with the advent of the first child. Later in life other things may assume more importance, and these may be accompanied by boredom with teaching especially if the teaching environment has changed in respect say, of discipline and motivation. As personal goals change so the teacher may come to rely more on experience and less on creativity in planning.

Most of us have to find ways to reduce the tensions and sometimes conflicts that arise from having to function in a plurality of social systems if we are to maintain a satisfactory performance at work. It is not surprising that the perceptions that people have of us are a function of the behaviours we display. To the observer it may appear that we change personalities as we occupy different roles.[7] It is part of the task of management to recognise factors like this which effect our performance and to take steps to alleviate them if possible, and in some case this may mean a change of role. Sometimes teachers avail themselves of career breaks in order to resolve these tensions; policy-makers have accepted that such breaks are valuable irrespective of the problems they create for school management. However, many teachers are unable to avail of such breaks and principals have to take such steps as they can to maintain performance.

In the past teachers have perceived their professional role to be confined to the classrooms in which they teach. But this was an over simplification that has been detrimental to the development of the profession. Increasingly they are expected to adapt to team playing both within the institution and the curriculum, as for example when some form of interdisciplinary studies is introduced.[8] Thus, they have to move between sub-systems within the work organisation.

The problem is that although the nature of work undoubtedly influences our attitude to work the orientation we bring to work will be influenced by the other systems in which we interact. These orientations to work (as well as the other systems in which we move) are also influenced by personality. Taken together they contribute to the meaning that work has for us. Thus one of the most powerful influences on role behaviour are the expectations' that we have of roles irrespective of the persons who occupy them.

Role Expectations

A role may also be defined as the set of expectations about the behaviour of its incumbent.[9] (See also Chapter 2). It is a two-way process in that both the organization and the individual have expectations that have to be matched if an effective performance is to be produced. One of my graduate students wrote, *"the truly content person is the one who can rise to the expectations of each changing role and not be pressurised, the one who can make each role suit him."*[10]

Whenever we anticipate a role, we generate expectations of what will be expected of us in that role. For example, when a student in his or her school-leaving year is looking for a job, ideas about what will be expected of them in different jobs will be generated. However vague this understanding, these expectations will have a strong conditioning effect on the student's subsequent choice. When they, and for that matter any worker taking on a new job, actually work in that job, they will in all probability have to make some *role adjustments* in order to adapt and so be able to perform their task.

Whether or not their performance meets the expectations of others is a different matter, and can have profound implications for the performance of managers. For example in my university it is the custom for the academic staff to elect the Provost (the most senior person in the university). An election is held and the candidates visit departments to sell their wares. It is not uncommon for some of them to promise to visit each department when they are in office. But we know, and presumably they do, that this is an impossible task. However, they can raise other expectations. Some of these may create contradictory expectations among the electors with the result that soon after taking up office they will fall from the grace bestowed on them by some of the electorate. In the case of schools where the teachers have no say in the appointment of principals expectations are likely to differ considerably among them. The same thing is likely to happen, that is, some of the staff may become disenchanted with the new principal for no other reason than that their expectations have not been met. In these circumstances it is desirable for those responsible for the selection of a principal to publish a role specification since this can avoid some of the ambiguities that lead to false expectations (see later section on ambiguity). We shall return to the issue of job specification later.

Networks, Key Persons and Role Sets

A beginning worker or a person joining a new company will find that they are linked into formal and informal networks of other people. Sometimes the bonds in these networks will be 'tight' sometimes they will be 'loose'. Sometimes they will find their dependence on another will be 'strong', sometimes 'weak'. They will not be able to avoid making contact with other people. This applies as much to classrooms as it does to other networks among teaching and ancillary staff in a school. The bonding between a teacher and his/her pupils is an important factor in the enhancement or impedance of learning. This is as true of the corporate manager, the assembly line worker, the refuse collector or the postman as it is of the teacher. These networks have a profound influence on an individual's behaviour. Therefore, we can only understand the behaviour of individuals within the social context in which they operate, and in this respect we have to take into account the perceptions that the individual has of his or her own behaviour and of the others in his or her network.

The social or organizational context may be complex. Sometimes, it is possible to identify key persons who are at the focal point of a number of roles (individuals) necessary for the key person to perform his or her task. This grouping is called a role-set.[11] In schools one such key person is the principal. Among the individuals or groups in the principal's role-set will be the teachers, the Board of Management (Governors), the unions and the parents, that is the so-called 'partners' in education.

But there will also be officials of the Department of Education, and Local Authorities if these are involved in the governance of the school. A vector diagram with the principal at the centre would indicate the relative strength (power) of the various role players on the principal, and it would also indicate the effect on the principals executive (i.e. day to day decision making), and strategic (i.e. long term policy making) functions. It would be possible to draw two overlapping role-sets that distinguish between the two functions.

Each person in the middle-management team in a school will be the focus point of a network. For example a 'year head' will be bound to tutors, subject teachers, special education teachers, student councillors, and parents. This role-set will overlap with the middle management role set. In such a structure the bonding between the year head and the principal will be relatively loose because of the delegation such an arrangement requires if it is to perform well. This assumes that the task is well defined.[12]

Taking all the role-sets together an organization may be viewed as a matrix of over-lapping role sets. It is a plurality of social systems. Just as individuals vary in their bonding within a role-set the role-set will vary both in degree of bonding (dependence) and distance (closeness in organizational terms) with other role sets, as for example, the distance between a board of management and the year heads role-set.

Any person who takes on a management role needs to quickly analyse the structure in terms of the role-sets in which they have to work and to elicit how power is distributed in these networks. They need also to recognise that for the efficient and effective running of the organization that these groups are interdependent on each other just as the individuals in any role-set are interdependent on each other for its effectiveness. One of the problems which many heads of university departments face is that the academics for whom they are responsible do not consider themselves to be part of an interdependent network.

They each fight for their own territory and find it difficult to take a common ground. This can be true of small post-primary schools where there are no subject departments and each teacher is responsible for a different year. They may see no need for interdependence. It is only when they are threatened that they may see a need to pull together as for example in a situation where enrolments are declining rapidly and putting their posts at risk. An incoming manager (principal) who is intent on change, for whatever reason, would do well to plot the role-set of interdependence that he/she perceives to be at work. Understanding the roles that teachers play in a staff-room and thus at staff meetings enables the principal to anticipate problems and develop strategies for dealing with them.

At the level of the formal organization there are occasions such as when post-holders leave their posts that a principal may take the opportunity to re-assess the tasks of the post-holders. In Ireland a Board of Management (Governors) may ask the principal to review the duties of holders of posts of responsibility. Day, Whitaker and Johnston[13] describe functional and developmental approaches to the structuring of responsibilities. Their functional approach is designed to be undertaken each year and it relates to the management tasks outside of daily classroom tasks. This approach proposes that posts are created for the purpose of achieving a specified set of objectives. In the developmental approach the responsibilities of the posts are linked to staff development needs required for the development of the whole school plan. Both are radical approaches and to be successful would require the commitment of every teacher for both require a high level of interdependence for their success.

Jeffrey Pfeffer of Stanford University considers that the failure to diagnose interdependence often leads to the collapse of new strategies and developments. He suggests a series of questions that a change agent needs to ask. They apply to any role-set where the focus person is seeking change. They are

1.   Whose cooperation will I need to accomplish what I am attempting? Whose support will be necessary in order to get the appropriate decisions made and implemented?

2.   Whose opposition could delay or derail what I am trying to do?

3.   Who will be affected by what I am trying to accomplish, in either (a) their power or status, (b) how they are evaluated or rewarded, or (c) in how they do their job?

4.   Who are the friends and allies of the people I have identified as influential?[14]

A new principal can learn much at the first meeting he/she has with staff that deals with school business by seeking answers to these questions.

Pfeffer points out that often (he says 'inevitably') any innovation changes power structures and requires the mobilisation of support. In schools the informal networks (or organisation-see Ch 4) may be powerful impediments to change.[15] A new principal will want not only to understand the sources of influence (power) but find a mechanism for removing them if they are creating problems. Very often persons in this situation will seek to divide and rule while trying to avoid conflict

In Irish schools that are medium and small sized the important role-sets have been the principal's and the Staff (room). Within the latter several small role-sets are likely to have functioned. These are likely to have formed friendships around particular goals (e.g., a golfing set). However, the principal is primarily concerned with the combined effects of these role-sets when he/she has to meet them together at a staff meeting for the purpose of making decisions. Irrespective of the size of the school the 'informal' organisation among the staff creates its own culture and this can create an environment that welcomes or inhibits change, and this will depend on the role-players in each set. A new principal will want to discover if there is a power group who effectively run the school.

Groups take on a life of their own and behave as if they were individuals. There is the *enthusiastic group*. They are like the children who always have their hands up and shout "Miss, Miss......Sir, Sir..." They can achieve their goals through shear noise and bombast. Group pressure can lead to non-cooperation particularly if its members are disinterested. There is often a *moaning group*. Rae suggests that this group emerges when an organisation is in a state of change and have strong feelings about the change particularly if they don't want to do any extra work.[16] I have found that irrespective of what is on the table there are persistent *moaners*. Perhaps *grumbling* is a better descriptor.

As indicated individuals play the same games. Principals would be well advised to familiarise themselves with Berne's now famous *Games People Play* - for individuals do play games at meetings and often for the purpose of being destructive but without seeming to be destructive.[17] Often this is achieved by setting up someone else in that persons role-set to do the destruction. In this way the perpetrator avoids blame. In the literature on meetings many negative roles have been identified. For example:

The aggressor	A person who increases his or her status at the expense of others, H/she blames, criticises and is generally hostile.
The blocker	A person who disagrees with every thing without good reason
The comedian	A person who messes about, and may make negative jokes.

The competitor	A person who challenges others.
The devil's advocate	A person who can be useful but may turn the group to his/her own way of thinking.
The digressor	A person who cannot stick to the point whose contributions can be longwinded
The dominator.	A person who makes loud and lengthy interventions.
The side-talker	A person who continually whispers to his/her next door neighbours.
The under-contributor	A person who contributes little or nothing to the meeting.
The withdrawer	A person who might be expected to make a contribution but doesn't[18]

The principal should be concerned to ascertain those who will give him support. Sometimes a person from whom support is expected will not make a contribution *(The withdrawer)* and nothing can be more annoying. Sometimes a *dominator* also creates fear among some persons to the extent that they don't contribute or withdraw. One feature of group behaviour can be a general reluctance to break what appears to be the general consensus. This may create difficulties in circumstances where change is sought. These comments apply in particular to schools where there is no middle management structure as was the case, until recently, with many small and medium sized secondary schools in Ireland. The introduction of community and comprehensive schools with larger numbers of pupils brought with them the possibility of year-heads and the organisation consequent on that role, as well as the possibility of subject departments.[19] Middle-management structures of this kind require teamwork and that is new to staff in Irish schools. Of course all is not as gloomy as this picture might have conveyed because there are those who play constructive roles in schools as the next section will show.

Teamwork

The need to create teams is illustrated by an experienced teacher who found that the job of a year head required numerous qualities and the ability to organise a team. She wrote that her job: *"includes encouraging curriculum development within the group, promoting the positive aspect of good discipline, subject to the principal and vice-principal. It also includes helping the students to respect each other, staff and those with whom they come into daily contact. The role of the year head also involves administration and organization of, for example, student files. Given these factors plus the fact that the year head is also class teacher for eighteen hours, the author has found the need to make a 'team' of those involved e.g. assistant year head, tutors, parents, subject teachers and other support structures like special education teachers, councillor etc"[20]*

Notice the scope of the team. It embraces all the stakeholders. From this example it will be seen that teams are formalised role-sets. As such they have to be chosen with care. An all-embracing definition of a team is a "small number of people with complementary skills who are committed to a common purpose, set of performance goals, and approaches for which they hold themselves mutually accountable."[21] An effective team will not only meet its needs but is likely to meet the psychological needs of its members. However, the personality profile (mix) of the group can either enhance of impede the effectiveness of the group.[22] Therefore, selection to a team is not a minor matter.

Peter Drucker, the management guru, has argued that the *"purpose of a team is to make the strengths of each person effective, and his or her weaknesses irrelevant."*[23] R. M. Belbin showed that effective teams were composed of people who collectively employed the eight roles now described.[24] In brief, the *chairman* is concerned with the attainment of objectives. Character-wise, while dominant, he or she will not be assertive, and will utilise the strengths of the team members. The *shaper* is the person who, in a group, always wants to bring everything together so that a project can be initiated and completed. *Shapers* are bundles of nervous energy able to challenge and respond to challenge. The *plant* is the person with imagination who, when the team is bogged down, looks for new ideas. Together with the *monitor-evaluator*, he or she is highly intelligent. The *monitor-evaluator* brings dispassionate critical analysis to the problem. Tse calls him or her, a 'cold fish.'[25] The *company worker* is the individual concerned with practical implementation. His or hers is a disciplined approach that requires plenty of character. The *resource investigator* looks outside for ideas and brings them back to the group while the *team-worker* is the one who understands the emotional needs of the group. The *team-worker* tries to promote unity and harmony. The *finisher* is the anxious one: the person who worries about detail and who wants things done properly.

Unfortunately, given the awkward squad listed previously, similar types to these will be found in any group, and teachers in departmental or staff meetings are no exception. They will be found in gangs of children. Each type has the strengths and weaknesses that Belbin has documented. While it would appear that individuals have a natural pre-disposition to certain roles and always behave in ways associated with the role, it is possible in training exercises to help them to play other roles. Belbin distinguishes between primary and secondary roles, and also between functional and team roles. While presenting the functional dimension the role player will do this within one of the frameworks of one of the eight pre-dispositions. It may be an advantage to the effectiveness of the group if some, if not all, of a team are able to play more than one role.

Belbin developed a *Team Strength Audit* to determine the strengths of a team. It assesses a person's capability along eight dimensions that relate to his roles. The strengths (dimensions) are *investigating, innovating, evaluating, focusing, implementing, finishing, supporting, co-ordinating.* For example, the capabilities associated with *investigating* are the ability to look for the latest ideas and developments, and to open up discussions that stimulate thinking. The *supporting* dimension illustrates the importance of social skills in team participation. It requires the ability to develop good relationships and to work well with different people. Teaching staff can be categorised in this way.

Teachers can reflect on teamwork from observing students working in team projects and having to assess such work. Studies of teamwork in industry and of its use and assessment in 16 plus education are highly relevant.[26]

Another teacher, Matthew Hynes described how he and his six colleagues who had been selected to manage and implement the national Curriculum project in Leaving Certificate Business used Belbin's Team Strength Audit to establish the team's strengths. Ranked in order, they were first, *supporting* and *focusing*, second-*finishing* and *investigating*, third- *implementing*, fourth-*innovating*, fifth- *co-ordinating*, and sixth-*evaluating*. Hynes suggests that the reason for the low level of the co-ordinating and evaluating dimensions was because there was no team leader and evaluation was seen as the responsibility of the programme administrator and the steering committee. His evaluation showed that the team had been very supportive and was highly focussed. He pointed out that the emphasis on *finishing*, *investigating* and *implementing* was borne out by the fact that all deadlines were met.[27]

Team Development

Individuals posted to a team cannot just expect it to work. They have to do things to help it work, and they can be trained to work in teams. Much effort has been expended on developing exercises to help individuals work in teams. These range from a variety of activities to assessment schedules that help the individual examine his/her performance.[28] Teams have to be developed and Lewin's ideas about individual development can be applied to teams. He suggested that in learning we first cling to existing knowledge, then we explore ideas, issues and approaches, then we identify, utilize, integrate values and skills with those held previously. These three stages were aptly called *freezing, unfreezing, and refreezing.*[29]

Perhaps the best known description of stages of team development is that described by Tuckman who called them *Forming, Storming, Norming* and *Performing.* Others have described the first stage as being one of confusion in which the individual seeks *orientation.* The second stage has been described as one of *experimentation,* or *conflict,* or *dissatisfaction.* The third stage has been described as *consolidation,* or *cooperation* or resolution, and the final stage as *commitment* or *production.*[30]

Hynes reported that when the curriculum team had been inducted into the project they were given a one-week training session which was organised by the In-Career Development Unit of the Department of Education. The team was briefed by one of theother curriculum team members who had had experience of this kind of work. Because school visits were to be a large component of the project they were able to discuss issues with a person who would have to accommodate these visits, and in particular how to identify a 'school principal's needs. A facilitator explored the team's strengths and weaknesses. Hynes reports that this analysis proved beneficial later on.

At this stage *"the team was the driving force and not any one individual."*

Subsequently, and early in its development the team prepared a mission statement and contract.

The teams mission was *" To provide guidance and support to teachers in the introduction and implementation of the new Leaving Cerificate Business Syllabus (syllabus support pack)."*

The team contract required its member's to-

Be loyal to fellow members, support and respect each other personally and professionally.
Abide by consensus decisions made by the team, share knowledge and expertise.
Trust each other and maintain confidentiality within the team.

Hynes considers that this was a very important moment for the team because *"the defining characteristics of a team is that its members voluntarily co-ordinate their work in order to achieve group objectives (Bell and Day, 1991)."*[31]

He completes his description thus
The team was extremely lucky in that it moved through the various stages of its development without too much upheaval. The identification of potential conflicts which might arise from the strengths of individual team members was key to building a successful team. A conscious decision was made by the team that rather than letting team strengths be a source of conflict they should be put to the advantage of the team, for example, when sample questions were being developed the members with examination expertise were able to identify pitfalls such as ambiguity in wording.

A decision to rotate the chairing of each meeting and representation at Steering Committee meetings ensured that no one mem-

ber dominated meetings or members. The team took responsibility for its own further training and development needs. Each member undertook to organise an element of this training. This training consisted of the following elements, communications course, information technology, links with Leaving Certificate Applied and Vocational Programmes, writing up case studies, mixed ability teaching and classroom management and reorientation back to teaching.

By identifying and meeting the teams own training needs the team set out it's approach to the provision of professional in-career development.[32]

The evaluation surveys of teachers who participated in the scheme and the principals of their schools suggest that the team was highly successful in achieving its outcomes.[33]

The idea that teams run smoothly is not one that is born out by experience but we can learn from bad experiences. Sanghera draws lessons from the Formula 1 Motor Racing team saga surrounding the Mclaren Racing Team and its young contender for the world title, Lewis Hamilton.[34] There was little evidence of any team spirit. *"In real life teamwork is rarely how it is presented in corporate brochures all smiles and hugs between people of different racial backgrounds. Often as at MacLaren teams are riven with tensions and sometimes our closest colleagues are the people we can least stand"* Sanghera draws a number of conclusions the first of which is, that difficulties in a team should be acknowledged. Feuds need to be acknowledged. He suggests that however difficult it may be that if you are involved in a feud take the moral high ground without appearing to be sanctimonious. It is equally difficult to dismiss a feud from one's work. *"A smile is contagious but backstabbing is more so. A dispute between two individuals can wreck not only the atmosphere of a department but of a whole [school]."*[35] Sanghera goes against some management thinking. He argues: *"Realise that a reconciliation may not be in your interests. Ca-*

*reer advisers will emphasise the importance of clearing the air.
But the fact is that sometimes it is not possible to mend fences,
and the only solution is for one of you to leave. You don't want
that person to be you.*"[36] Easier said than done in the school
situation, but situations like that can and do occur in schools.
So what about conflict in organizations.

Conflict

Conflict and tension are normal consequences of living in systems, be they as small as the family or as large as an industrial
organization. It can be positive, negative or neutral in its effect.
At its most simple, conflict may occur when there is a difference
between expectation and reality. A teacher writing to me about
the problems of homework in his inner-city school, said:

> *Homework is tied to a certain extent with discipline. Stu-
> dents expect to get homework to do and the amounts to in-
> crease with the proximity of the exams. However, when stu-
> dents fail to provide even miniscule amounts of homework,
> teachers come to rely on the work done in the class. This subject
> is a very great source of worry for teachers and pupils because
> both wish for more homework but because of human failings,
> it cannot live up to expectations in reality. This causes what
> is known as 'conflict'- expectations and reality are in conflict,
> which gives rise to feelings of guilt for both parties.*

Some individuals are particularly creative in conflict situations. Thus conflict may prevent stagnation, or it may cause a
group of individuals to remain united and establish relationships that would not otherwise exist. Schools are open to this
problem when principals for one reason or another manage
to align a staff against them. Such a situation can be brought
about by the failure to delegate The task of the principal is to
find a problem which can unite the staff in finding a solution.
For example, the whole area of discipline can give rise to tension. One school examined its policies for discipline to see if
they could be improved.:

Staff were divided into six groups (there are sixty members of staff), each one being chaired by a post holder in the school. The [ ] post holders met prior to this to develop skills in group task and maintenance and to prepare for possible conflict situations and their resolutions that might lead the group to lose sight of the main objectives. Throughout the course of the group sessions, a number of areas were discussed and recorded, such as the main areas of concern and suggestions for improvements etc. Following this, the post-holders or middle management team met with the principal and vice-principal to discuss findings. Management, together with staff drew up an agreed set of approaches, many involving teamwork. For example, subject departments agreed to draw up sets of work which could be used with classes in the event of their teacher being absent, thereby allowing students to continue their normal classwork and avoid conflict for those teachers supervising. Year heads together with tutors agreed to do a regular 'blitz' of reminders of general school rules, procedures and sanctions.

Another outcome of this initiative was to form an 'incentives' committee drawing on the skills of all departments and levels within the staff to promote the positive aspects of student behaviour.

This initiative served many purposes successfully, apart from its main objectives, it drew together all staff, at all levels and of all experiences, in an area which can cause much stress and isolation for teachers. Staff became very motivated and re-energised. This was largely due to the willingness of management to listen to staff's frustrations, to the preparation in ensuring all sessions were conducted in a fair manner, inviting all opinions.

It is evident that the day-to-day running of organizations can be impaired by conflict. It is not so much the large official strike that is likely to do the damage but the little unofficial stoppages that last for one or two hours and disrupt the flow of productivity. Conflicts between teachers and the organization can be to the detriment of the learning of the students involved.

In the same letter quoted above the teacher also wrote:

In the past year, the principal has become much more involved with the Leaving Certificate students and has taken a personal interest in them. She has stated her expectations of them plainly. They are, punctuality, attendance, homework and effort during the class. She also threatened to suspend the two lowest scorers in the Christmas tests. Even though they thought that she could not carry out his threat, they were still quite worried about it while at the same time they sought the easy way out by getting good marks in such subjects as physical education and religious knowledge...

The students see obvious conflict between what the principal expects by way of timekeeping and what teachers are giving. It is no wonder therefore that there is confusion in their minds because they do not see unity of purpose from the teachers. We have already spoken of homework and effort which is a 'two-way street' within the classroom itself. The principal has never stressed to the teachers the need for homework or her feelings about it or indeed sanctions for not doing homework. Some of the teachers feel that it takes a lot more effort than they are willing to give, to try to drag homework out of students and they feel that this mothering of students is bad training in that the way to get the students to be responsible starts with homework.

Conflict situations, can therefore, cause strain and tension between members of an organization. Role conflict can arise in a variety of circumstances.[37] One condition of role conflict arises when the actions of two individuals, who have a common goal, are directly opposed. In a role-set the person at its focal point may not be able to meet the different expectations of the members of his or her role-set.

This point is illustrated by an evaluation of the role of subject leaders in England. Within the team teachers retain personal autonomy to which the subject leader has to respond. He/she will in all probability have to cope with team members who have different opinions about how the role should be carried out. This can cause tension which can be accentuated by a tension between meeting the demands of the team and senior teachers who want the subject leader to widen their role within the school more generally.[38]

In universities that encourage participative management many conflicting demands may be made on persons at focal points of role-sets. For example a professorial head of department who is required to undertake administration, teaching and research is often placed in mental conflict because of the heavy demands made on him or her, especially those of administration, with the result that very often his or her teaching and/or research suffers. In schools a year head can be delayed in getting to class by a sick pupil.[39] A series of such instances arising from the pastoral role of the year head can lead to stress. In a university the central administration can also place the head of department in conflict with his/her colleagues by requiring actions that some staff are not prepared to carry out. At the same time the head of department is given no power of sanction. In such circumstances the individuals who make up the department continue to carry on as they did before, and it is exceptionally difficult to manage them even by participation.

School principals can find themselves in much the same position. As Dunham points out, the principal *"is at the centre of all internal and external transactions in the school. In consequence he/she is continually having to make rapid adjustments as he/she meets with pupils, parents colleagues, governors, managers, administrative staff, caretakers', representatives of the Department, building contractors and so on."*[40] Yet most of the problems that have to be solved are relatively small. They take up an inordinate amount of time and strategic planning suffers at the expense of executive decision making. The trouble is that they are continuing, and because they are so demanding, there is a tendency for principals to develop skills in handling the trivial. This may cause them to make mistakes when they are called on to deal with strategic matters-as for example, trying to change the direction of the curriculum. As Trim says *"managers can become so thinly spread as time devoted to [trivialities] has an opportunity cost in the sense that time and energy are not spent equally on important issues, and detract from forward thinking and planning."*[41] The requirement in Ireland, for example, that schools should complete a school plan should enable both principals and teachers to focus on the strategic.

Role conflict may be a product of the culture (organizational climate). For example, as is the case with many schools in Ireland where

"so many staffs are growing old together in a situation where there is little room for movement outside of one school, a sense of claustrophobia can develop in which even the most superficial conflict may have a deep or undisclosed or even unconscious agenda. A hidden dimension may be suspected if a minor dispute leads to an extreme emotional reaction. Much conflict has its origins in a power struggle where one party wants to feel that they have imposed their will on another. An example of this might be a year head who presents the vice-principal with a problem and then advises him or her how it should be handled. Another instance might be a subject teacher who demands of management that a student be suspended as a result of a breach of discipline. A wider view of the situation which the principal may possess could view this demand as an over-reaction and hence the possibility of conflict"[42]

Role conflict is not always harmful and may occur without conflicting role-expectations. This is very often the case with teacher-pupil interactions in the classroom, when sanctions are imposed on a particular pupil for behaviour regarded as deviant. The class may not like them but, nevertheless, acquiesce because that is what is expected to happen. Similarly, management and labour may take different views about when the dismissal of personnel is justified, for there is likely to be a conflict of interests and functions. This has been a particularly thorny issue in Irish Schools.

Within organizations there are many sources of conflict. They are frequently due to poor communication, which is often a function of the structure of the organization. The organization can accentuate personality clashes and power struggles among its members, and external pressures dictated by customers (stakeholders) can set them on the run. I have seen an organization changed by merging two departments so as to overcome difficulties created by certain of the role holders. But no attempt was made to change the role holders so the difficulties remained. The possession of a middle-management structure of itself will not ensure effective communication. If delegation is to work, those to whom powers have been delegated have a responsibility to keep management informed. Very often this does not happen and management can be left having to defend the indefensible when they have to take responsibility for the actions of subordinates who have gone beyond their brief.

Conflict, therefore, that takes place between role players in an organization, or sectors of an organization, may have either harmful or beneficial, or for that matter, no effect on the efficiency of an organization

Heller and Wilpert have gone so far as to argue that *"conflict may be a necessary and crucial ingredient of organizational life, if the mobilisation of adaptive resources to changing conditions is to be ensured. For this reason management has to learn techniques for resolving organizational conflicts that cause the groups involved to make compromises which aim to help the organization survive."*[43]
Because conflict arises from the interactions individuals have with each other, it is important to understand the internal and

external factors that influence an individual's behaviour, that is, personality on the one hand, and role interaction on the other.

The Management of Conflict

It is not part of the purpose of this book to enter into a treatise on the management of conflict. There are many practical paperbacks that have been written on this topic that may be of help to those who engage in conflict situations. A list of these would include books on negotiations and obtaining a solution to conflict will require negotiation. Negotiation *"is that process through which an elegant win/win solution is reached which meets the differing needs of the two or more parties."*[44]

That books of this kind can be helpful is illustrated by a teacher who found herself in an on the ground management role in her school in association with the principal and vice-principal.[45] She found that the principles in the literature began with the view of negotiation described above. The next step was to confront the conflict because if it is postponed it could fester into something more intractable.[46] It is not an easy thing to do as another principal of a three teacher rural school explained of himself

It is ironic, that although I classify myself as having a good inter-personal style. After perusing the literature on the qualities of the authoritarian head, I have to admit one feature stuck in my memory, and continued to unsettle me: "the authoritarian head seems to have an almost pathological abhorrence of confrontation" (Ball, 1987). Granting that pathological might be a little strong in describing my aversion to confrontation, nevertheless, I feel that I usually try to side-step any show downs or otherwise work in such a way as to avoid conflict in the first place. "Many principals expect or feel that they are expected to keep everyone happy by running an orderly school, and this becomes the major criterion (expectation) of the principal's ability to manage." (Fullan, 1991). Both colleagues af-

firm that this is very much my manner when dealing with pa-
rental issues and that I thrive on having cordial associations
with parents.[41][47]

I suspect that many of us would report similarly. We want to
avoid conflict if we can, and this is reinforced by the fact that
many of us have received no training in dealing with conflict
and have to rely on reading for help.

Very often things go wrong because the problem is not clearly defined. This can happen when someone (parent, pupil or
teacher) bursts in the door demanding a hearing. It is important in such circumstances to win time in order to be sure that
the problem has been understood and that all the parties involved agree that that is the case.[48] (See chapter 2). In so doing
it will be necessary to listen and come to an understanding of
the other person's point of view (i.e. demonstrate empathy).[49]
To do this and at the same time to be objective one has to ditch
one's own feelings and prejudices and focus on the issue and not
the person or persons involved.[50] To be above one's prejudices
and search for and evaluate alternative solutions is called 'helicoptering'. Finally when an agreement is reached each person
involved needs to be sure that their understanding of the agreement is the same as the others.

A teacher reporting in an in-career assignment said that she
had found all of these principles helpful, and, in particular, that
John Crawley's exposition assisted her to understand the role
she had been asked to undertake because he made a distinction
between the conflict manager and the conflict participant:
The former seeks facts, views a situation from several angles,
gets others to explain their position and looks for what is best
overall. The conflict participant, on the other hand, tends to
make assumptions, has a narrow point of view, does not lis-
ten and singularly pursues his own ends. Throughout the past
year, I have found myself developing as a conflict manager and
evolving skills to assist me in this process. Crawley suggests an

approach which I found to be very useful. This involves four elements: self, others, situation and consequences. Probing questions can be asked in relation to each of these so that in relation to self one can ask What can be done? Or What do I want to do? In relation to others you can consider what they are doing?, what do they want? Having considered your own position and the needs of the other, you can then consider the situation itself and what limitations it puts on action. Then finally, the consequences have to be estimated. This approach is useful because it enables the conflict manager to become more a facilitator stepping back emotionally from the situation and focusing on the future where change can occur rather than on the past which is locked in conflict.

This teacher found that her role became defined in situations where conflict had to be resolved between staff and students. In one of her case studies she describes a situation requiring a quick decision thus:

Background

Most of the problems we encounter from day to day in schools are not in themselves enormous issues when looked at from a perspective outside the organization but they can be quite intense due to the apparent suddenness with which they tend to manifest themselves. During my first term in my post, I found myself constantly in positions where decisions had to be made without delay which was complicated by the fact that I had to be ever-mindful of the need to balance a natural desire to be seen by staff members as effective against the imperative of helicoptering above the situation and taking all factors into account.

The conflict

A long-standing colleague came to my office in a state of extreme exasperation at the rude way a in which a fifth year boy

X, had blankly refused to tidy up chairs in a classroom he was going into for a new young teacher, Ms Y. In a heightened state, this colleague informed me that something would have to be done about it and that we simply could not have pupils treating teachers like this. I was aware that my gut response to this was to feel personally challenged to do something, while at the same time, I agreed with the principles which had been expressed.

Intervention

Having absorbed what the circumstances were and knowing how I felt myself and what my own prejudices were, I then met with the student whose general body language suggested *someone who was about to engage in explosive conflict.. The student was initially very defensive and angry at the whole system but finally relented and accepted that his behaviour was beyond the bounds of what was acceptable either in school or at home. He expressed frustration at having to do Irish, having failed it in the Junior Cert. And was fatalistic about his chances of success in the forthcoming summer exams. When the new teacher joined us, she informed me that this type of attitude was ongoing with this student but that she had not reported it to the Year head. Ms Y's manner towards X was fair and not unkind so that X finally accepted that he had taken out her hostility of the subject on the teacher.

Resolution

Since X had never been in any trouble before in this school, I was able to be positive about his situation and point out to him that she would get a very good reference in due course and why spoil a good record by losing his head in relation to one subject. We discussed the fact that he had not tried at the subject and also ways he might get some revision done before the exam. While on this occasion no sanction was imposed, I made it clear to X that if there was a recurrence, the situation would be different. Before he left the office, I made an appointment to meet with him the following week to find out how things were going. Ms Y was present for all of this interview and after X left, I expressed my view that she had been fair in her treatment of X and reassured her of my support if such a situation occurred again.

*This also provided this young teacher with an opening to discuss problems she was having in various classes. In so far as X was concerned he was provided with a teacher listener and prospect of positive follow up. This conflict actually cleared the way for better communication and eased tension.
(*edited for purposes of this text).

Very often while the purpose of a role is understood the person who is appointed to the role has to develop the role and where there are ambiguities this can be a difficult task. It seems that role ambiguities of this kind have been experienced by"subject leaders" in secondary schools in England. The tensions they caused were summarised in an earlier paragraph. It seems that similar difficulties arise in primary schools where the concept of subject leader is difficult to clarify since teachers teach all subjects.. *"obviously the concepts of middle manager' and 'subject leader are not synonymous within a set of standards that appears to cover every one. Bennet has noted that the concept of middle management development is deeply problematic since the role in primary education of middle manager probably does not exist. If one takes this further one might ponder at what point does a middle manager become a senior manager and as Glover et al have noted "The distinction between middle and senior management remains blurred and demarcations of leadership functions are still not adequately delineated or defined.""*[51] One might argue that such demarcation should be a matter for the principal and the Board of Management. Given that Reading's point was made in the context of management training for these roles it might also be asked if there is any necessary distinction to be made in the training of senior and middle management given the limits of management training as elucidated in previous chapters.

Negotiating

In the example above the teacher carried out a negotiation. It is important to realise that those who enter into negotiation must possess 'something' with which they can negotiate. For example if there is a demand for money and management has no money to offer negotiation is rather pointless. Similarly staff meetings in schools are often held for the purpose of negotiation. The partners have to enter into negotiation in the spirit of give and take. If a principal holds a meeting for the purpose of obtaining consent but has no intention of changing his or her position the result is likely to have a negative attitude on relations as the example supplied by another teacher shows.

Principal X manages an average sized pupil number and staff number school. There are no obvious uniting issues or problems amongst the staff, except that of X

There is a begrudging respect for the many talents that X has, however this is overshadowed by a massive negative emotional swell that occurs particularly around the time of a meeting. X does not freely associate with the staff. It is possible to talk to X but this is often an uncomfortable event. Because of the distancing between X and the staff X is very difficult to read and has difficulty accurately reading staff. There appears to be little interest in getting to know each other well enough to destroy any misperceptions. X's value system has a great impact on the way people are treated. This formation of ideas about people, based on X's values alters dramatically X's behaviour and attitude toward certain individuals. This is felt not only by the people involved, but also by those watching from the sidelines. It adds to the negativity which increases hostility towards X and to the suspicious nature with which X's suggestions are greeted.

By and large X treats staff with calm and respect and restraint, but the distancing arising from previous experience causes a great strain. Staff are willing to work with X only for so long as it is of benefit to them or will not disrupt their daily activities. Some will actively support X in order to gain power from familiarity, others will be acquiescent. Others again will actively try to get in conflict because (a) X thrives on a good fight and (b) it is a good pay-back for previous incidents or it will be a good game of diversion for as long as it lasts. Therefore, before any staff meetings, of which there are few, battle lines are drawn in all quarters and sides are taken. Few will ever enter a meeting with any real hope of negotiating. Unsurprisingly, there is rarely any real negotiation that can take place either. Meetings will start off with attempts at a democratic format but all too soon it resorts to a process of informing staff of the decisions that have been made for them. While this saves time, gets things done and avoids open conflict, it does nothing for the feelings of suspicion and hostility.

Prior to a staff meeting to negotiate supervision at an open-day some elements among the staff arranged in advance to use the meeting as a forum to drag up old war wounds, as they usually did. Others decided to or were warned off to remain quiet. With less input it was hoped that the meeting would last a shorter time and so would be 'done and over sooner.'

X arranged the seating in a circle before the meeting, and then took up a position randomly in one of the seats. The meeting was opened by trying to focus peoples minds on the reason for being there. Things progressed smoothly until the conflict-group began their performance.

While they are a destructive force, they are given reign by the others as they merely vocalise the feelings most hide. Once the tirade began most switched off, offering no support to either co-workers or management. Power was swung, by virtue of numbers, away from X into the hands of the dissenters. To regain control X reverted to old habits and a commanding stance. A win-lose situation was set into action and the aim of the meeting was lost to a power struggle. It ended, as many meetings before, by X telling people what to do or reminding people what they had agreed to do, as if they were giving in to an order, and not offering from their generosity. Generally feelings were low.

While the tactic was efficient and accomplished what was needed to be done, it was not effective. Feelings had not improved, nor had relationships between manager and subordinates. There was no negotiation.

The writer does not tell us, unfortunately, or even surmise, as to what would have happened if the conflict-group had not intervened. Would there have been negotiation in those circumstances? The case does, however, illustrate the points made in this and other paragraphs about negotiation. Unfortunately behaviour of this kind is not unusual. Another writer provides an example of what he considered to be effective negotiation. In this case X was a principal who managed a small sized staff with corresponding pupil numbers. There were problems with staff-pupil ratio and the school had to be marketed. The need to maintain numbers and the external threat of a reduction in numbers to some extent unified staff and management.

X makes a habit of listening to staff regularly by meeting them at nearly every eleven o'clock tea break and through regularly scheduled one-to-one meetings. X's body gestures and ritualised responses are well understood. This manager is easily read by the staff and the knowledge means that X can always read them equally well. Despite this familiarity, X is obviously the one in charge and makes the ultimate decisions, whilst being willing to listen to and consider alternatives that might be suggested. X has preconceptions of what hidden agendas the staff are fighting during any meeting, and can let this cause stress and uncharacteristically close-minded approaches to some in-

dividuals ideas. However, generally when in deadlock, X will stop the meeting and suggest a tea break so as to allow all parties time to rethink. Time, while valuable, is the tool of X not the master. X encourages all to have their say, and draws out the quieter members, while not being afraid to refer to more expert members of the group or to delegate. Amongst the staff, despite occasional clashes, there is general feeling of respect towards X and trust that X is doing things for the good of the school, and so indirectly for the good of the staff. Small suggestions made by X to individuals, on a daily basis, are listened to and mostly accepted. Conflict is avoided for the good of the small numbered group. Usually one of the more powerful characters within the staff solves the problems before they come to X's doorstep.

Here he (X) is at work

A staff meeting was called to examine how time could be taken from subjects to allow one particular subject either to satisfy the basic requirements of the Department of Education or to be dropped. If the subject were dropped it would mean one less teacher and less choice for students. This in its turn could lead to a possible reduction in numbers, and a specialist teacher would have to be re-deployed.

X introduced the problem at an earlier staff meeting to allow people to think about the issue. At the actual meeting X represented the needs of the Department of Education, of the parents and pupils and of the teacher whose subject was in danger, and of the one who would be in danger of redeployment. Certain other teachers represented their needs and the needs of their subject and students. The rest of the staff either took sides or sat on the side-lines observing, listening thinking and feeling for their fellow co-workers.

X entered the meeting with official documents and the previously expressed thoughts of those involved printed on paper for all to examine. Staff entered with thought out alternatives and fall-back positions. Timetabling information and govern-

ment guidelines were also provided as visual aids shortly after a statement of the issues at stake had been made.

Prior to the meeting staff had managed to work themselves up into a state of paranoia. The negotiations started calmly, if not coldly, suspicions were guarded and tightly controlled so as to hear X out. Soon, tempers flared and sight began to be lost as to exactly what was to be achieved. Control of the situation began to slip.X became more anxious, which was easily read by all, making matters worse. For some this was a sign to go for the jugular, for others it was a sign to retreat altogether. A tea break was called.

When all regrouped, the air was more controlled again, but there was now an element of having to come up with a solution. There was a fear that if protracted X would disempower the staff on this issue and take the decision. By the end of the meeting everyone knew what the outcome would be but X gave everyone time to think and win over those who had not yet made up their minds by adjourning the meeting for a week. At that meeting the staff agreed to take time off from other subjects.   All came away as winners and no permanent damage had been done to anyone's standing in the group.

The teacher who described this case pointed out that *'management and negotiation have much in common.'* In the case of the proceeding report, the teacher wrote *'became clear how little true negotiation actually takes place, and how often people feel dissatisfied with outcomes because the process is not true to its self.'*

Apart from illustrating differences between negotiation and non-negotiation these examples show two very different management styles at work. Some styles, it would seem, can shape the environment in a positive way while other styles are likely to shape an environment in such a way that it has a negative effect on performance. But environments can only be shaped when the network or team has a clear understanding of the roles of each individual in that network or team.

Role Ambiguity and Power [52]

Ambiguity and role conflict can cause stress. Even if individuals do not suffer stress, they may react in ways that make the goals of the organization more difficult to achieve. As we saw in the last chapter ambiguity can be a source of difficulty between people, for such ambiguity lies in the perception of the role that either the role player, or the participants in the role-set have of the player's role. Ambiguities are inherent in life and therefore organizations. Indeed management could be defined as the "management of ambiguity." Sometimes role ambiguity can be beneficial especially when it allows person to grow into a role. For example in primary schools in Ireland the deputy principal has had to teach. However, recently in very large schools administrative deputy principals who do not teach have been allowed. There is very little literature available about the exact role of the Deputy. So the principal and deputy principal have to work out for themselves what to do. One report that describes this situation reports how a principal allowed the deputy to grow in the role so that between them the role of the deputy was established over a period of time.

The negative consequences of role ambiguity often occur when a person is deprived of information. This may be deliberate so as to isolate the person (role isolation), or it may be due to the fact that the appropriate information is not available. One of the consequences of the division of labour is that management comes to believe that broad information is unnecessary for most jobs. However, as soon as a teacher is made a post-holder, difficulties can occur if the post is not adequately defined.

A report on the duties of year heads in a post-primary school in Ireland showed that whereas there were five main duties listed for the role of the year head in practice the role was minimal. *"It amounted to the checking of absence notes and the occasional warning given to students regarding their behaviour."* When the reporter questioned them about this discrepancy the year heads told her that there had been *"no systems or structures in place for them to carry out their tasks and as a result their job description was unmanageable."* They reported that at that time the role was negative and caused them to have negative relationships with their students. They also considered that two of the five items in the job description were vague and ambiguous- *"Generate ambition in the student body"* and *"Build up student self-image.*

Subsequently, in consultation with them the job description was clarified and supporting structures were put in place. Three areas of responsibility were defined. These were Administrative, Pastoral and Disciplinary. In respect of the pastoral dimension they were expected *"to build students self image/ self esteem."* To achieve this goal management agreed to support extra curricular activities set up by the year head and to make available student reports so that the year heads could review and track progress. This related to the second dimension of pastoral care, namely that they should *"monitor the academic progress of students."* They were encouraged to discuss their concerns with management and to meet parents. The new system apparently changed their attitudes considerably. It is reported that *"as they made more decisions about their role they became more confident in their own abilities"* – *"They began to operate as a team supporting each other in completion of tasks,"* and they became more involved with the students in their year group.

The consequences of role ambiguity may be profound for the individual. Uncertainty about the way in which our work is evaluated, and opportunities for advancement, can lead to deep frustration. The responsibility we have, and the expectations of others about our performance, may cause low job dissatisfaction, low self-confidence and a high sense of futility. Such factors may cause stress, which can lead to anxiety and depression. Role conflict and role-ambiguity tend to be greater at the higher levels of hierarchical systems of management, and when they cause work overload. They may become important elements in job stress.

When a role is ambiguous it can be manipulated. One case study quoted by Jaques, showed how patients in psychiatric hospitals were able to manipulate doctors, nurses and orderlies who were not clear about their accountability or authority.[53] This can happen in schools especially in relation to the procedures for discipline. All of which suggests that there is a need to define roles. The advantages of job definitions are that they can avoid mismatches between the capabilities a person brings to a job and the requirements of a task. A mismatch occurs when there are no or inadequate resources to do the task that is wanted, and/or the organization has not been adapted to allow the task to be done. In contrast stress may occur when the job is too easy because of an excess of resources. Similarly, if in cognitive terms a task is too difficult and beyond the capability of the individual, or too easy, there is a mismatch, and such mismatches can cause stress. In Irish schools under-utilisation can cause stress as for example when a teacher who feels him/herself to be able to teach Leaving Certificate Examination classes is continually required too teach non-examination classes. If persons are kept in the same role for too long because they are thought to be good in that role they can become frustrated. In primary schools teachers can become frustrated when they are not moved so as to experience different year groups but are always required to teach the same year group year in and year out.

In the Irish system, even with new legislation, the post of vice-principal has been highly ambiguous although the picture is changing. More recently they been called deputy-principal. One study called for the profile of the deputy principal to be raised so that the norm is for the deputy principal to share more significantly in the management of the school.[54] Another study recommends that deputy-principals should not teach because they so often miss classes. But there are also those in the in Ireland and UK who believe the deputy principal should teach because it is a source of pride. It is important for other members of staff to know they are dealing with some one who understands the teaching problem.[55] Leader and Boldt in Ireland suggested *"that it can be very satisfying to spend an hour or so of uninterrupted time with students, maintaining teaching skills and keeping in touch with the curriculum of one's own subject."* [56] One of the many studies of stress in teaching that has been made reported that deputy principals who had responsibility for curriculum development reported far lower stress levels than those whose main responsibility was for administration.[57]

However, there is a case for allowing roles to develop. The examples below support this view. In the first example a person who was appointed deputy principal agreed with the principal

"not to assign a set of functions to the deputy principal but to allow her a period of time to become familiar with the functions of the former deputy principal and to work within areas of management in which she felt most comfortable and competent. During the first year, the principal and deputy principal met several times to discuss and agree on a definition of their respective roles, exploring the cross-over and the differences. A draft document relating to both roles was agreed for inclusion in the staff handbook." (see exhibit 3.1)

However, not content with this the deputy principal who was conversant with the literature in the field decided to keep a diary during one week and to analyse her work. She used a threefold classification suggested by Torrington and Weightman for her analysis.[58] It distinguished between technical, administrative, and managerial work to which she added personal. After a very detailed analysis the summary table shown in exhibit 3.2 was produced.

To her surprise 39% of her time was spent on technical work, that is, to do with the actual craft of teaching. 31% was spent on administrative work most of which was spent arranging substitution for absent teachers. This is executive work it is not strategic.

"The work of covering classes and facilitating room and time arrangements can be very time consuming, frustrating and disruptive of the normal duty timetable."

At the same time she points out that some of these tasks overlap with the managerial functions that are concerned with the professional development of colleagues because she had to meet teachers and on these occasions there were times when she could encourage and support a particular teacher.

25% of her time was spent on managerial tasks. These are strategic as opposed to executive tasks as for example planning the curriculum for the next year. She found. as have many others, that the solution is to leave the school with the principal and go to an alternative venue to plan for staff meetings curriculum and staff development. This they did on one day per term.

As a result of her study she felt that she would have to reduce her teaching commitment in order to allow for more time for management that would include the development of a leadership role.

Another study showed the potential for role ambiguity and conflict when a second vice-principal was appointed.

The two vice-principals met with the principal and the duties associated with position were shared. It was extremely difficult to make any differentiation between the two positions and the best way forward for the school was for each of the vice-principals to set out certain roles for themselves in their first academic year. A review of these roles would follow after a year and changes would be made if necessary.

Support for this position could be found in the report of the National Education Convention that said

Ideally the principal and the vice-principal should operate closely as the senior management team in the school, sharing duties on an agreed basis so as to ensure the smooth running of the school in the absence of either. For this reason it was felt that the duties and responsibilities of the vice-principal should not be specified in detail but rather should be agreed in accordance with the particular needs of the individual school. In general it was reported that the vice-principal operated more or less as a front house manager in the school, assuming the main responsibility for drawing up and implementing the time table, organising classes, managing substitute teachers as well as for a broad range of student related issues such as time-keeping, absences, pastoral care [...]59

In this example the need for role clarification was evident for both vice-principals had been year heads and they both felt that in reality the teachers still expected them to do the duties of year heads as well. When they were appointed they found it a time of stress.

"*We both tried extremely hard to keep to our defined roles and duties but quite often we adapted to circumstances as they presented themselves,*" and a questionnaire which was circulated showed that the staff saw both roles as similar:

-Responsible for the day to day running of the school and timetabling.
-Responsible for administration, pastoral duties and hands on participation in situations as they arise.
-Dealing with major disciplinary problems and general management of resources.
-Very visible in the school, always in close contact with the teachers.
-Delegating as much routine work as possible but always ensuring that the work is completed properly in accordance with school policy.
-Having a close liaison with Year heads and department heads.
-Enforcing standards required for a learning atmosphere.

We are seen as the management whom staff can relate to, a link between the principal and teachers, and we are seen as the people in the fore-front in decision making and implementing policy by creating practical systems to ensure the efficient running of the school.

Although the year head is the person who is most closely acquainted with the students the very fact that the vice-principals are managing on the shop–floor means that the students will have an image of them. In this study a questionnaire to students found that they understood the particular roles that these vice-principals had undertaken. These vice-principals argued that where this is the case, this is likely to lead to the effective functioning of the school.

In spite of the rather rigid system of post-holding in Ireland there have been several examples where experienced teachers have been asked to undertake duties associated with a senior position by without a post. Such innovations create tension. One teacher placed in the situation reported that the role had to unfold in a situation where there was *"not open hostility but a certain degree of begrudgery."*

"In this school the principal deals with the administration of the school, while the vice-principal handles on the spot discipline. Hence my role developed into one of hands on deck at all times and visibility was all-important to building up the role with both staff and students. The chief role difficulty was the fact that, at one level I became part of the management team, but since the role lacked official Department of Education sanction it had no authority in relation to staff. The task of the first term became that of performing in such a way that respect would accrue to the role based on the fact that it made the day to day running of the school smoother. If staff members find that a role is supporting their work in a tangible way, negativity towards the role will and, hopefully did fall off. At the same time, as the role unfolds, it is important that it is established as

being independent and not simply rubber-stamping the wishes of those whom it seeks to serve. In the case of this role, it was in the handling of conflict situations between staff and students that the role became defined."

In this way this teacher shaped the environment. This case and others show that even in rigid situations it is possible to be creative and innovative.

Shaping Our Environment

Clearly personality plays an important role in our ability to shape and control our environments. In some environments we will adapt, others we will try to shape.

Personality is a complex characteristic. This may be demonstrated by a study by Heller and Wilpert.[60] They asked managers to describe the skill requirements of their job in terms of twelve attributes. These were knowledge of technical skills, close contact with people, knowledge of human nature, imagination, self-confidence, responsibility, decisiveness, tact, adaptability, forcefulness, intelligence, and initiative. Most of these are factors that, when equated together, would be called personality, or at least dimensions of personality. So if we are to shape our environment, we have to understand how these traits are acted by and in ourselves.

The vice-principal is the person who, under the direction of the principal, shares the duty of co-ordinating the work of all sections of the college.

1. *The principal and vice-principal are seen as a cohesive management unit in the college.*

2. *The vice-principal discharges all the duties of the principal when the latter is absent.*

3. *The vice-principal makes decisions consistent with the ethos of the college.*

4. *The vice-principal helps to foster unity, dialogue and good communications with the staff and the school.*

5. *The vice-principal through leadership, promotes and encourages high academic standards among staff and students.*

6. *In working with the principal, year heads, and tutors, the vice-principal values, promotes and develops the strong pastoral care tradition of the college.*

7. *In attending to the vice-principals teaching duties, an example is set for good practice in attention to agreed procedures and academic and pastoral excellence.*

8. *The vice-principal deals with parents as significant partners in the education of young people and with the respect due to them as such.*

9. *The vice-principal in exercising the authority and functions of the post has the respect, loyalty, and support of the principal.*

Continues over

10. While the position of vice-principal is an important, influential and onerous one, final management of the College rests with the principal under the Board of Management.

11. The vice-principal has devolved responsibilities for specific sections of the school on a daily, weekly, monthly, term and annual basis.*

The functions of the Vice-Principal.

1 Teaching. Load specified

2 Substitution

–arrange substitution of classes of absent teachers, teachers involved with classes in 'in school' or 'out of school' activities and teachers on in-service-courses. Parent/teacher meetings or other meetings
-arrange room adjustments for above.
-teach or supervise classes for absent teachers if no part-time teacher is available.
-work with part-time teachers to ensure effective substitution for absent teachers.
-organize availability of resources to be used in substitution classes.

3 Plan and arrange, with post holders, the timetable, supervision and locations of all in-house examinations.

4 Draw up and monitor rotas and procedures for
-morning and lunchtime supervision
-morning and afternoon registration

Continues over

5   Recruit and interview part-time teachers. *Ensure that new teachers become familiar with a all aspects of the school and its structures- introduce them to a 'link' teacher on the staff*

6   Update staff hand book annually.

these were specified in detail in the handbook. In the annual section there is a requirement to advise and assist the principal in curriculum development and general educational needs of the college.

Exhibit 3.1. General guidelines (and functions) for the role of a Vice-Principal as set out in a staff handbook. These might be compared with a recently published Trade Union view of the role (White, J (2008). The role of the deputy principal *ASTIR*, 26, (1), 12.

Activity	Monday	Tuesday	Wednesday	Thursday	Friday	
Social	27	10	15	20	65	=137
Technical	335	179	245	180	95	=1034
Administrative	203	95	255	137	170	=860
Managerial	100	226	55	188	125	=694
Personal	0	0	0	10	0	=0
Total	665	510	570	535	455	=2735

Exhibit 3.2. Time (in minutes) spent on each activity each day..

A beginning can be made with the subject of previous paragraphs: conflict. Psychoanalysts are concerned with conflict within ourselves. Such conflict may create a tension that is a source of disintegration in opposition to the 'integration' we require. If we find ourselves disintegrating we will try to re-shape our environment to restore within us that lost sense of 'integration' (provided that the disintegration has not become completely pathological). Stability and security demand consistency of behaviour and whether we are managers, teachers, parents, workers or pupils, we require consistent and controlled behaviour from those with whom we associate and, in return, we need to show a similar consistency. The problem is that sometimes we may be too rigid and in situations that demand change we may find ourselves unable to adapt. Or, it may be that we become too tired with the job. There are examples of principals who have provided considerable leadership immediately after they were appointed who let things go to the detriment of the school and its culture. Circumstances such as these have led to the idea that individuals should change their jobs at regular intervals. In British Columbia Principals change schools at regular intervals, and it has been suggested that this should happen in Ireland. In Portugal the President and vice-presidents (principals and vice-principals) are elected for three years by a Council of Teaching Staff and parents. In traditional systems, organizationally such movements of the kind operated in British Columbia are likely to prove extremely difficult to achieve in practice, and for this reason some mechanism for principal renewal needs to be found, and teachers need to remember that principals have the same 'life' problems as themselves. At least one study in Ireland has shown how teachers can assist with principal renewal which was made necessary by the competition the school was experiencing for pupils. This was achieved by a member of staff designing, implementing and evaluating a questionnaire which sought to determine the culture of the school and to see what changes, if any, would be required to restore morale if morale had been lost. This was done with the permission of the principal and the results led the principal to make changes that it was thought would be helpful.[61]

We have, therefore, to learn about ourselves. Reflective thinking should yield observations that will help us cope with other people and groups. For example, when do we embark on aggressive behaviour and what effect does it have? A person who has a strong need for affiliation is unlikely to adopt behaviours that would lead a group to exclude him or her from membership.

A person who might otherwise respond to a request from a beggar might, if he or she is with his or group, abuse the beggar.

We avoid embarrassing situations and to do this we use an ego-defence mechanism. The ego- defence-mechanism used by the person who is forced to interact with the beggar is called *infavoidance*. Ego-defence mechanisms, according to Lazarus, are learnt behaviours.[62] They are mental devices that help us to cope with the mental stress arising from conflicting needs. There are many ego-defence mechanisms. Freud held that *repression* was the most important ego-defence mechanism. It is a form of self-deception in which the ideas and problems facing a person are chased away below the preconscious into the unconscious. *Self-deceptions* are common and help us to live reasonably comfortable lives- similarly with *sublimation* which, in its broadest sense, is the redirection of a motive from a relatively unacceptable goal (however desirable as a need) to a more acceptable one. These defence mechanisms help us to control our behaviour. It is evident that individuals are capable of controlling their actions. However, some persons under-control, that is, tend to act on the spur of the moment, while others who are slow to make up their mind and carry out detailed planning of future actions, may over-control themselves and the others over whom they have control. Others may *regress* (i.e. retreat to the behaviour of an earlier developmental level causing them to make less than mature responses to the situation).

There are many occasions when we wished we had behaved as others do in certain situations. We would wish for more certainty, more direction, more firmness, more control, and so on. We would like to be less hot-headed or more able to perceive all facets of a problem.

While there is a lot of truth in the view that the dispositions of personality are deep and persistent, the evidence would support the argument that we can develop skills that can direct and control our behaviour. Role-playing is a technique that has as its aim the achievement of these goals.[63] Conducted well role-plays should help with the development of skill in reflection which is the key skill required by those who would improve their understanding of their own behaviour. Of course this skill can be developed in a number of ways. For example various types of self-assessment inventory have been used and one way of developing skill in reflection is to ask not only if one's contribution to a formal discussion that is seeking to solve a problem was potentially helpful to the case or destructive but why. Was I bloody minded or cooperative? Was I quarrelsome or benign? Rigid or flexible? Intolerant or tolerant? Closed minded or open minded? Talkative or silent? Dependent or independent? And, lacking in information/knowledge or well-informed? In *Learning, Adaptability and Change* (p49) I showed a questionnaire based on these dimensions that had been designed for individuals in negotiating teams to evaluate their performance after they had seen a video replay of the action.[64] But these same dimensions apply equally to performance in staff meetings and their answers don't have to await a viseo playback. At the same time one has to be prepared to try and change if this is thought to be necessary and to try it again. Reflective practice is a continuous process of learning.

Role-playing gives us an understanding of power. We cannot and should not shirk away from the issue of power for, as Hunt says, *'Role systems exist for interpersonal relationships, which depend on influence, which depends on power. Power is a resource, while its effect is influence. The effects of influence are co-operation, love, hate, fear, jealousy, and all those other emotions encountered in role systems.'*[65] How do we exercise power and how do we respond to power? Do we try to create fear in one way or another by the use of coercive power? Would we, if we could, exercise remunerative power through the dispensation of rewards and/or patronage? Or do we rely on the legal power vested in the positions we occupy? Are we able to use expertise as a means of power? Not every expert is able to exercise power. How do you respond to power? Do those whom you admire influence your decision? To what extent do you exercise and are influenced by charismatic power? And, finally what do you do to acquire power? We have already alluded to some of the answers to the last question in earlier sections of this chapter.

Principals who want to lead have to learn the proper exercise of power for without power they cannot lead. It may be uncomfortable. Schools, principals and teachers are no different to the organisation and its personnel about whom Pfeffer wrote that:

"It is easy and often comfortable to feel powerless-to say, "I don't know what to do, I don't have the power to get it done , and besides, I can't really stomach the struggle that may be involved." It is easy, and now quite common to say, when confronted with some mistake in your organization, "It's not really my responsibility, I can't do anything about it anyway,......... Such response excuses us from trying to overcome opposition, we will make fewer enemies and are less likely to embarrass ourselves. It is, however, a prescription for both organizational and personal failure. This is why power and influence are not the organization's last dirty secret, but the secret of success for both individuals and their organizations. Innovation and change in almost any arena require the skill to develop power, and the willingness to employ it to get things accomplished. Or in the words of a local radio newscaster, "If you don't like the news, go out and make some of your own."[66]

Do not suppose that exercise of power is best accomplished with the aid of a bull-dozer. Cooper has been led to the view that men's style of management contributes to stress. Moreover, it tends to stop workers from doing their best. *"Stress at work is closely related to the amount of control people feel they have over their area of responsibility. British management-(mostly men)- are not, in general, too good at allowing their subordinates this kind of freedom, because they are too sensitive about their own power."*[67] For this reason Cooper felt that women were likely to be better managers in the future. A woman principal of an Irish school when asked if it was possible for each principal to put his or her own stamp on their role replied that, as a woman, she had a different approach to leadership than many men she had observed. She felt that power was not as important for her as for others. She was more interested in how she could influence staff and students by delegating and supporting. She observed that many men seemed to get a personal feeling that the role of principal made them powerful. She viewed the role as being a way of doing things. She favours a partnership approach rather than a hierarchical one, *"emphasising the responsibilities of the role rather than the power attaching to it."*[68] But, this principal's notion of power is rather stereotyped. If we agree with Pfeffer's definition that *"Power is the potential ability to influence behaviour, to change the course of events, to overcome resistance, and to get people to do things they would not otherwise do,"* then according to the report, in which this principal was quoted, she had been successful, and she had exercised power.

As Pfeffer says:

"Individual success in organizations is quite frequently a matter of working with and through other people, and organizational success is often a function of how successfully individuals can coordinate their activities. Most situations in organizations resemble football more than golf, which is why companies often scan resumes to find not only evidence of individual achievement, but also signs that the person is skilled at working as part of a team. In achieving success in organizations, "power transforms individual interest into coordinated activities that accomplish valuable ends." [69]

Which is to bring us back to where we started namely that one of the principle tasks of management is the co-ordination of roles and a year head, as we have seen, has to do this just as much as a principal as does any group leader.

If we are to shape and control our environment, we need to understand how we perceive and develop and adapt our roles to meet differing circumstances with which we are continually faced.

While adaptability may be regarded as a skill, our use of that skill depends on our dispositions. Nevertheless, we can be helped to develop this skill. To be able to adapt within an organization, and to understand how the skills of the 'others' in our role-set can best be utilized. To achieve this goal, we will require an understanding of how jobs can be designed or redesigned to serve better both the individual and the organization. The more we understand behaviour in organizations, the more we are likely to benefit from such exercises and the more we shall learn to help our selves change.

The view we take of why individuals are motivated to work underpins the judgements we make about organizational structure, the role of the manager and thus to the meaning we give the managerial role. It is with the nature of motivation at work that the next chapter is concerned.

Notes and references

[1] This paragraph is based on Barbara Engler's study of George Kelly in Engler, B (1979). *Personality Theories. An Introduction*. Houghton Mifflin, Boston Chapter 13.

[2] This is but one typology (due to Bey) of the orientations that students can adopt: Bey, C. (1962) A social theory of higher education in N. Sanford (ed). *The American College*. Wiley, New York. Another orientation that has become important is *"strategic"*. A *"strategically* oriented student is similar in some respects to Bey's *academically* oriented student in that the *strategic* student works out what is required of him/her to get satisfactory marks (as defined by the student).

[3] Handy, C (1993). *Understanding Organizations*. 4th edition. Penguin, Harmonsworth – Holland, J. L.(1973). *Making Vocational Choices. A Theory of Careers*. Prentice hall, Englewood Cliffs, NJ

[4] Kolb, D. A (1984) *Experiential Learning. Experience as a source of Learning*. Prentice Hall, Englewood Cliffs, NJ.

[5] for example-. In an assembly line a worker may develop an *instrumental* attitude toward

work particularly if it is repetitive and unpleasant. Workers will tolerate such work provided that the rewards are sufficient to allow them to look for satisfaction elsewhere and not at work. Another person in these circumstances may be *solidaristically* inclined and seek satisfaction through membership of a group associated with work such as a trade union. Work enables the individual to share in a group activity from which he or she obtains meaning. Other individuals particularly those in supervision and management whose jobs give them some satisfaction are likely to have a bureaucratic orientation to work and give service to the organization. Motivated by interest, this type of worker uses his or her work for steadily increasing income, social status and for long term security. These orientations will be found in Goldthorpe, J et al (1970). *The Affluent Worker; Industrial Attitudes and Behaviour.* Cambridge University Press.

[6] phrase due to Burns, T (1966) On the plurality of social systems in J. R. Lawrence (ed) *Operational Research and the Social Sciences.* Tavistock, London

[7] One of my post-graduate students suggested that *"each role forces one to change personality a little, to put it on a façade, act very differently."* But if personality is the aggregate of our dispositions it may be argued that each role draws on different dimensions of our personality

[8] As for example in Ireland in the Transition Year

[9] Cohen, A (1992) Managing people: the R factor in E. Collian and M. Devanna (eds). *The Portable MBA.* Wiley, New York

[10] From a post-graduate assignment, 1998

[11] Role-set, role conflict and ambiguity were originally discussed by R.L. Kahn. See Kahn, R.L. (1973) Conflict: ambiguity and overload: three elements in job stress. *Occupational Mental Health*, 3, (1), 191-194. Role-set is both a psychological and a sociological concept. A sociogram of a class is in part a representation of the role-set among a group of students.

[12] In Ireland this is not always the case. See O'Kelly, P (2005) The Role of the year Head in the schools of one VEC (Vocational Education Committee). Towards an Improved Role. MSt Thesis. University of Dublin, Dublin.

[13] Day, C., Whitaker, P and D. Johnston (1990). *Managing Primary Schools in the 1990's. A Professional Development Approach.* 2nd ed. Paul Chapman, London.

[14] Pfeffer, J (1992). *Managing with Power.* Harvard Business School Press, Cambridge, MA In respect of item 4 These may be ideas of his or her own, or they may be requirements of the management board, or policies that the State wishes to implement

[15] ibid

[16] These groups are described by L.Rae (1994) in *Lets Have a Meeting.* McGraw Hill, New York.

[17] Berne, E (1964). *The Games People Play. The Psychology of Human Relationships.* Penguin, Harmonsdworth

[18] Hodgson, P and J. Hodgson. (1992). *Effective Meetings.* See also Rae, L.(1994). *Lets Have a Meeting*

[19] In Ireland the secondary (denominational) schools were, in the case of Catholic Schools, run by Religious. A Priest, Brother or Sister would be the principal. They were supported by other religious who undertook the extra-mural work required by the school. In consequence the lay teachers had no responsibilities. There was no possibility of promotion. In 1968 The Trade Unions obtained an agreement with the Government to the effect that senior personnel would be rewarded with a post of responsibility. There would be two grades (A and B). The number of posts would be a function of the number of pupils in the school. The most senior person in the school would be appointed to the next post to come available. The duties were then agreed. Some of the tasks were non-tasks i.e., little or no work was required from the incumbent. The posts related to the particular school in which they were given and could not be transferred. Neither could they be advertised or awarded on merit. They had to be given to the most senior person. As the number of religious declined they withdrew from the schools but remained as managers and trustees. This meant that lay persons could now become principals. Many of these lay principals found that the staff expected them to do all the work that the religious had done in the

past. In consequence they became heavily overloaded. This drew attention to the lack of middle-management and some schools initiated experiments which showed the value of such structures. One outcome of the Education Act of 1999 was to provide for middle management structures as a development of the previous system.

[20] From a post-graduate assignment 1994

[21] Katzenback, J. and D. Smith (1993). The discipline of teams. *Harvard Business Review*. March/April

[22] Freeman. J and J. Sharp (2001) Group Dynamics and the Learning Process in J. Heywood et al (eds). *Improving Teaching in Higher Education*. University of Salford, Salford UK pp 128 – 143

[23] Drucker, P. (1993). *Managing the Non-Profit Organization*. Butterworth-Heinemann, London

[24] Belbin, R,M. (1981). *Management Teams: Why they Succeed or Fail*. Heinemann, London. See also Eales-White, R. (1996). *How to Build a Team*. Kogan Page, London. There are other typologies

[25] Tse, K.K. (1985). *Marks and Spencer. Anatomy of Britain's Most Efficiently Managed Company*. Pergamon, Oxford.

[26] Smith, K. A. (2004) *Teamwork and Project Management*. 2nd edition. McGraw Hill, New York. for a review of teamwork and its assessment in 15 plus education see Heywood, J (2005) Ch 13 of *Engineering Education. Research and Development in Curriculum and Instruction*. IEEE/Wiley, New York.

[27] Hynes, M (2000) Curriculum Support Teams as vehicles for the provision of In-Career Professional Development for Second-Level Teachers. M.ST Thesis University of Dublin, Dublin.

[28] Woodcock, M. (1993). *Team Development Manual*. 4th edition. Gower, Aldershot.

[29] Lewin, K (1947). Group decision and social change in T. M. Newcomb and E. L. Hartley (eds). *Readings in Social Psychology*. Henry Holt, New York.

[30] Tuckman, B.W. (1965). Development sequences in small groups. *Psychological Bulletin*, 63, (6), 384-399. Woodock see note 28. Eales-White see note 24. Blanchard, K (1994) *Leadership and the One Minute Manager*. Harper-Collins, London.

[31] *ibid*: Bell, L and C. Day. (1991). *Managing the Professional Development of Teachers*. Open University. Milton Keynes

[32] *ibid.*

[33] *ibid.*

[34] Sanghera, S. (2007) Hamilton gives us all food for thought. *The Times* p 67 October 6th.

[35] *ibid*

[36] *ibid*

[37] See Kahn ref 11. See also Cooper, C and J. Marshall (1977). *Understanding Executive Stress*, Petrocelli, New York. Intra sender conflict exists when someone is asked by another to accomplish two objectives that are in apparent conflict. Inter-sender conflict occurs when a person receives contradictory instructions from two or more people. Inter-role conflict occurs when an individual has to take on incompatible roles.

[38] Poultney, V (2007). The role of the effective subject leader: perspectives from practitioners in secondary schools. *Management in Education*, 21 (2), 8 – 18.

[39] Calderwood, D. (1989) Some implications of Role Conflict and Role Ambiguity as Stressors in a Comprehensive School. *School Organisation*, 9, (3), 311-315

[40] Dunham, J. (1984). *Stress in Teaching*. Croom Helm, Beckenham

[41] Trim, P (1997). Strategy saves the day. *Management in Education* 11, (4), 29 – 31

[42] From a. Post-graduate assignment(1996) by an experienced teacher.

[43] Heller, F.A. and B. Wilpert (1981) *Competence and Power in Managerial Decision Making*. Wiley, New York, NY

[44] Helps, V (1992). *Negotiating. Everybody Wins*. BBC publications, London

[45] At the time this teacher was appointed to this post the Department of Education did not sanction a second vice-Principal in the school because it was just under the size which allowed for such an appointment. It was a community school with 800 students and a

fairly high proportion came from problem family backgrounds. A need was felt for a third person apart from the Principal and vice-Principal to deal with this issue on the ground management in the school. This teacher was, therefore, given the title of senior dean with greatly reduced teaching hours.

[46] *ibid* Helps

[47] From a post-graduate assignment that quoted Ball, S.J.(1987). *The Micro-Politics of the School. Towards a Theory of School Organization*. Methuen, New York. And Fullan, M (1991) who was quoting Sarason. *The New Meaning of Educational Change*. Cassell, London

[48] Everard, K. B and G. Morris (1990) *Effective School Management*. Paul Chapman, London.

[49] Tillett, G (2000). *Resolving Conflict. A Practical Approach*. 2nd edition. Oxford University Press, USA.

[50] Crawley, J (1993). *Constructive Conflict Management. Managing to make a Difference*. Pfeiffer, San Diego, CA.

[51] Reading, M. A (2002) Middle management leadership development in English schools. Bulletins of the EFEA.No 3, 73 – 80. European Forum on Educational Administration. He cites Bennett, N (1995). *Managing Professional Teachers: Middle Management in Primary and Secondary Schools*. Paul Chapman, London. Also Glover, D, Gleeson, D, Gough, G. and M. Johnson (1998). The meaning of management. *Educational Management and Administration*, 26, (3), 181 – 195.

[52] This is a continuation of the section in chapter 2 on ambiguity

[53] Jaques, E (1970) *Work, Creativity and Social Justice*. Heinemann, London

[54] Leader, D and S.Boldt (1994) *Principals and Principalship*. The Marino Institute of Education (Christian Brothers), Dublin

[55] Torrington, D and J. Weightman (1989). *The Reality of School Management*. Blackwell, Oxford.

[56] *loc.cit*

[57] Knutton, S and A. Mycroft (1986). Stress and the deputy head.. *School Organisation* 6, (1).

[58] *loc.cit*

[59] *Report of the National Education Convention* (1994). Government Publications, Dublin.

[60] *loc.cit* ref 10

[61] Purcell, C (1998). MSt Thesis. University of Dublin, Dublin

[62] Lazarus, R. S. (1963). *Personality and Adjustment*. Prentice Hall, Englewood Cliffs, NJ

[63] For a description of a role playing course in the M.Ed degree at Trinity College see Fitzgibbon, A and J. Heywood (1986) The recognition of conjunctive and identity needs in teacher development: their implications for the planning of in-service training. *European Journal of Teacher Education*, 10, (2), 163 – 178.

[64] Taken from Heywood, J. (1989). *Learning, Adaptability and Change*. Paul Chapman, London. It was designed by J. Heywood, W. Humble of the British Steel Corporation and J. Freeman of the Department of General Practice, The University of Manchester. There are many similar inventories of this kind. See for example the latest edition of *The Team Development Manual* Gower Press, Aldershot) by M. Woodcock

[65] Hunt, J (1979). *Managing People at Work*. McGraw Hill, Maidenhead.

[66] *loc.cit* ref 10

[67] cited by J. Spicer (1988) Women are better managers. *The Times* 6, January

[68] *loc cit* ref 10. Pfeffer. The last sentence is quoted from A. Zaleznik and M. F. R de Vries(1975). *Power and the Corporate Mind*. Houghton Miflin, Boston

[69] *ib*

CHAPTER 4

EVERYONE A MANAGER

Introduction

The view we take of why individuals are motivated to work underpins the judgements we make about organizational structure, the role of the manager and thus the meaning given to service in the managerial role. The same applies to teachers and their evaluations of why students learn. Teachers are managers of learning. Various stereotypes of workers (learners) are used to demonstrate these axioms, and from the evidence it is argued that there is no simple model that accounts for the motivation to work or to learn. However, individuals behave in different ways, and at different times according to the circumstances in which they find themselves. Accordingly, each model of the individual has something to add to our understanding of human behaviour and the reasons why some people adapt and others resist change. None of these models excuse management from providing a technology of learning or production that is a challenge to the student or worker. For many people, to do this, requires considerable changes in attitude towards learning and work and its organization among managers. Such change may be brought about by an understanding of the inherent capability of individuals for decision- making, and the necessity for them to use management skills in every role and task they undertake. This argument is supported by a discussion of the nature of decision-making and the learning process. Everyone is shown to do managerial tasks, and a model of the individual as manager is proposed. In this chapter some of the ideas presented in chapters 2 and 3 are developed further.

The Rational-Economic Individual

If I were asked to say what it is that boys and girls and men and women do most, apart from sleep and work, I think I would answer very quickly and without much thought, "gossip". When we seek another job we often try to work out who the competitors are, particularly if we operate, as some do, in a relatively small group of schools or, say university professors as I do. The communication network is particularly adept at conveying gossip, true or false. And, when a person is appointed, we are apt to spend much time with our colleagues wondering why this or that principal or manager, or chairperson of governors was appointed. Anyway, often there are unexpressed but uneasy feelings in our mind because we are not sure, never having done the job, what the job demands. We find it difficult to describe readily our mythical models of the manager, or principal. The more rarefied the job, say, a head of a university, the more difficult it is to come to grips with the nature of the job. So too, is the "fall" of a senior person cause for gossip. In this respect men are no different to women, although, as might be expected, the way in which women perceive men often differs from the way in which men perceive women. More striking is the fact that the way we perceive the actions of workers in a strike situation is likely to be very different from the way in which we would perceive the same workers on the golf course or in a bar. Think of any teachers' strike in this respect. As we saw in chapters 2 and 3 expectations vary as people change their roles.1 We associate one set of expectations with the work role, another with the friendship role, and so on. Our family has totally different expectations of us from those of our manager, or of our teacher, or of our colleague. We should also be aware that we ourselves create expectations and these have an impact with those with whom we have to deal both at the level of the school and the classroom. The task of the principal in so far as is possible, is to ensure that the teachers' expectations of their work are met. A caveat arises from the fact that there are important features of the task that may be outside the control of the principal, as for example the curriculum, and the monetary rewards they receive if they work in a public system of education.[2]

If we try to analyse our expectations in depth, we find we are thinking about the way in which a person will behave in those particular circumstances. Moreover, we draw conclusions about the way in which those concerned with that person and his or her behaviour should behave. These expectations are often biased and stem from the deeply held beliefs acquired during a lifetime. The pictures associated with these beliefs we call stereotypes, and it is such stereotypes that often guide our behaviour in relation to our judgements about the performance of learners and workers. In this respect, our views of why individuals learn and work are important for they underpin the judgements we make about organizational structure, the role of the manager and thus the meaning given to service in the managerial role. Views about the reasons why individuals work run deep, and many managers undoubtedly believe in the rational-economic learner or worker described by Schein.[3] Here is Schein's description (slightly adapted):

1. The individual is primarily motivated by economic incentives and will do that which gets him or her, the greatest economic gain.

2. Since economic incentives are under the control of the organization, an individual is essentially a passive agent to be manipulated, motivated and controlled by organization.

3. The individual's feelings are essentially irrational and must be prevented from his or her rational calculation of self-interest.

4. The organization can and must be designed in such a way as to neutralize and control the individual's feelings and therefore his or her unpredictable traits

This model is very similar to McGregor' Theory X which Schein also reports thus:

1. An individual is inherently lazy and must therefore be motivated by outside incentives.

2. The individual's goals run counter to those of the organization, Hence, the individual must be controlled by external forces to ensure his working toward organizational goals.

3. Because of his irrational feelings, an individual is basically incapable of self-discipline and self-control.

There is no escape from the fact that many owners and managers do react to individuals in this way. Hierarchical structures where commands move from the top- down and communications flow-up (figure 4.1) are one result. At the present time call centres seem to exemplify this approach. When making a hotel reservation we are often told that the call may be monitored with a view to improving the service. We are told by those who work in such centres that they are tightly controlled even to the amount of time that they should spend with a client on the telephone. One would expect there to be a high turnover in such systems. Management would not be bothered by such losses if there is a reasonably plentiful supply of labour and training is easy. In the classroom the equivalent of turnover is "turn-off". It would be wrong, however to assume that some people will lack motivation in these situations for some take an instrumental attitude to work. It would also be wrong to assume that motivation should be equated with happiness. Some people are miserable whatever their work situation and some of them can be very clever. For example, currently many British commentators cite the example of a British Prime minister![4]

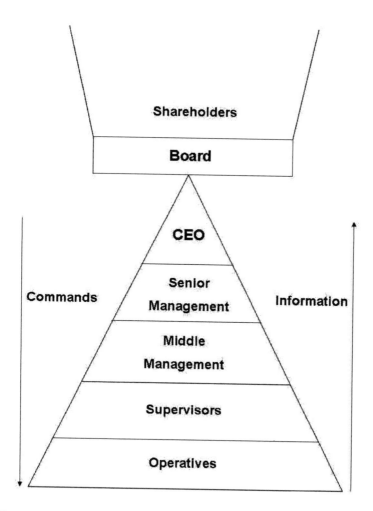

Figure 4.1. Communication in a hierarchical organization.

Similar views are to be found among teachers about their students. Thus the theory X model of the student is,

1. The student is primarily motivated by academic incentives and will do whatever gets him or her, the greatest academic gain.

2. Since academic incentives are under the control of the institution, the student is essentially a passive agent to be manipulated, motivated and controlled by the organization.

3. The student's feelings are essentially irrational and must be prevented from interfering with his or her rational calculation of self-interest.

4. Institutions and their organizational (curriculum) arrangements can and must be designed in such a way as to neutralise and control their feelings and therefore, their unpredictable traits.

Extrinsic incentives, such as regular testing, may be used to encourage students. Chalk-and-talk methods of lecturing will probably be employed.

The implications of theory X attitudes for managers, and indeed teachers are profound. Managers and teachers *must* plan, organize, motivate and control their personnel without reference to the feelings and needs of their workers and pupils. It leads to a rationalist approach to management that is to be found in many companies and educational institutions[5] In what became a best seller. Peters and Waterman in- In *Search of Excellence* said, that the analytic approach of rationalist management, with its emphasis on quantitative techniques and factual data, has been to the detriment of excellence in many American companies.[6] They blamed along with many others the American business-school curriculum for this state of affairs. But in schools where it is not matter of large sums of money and quantitative techniques, but a matter of struggling to get by it is the psychology of human behaviour inherent in such judgements that is worrying. It can for example reinforce the isolation of teachers in their classrooms to the detriment of a corporate mission to educate children. Such dispositions can reinforce "them" and "us" attitudes.

The Social Aspects of Work

Sometimes it is the social aspects of work that influence behaviour. This was illustrated in the Hawthorne studies that could be said to be the founding studies of industrial social psychology. These studies conducted in the late nineteen twenties and early thirties and directed by Elton Mayo are named after a factory in Chicago operated by the Westinghouse Electric Co.[7] This factory gave its name to the "Hawthorne Effect" which is an important phenomena in social research .and described in detail in the note.[8] Here we are mainly interested in another of the Hawthorne Studies. In this one, briefly, men who wired and soldered wiring banks, together with their supervisors (fourteen persons in all), were watched for a long period by a trained observer. After a period the observer's presence was ignored. He found that within the group there were two sub-groups related to the front and back of the workroom. Some workers did not belong to either group. The workers at the front felt they had more status than those working at the back of the room because they believed they had a more difficult job to do.

The group developed norms behaviour, that is, unwritten rules about behaviour and performance to which the group would conform. Thus, they had norms about the amount of work that should be done in return for the pay they were offered. This, according to the observer, was well below that which could have been achieved, although the output satisfied the company. *"The attitude of the members of the group towards the company's financial incentive was one of indifference."*[9] Anyone who worked at a rate above the norm was called a *'rate buster'*, while those who worked at a rate that would produce below the norm were called *'chiselers'*. Deviations from the norm led to pressures on the deviants to get back in line. The high status group were high-producers who thought the low-status group were social isolates. Neither dexterity nor intelligence tests correlated with individual output. The social mechanism that restricted productivity appeared to be the fact that the low status group resented being called 'chiselers' by the high status group. So they decided that the best way to get their own back was to reduce their rate of production, the net effect of which was to get the backs up of the high status group with the same result.

It was also understood within the group that those in authority (the supervisors) must not act officiously or take advantage of their authority position. An Inspector who deviated was transferred to another department because of the pressure put on him. The supervisors were regarded as no better than anyone else and they acquiesced in the behaviour of the group. The group also undertook other activities that were contrary to company policy. For example, they exchanged jobs. Soldermen sometimes did wiring while the wiremen sometimes did soldering.

One of the concepts that derived from these studies was that of the *"informal organisation"*. These workers created their own organisation independently of but within the "formal" organisation of the company. Although this concept seems to have gone out of favour every principal on joining a school will want to understand the informal structures that develop in the staff room. They are likely to affect both the conduct and outcomes of staff meetings, and in consequence effect the extent to which the school achieves its mission. Because schools are organised for isolates (single teachers in single classrooms) and not for teams the staff room is the place where they discuss all the other activities of schooling but not what they do by themselves in their classrooms.

These studies indicate the importance of social relationships at work and Elton Mayo was led to assume that individuals were primarily motivated by social needs, and would therefore be more responsive to their peer groups than to management. Therefore, management should try to meet an individual's social needs, and this will enhance motivation. Schein's description of Mayo's model of the social person is[10]

1. The person is basically motivated by social needs.

2. As a result of the rationalization of work, meaning has gone out of work and must be sought in social relationships on the job.

3. The focus of the work group will do more to influence behaviour than the incentives and controls of managers.

4. A supervisor will only be effective to the extent that he/she can satisfy his subordinates' social needs.

Everyday observation of people at work provides evidence of the importance of social relationships. But it also suggests that they can have an inhibiting effect on performance, as any observation of classroom behaviour will show.

The finding of the experiment that established the "Hawthorne Effect" was that if individuals perceive that the organization has an interest in them they are likely to work hard. This model of motivation replaced the rational-economic person model. It was the pillar on which the human-relations school of management was built. It was found to be too simplistic and was replaced by other models, in particular theory Y and Self-actualisation.

Theory Y and Self-Actualisation.

Theory Y is the opposite of theory X. McGregor lists the assumptions of Theory Y as follows.

1. The expenditure of physical and mental effort in work is as natural as play or rest.

2. External control and the threat of punishment are not the only means for bringing about effort toward organizational

objectives. A person will exercise self-direction and self-control in the service of the objectives to which he is committed.

3. Commitment to objectives is a function of the rewards associated with their achievement.

4. The average human being learns, under proper conditions, not only to accept, but to seek responsibility.

5. The capacity to exercise a relatively high degree of imagination, ingenuity and creativity in the solution of organizational problems is widely, not narrowly, distributed among the population.

6. Under the conditions of modern industrial life, the intellectual potentialities of the average human being are only partially utilized.

As will be seen Theory Y is the opposite of Theory X. The principle of Theory X is The Little Oxford Dictionary's definition of management as "direction and control". The central principle of theory Y is that of integration. To quote McGregor, *"It is the creation of conditions such that the members of the organization can achieve their own goals best by directing their efforts towards the success of the enterprise."*[11] Thus, the task of the principal is the reconciliation of the goals that each of the teachers has with the goals of the school, and the question is how best might this be done. Is it by means of an approach based on teachers primarily as rational-economic individuals, and its derivative Theory X, at one end of the spectrum? Or, at the other end of the spectrum, is it the kind of organisation that emerges if the integrating principle of Theory Y is applied?

A principal on a management course as part of an assignment gave a rating scale to some students in his school that was designed to distinguish between Theory X and Theory Y behaviour. He asked them to rate their teachers and themselves.

Surprise, Surprise! They rated their teachers as Theory X and themselves as Theory Y. Of course there may be some truth in this if these perceptions are based solely on the classroom behaviour of teachers. But it needs to be remembered that the organisation can cause the teacher behaviour rated as Theory X. For example, the belief that examinations test rote knowledge leads to the belief that the classroom is best arranged for children to learn by rote. And, this implies teacher centred as opposed to student centred learning.

A teacher wrote, that a principal whose beliefs about motivation follow theory X may *"not feel compelled to consult with staff or take their views and feelings into account when planning and organising"*. A principal whose beliefs are similar to those of Theory Y *"will see the need to consult and delegate and create an environment conducive to learning, personal growth and advancement"*. She classified her own principal as Theory Y because he is *"easy going, democratic and believes in theory Y style management. In his opinion people are motivated by responsibility and like to be consulted on decisions which affect them. He believes in delegation, shared responsibility and continuous learning"*. This means, in the case of her school that, *"teachers with special duties and the deputy principal play a vital role in the day to day running of the school"* [12] There is, however more to running a school than this because the principal is at the centre of a system where external relationships are also important.

One of the problems for principals whether of theory X or Y dispositions is when they become office bound because of the minute by minute problems that a principal has to face. In these circumstances they can become isolated from the school, its teachers and staff. Consider the case where it was argued that the *"principal sets the tone of discipline for the school"* then if that is the case the principal has to know what is going on and he/she has to have a system of communication to achieve this objective. In the case study the principal had delegated the task of developing and introducing a new scheme of discipline to the deputy-principal. Neither the principal or the deputy-principal were aware that the scheme was not working well until the staff became so frustrated that they went to the top. Delegation does not relieve the delegated from informing the delegator of what is happening and of evaluating progress. *"Evaluation is the key to any policy being successfully implemented."*[13] In this case the degree of commitment of the teachers to an effective discipline policy was very high.

McGregor points out, that acceptance of Theory Y does not imply abdication, or 'soft' management, or 'permissiveness'. We should perhaps add 'happiness.' As was indicated above, such notions stem from the acceptance of authority as the *single* means of managerial control, and from attempts to minimize the negative consequences. *"Theory Y assumes that people will exercise self-direction and self-control in the achievement of organizational goals to the degree that they are committed to those objectives. If that commitment is small, only a slight degree of self-direction and self-control will be likely, and a substantial amount of external influence will be necessary. If it is large, many conventional external controls will be relatively superfluous, and to some extent self-defeating. Managerial policies and practices materially affect this degree of commitment."* [14]

McGregor's theory Y followed in the wake of a humanistic model of motivation called self-actualisation. This was based on the idea that there are human needs that have to be satisfied if a person is to be motivated.[15] Maslow suggested that people are motivated by five types of need. Although it was not proposed either for management or teaching many managers and teachers are familiar with the theory. Interpreted for work it says than an individual is motivated to work as his or her needs are met. But, the primary physiological needs have to be met before the secondary psychological needs- the needs for self-esteem and autonomy have to be met before self-actualisation, when an individual is fully occupied and satisfied with what they do[16] (See figure 4.2). In theory Y the individual seeks autonomy in the work that has to be done, and given an appropriate challenge will be motivated to meet the new demand, and this will make the organization more effective. The manager's task is, therefore, to arrange that the organization brings to the worker an environment and resources that will help the individual strive towards self-actualisation. Barnes has argued against this hierarchical concept of need-fulfilment on the grounds that self-actualisation (that is, to become everything that one is capable of becoming) is unlikely to be possible operationally. He also argues that the safety needs overlap the higher needs because whenever one of these is threatened, so is the individual's safety.[17] Looked at from a behavioural point of view self-actualisation may be reached at some optimum level of motivation. Any attempt to increase motivation above that level will reduce motivation. Moreover, the level at which this optimum is reached may be a function of personality. For example, a recent and on the whole successful attempt to persuade a number of primary schools in Ireland to attempt to develop skills associated with enterprise using a project approach caused some schools to over reach themselves. Whole schools were involved by their teachers but the effort and enthusiasm of their teachers led them to put so much time into the project that they became, in a very crude sense, "burnt out". This meant that some of them did not want to do the project again because of the heavy workload. They had overshot the point of optimum motivation.[18]

It would seem that a teacher is ideally placed to aspire to self-actualisation. They have no one to bother them, except the class or classes they teach, and there is no doubt that many teachers enjoy their work and get fulfilment from it. Unfortunately, it is also true that many teachers do not enjoy their work. In recent years in many countries teachers have been required to respond to what have been significant changes in their work. In this respect, Ireland is no different to any other country. Secondary teachers in Ireland have had to respond to the broader range of ability their schools now admit.

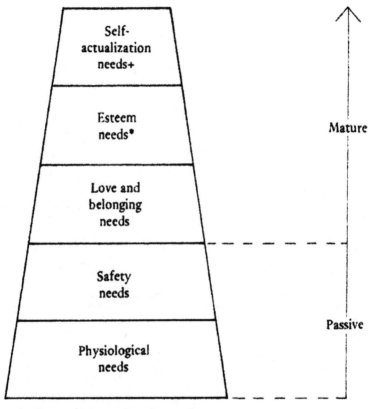

+ Desires to know and understand
* Desires for achievement recognition

Figure 4.2. Self Actualisation

They have also had to respond to the changing attitudes that children of all abilities have toward discipline. So there is work for a principal to do to keep "the show on the road."

One of the ideas to come from humanistic psychology is the idea of "intrinsic" motivation. It is the motivation we generate inside ourselves because we want to do something. Quite clearly it depends in no small way on interest. So a principal who accepts that intrinsic motivation is important will want to ensure that the teachers in his/her school maintain an interest in their subject. In Irish secondary schools this is a very difficult task because the principal has been effectively barred from taking such an interest. The principal is required to be more of an administrator than senior pedagogue *(primus inter pares)*. From the perspective of management it is important that the encouragement of intrinsic motivation does not drive the respondent beyond that respondents optimum level.

While Maslow's theory has never been validated empirically it has influenced managerial writers such as McGregor. Another study by Herzberg and colleagues continues to receive much attention although it has not received much support from empirical research. Indeed, McGregor draws attention specifically to this work. Herzberg's two-factor theory as it is known describes the factors that lead to job satisfaction and job dissatisfaction. The data was obtained from engineers and accountants who were asked to recall "critical incidents" that were associated with especially good and bad feelings about work. The theory derived from these interviews makes the assumption that individuals have *motivator* needs and *hygiene* needs. The *motivator* needs are intrinsic to work, and the *hygiene* needs are extrinsic. Herzberg and his colleagues argue that if the hygiene needs are not met then a worker will be dissatisfied. But, even if they are met this does not produce a state of satisfaction. As we saw in one of the examples in chapter 3 lack of policy for year heads was a cause of disatisfaction but policy by itself will not resolve the issue unless the resources are provided for it to be achieved. It is only when the *motivator* needs are met that an individual becomes satisfied.[17] The components of these two factors are tabulated in exhibit 4.1.

Satisfiers (motivating factors, elements that increase job satisfaction)	Dissatisfiers (hygeine factors, elements that dimish job satisfaction)
1 Achievement 2 Recognition 3 Work itself 4 Responsibility. 5 Advancement	1 Company policy and administration. 2 Supervision-technical 3 Salary 4 Interpersonal relations supervision 5 Working conditions

Exhibit 4.1. Herzberg's Satisfiers and Dissatisfiers.

As with Maslow's theory Herzberg's theory has not received much support from empirical studies.[19] However like Maslow's theory it continues to be of interest because it focuses attention on the influence of motivators. It continues to interest teacher researchers. Swan[20] for example in an exploratory study of teacher retention in Ireland and Texas came to the conclusion that in spite of criticisms by Nias[21] Herzberg's theory would be a useful starting point for a study of the retention of teachers. She found some evidence that teachers stayed on because they were enthused by the work they do (satisfier). Interestingly they had not sought promotion to principalships or deputy principalships. There was some evidence that principals who were sensitive to the needs of teachers could produce a 'satisfier' response from teachers.

Nias found that the hygiene factors could satisfy teachers' which is in contradiction of Herzberg. Evans[23] suggested that there was difference between the interpretations as to what constitutes job satisfaction. Evans in a reappraisal of the two-factor theory concluded that there were two components of job satisfaction job comfort and job fulfilment. She also thought that there was a link between the hygiene factors and the lower order needs (job comfort) of the Maslow hierarchy and conversely between the higher order needs and the satsifiers (job fulfilment).

An experienced teacher interviewed her colleagues to try and establish what motivated and what de-motivated them. She was aware that the staff might not have expressed their "true" feelings to her. Nevertheless, she concluded that her colleagues had a predominantly "Theory Y" interpretation of human behaviour. *"From the interviews it could be said that many of the staff have "unrealised" potentials, they seek more responsibility and not necessarily a financially rewarded one".*

She listed the following motivators-

(a)   Teachers felt they had an influence on children's lives- therefore gained satisfaction from seeing a pupil learning and developing as a result of the teacher's efforts.

(b)   Extra-curricular activities inspired some members and the excitement was shared by colleagues.

(c)   Although limited enough, the promotional aspects of the teaching profession provided an incentive for greater motivation.

(d)   Compliments and praise are great incentives to "keep up the good work" while they may only be given occasionally, they are always welcome.

(e)   Teaching by its nature can become stagnant, for this reason the staff felt that on the whole "challenges" to their professional skills can be very welcoming.

(f)   A is a modern, well-equipped school and the teachers felt this had a positive influence on their working day.

(g)   Most of the teachers felt that being given a chance to take responsibility for events outside the classroom was refreshing as it conveyed a measure of trust and recognition from the principal.

(h)   Two teachers felt there were occasions when their needs were not met that conversely acted as motivators. For example, the shared remedial teacher in the school for 14 years, expressed a desire to return to mainstream teaching, but refused to teach infant classes which was the standard offered to her by the principal for various reasons. As a result the teacher stayed in remedial education but decided to take a fresh look at her job. She has provided herself with new challenges and skills and her work has now a much more positive affect on the school in general.

(i)   Holidays and short hours were seen as important motivators.

(j)   Autonomy in the classroom was welcomed and seen as having a positive effect on job satisfaction.

(k)   Time to pursue personal and academic interests was viewed by the teachers as very necessary in the light of teaching being such an intensive and sometimes stressful job."

The de-motivators were-

(a)   Stressful situations whether it involves children, teachers or parents were seen to be the cause of the "burn out" feeling experienced by teachers from time to time.

(b) Not being given enough responsibility, despite a willingness to take it on.

(c) While quite rare in our school, lack of support by colleagues and management contributed to a feeling of dissatisfaction.

(d) Lack of consistency and fairness by management created negative feelings among the staff.

(e) Lack of honesty among staff and management. People not speaking their mind can lead to ambiguities and to negative attitudes.

(f) The work done by teachers is "taken for granted". "Teachers have a short working day and are well paid for it!" "Compliments are rare enough"

(g) Extra work to cover and poor time management = frustration and a feeling of dissatisfaction.

(h) Not being paid enough for the responsibility they carry and the extra "homework".

(i) Lack of change within the school.

(j) Discipline problems.

(k) Externally imposed changes".

She felt there were a number of things that the principal could do but they were related to the hygiene factors, as for example, *"alleviate the workload by encouraging the teacher to prioritise."* From this study she concluded that principals should be aware of theories of motivation, and among other things she counsels *"be flexible and ready to change re- approaches e.g.*

what motivates today may not succeed tomorrow, or two people may require different motivators ".

Another experienced teacher asked a number of her colleagues in a questionnaire to mention five positive good experiences of their work in school. She found that most of the responses centred around- *"affirmation, responsibility, acknowledgement, social ease and interaction ".* She said that some affirmation came from students but not from management. She also asked them for negative experiences. The responses were linked to ignoring opinions, issues being democratically discussed but autocratically decided, and not being given responsibility.

In the UK it has been reported in the newspapers, and the BBC considered the issue in a news bulletin that there is a shortage of applicants for head teacher appointments even though salaries can rise above £100, 000, a figure that is high historically. It was argued that the conditions of work put people off. Evidently some potential applicants believed there was not enough job satisfaction.

Pfeffer and Sutton point out that whereas one might think that the use of financial incentives to improve performance decisions would be made on the best and substantial evidence, they are not. Indeed, they argue that incentives are often recommended in complete disregard of the facts and they suggest that when Chief Executive Officers are paid several hundred more times than the average employee that this sends out debilitating messages to the employees. *"If front line people think that what they do doesn't' matter very much for the organization's success or in the opinion of senior management, why bother to worry about how well they are doing their job?"*[24] Getting the incentives right at all levels of the organization is important, and no less so in education.

The findings reported by these two teachers support the importance of some of Herzberg's motivators in particular the first two. At the same time they also support the view that the meaning that work has for the individual is an important factor in satisfaction. It is possible to do jobs that others would find quite terrible. Thus, a worker with an *instrumental* disposition to work may find self-actualisation at home in the family and / or in a hobby.[25] It follows from the fact that individuals live in a plurality of social systems that what is important to them at particular times, and in particular places varies throughout the life span. So when we try to understand a worker's (teacher's) motivations *"the critical question is not the one so frequently posed of what are people really interested or most interested in or whether they are more interested in job satisfaction and intrinsic rewards than money and extrinsic rewards, but rather when are they interested in intrinsic rewards and when are they interested in extrinsic rewards".*[26]

We have only to look at how our attitudes change through life to see that this is so.[27] So it is that one of the problems that principal's have to face is that often schoolteachers in their schools are of different ages, and in consequence, have different social needs. The young enthusiastic "new" teacher who is unmarried will put in a great deal of work to become effective. The newly married teacher will want to spend more time at home especially if there are children. The person whose children are grown up may be fed up or burnt out. Although there is no necessary correlation between age and these states of affairs a principal has to be conversant with the teaching staff and their needs if he/she is to ensure that the school is self- renewing. To some extent the principal can learn how to do this from an understanding of theories of motivation, and to recognise that individuals are complex.

The Complex Being.

The situation in school or university is no different for students. The motivation to study in the first year is different from that in a year in which there is no major examination to be taken, or in systems of continuous assessment where it is evident that the pressures to study are different. Moreover, motivation in examinations is strongly influenced by an individuals emotional disposition, and there is no reason to suppose that this is not true of other workers. The individual's reaction to any situation is complex, and the only model of the learner or worker that satisfied all conditions, is to quote Schein, "complex." My adaptation[28]of his model is as follows

1.   The learner (teacher or principal) is complex: the individual is highly variable, and at any time has many motives, some of which are more important than others. Since an individual's motive patterns are complex, the individual's response to incentives will also change with circumstances.

2.   The learner (teacher or principal) is capable of learning new motives through his or her learning, curriculum, teaching and institutional experiences. The psychological contract that an individual makes with his/her peers, teachers, principal is the result of a complex interaction between perceived needs and learning (work) and institutional experiences.

3.   The learner's (teacher's or principal's) motives in different institutions (schools) or different sub-systems of the same institution (school) may differ. The student (teacher) who is alienated in the formal structure may find fulfilment of social and self-actualisation needs in the student union, trade union or other institutions in the social system, or outside the system altogether as, for example in the family or in a hobby (e.g. golf). If the curriculum or work is complex, in respect of perceived needs or apparent abilities, some parts of the curriculum (teaching) may engage some motives, while other parts engage other motives.

4.   The learner (teacher or principal) can become productively involved with the curriculum (teaching, administration) and institution (school) on the basis of many different kinds

of motive. The individual's ultimate satisfaction in the institution (school) depends only in part on the nature of personal motivation. The nature of the task to be performed, the abilities and experience of the learner (teacher, principal), the nature of the actors in the institution (school), all interact to produce a certain pattern of work and feelings.

5. The learner (teacher, principal) can respond to many different kinds of learning (teaching administration) depending on his or her own motives and abilities and the nature of the task. There is no correct learning (teaching, administrative) strategy that will work for all learners (teachers, principals) at all times.

There are many models of individual behaviour. Each of the models referred to above, throw some light on individual behaviour, and the actions of individuals as they react to particular management styles, and organizational structures irrespective of whether they are schools or factories. It is clear from all the books written on the topic-despite all the investigations that suggest that individuals are badly managed- that many organizations (schools) continue to be ineffective for this reason.

Inspection of the rational-economic model of humanity shows it to have an affinity with those psychological theories that consider individuals to be impelled by appetites, drives and incentives: at the extreme they are also "automaton" in their response to the world. Habits are easily ingrained. While we may react strongly against this view of humanity in the sense that it is perceived to be totally deterministic and a denial of the 'free will' to determine actions, it contains an element of truth. There is as we have seen, more than an elementary case for the rational-economic model, particularly where the worker is a machine minder in an automated system. Indeed a recent book by Kenston that had as its primary aim an attack on the motivation industry (books and courses- with which I sympathise) argued that theory Y is a myth. Fear, low self-esteem, moderate expectations, and despondency also get good results and cost nothing.[29]

But people do act apparently of their own free volition, and sometimes the actions they take bring them into conflict with the work they do, and this is becoming increasingly the case among professional people. Neither should we be surprised at this for few individuals are entirely passive. And, this applies as much to pupils as it does to teachers and principals. Therefore, we should look to models of the individual that are active not passive. Necessarily they will be based on analyses of what people do when they act, be it at work or play.

Individuals at Work

Work can be analysed in a variety of ways. We can observe what a person does and this is often done by time and motion study. We can infer what a person does in solving problems from the process related to the activity area in which the problem is set. That model is likely to be a simplification of what actually happens. It is also likely to be based on some concept of information processing in order to make decisions. This can be demonstrated by comparing the skills involved in the processes of engineering design and science. Figure 4.3 (a) and (b) demonstrate this point. These two activities are remarkably similar, yet most of us probably have difficulty in accepting that this is the case. This is because in everyday life the fundamental skills involved in these processes are overshadowed by the content to which they are applied, and the content of scientific analysis is different to the content of engineering design and arises from the different philosophies that engineering designers and scientists have. This is of course an oversimplification, and protocols of how we solve problems suggest that we probably don't follow a linear process in solving problems but we will use the skills that are inherent in those processes, and these are skills of learning. At the same time it is clear that some children benefit from using heuristics of the kind described in these models.[30]

For example the SCOOPE project sponsored by the Tipperary Leader Group in primary schools in Tipperary wanted schools to use projects to develop the skills of enterprise.[31] The objective of SCOOPE was *"to sow the seeds and develop the skills of enterprise at a very young receptive age i.e. primary school level. The hands-on experience of developing a project facilitates the students to develop skills required to operate a business with regard to the generation of ideas, team work, research, management, marketing skills, selling, record keeping etc. It is hoped that each student, while passing through the various classes, will get hands-on experience in all these areas."* [32]

Generating ideas assists divergent thinking processes and these are needed at some time or another in very many activities. Undertaking research involves skills in seeking out information, sorting alternative solutions and making hypotheses or judgement. Marketing and selling also involve the evaluation of products. Skills such as the ability to "apply", "to select from alternatives" (in today's language "to make choices"), "to evaluate" (to make a judgement) are the basic skills we need to learn let alone make decisions, and it is in this sense that learning and decision making are the same thing. They are also 'goal' (target, if you prefer) directed. Learning and decision making are directed at "ends" to be met. Management is the mechanism that we use to direct and control the process in search of these ends. Sometimes this process is ill thought through and leads to delays when it is implemented such as those experienced in building the Channel Tunnel (Folkstone – Calais). It may involve the setting of the goals in the first place and that is inevitably the case in self-management. In this sense management is about learning, and in the same sense teaching is about decision making and therefore about management. This point is illustrated in figure 1.5 which was adapted from a textbook of educational psychology and is about the planning and decision making involved in preparing and managing a lesson.

Learning is about the development of understanding and, therefore, the acquisition of new goals. We have to assemble new information so that it relates to and adds to existing frames of reference. Any decision-making exercise involves us in the same mental activity. The results of the activity, when analysed, are new learning, which is placed in the memory store for future reference. The skills of decision making and the skills of learning are the same and fig 1.5 illustrates this point. Just as it is very difficult to avoid learning so it is very difficult to avoid having to make decisions. We can't help being decision-makers, yet I suspect that most of do not think of ourselves as decision-makers even though we possess and continuously use these so-called executive skills.

Many years ago a team of us studied the jobs that engineers do.[33] Our intention was to derive a taxonomy of training and education objectives for technologists and technicians. When I interviewed those in engineering functions I was very impressed by the way in which, individually, they not only "managed" but also had to "manage" their jobs. They told me of how, by necessity, they had to widen the scope of their initial brief through communication and co-operation with other people. Their role definitions were inadequate. In these cases ambiguities it seemed were an advantage. Often, in order to get a job done, a person would have to persuade another, over whom they had no authority, to do a job. In one case, no formal systems existed for this work, yet if it were not done, a contract might have been broken with serious consequences. The person concerned had to develop his role to achieve this goal. In so doing he used management skills. Other similar situations came to light in these interviews.

The organization was rather more a system of persons in relations rather than a hierarchical structure. And that is how, slowly, we are coming to view schools. It is in such experiences that feelings of responsibility are acquired. When there is a demand for such systems, as seems to be the case with schools

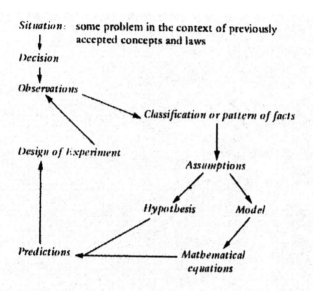

Situation: some problem in the context of previously
accepted concepts and laws

Decision

Observations

Classification or pattern of facts

Design of Experiment

Assumptions

Hypothesis   *Model*

Predictions   *Mathematical
equations*

After a number of cycles there may emerge new *concepts,
laws,* or *practical applications* of this knowledge.

(b)   *A model of the design process*

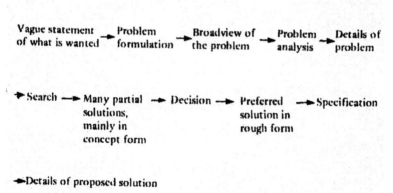

Vague statement → Problem → Broadview of → Problem → Details of
of what is wanted formulation the problem analysis problem

→ Search → Many partial → Decision → Preferred → Specification
solutions, solution in
mainly in rough form
concept form

→ Details of proposed solution

Figure 4.3 (a) and (b). A Model of how a scientist solves problems compared
with a model of the design process.

and schoolteachers, some of the participants seek responsibility, and if it is denied may not act positively toward their work. It may be, that like the designers in our study, that it was not so much status that is sought but responsibility.[34] It was almost as if they had to justify to themselves that they were doing something worthwhile by measuring it in terms of responsibility.[35]

It is not unreasonable to suppose that the perceived activity of management is as much an attraction of the job as salary. In our study, everyone was involved in direction and control, and, hence, in management. But they too were subject to direction and control. Thus it is that the extent of job satisfaction may be a measured by the degree to which individual needs for direction and control are satisfied, whether it is directing and controlling or being directed and controlled. This in turn is as much a function of personal history, ability and interest. What is an acceptable goal for one person will not be to another: some want to be stretched, others want a strict routine. No two persons in a work group will be exactly alike. In the same group there will be aggressive people and timid people who, if they are taken outside the sphere they are capable of controlling, will have to be supported. Sometimes people of high ability find themselves in this situation.

A person is a psycho-social system. Within the boundaries of that system, most individuals wish to be 'organic', to use a term first suggested by Burns and Stalker.[36] They wish to be able to take actions and decisions as well as mature. The boundaries of these psycho-social systems are a function of the needs of the job and the needs of the person. From the perspective of a principal the situation is complex because teacher's needs change with time. A principal has to take these changes into account, and in so far as it is within his/her capability try to keep him or her motivated to achieving the goals of the school.

When these needs are matched for each person in the organization, a hierarchical system becomes structured by individuals who are organic within their own sub- systems.. The system itself becomes organic if it can respond to the needs of individuals. Both systems have to be self-adjusting. Within these systems every person is his of her own manager. The implications of this view are profound. Not everyone wants to be a 'manager' in the traditional sense, but they do wish to be given the dignity of a human being, capable of decision-making.

The idea that every person is a manager receives general approbation, yet when I put this idea forward as a significant model of human behaviour I was regarded by some as naive. The reason for this is not very hard to see, for the stereotype of a manager is not related to direction and control as described in the foregoing paragraphs. Management is thought to be a role in which the individual is authorised to get work done through an employed subordinate for whose work that individual is held accountable.[37] It is a view that assumes that management is an overt activity of control in a downward direction. In a hierarchical organization instructions are handed down and communications sent up. This was very much the way secondary schools in Ireland functioned when they were managed by religious.[38] At the same time in such organizations other persons are able to exercise some control, as for example the secretary to the principal. The discretion she or he has as an intermediary can be considerable. The teacher exerts considerable direction and control of the pupils in his/her class. When we play our roles in the family, with friends or in the work group, we exert direction and control, sometimes at a very high level of influence.

Replacing a tap, cooking, planning a holiday are all activities that require the utilization of decision-making skills to which we draw attention only when a person is said to be managing. Because this is not recognised we do not try to develop these capabilities. Thus, in every role there is a management (servant) component as well as a learning (gift) component. At one time one will predominate, and at another time, the other. The roles we adopt, the perceptions we have, and the attitudes we acquire affect our performance. The trouble is that, for much of the time, these capabilities remain dormant and in consequence we do not acquire dispositions that help us to prepare for and control change. Decision-making and problem solving skills are of no avail if they do not generate action. Thus it is with the potential for action that principals are concerned, and in particular with the best organization of the means of involvement in the general pursuit of the organisations goals.

However, in the situation in many Irish schools where some teachers are demanding a high level of involvement in decision making, rights, as they would see them also bring responsibilities. Democracy can easily become anarchy and the desire of a group to run a school can put the principal in a position where he/she is simply not allowed to make decisions. In this case the organization is not learning; neither is it adapting. In order to be able to adapt each person in the system has to be a learner, and the lesson that has to be learnt by individuals and groups in this circumstance is that it is a management decision to let managers manage.

Drucker writes that *"implicit in all this is that different groups in the work population have to be managed differently, and that the same group in the work population has to be managed differently at different times. Increasingly "employees" have to be managed as "partners"- and it is the definition of partnership that all partners are equal. It is also a definition of partnership that partners cannot be ordered. They have to be persuaded. Increasingly, therefore, the management of people is a "marketing" job. And in marketing one does not begin with the question "what do you want?". One begins with the question "What does the other party want? What are its values? What are its goals? What does it consider results?"*[39] And this is neither Theory X or Theory Y, nor any other theory of managing people. But even in such circumstances someone has to be able to make decisions otherwise the search for consensus will lead to the lowest common denominator of mediocrity.

Heller and Wilpert have pointed out that if participation is to be effective, the skill level of the workforce will have to be high.[40] and many teachers do not possess these skills. Such skills involve both the cognitive and affective domains as the diagram in figure 1.1 shows. It is for this reason that students while still at school, should be exposed to a variety of learning techniques as in the case with the SCOOPE project. Moreover, at some time during the later stages of their schooling they should have to negotiate a component of their curriculum for independent study.

The next chapter reviews in more detail some of the studies that have been done on the organization of work and their implications for the world of the school and the social system in which it exists.

Notes and references

[1] This follows on from the discussion of expectancy in perception in chapter 2. Expectancy theory can be illustrated in the classroom. As defined by de Cecco and Crawford expectancy is a momentary belief that a particular outcome will follow a particular act. In relation to classroom teaching, it is useful to think of the expectations which pupils have of what will happen in the class, as well as the ability of the teacher to create expectations within the class. But this is to lose the "momentary" aspect of the definition as has been done in the main text. The value of the "momentary" is that it relates our instantaneous behaviour to what we are. If there is a discrepancy between what we see and what we expected to see, we may become angry. For instance, if we enter a classroom and find pupils jumping on the desks when we expected to see them sitting and reading, then there is a discrepancy between expectation and perception that could cause anger. Such discrepancies are sources of arousal. It has been suggested that a small discrepancy may cause us to feel pleasant while a large discrepancy may cause unpleasant feelings. This could happen to a teacher who is asked to visit the principal. Or, it could happen to the principal when visiting a classroom. Expectancy is also accompanied by estimates of the level of satisfaction attained. Psychologists call this characteristic *valence*. This is not the same as enjoying the outcome when we have it. De Cecco and Crawford illustrate *valence* with the example of *under-achievers*. A pupil who has the ability to achieve academically has a high expectancy of success. If he or she does not get satisfaction from academic success (*low valency*), he or she may not do as well as potential suggests. Such persons are called *under-achievers*: they are not motivated to achieve, nor do they expect to succeed. Even the prospect of failure will not produce a high level of drive. This applies equally in particular work situations and to teaching. If the work environment is changed expectations may be changed. Thus, in the classroom, the teacher has to maintain the students in a state of willingness to learn. This is achieved through teaching strategies, which range from simple questioning to complex projects. The teacher achieves the expectancy function by first defining what is expected of students and then modifying the students' expectations in such a way that they are encouraged to pursue teacher's

objectives. Principals can do the same thing in relation to both teaching staff and students. This activity is related to the incentive function, for pupils often value their achievements of their success and failure. The same is true of staff. But it is a major problem for principals in schools where they are not allowed to watch their teachers teach (as is the case in Irish secondary schools). How can they praise teachers in such circumstances? The paradox is that teachers want to know that their work is valued. It is for this reason that it is argued that students should be told where they are going either through properly designed advanced organisers or a statement of objectives. Similarly, with teacher appraisal. If appraisal is to be beneficial the appraiser and appraise should agree objectives that have to be achieved over a period of time. This enables work to be valued. De Cecco, J.P. and W.R. Crawford (1974). *The Psychology of Learning and Instruction*. Prentice Hall, Englewood Cliffs, NJ
For a brief discussion of culture, expectations and schools success in the American context see. Gage, N. L and D.C. Berliner (1988). Educational Psychology. 4th Edition. Houghton Mifflin Co. Boston, MA.
[2] see for example Chapter 7 on Pay for Performance in Kohn, A (1993). *Punished by Rewards. The Trouble with Gold Stars, Incentive Plans, as Praise*. Houghton
[3] Schein, E.H. (1965). *Organizational Psychology*. Prentice Hall, Englewood Cliffs, NJ
[4] Sanghera, S (2007) Cheer up, were only happy when we are miserable. *The Times* October 20th p 65.
[5] For a discussion of rationalist (modern) approaches to management and motivation in education versus post-modern concepts see Taylor, P. R and C. E. S. Taylor (2005) Leadership and Motivation: A Rational Process, Delusion or Subjective Rationality. In P. Taylor and J. Heywood (eds) The Motivation and retention of teachers. *Bulletins of the EFEA* (European Forum on Educational Administration) No 8, 117 – 126.
[6] Peters, T and Waterman, R.H. (1982). *In Search of Excellence Lessons from America's Best Run Companies*. Harper and Row, New York
[7] Elton Mayo is credited with being the founder of the human relations movement in management and industrial sociology (see Pugh, D. S et al (1983). *Writers on Organizations*. Penguin, Harmondsworth – pp 161 – 163 Elton Mayo and the Hawthorne Investigations). See in particular Roethlisberger, F. J. and W. J. Dickson (1939). *Management and the Worker*. Harvard University Press.,Cambridge, MA. These studies have been described in several books. See in particular Brown, J.A.C (1980). *The Social Psychology of Industry*, Penguin. Harmondsworth., See also D. S. Pugh (1974). *Organization theory. Selected Readings*., Penguin , Harmondsworth ,London., and references at the end of footnote 8.
[8] Long before the bank wiring room experiment the company had of its own volition varied the conditions of work experienced by female workers. The method was to vary the lighting. It was found that irrespective of the conditions good or bad productivity did not change. It was expected that the poor conditions would lead to a loss of productivity. It did not. It was this finding that led to management's invitation to the Harvard school to investigate the problem in more detail. They carried out a very sophisticated experiment over a period of five years and found similarly. In both cases the girls had been specially selected and segregated in a special room. The changes, which included incentive payments, were fully discussed with them before the new scheme was introduced. With each change that was made there was an increase in output. After a period the girls were asked to revert to the original conditions- a forty eight hour six day week with no incentives, nor rest pauses, and no refreshment. Conditions were terrible by today's standards. Yet, production increased again. The interpretation of this finding was that the high productivity was due to a large increase in job satisfaction arising from the freedom provided by the researchers in the new environment in which the researchers played an active role. Such was the trust between the girls and the researchers, that the girls provided norms of output they thought the investigators wanted. Apart from that the supervisors developed a sense of participation that radically changed the pattern of working. That individuals are likely to act differently when they are being appraised or

observed is the "Hawthorne effect" and this has to be taken into account in research design. It also has to be taken into account in practice, as for example, when a teacher is being appraised or inspected. In the experiments that my student teachers have done on classroom teaching there is no doubt that the success of some them was due to a Hawthorne effect in which their pupils wanted to do their best. This effect would be created, for example, if they told their pupils that they were doing the study for their assessment for their teacher's certificate. It might be argued that all teaching should be seeking to create a Hawthorne effect in terms of learning! (See any research text, for example, Easterby-Smith, M (1994) *Evaluating Management Development, Training and Education*. 2nd Edition. Gower, Aldershot,).

For a more detailed description of the experiment see Pugh et al (note 7). Handy, C (1993) *Understanding Organizations*. 4th Edition, Some of the Problems with the Hawthorne Studies have been summarised by Morley, M et al (1998). *Principles of Organizational Behaviour. An Irish Text*. Gill and MacMillan, Dublin

[9] Pugh et al note 7.

[10] *loc.cit* ref 3

[11] McGregor, D (1960). *The Human Side of Enterprise*. New York, McGraw Hill. The relevant chapters are reprinted in Pugh. D. *Organization Theory*. Harmondsworth, Penguin

[12] Extract from an assignment in a post-graduate diploma course

[13] Quotations from an assignment in a post-graduate course

[14] quoted from McGregor (1960) *loc.cit* note 11

[15] Murray's list of needs published in 1938 will be found in Heywood, J. (1982). *Pitfalls and Planning in Student Teaching*, London, Kogan Page

[16] Maslow, A. (1954). *A Theory of Motivation and Personality*. New York, Harper and Row

[17] Barnes, L.B. (1960). *Organizatoional Systems and Engineering Groups*. Cambridge, MA., Harvard Business School.

[18] The principle underlying this statement is due to Yerkes-Dodson. See Furneaux, W. D. (1962) The psychologist and the university. *Universities Quarterly* 3, 33

[19] Herzberg, F., Mausner, B., and B. Snyderman (1959). *The Motivation to Work*. New York, Wiley.

[20] Swan, V, Heywood, J., and K. E. Mayo (2005). A comparative study of the factors influencing the retention of teachers in the Republic of Ireland and Texas *Bulletins of the European Forum on Educational Administration* (EFEA) No 8 pp 71 – 116.

[21] Nias, J

[23] Evans, L (1998). *Teacher Morale*. Paul Chapman, London.

[24] Pfeffer, J and R. I. Sutton (2006). *Hard facts. Dangerous Half-Truths and Total Nonsense. Profiting from Evidence Based Management*. Harvard Business School Press, Boston, MA p 133. See whole of Ch 5 on financial incentives.

[25] See Ch 3., for meaning of instrumental in this context

[26] from Daniel, W.W. and N. McIntosh (1972). *The Right to Manage*. Macdonald, London.

[27] See for example Mant, A. (1970). *The Middle Aged Manager: A National Resource*. British Institute of Management, London. Also Hunt, J. W. (1979 or later edition).*Managing People at Work*. McGraw Hill , Maidenhead

[28] Second edition Heywood, J *Assessment in Higher Edition* (1989). , Wiley, Chichester

[29] Kenston, L (2005). The art of Demotivation. www.despair.com Reviewed in *The Times* by Toby Moore, 18th July 2006.

[30] Student teachers using a heuristic on higher diploma courses found that some children especially average and below average achievers liked the structure of simple heuristics like those of Polya, and Wales and Stager. See Heywood, J. (1996) An engineering approach to teaching decision making skills in schools using an engineering heuristic. Proceedings *Frontiers in Education Conference* (IEEE) 67 – 73.

[31] SCOOPE is the acronym for the School Children Operating and Organising Profitable Enterprise project sponsored by the Tipperary Leader Group Ltd. Its purpose was to create an enterprise culture among primary school children in Tipperary. It was regarded as a pilot project, and was sponsored for a period of three school years beginning in 1997 and ending in the summer of 2000.

[32] From the SCOOPE annual report to schools for 1997/98.

[33] In an extensive study of an industrial organisation, we attempted to analyse the work done by each engineer. The Company called everyone in its engineering operation an engineer, so the term embraced a number of people who would not be regarded as professional engineers (for example, technicians, draughtsmen, contracts clerks, certain personnel in stores). Wages and salaries were measured against different grades (levels) of engineers. We found that the 200 people in engineering functions performed about 450 operations. Some of these were "small" and some were "large" in executive terms.

[34] I know of no Irish study that has looked at this issue in respect of posts of responsibility

[35] Monk, J. D and J. Heywood (1977). The education and career patterns of mechanical engineers in design and management. *The Vocational Aspect of Education*, 29, (72), 5- 16.

[36] Burns, T and G. Stalker (1961). *The Management of Innovation*, Tavistock, London

[37] Jaques, E (1970). *Work Creativity and Social Justice*. Heinemann, London

[38] In the Catholic Church this term used to denote members of a religious congregation order. Most Catholic schools are run by religious congregations or orders although there are diocesan secondary schools. There are also Protestant secondary schools.

[39] Drucker, P.(1999) *Management Challenges for the 21st Century*. Harper, New York

[40] Heller, F. A and B. Wilpert (1981). *Competence and Power in Managerial Decision Making*. Wiley, New York.

Chapter 5

Patterns of Work

Introduction

In the last chapter we saw how the views we hold of why people *and students are motivated to work and learn can influence our behaviour. It became clear that those views influence if not dictate the organizational structure we employ to motivate workers It also became clear that social relationships at work are an important factor but not the only factor in the motivation to work. The argument that all jobs involve some degree of management when it is defined as direction and control was continued. In this chapter we look in particular at how organizational structures can influence our behaviour at work in order to understand better both our own situation as well as to design an organization that functions effectively. To achieve this goal, some of the major investigations of organizational behaviour are briefly discussed with reference to the circumstances in which they are regarded as successful. An open/organic system is more likely to be more innovative than a closed/mechanistic system Some principles of job enrichment that apply to most occupations are listed. These findings would seem to apply to innovation in educational institutions but the principal/head plays a key role in the encouragement of innovation. The significance of organizational climate and culture is discussed in relation to structure and the type of personnel that fit such structures. However, organizations are not possessed of a unitary structure. Rather persons live in a plurality of so-*

*cial structures and management's task is to gather the cultural
forces together using the strength of each in the right places.
The chapter ends with a note on the physical environment and
the importance of building design for learning- a thing that seldom happens.*

Social Relations at Work

Reference was made in the previous chapter to the Hawthorne
studies that gave rise to the social model of the person described
by Schein. Motivation, productivity and quality, it was postu-
lated, are related to the social relationships between workers.
But these studies not only illustrated the importance of social
relationships at work, it also showed that there was an informal
system of work that was as important as the formal. It is easy to
deduce that change is not likely to be accompanied with ease in
such circumstances. As Rosemary Stewart pointed out *"When
the informal group is strong, its sanctions are likely to be more
compelling on a group member than those of management,
since they are more certain to be applied."* [1]

Informal organizations are to be found in classrooms and
staff rooms in educational institutions, and they can have a
powerful influence on learning and the direction the school
takes. There is also both a formal and a taught curriculum that
is the official statement versus actual practice. But there is also
a 'hidden curriculum' in which students learn a variety of ideas
that are not related to the syllabus (content). For example children learn how to get on well with their peers as well as their
teachers. Their peers may expect them to cheat or refrain from
achieving high marks. The same type of process is at work as
those in the Bank-Wiring Room. The idea of the 'hidden agenda' is now part of everyday vocabulary.

The games people play in organizations or its micropolitics
can have a powerful influence on the direction and organisation
takes. They are part of the power play in the school. Part of
the search for influence. And they take place both formally and

informally with the intention of influencing the formal as any observation of a staff meeting will show. Groups can impede or enhance the work of a school. Principal's have to learn to engage with the micropolitics of the organization.

Socio-Technical Systems

The concept of the socio-technical system derives from studies undertaken by the Tavistock Institute of Human relations that investigated the effects of three different systems of mining on the production of coal.[2]

Traditionally, coal-miners worked in small groups. A miner and his mate cut the coal, which was then taken away in 'tubs' by labourers. Together they formed a group or team. Members of the group (team) were selected by the miner. It was he who cut the coal. In today's jargon he was the team leader. Clearly selection depended on the acceptance of mutual responsibility. It led to the establishment of long-term relationships and deep emotional bonds that would include the care and welfare of a sick man in the group and/or his family. The coal-face was mined in small sections from which the description 'shortwall' comes. The better the section, the greater the return when a piecework system is in operation. Thus there was conflict and competition for the good sections between these working groups.

When the cutting process was mechanized it changed, as you can imagine, the structure of the work group considerably. Instead of small coherent groups, forty or so men came under supervision of one person. Moreover, the workers were spread out over the length of the equipment, which was of the order 180m (200 yds), in conditions that were far from pleasant: considerable heat, dust and noise in a tunnel that was often very small (in diameter). Sometimes the miners were committed to a single and sometimes part-task. Those who cut the coal gained the highest status, while the other small groups were differentiated by the particular tasks they did. Contrary to expectations productivity was low and the quality of work poor. The investigators from the Tavistock Institute found a state of *anomie* (loss of meaning). The old emotional ties had been broken and there were many difficulties in the way of completing the tasks they were given.

With the help of these investigators the National Coal Board redesigned their mechanical system for 'longwall mining' into a composite designed to make work more meaningful by increasing the number of tasks done by each miner, and also by arranging the grouping of tasks so that emotional needs could be met. It increased productivity. Once again the social needs of the workforce were shown to be important. But the study also showed that the technology of production also creates a social system. Thus, in any organization there is both a technical system and a social system. Moreover, technical systems can be designed in such a way that they either tend to impede or enhance the satisfaction of social needs.

An organization in this perspective is regarded as a socio-technical system. Classrooms may be analysed in the same way. Benches or desks that are arranged to face the teacher at the front of the class will produce a different teaching system from one where tables are used with four or more students sitting at them. Teaching methods are limited when the desks are fixed so as to face the black (white) board. Small group work can help teachers when the range of ability in a class is very wide. It is also much more suited to project work designed to help develop executive skills. Just as it is that different methods of production change the role of the worker so it is that different arrangements of the classroom may require a change in the role of the teacher if they are to be effective. The teacher's task is to choose the instructional strategy that will best achieve the learning objectives to be obtained. The teacher can be a manager or facilitator of learning. Thus there is a choice between being the creator of work, the motivator and controller or the facilitator and sympathetic supporter, to quote Schein. [3]

The idea of a socio-technical system is a very different concept from that of informal organization, although informal organisations can and do exist in socio-technical systems as for example, the organization that develops among students during break periods. Even so the administrative arrangements for breaks (for example supervisions, use of rooms) are part of the socio-technical system. An important consequence of this concept is that the designer of a classroom should take into account the effects of the technical system on the social structure of organization. Often the design of classrooms is based on myths about how people learn that have been handed down over the last hundred and fifty or so years and many rooms, particularly in second and third level education are unsuited for any form of effective group work. These studies highlight the importance of the peer (work) group as a controlling agent in learning (productivity). These investigations show how learning (work) can be restricted.

Organizational Structures and the Work of Professional People

At the other end of the job spectrum there were several studies of the factors that enhance or impede creativity and innovation among people we commonly call 'professional' at work, and. In the USA, for example, it was found that there were more positive attitudes and output from engineers when their work was arranged in an open system.[4] In a similar study in Scotland, it was found that companies would more likely innovate if they were organized in an organic, as opposed to a mechanistic way[5]

The mechanistic type of organization described by Burns and Stalker is very similar to that of a bureaucracy. Indeed the starting point of their study is with Weber's study of bureaucracy. As exhibit 5. 1 shows in a bureaucracy every person (official) is subject to impersonal orders that guide their actions. They operate within a framework of rules that have been specifically developed for this purpose. Their actions have to conform with these rules; thus they have to have a specified sphere of competencies in which obligations, authority and obedience are strictly defined. They conduct their business by means of written documents. While it may be efficient it does not take into account the human factors involved in any work situation. It is very much theory X. It is a mechanism for controlling people. In a bureaucracy the role players become concerned with their position in the hierarchy. The emphasis on power and status that accompanies such concerns will inhibit drives for change and innovation.

---

1 *Members are personally free and are subject to authority only in their impersonal obligations.*

2. *They are organized in a clearly defined hierarchy of office*

3 *Each office has a clearly defined sphere of competence.*

4 *The office is filled by free contractual relationship.*

5 *Candidates are selected on the basis of technical qualifications*

6 *They are renumerated by fixed salaries, in money.*

7 *The office is treated as the sole, or at least primary, occupa tion of the individual*

8 *It constitutes a career, with promotion according to seniority and achievement.*

9 *The official is excluded from ownership rights.*

10. *He/she is subject to discipline and control in the conduct of his office.*

Exhibit 5. 1. Bureaucratic model proposed by Weber in Weber, M (1947) *The Theory of Social and Economic Organization*. Free Press, Glencoe, Il. Translated by A. M. Henderson and T. Parsons p 337.

Because they are unable to function outside this framework, communications between bureaucrats and the public are often accompanied by friction. Not knowing the rules, the public are unable to determine whether anything can be done, or even know if the official with whom they are dealing, has it in his or her power to refer the matter to higher authority. Officials, in their turn, can hide behind the prescribed rules for their role. During the last twenty years there has been much loosening up in this respect and officials have become more helpful and friendly although there remains considerable antipathy toward the bureaucracy of government. If officials have become more flexible then while it is generally held that it is difficult to change or innovate in such organizations there is the possibility of change and innovation. A strategy for change will involve the possibility of role change since innovations are likely to require role change as well as attitudes and values. The strategy will also seek to reconcile professional values with those of the bureaucracy. Professionals seek autonomy at work and expect their peers to measure their professional growth and not a superior who may not be qualified in the field. They also value the acquisition of new knowledge.

Burns and Stalker found that most of the companies they studied were organized in this way. In these *mechanistic* organizations (as they called them) there is specialized differentiation of functional tasks. Each task is pursued by persons with techniques and purpose, more or less distinct from those of the concern as a whole. This means that reconciliation of these distinct tasks has to be accomplished by some form of management or supervision. Groups of performances have also to be reconciled, and this is achieved by a hierarchical structure of control, authority, and communication. In such organizations the location of comprehensive knowledge is at the top. It will be appreciated that there is a minimum of interaction between peers. Information is sent vertically upwards and commands downwards. There is very little lateral communication. Such organizations encourage an authoritarian or Theory X type of management.

In these organizations there is little lateral communication and worse when there is supposed to be communication between sections this may not be effective because the different sections speak different specialised languages. Burns and Stalker found that qualified personnel working in research and development had difficulty in communicating with manufacturing personnel whose origins were in apprenticeships. Teachers in secondary schools that are organized into subject departments speak the language of their subject. Since there is not a common technical pedadgogy change across the curriculum can be difficult. Many post-primary schools are typically organizations of this kind although the search for distributed leadership (see below) necessarily reduces the hierarchical element in favour of much more collaboration.

But Burns and Stalker also found organizations in which individual workers understood their role in terms of the general aims of the organization. Such systems were organized so that every one contributed to the common goal of the organization. Individual tasks are related to the total situation of the organization, so they have to be adjusted and continually redefined as they interact with each other. To maintain this situation, control, authority and communication are allowed to derive from the mutual relationships between the group rather than from the contractual relationships of specified roles to be found in a bureaucracy. In such organizations the head is not omnipresent. Burns and Stalker argued that *organistic (organic)* systems of this kind were more open to innovation than mechanistic systems.

My impression of the highly innovative company in the aircraft industry we studied (see page 167) and of some schools I have visited leads to me to enter a caveat to that theory. It seemed to me that the firm was moving towards an organic framework- although it still operated within a broad mechanistic structure.[6] It seemed to be midway between the two and at the same time was innovative. As one authority puts it, *"real life organizations tend to occupy intermediate positions in the grey areas between one extreme and another."*[7] Such situations are as of true schools as they are of other types of organization. Much, it would seem depends on management and the leadership it gives.

Inspection of the differences between mechanistic and organic systems shows that a person would be required to make radical change in his or her role if he or she were to move from one system to another. This would have to be accompanied by a substantial change in attitudes if the person is to adapt to the new role. There is probably some truth in the view that individuals are more comfortable in a *mechanistic* system than they are in one that is *organic*. Children when they reach the age of 11 or 12 like the rather more structured teaching they receive in post-primary schools as compared with the *organic* systems that characterise many primary school classrooms. There is a high level of security attached to highly structured roles. In less structured roles that have some freedom, a high level of adaptability and flexibility is required. New attitudes have to be learnt and that can be difficult.

Open versus Closed Systems

An open system is one that is in exchange with its environment where as a closed system is one that has no exchange with its environment. A closed system will eventually die, whereas an open system maintains itself because it is able to export and import 'material' from it's the environment. This description of biological and thermodynamic systems[8] may be applied to organizations. An industrial or commercial organization is in exchange with its market. If it does not respond to the market it will die. Within the market it also has to choose how it competes. Will it compete with the same type of 'good' companies over a range of products, or only in product areas where it has a technical advantage? The same applies to schools as the principal of a primary school in a rural town wrote *"In a climate of competition, marketing is unfortunately a necessary part of school management. In our school, we have just produced a promotional brochure. It is bright, eye-catching, relevant and informative. It would be great, if we could say that our strengths were strong enough to sell our school, but that is not the case. Addressing our weaknesses and threats is the challenge facing us if we are to reinstate ourselves as a competitive school."* This school was behaving as an open system.

The way in which the senior management of an enterprise views the environment may also condition attitudes within the organization. In the United States in a study conducted around the same time as the Burns and Stalker study Barnes described the attitudes of management and its effects on a particular section of a company in the electronics industry.[9] This company not only had to operate in a highly competitive way but also had to meet the goals of its parent organization. The pressure on the general manager was for low prices and high quality with the effect that engineering management believed that productivity was much more important than quality. This meant that development work in the department investigated did not have a high profile, even though it seemed that development work was required and engineers wanted to do such work.

Barnes shows how the chief engineer and supervisor were placed in middle-management roles. Management and business values (practical engineering and productivity) were stressed to their subordinates, whereas to their seniors in contrast, they emphasized the value of the scientific approach to engineering, thereby reflecting the views of their staff. On the one hand, the supervisor *"stresses scientific principles and deplores production engineering's knob twisting approach. On the other hand, he builds up subordinate resistance by asking them to turn out more 'quickies', to get out into the factory, and to be scientifically less rigorous."*[10]

In contrast, Barnes described another company in the same business that was also highly competitive but making products in which it had a technical advantage. It is not surprising to find that in this company technical and scientific knowledge was valued. The field engineer, who was the equivalent of the chief engineer in the first company, did not present one face to the engineers and another to management. There were no pressures on him for productivity and practicality. The pressure that came through, if it can be called pressure, was management's encouragement of individual development. Officials at the top of the organization put down company success to informality that spread across the organization. So the field engineer in responding to this, arranged for his subordinates to have high autonomy while at the same time ensuring interaction between himself and his engineers so that a system of mutual influence was created.

As things stood, according to the measures used, the second company was more efficient than the first. Barnes put this down to their different organizational structures. The first was a relatively 'closed system', he stresses the term relatively, while the second was 'relatively open.' In the first organization the engineers thought they should be doing engineering development whereas the pressure was on them to worry about production. In the second there were no explicit pressures for productivity and practicality of the knob twisting kind.

Of particular interest is the fact that the organization of the first department seemed to highlight the different value dispositions between the individuals and the group. Those who were oriented towards the values of science (for example, truth and knowledge) tended towards relatively low non-work activities, low interactions and low mutual friendships. Those who wanted to attain promotion, acceptance and prestige within the organization tended toward relatively high interaction and high mutual friendship. Barnes called the former group 'professionals' and the latter group 'organizationals.' A third group who wanted popularity and acceptance by the high-status groups he called 'socials.' They were characterised by high non-work activities, high interactions but low mutual friendships.

In the second department, there was much mixing between the grades, and there was a higher level of participation in non-work activities. The two structures influenced the way in which individuals in the departments behaved and worked, and they in their turn were influenced and reinforced by that mode of work. Professional values were taken into account whereas they were not in the first organization.

Given the previous discussion the reader will not be surprised to learn that the department that was relatively closed was organized hierarchically. It was organized into 5 sections each with a section head. Each of the sections, except one were supported by technicians. The sections specialised and were kept to their specialist tasks. Work was not shared so there was no cross communication and learning about other tasks. In the open department the engineers were organized in a single group. They undertook whatever task they were given by the supervisors. They could obtain the services of a technician. The technicians were organised as a group under a foreman. In this department there was a great deal of communication. Clearly it was better organised for learning. The combination of structure and the attitudes of senior management undoubtedly influenced the style of the departmental managers.

Clearly schools are relatively open or closed in their environment but they can be open or closed in their internal management. For example in relation to the development of a transition year (TY) it was recorded that *"we have here staff operating in line with McGregor's Theory Y and the school authorities starting out with a collaborative approach. However it would seem that the authorities came to the question of TY with a set of beliefs as to what was best for the school and their sincerely held beliefs were not open to change. As these sincerely held beliefs were challenged the focus of their activity became how to get them implemented. At this stage collaboration and collegiality was very little in evidence as the authorities ensured that they retained control rather than sharing power through shared decision making. Pragmatism rather than Covey's principle centred leadership seemed evident in the decision to recruit a compliant member of staff to lead TY."*

"The central question of whether this placed the organization towards the closed end of the open-closed continuum depends on how effective the adaptive changes were. The TY as implemented involved a relatively low level of creative input by teachers causing disappointment on the part of the students when they found that TY differed very little from other years. The circumstances surrounding the appointment of the TY coordinator lessened his ability to provide leadership to staff. Student dissatisfaction moved the TY leadership to avoid meeting parents until as late as possible in the year resulting in a weak parent-school partnership. A concrete indication that the quality of TY was poor, was a decision by the TY co-ordinator and the school authorities to take on board, for the second year, suggestions that they had previously rejected." The commentator drew the conclusion that *"lack of learning and a non-collegial approach made for less effective adaptation and placed the school away from the open-end of the continuum."* Subsequently a new management brought about a more collaborative environment and changes in the way the transition year was run with the result that it gained the approval of parents. The system became more open.

Marketing Schools

At first sight it would seem that schools may be exempt from an open systems framework but this is evidently not the case. In the UK the middle classes in particular will move home so as to be in the catchment area of a school that is 'perceived' to be good. The turn around in the last twenty years of so called faith schools, and in particular Church of England and Roman Catholic Schools has led parents to nominally accept that faith as a condition of their children's entry to those schools.

Voucher systems in which parents can spend on the school of their choice are clearly designed to function in an open system and schools that do not attract children will clearly die in such systems. They believe schools will have to learn to market themselves and respond to market demands at least that is the hope of those who propose such systems. Failing schools they believe will spurred on by the competition and turn themselves round.

In Ireland schools are paying increasing attention to marketing. X is a small primary- four- teacher school with just under 100 pupils. Most pupils come from a small catchment area within about one and a half miles. Yet within a three-mile radius there are four other primary schools and because they maintain a high profile X is constantly aware that it must always have an attractive and viable strategy to maintain sufficient numbers. *"A vital cog in the marketing strategy is to provide areas of the curriculum where certain teachers excel [...] Music and singing has been one such forte and it has been central to our marketing strategy. The school boasts two eminently qualified bands and its' many fine singers and musicians have been prominent in recitals and competitions both locally and provincially. The success of this strategy can be seen from the fact that the school maintains a very high profile at all times and that the enrolment has actually increased in recent years"*. Parents can exert powerful pressure on schools in such circumstances. In the Irish context post-primary schools are often in competitive situations too which they have to respond.[11]

It is clear from previous analyses that the components that that make up any school (eg subject departments, year groupings, classes) can from a managerial perspective, that is, the perspective of change and improvement be relatively open or relatively closed.

Job Enrichment

Socio-technical systems theory pointed to the fact that when workers only undertake part tasks their commitment to the goals of the organization is reduced. And as the Goldthorpe study showed they are likely to take an instrumental attitude toward work (see page 48). Assembly line methods are likely to exacerbate this tendency. No wonder that in the sixties and seventies there were attempts to revive the system of cottage industry. In the small workshop of cottage industry everyone knew what everyone was doing and this ensured high quality work, since faults were easily corrected and quickly spotted.

Williamson also drew an analogy between the small workshop and the human cell.[12] Cells in living organisms do not increase in size but duplicate themselves as the organism grows. *"If an abnormally large cell does occasionally form as they sometimes do, the cancerous growth with which they are associated may result in the death of the organism."* His message for large-scale traditional batch-production methods with their lines of milling machines, lathes and other devices is clear. Errors, he argued, can go undetected until the final stage of manufacture, because no one sees the total process of manufacture of an artefact from start to finish, wasteful work planning goes undetected unless there is a serious failure in manufacture. He went on to suggest that 'cellular' manufacture should replace single-unit manufacturing enterprises. People and machine tools would be grouped into special cells manufacturing one category of component or very limited range of components. At first sight it seems that the people would be just as limited as in traditional systems, but it is clear from his description of cellular organization that in such cell systems they have more responsibility. He wrote *"Each component is classified in such a way that it is issued into the cell most appropriate for its manufacture. Such specialisation would bring its advantages on the human side, in familiarity with the components, resulting in more-detailed know how, and a higher concentration of skill: and on the ma-*

chine tool side in the ability to use simpler machine tools specially suited to a limited range of components, supplemented by appropriate specialise tooling. An operator in a cell could use more than one machine tool, and in general there would more machine tools than operators."[13]

Attempts to organize manufacturing along these lines have been variously called 'group technology, 'autonomous working groups' and 'cellular organization'. One of the most publicised of these arrangements were the arrangements for the manufacture of engines by Volvo and Saab. Of interest to this text is the fact that such arrangements can provide a mechanism for enriching the jobs of the blue collar workforce.[14]
Taken together the studies reported in this chapter suggest, that management should

- Provide a worker with adequate elbow room (e.g in choice of methods of teaching)

- Give opportunities for learning on the job (e.g. teaching as research)

- Design work for an optimal level of variety (e.g. variation in classes taken)

- Arrange the work environment so that workers can and do get help from their work mates

- Help workers to obtain a sense of their work as contributing to social welfare.[15]

For example one way in which teachers may be given opportunities for learning on the job is to encourage them to view their classrooms as laboratories for research. This is a problem that will be discussed in more detail in chapters 8 and 10. As for Irish primary schools sometimes teachers teach the same class level (age group) all the time and are not given the opportunity to work with other groups. Of course there may be good reason for this such as lack of competency but the practice is much more widespread than one might suppose competency problems would produce. In post-primary schools some teachers can be disadvantaged by the structure of the timetable.

One can substitute teacher or student for worker in this context. The principles apply to learning in the classroom as earlier chapters' showed.[16] For example, in respect of the student the fourth point relates to the use of cooperative learning in the classroom. All of them relate to project based learning. In any case if workers are to take more responsibility for their own work then they will need to be trained for this and such training should begin in school. Neither is such training at odds with the goals of liberal education.[17]

For example, team project work is designed to achieve this objective and is much encouraged. The *Technologie* programme in the junior cycle French curriculum was based on the project method.[18] Children, from the age of 12, market research a product, which they then make. The class is split into several groups responsible for managing, making and learning. For example, if it is decided to manufacture 100 small electronic alarms to meet market demand, the children will order the components, fabricate the box, wire up the electronic equipment and learn the principles of electronics at the same time. This project method was carried through the whole junior cycle. Each project is substantive in terms of the time deployed. It may with some justice claim that this is preparation for work and life. The group work I saw suggested to me that they are likely to experience the same problems of motivation that are experienced in industry, unless they are carefully managed. It is possible even at this age for students to take over from teachers' responsibility for the project, but this would require a very substantial shift in perception on the part of the students and their teachers. The Tipperary Leader Group believed that the skills of enterprise had to be acquired from a very early age and sponsored project work in primary schools that could involve a class of students or the whole school.[19] (See chapter 4). However, much is lost if the students do not rigorously evaluate their experience of running their own ventures. For this they need to acquire skill in self-assessment, and this it seems is most difficult to develop. Work in Ireland has suggested that young students in mini-companies are likely to benefit from an appropriately designed formal course in management studies prior to mini-company activity.

At issue here, is how if at all can one enrich the jobs of teachers? Clearly some school managers restrict the potential of teachers while others encourage personal and academic development as the stories in this text show.[24]

Innovation in Schools

MacMahon[20] undertook a study in four schools in Dublin to see if organizational structure would influence the potential for innovation. At the time new community and comprehensive schools had been introduced they were able to develop different organizational structures if and they wished. There was also some curriculum innovation particularly in these schools. He was able to distinguish between innovative and non-innovative schools. He found that there was little difference in the characteristics of the teachers in the various schools and that they shared many ideas in common including the view that there was a need for change. Teachers were not opposed to innovation but in the non-innovative schools they were not given the impetus so to do. MacMahon did however find important differences between the teachers regarding the functions of public examinations and the role of school-based assessment. He thought that teachers in the innovative schools were frustrated by the examination system.[21] there were also differences between the teachers on the approaches offered to the development of pupil abilities which he put down to differences between subject and pupil oriented approaches to teaching.

He found that the ways teachers related to the overall task of the school were similar to those found in mechanistic and organic organizations in that in the non-innovative schools teaching was oriented only to that which was specified in the syllabus.

He also found that the following organizational variables contributed to the effectiveness of innovation.

"1. *The existence of a two-way network of communication between principal and teachers and between the teachers themselves.*

2. *The encouragement and support of the principal for the innovation.*

3. *Cooperation between the teachers.*

4. *An absence of precise regulations about the work of the teacher.*

5. *Flexible structures of organization.*

6. *A favourable attitude to innovation among teachers.*

7. *Teachers involvement in the overall task of the school.*"

MacMahon concluded that *"The indications from the survey are that leadership and encouragement are necessary from people in authority if innovation is to occur. The initial impetus may come from the teachers but unless it receives support and encouragement from the authorities it has little chance of surviving."* Hence the importance of senior management, and if the innovation is in curriculum and teaching the need for the principal to understand the principles of curriculum and instructional leadership (see chapter 10).

MacMahon found that the schools in which innovation took place tended to have an organic pattern of organization. He compared his findings with those of Burns and Stalker and drew up the charts shown in exhibits 5.2 and 5.3.

Glover and Miller[22] in a small-scale study of the introduction of whiteboards into post-primary school classrooms came up with similar findings to MacMahon. They distinguished between three kinds of culture, and three types of approach to the introduction of the whiteboards. There was a *traditional* culture characterised by didactic teaching and an *interactive* culture characterised by *"interactive learning, exploration of ideas, group activity and pupil enthusiasm."* Between these two was a *transitory* culture. Notwithstanding the difficulties inherent in observing lessons they contended that there was sufficient evidence to support the view that backed up by thoroughgoing professional development the introduction of this technology has the power for positive change. They classify such development as *innovatory.*[23] That is, if it is accepted that theory Y teaching is preferred to theory X instruction.

Matrix Organizations

"Each era of management evolves new forms of organization as new problems are encountered." One of those that evolved in the eighties was the matrix organization. It has many similarities with the Barnes open system for it is designed for both flexibility and easy decision making. Moreover it can be a unit within an organization. Galbraith is considered to be the 'father' of the Matrix concept. He was particularly concerned with the development of lateral relationships in organizations.[27] Matrix organizations have to be able to reconcile several conflicting objectives, especially when a company has to respond to two sectors simultaneously, or when the uncertainties of the market creates demand for large amounts of data, or when there are strong constraints on resources. Matrix organisations can handle several projects simultaneously and their teams combine both function and line tasks and project managers acquire experts as required. When the expert's task is finished they become available for work in other parts of the organization. One characteristic of a matrix organization is that some project managers may report to two bosses. In a dual command and con-

trol situation managers have small formal authority but a great deal of responsibility. Their task is integration. Power is shared equally between project needs and the people requirements of the organization. Administration can be operated in large educational institutions on a matrix basis. A major difference between companies and schools is the time scale of adaptability. It is short for industry and long for educational institutions.

Organizational Climate and Culture

Every institution is different. When we apply for a job we want to know and try to find out what the institution is like. The questions we have in mind are about the values the institution has and the way the institution is managed or how we are likely to be managed, its management style and the style of its management. We will want to know

1. Do I know what is expected of me in work?

2. Will I have the equipment and material I need to do my work right?

3. At work, will I have the opportunity to do what I do best every day?

4. Will my supervisor or someone at work seem to care about me as a person?

5. Will there be someone at work who will encourage my development?

6. Will my opinions count at work?

7. Will the mission/purpose of my company make me feel my work is important?

8. Will my co-workers be committed to producing quality work?

And so forth (adapted from Diggins; 2002).[28]

Characteristics of organic organisations adapted from Burns and Stalker	Characteristics of innovative schools MacMahon
1. Contributive nature of special knowledge and experience to the common task of the concern. 2. The "realistic" nature of the individual task which is seen as set by the total situation of the concern. 3. The adjustment and continual redefinition of individual tasks through interaction with others. 4. The shedding of 'responsibility' as a limited field of rights, obligations and methods. 5. The spread of commitment to the concern beyond any technical definition. 6. A network structure of control, authority and communication. 7. Knowledge may be located anywhere in the network 8. A lateral rather than a vertical direction of communication. 9. Information and advice rather than instructions and decisions. 10. Commitment to the concerns task. 11. Cosmopolitan (external) prestige.	1. An interdisciplinary approach & and knowledge and emphasis on...... 2. Teacher cooperation; involvement of teachers in defining goals of the school. Teachers do not limit themselves to teaching only what is specified in the syllabus and they cooperate with other teachers. 3. The curriculum is subject to regular evaluation and development by the teachers. 4. Clear rules and regulations are not prescribed for the teacher. 5. Involvement in innovation denotes a commitment to the task of the school which goes beyond the traditional role of the teacher. 6. Teachers are involved in the decision-making process. 7. Teachers are involved in developing the curriculum. 8. Teachers are asked to make recommendations on specific matters. 9. Rules and regulations are not prescribed and there is a high degree of cooperation. 10. Involvement in innovation is an indication that teachers want to improve the effectiveness of their teaching. 11. Teachers have experience working abroad

Exhibit 5.2. MacMahon's findings on innovative schools compared with his adaptation of Burns and Stalker's organic organization.

Characteristics of mechanistic organizations	Characteristics of non-innovative schools (MacMahon)
(a). Specialised differentiation of functional tasks.	(a). A subject-based curriculum with teachers concentrating on their subject.
(a). The abstract nature of each task which is pursued without reference to the overall task of the concern.	(a). Each teacher works largely on his own, with little cooperation from other teachers
(b). Distinct performances are reconciled at each level by immediate supervisors.	(b). The work of the teacher is coordinated by an immediate superior (principal).
(c). Precise definition of rights and obligations	(c). Clear rules and procedures are prescribed for the teacher's work.
(d).Responsibilities related to a functional position.	(d). Teachers concentrate on teaching a particular syllabus.
(e). Hierarchical structure of control	(e). Teachers not involved in decision making.
(f). Knowledge located at the top of the hierarchy.	(f).Teachers do not suggest new ideas to each other.
(g). Vertical interaction between members; downward communication.	(g). Little cooperation between teachers.
(h). Work governed by instructions and decisions from superiors.	(h).Teachers not involved in decision-making
(i). Loyalty and obedience to superiors.	(i). No data on this
(j). Importance attached to local (internal) knowledge.	(k). No data on this.

Exhibit 5.3. MacMahon's findings on non-innovative schools compared with his adaptation of Burns and Stalker's mechanistic organization.

We are interested in the psychosocial climate of the organization. We would like to find, to quote Diggins: *School cultures that ooze respect, and where leaders are focused on the learning needs of students"* that it will be a place where *"personal development takes place."* A place *"that provides a safe haven within which to experiment, to risk being wrong, to learn from and with each other in a humane atmosphere."* A place that *"cultivates the leadership qualities of other and so enhances its own capacity to be effective."* [29]

As might be expected schedules have been developed for evaluating peoples' perceptions of organizational climate.[30]

My first introduction to this idea was in the Merchant Navy when I was told that some ships are "happy" and some "unhappy". Subsequently experience taught me that these were good characterisations of ships. I also found that "happy" organizations were not necessarily the most effective or efficient though it helped. It also taught me that in hierarchical organizations, for that is what ships' are, the "boss" contributed greatly to whether a hierarchical organization was "happy" or "unhappy" and efficient or inefficient. A change of commander could make all the difference. The games people played in the former were different to the games they played in the latter. I make no judgement about the validity of such perceptions since they can be dangerously misleading Much the same can be said about schools. While most people will say they have an intuitive feeling about an institution or different institutions and although the concept of "climate" may be theoretically vague and lack objectivity it is those feelings that often dictate attitudes toward the organization irrespective of their rationality. Perhaps the organization has a "personality".

Much the same may be said of the concept of culture This invaded management theory after the publication of Peters and Waterman's *In Search of Excellence*.[31] They had concluded that cultural leadership was the major factor in the success of the companies evaluated. They contended that successful organisations are rich in legend and parable, whereas unsuccessful companies were not. The leaders gave the culture shape through the creation of language, ideology and ritual. Evidently some schools tried to create such cultures and Hoyle and Wallace summarising other research drew attention to schools that talked about the 'X' way.[32] Most of us will have heard of the 'Walmart Way". However, many of the successful organisations studied by Peters and Waterman went on to fail and Miller's research into failing firms led him to the conclusion that *"focused cultures and strategies, and orchestrated configurations, contribute mightily to outstanding performance. But they carry with them daunting risks of rigidity and isolation. To compound the problem, it is terribly hard to distinguish between the concentration needed for success and the narrowness that guarantees excellence. Managers of thriving organizations must forever remain alert to such "perils of excellence."*[33] This view applies as much to schools as it does to industry.

Hoyle and Wallace attempt to clarify the meaning of culture. They cite Smircich's distinction between *"culture as what an organization is and culture as what an organization has...... If an organization has a culture, then it is readily conceivable that this culture can be instrumentally manipulated. But if an organization is a culture, then cultural change implies a much grander but less manageable undertaking: nothing less than altering the nature of the entire social construct that the organization constitutes."* (p 114).[34] But one could go on. For example it is possible to distinguish between a culture that is at a surface level of an organization and culture that is at a deep level. It might be relatively easy to change a surface level culture as for example the discipline culture of an organization but not the deep culture that persists and is less malleable. An example of the latter in Ireland is the opposition to promotion by merit instead of seniority among school teachers.

It is in the latter sense that Handy and Aitken distinguish between four types of organizational culture.[35] The first is called the *club culture*. They describe it using the analogy of a spider's web. It is an organization designed to extend the power of its creator. In the analogy, the spider, the closer a person is to the centre of the web the greater their influence. The circles of the web represent degrees of intimacy with the centre. The other lines represent levels of responsibility and functions within the organization. If the founder of the organization could do everything himself/herself he/she would. But organizations grow so the founders employ people to do the tasks that they cannot. They employ people whom they believe they can trust to ensure they the orgnization develops in the image of its founder. *"Club cultures "* write Handy and Aitken *"are rich in personality. They abound with almost mythical stories and folklore from the past and can be very exciting places to work if you belong to the club and share the values and beliefs of the spider"* (p 86). In the fourth edition (1999) of *Understanding Organisations* Handy calls this culture a *power culture*.

Such organizations are good in innovative and crisis situations. Their dependence on informality means they are more suited to the small than the large. Evidently the founder of a new university department has the opportunity to create a *club culture*. The open system described above could well have had such a culture if the manager was perceived to have charisma.

But a better description of that department is the *task culture*. *Task cultures* derive from the need to solve problems.

In contrast to both of these is the *role culture*. Burns and Stalker's mechanistic organization is representative of this group. Such organizations are characterised by predictability and certainty. They find it difficult to change. They do not want to change or take initiatives. *"They want 'role occupants' not individualists"* (p88). In the organic and open system the personnel contribute to the tasks that have to be done individually, or in groups (or as they are often called today- teams). The task dictated the requirements for personnel in that department. The point to be made is that in large organizations that are departmentalised the individual departments may have different cultures.

Handy's fourth culture is the *person culture*. It differs in a major way from the other three in that its focus is on the individual and not on the goals of the organization. The organizations goals are arranged so as to make the best use of the persons talents. As was argued in chapter 2 all organizations ought to do that anyway. Theoretically a university is this type organization. Handy and Aitken point out that such persons mostly from the professions and vocations do not like the language of management. Doctors and lawyers use such terms as practice and chambers. Universities have in the past talked about faculties. But accountability has forced some of these professions to use managerial terms. Thus hospital matrons and sisters have become managers. There are even line managers in some universities. But as governments have found a person culture is very difficult to run in the ordinary way that accountability demands. It is significant that the term Matron has been re-introduced in some hospitals in England. Pring counsels *"change the language and you change your understanding of the situation – the values which are picked out, the qualities which are respected, the aims which are thought worth pursuing. The systematic transformation of the moral language of education into that of management and control necessarily brings with it a transformation of the ethos and culture in which we work."*[36]

It seems to be apparent that persons working in these cultures respond to different kinds of management.

In his book Handy relates these different cultures to four of the Greek God's of mythology. Thus, Zeus " *a very personal ruler with a habit of direct interventions"* is the God of the *club culture*. It is a culture in which a lot of time is spent selecting the "right" people mostly like themselves. *"Zeus after all saw himself as head of a family, and the same sort of feeling pervades these organizations at their best."*[37] (p88) Family organizations decline as their members' change. The Bureaucrats have as their God, the God of harmony, of rules and of order –Apollo.[38] The people required in such organizations are those who want to be trained for the role. Athena the goddess of war and patron of the commando leader Odysseus is the God of the task culture while the existential Dionysius puts individuals first and is the God of person culture. It seems clear from these examples that the management styles required for these different cultures will differ as will the qualities and value systems of their employees.

Handy and Aitken argue that organizations are seldom made up of one culture and that some have a mix of all four. One teacher examined the cultures in the staff-room of her secondary school. She concluded that *"the school exhibits all four typologies identified by Handy and Aitken to varying degrees but it appears that role and task culture are the most significant in this staff-room. Task culture is prevalent among staff. At staff meetings members volunteer their time and experience to do certain tasks. Two recent ones were: (1) The enrolment committee to conduct the school's open day, visit primary schools in the catchment area and induct the incoming first years. (2) Seachtain na Gaeilge is a week focusing on Irish culture, music and song orchestrated by the Irish teachers with the help of other volunteers. Role culture exists in the schools management structure from principal, deputy principal, year heads, assistant principals, special duty posts, chaplain and class teachers. The students and staff alike are conscious of these roles and know which staff members are in charge of which areas. To a degree the school is a Person culture where all students are treated and valued equally and the school endeavours to meet their needs. Each individual cannot be prioritised all the time or it would be impossible for the school to operate but certainly the school has each child's welfare at heart. Each child receives and education, grades, a summer and Christmas report, and is encouraged to participate fully in school events. In a person culture decisions are usually made on a consensus basis. Whilst this is true of many staff decisions made, the students are not included in the decision-making process.*

Club culture is evident among the staff to a small degree. Staff from the same subject areas form a "club" and the staff can be classified broadly into senior, middle and junior members in relation to their age profiles. Ten years ago, six staff members played bridge at every lunch hour claiming a table in one corner of the room. Excluded from the "club" were those who could not play bridge. This ritual died out in the ensuing year as one member retired, one resigned, one became principal and another became deputy principal so they no longer had time to play, and the remaining duo had too few players to continue. The new young members have formed their own club culture. Apparently role and task cultures are the most significant in the class room"

Many teachers would probably see their own school mirrored in this picture. But there may be situations where the need to function in more than one culture is essential and post-holders may find themselves in such a situation. Some individuals may find this difficult because they tend to be predisposed to one of these cultures and find it difficult to change to another. If change is necessary *"they often need a blood transfusion of new people if the culture is really going to change, and that is, of course is what tends to happen in the more cut-and-thrust world of business organizations. Where such dramatic transfusions are impossible, organizations tend to play around with the structure, partly to bring new people into prominence, partly to give themselves the freedom to set some norms of behaviour- that is to introduce a new culture."*[39]

Such a situation is analogous with the problem of teaching and its match with learning styles. Learning style theory suggests we have pre-dispositions to learn in particular ways (styles). It is argued that teaching styles should match learning styles but that is impossible in a class with a mix of learning styles so teachers have to learn and employ a variety techniques that will cause those with different learning styles to respond. Managers have to employ several styles and be able to function in different cultures.

It is clear that culture and structure are intimately related. If a culture is to be changed the structural change may in part assist cultural change.[40] A minute's reflection on the differences between theory X and Theory Y beliefs and structures should illustrate this point.

When Handy undertook research in schools he found that primary school teachers thought of themselves as being in a task culture. Secondary teachers however, showed themselves to belong to a role culture. Handy refers to another investigation that reported a collegial culture that is a person culture of individuals whose roles have to be coordinated *"in spite of themselves"*[41] His conclusion was that *"schools like other organizations, are pulled four ways by the demands of the different cultures. Sometimes it must feel as if they are being pulled apart. Management's task is to gather the cultural forces together using the strengths of each in the right places. It is no easy task."*[42] Management does this by helping everyone in the organization to learn, for as Schein in his definition of culture notes it places an emphasis on *"shared learning experiences which lead, in turn to shared taken-for-granted assumptions held by the members of the group or organization."*[43] And behaviours consequent there on. As Swan puts it quite simply *"teachers being teachers have shared learning experiences which result in a 'culture of teaching.'"*[44]

In chapter three the consequences for the pursuit of the goals of an educational institution of the fact the each individual lives in a plurality of social systems was considered. It was argued that it is not possible to get every individual to devote themselves wholly to the pursuit of an organizations goals because of the variety of priorities that individuals give to the social systems in which they live. It follows that an individual lives in a plurality of cultural systems and this is as true of school teachers and their pupils as it is of anyone else. Moreover just as we use technology to describe many things that a technologist might not recognize as technological so too can the term 'culture' be used. Just as we speak of the technology of the classroom (organization and layout as a socio-technical system) or even the technology of the timetable so to it is possible to speak of a variety of dimensions that contribute to the culture. In Hoyle and Wallace's terms a school 'has' dimensions such as discipline, timekeeping (on the part of teachers), school, spirit and learning that are open to manipulation.

A recent small scale study compared the culture of two schools along five dimensions proposed my Maehr and Midgely.[45] These dimensions are.

1. Style and Preference
2. Knowledge, technology and the tasks to be done.
3. Social organization.
4. Myths, artefacts and symbols,
5. Beliefs, values and goals.

Some idea of the meaning of these categories can be obtained from extracts from a comparison of the two schools referred to above. No judgement is intended. In respect of category 1 school A exhibited a formal style. *"The school uniform has been replaced with a school tracksuit. Staff dress patterns are individualistic and generally informal [...] movement around the school by students, staff and parents is relaxed, confident and constant Displays of student's work are uncoordinated and informal [...] School B- uniform was compulsory and movement around the school, was restricted and rarely encouraged outside of break time.*[46]

The recent death of Mary Douglas is an important reminder of the role of symbols in the development and maintenance of an ethos.[47] In respect of category 2 *School A has evolved a system of tasks where fluidity and overlap are common. Teachers move in and out of mainstream teaching and special resource teaching [...] Student's efforts are encouraged but there is lit-*

*tle focus on final outcomes.[...] School B was clearly expect-
ant of high standards in students; and teachers' work. Each
teacher took full responsibility for their students progress [...].*
In respect of category 3 *School A is renowned for being a place
welcome for all [...] social events for staff are important [...]
In School B social outings for the staff were not held. Visitors
had to be admitted by the secretary in response to a bell [...]
there was a real welcome for students from overseas as well as
genuine warmth towards the students in a special class of profoundly mentally handicapped children[..]* In respect of category 4 *School A is slow to celebrate its past. There are few class
and staff photos on display and there is no chronology visible.
The majority of the teaching staff has been together for twenty
years and collective folk memory exists but is not shared with
parents or students [...] School B was strong in its sense of
self. Photographs of past classes were prominently displayed.
Whole-school assemblies were held at least fortnightly."*

In respect of category 5 - Beliefs values and goals both schools
were committed to providing a catholic education first together
with high academic standards. It is a belief that education has
a moral purpose. The question of developing and maintaining
a Catholic/Christian ethos in schools has not only preoccupied
the authorities in Ireland but those in many other countries including Australia, Britain and the United States. Moreover it
has been the source of several important works on culture and
ethos.[48] Summarising research on school psychosocial environment (climate) research Dorman cited in particular, studies by
Flynn in Australia, Erickson in the United states and Rutter
and his colleagues in the UK4 9 Together they point to the
conclusion that effective schools of any type are characterised
not by elaborate facilities, extensively trained teachers, physical
resources, small classes or high levels of financial support but
by outstanding social climates.

Changing a Culture

The generally accepted view has been that school environment enhances student outcomes. An Irish project clearly believed that values inherent in any ethos could be implemented throughout a school community but that resources were needed if this were to achieved.[50]

The author of the study cited above suggested procedures that would bring about change in three dimensions of culture based on Schein's strategy for bringing about change.[51] Schein argued that if any part of the core structure is to change in more than minor incremental ways, the system must first experience enough disequilibrium to force a coping process that goes beyond just reinforcing the assumptions that are already in place. This is to make a distinction between first level and second level change described by Argyris and Schön.[52] (See chapter 7). To achieve this goal three steps are necessary. The first is to establish the will to change. For this the leader will have to provide " *(1) enough discomforting data to cause serious discomfort and disequilibrium (2) the connection of the disconfirming data to important goals and ideals causing anxiety and or guilt; (3) enough psychological safety in the sense of seeing a possibility of solving the problem without loss of identity or integrity, thereby allowing members of the organization to admit the disconfirming data rather than defensively denying it."* [53]

As Chapter 2 demonstrated it is all about changing perceptions and challenging their assumptions.

The next step is to engage in cognitive restructuring or redefinition of the prevalent culture, and the third and final step is to reinforce or refreeze the new cognitions and the production of new confirming data. In respect of learning an experienced teacher (post-graduate) wrote of a school that, *"clearly work needs to be done on learning outcomes. Following Schein's model for transforming this situation, a suitable modus op-*

erandi might be to conduct a full objective standardised test of Gaeilge, Maths and English. The results to be presented in school wide context with no relation to individual teachers or classes. This would allow the psychological safety for every teacher to reflect on the whole school performance and to suggest strategies to improve learning outcomes for all students. Cognitive restructuring in the form of new approaches to the management of students' learning might then arise. The refreezing would obviously come as improved performance by students is evident in follow up tests."

If one thing is clear from the case studies it is that cultures change quickly. One reported how after a new discipline policy had been introduced with the approbation of teachers and parents that after two years it had changed *"a warm school climate full of positive energy and enthusiasm into a stormy climate"* This was because the formal policies had broken down when it came to minor disruptive behaviour. *"The perception evolved that small problems go unpunished spread throughout the school community and a poor working environment developed. Students were of the opinion that this poor behaviour was acceptable in school and evidence of responsible behaviour. [...]Bypassing the record system meant that staff went to the head of discipline with their problems. An informal chat then occurred and the student would 'keep on the right side of the teacher for the rest of the day and say sorry.' There was no true acknowledgement on the student's behalf that this was inappropriate behaviour. Repeated offences were inevitable. A gulf of 'them' and 'us' developed"* [...]

Many teachers would say "been there, done (experienced) that."

It is clear that any attempt to change a culture must begin by understanding the present culture of the institution and starting from that point. Nowhere is this more important than when two schools are faced with amalgamation. Research suggests that all to often amalgamations are implemented at a speed that does not allow for the effective development of a new culture (see chapter 7). Moreover they can create a great deal of stress that could effect the performance of teachers.[54] It also suggests that those who cause mergers have little knowledge or understanding of the factors that will bring about success. That is because they did not understand amalgamation to be a process, and something that could not be brought about instantly.[55] A study of mergers in the UK by the Hay Group found that half of seventy three mergers of primary and secondary schools failed as measured by a decline in performance following the merger. The group had a contract to support the development of a single institution from the merger of two schools and the first thing they did was to undertake a culture review on both sites. *"This involved focus groups with staff, parents, pupils, support services and feeder primaries. It enabled everyone involved to appreciate fully the responses to the merger from both sides and identified differences in culture and outlook between the schools. More importantly, it also highlighted shared concerns and values. [...]"*[56] Finally from the world of business comes the view that *"organizational culture and the ability to operate effectively-successful implementation is much more important to organizational success than having the right strategy."*[57]

Twenty years later Hoyle and Wallace suggest that management theorists should not abandon the concept of culture altogether but their conclusion adds to Handy's. They say *"skilful school leaders are those who can achieve the minimal degree of consensus needed for the school to run smoothly whilst, as far as possible, enabling individual teachers to pursue their own values."*[58] However, the case studies suggest that this cannot be done without attention to the culture.

The Physical Environment

There is little doubt that the physical environment contributes to school culture. But there is little evidence that architects have any notion of learning. A building may be aesthetically pleasing outside but hopeless for learning inside. On several floors in the building in which I work the seminar and lecture rooms are totally enclosed with no outside light and inadequate ventilation. The corridor walls are of grey blocks and there is a heritage order on the building that they cannot be painted. Inspection of many educational institutions shows that they have been built with one particular model of learning in mind- information giving. Students are seated in rows facing a dais and are supposed to learn by listening and recording. Often the means for recording notes are poor as in our case a little piece of wood attached to a chair in an overcrowded room. There is no way that teachers can conduct satisfactory group work in such circumstances.[59]The idea that effective teaching demands the exercise of a range of instructional strategies is not understood.

In the UK Beard visited over 50 new schools and concluded that the *"briefs, and hence the completed schools, tend to be based on traditional models of teaching and learning. They have taken little account of how, for example, ICT will impact on methods. In conventional classrooms ICT provision normally means data projectors and interactive whiteboards, plus a handful of ICT suites with seried ranks of PCs. Linked to this the whole agenda of personalised teaching has yet to be addressed. The teaching spaces in most recently completed schools are still almost entirely 55- square-metre standard classrooms limiting opportunities to introduce new forms of teaching and learning."*[60] He shows what can be achieved. It does require that the managers of schools and their architects are educated in what learning is all about. It should not be an impossible task.[61]

Beyond that are the questions in what ways are organizations learning organizations and in what ways can they become learning organizations?

Notes and references

[1] Stewart, R (1986). *The Reality of Management*. 2nd ed. Pan/ Heinemann, London. p 110.

[2] See articles by Emery, F. E., an E. L. Trist in F. E. Emery (ed) (1969). *Systems Thinking*. Penguin, Harmondsworth.

[3] Schein, E. H (1965) *Organizational Psychology*. Prentice Hall, Englewood Cliffs, NJ

[4] Barnes, L. B (1960). *Organizational Systems and Engineering Groups*. Harvard Business School, Cambridge. MA

[5] Burns, T and G. Stalker (1961). *The Management of Innovation*, Tavistock, London.

[6] Youngman, M. B. Oxtoby, R., Monk, J. D. and J. Heywood (1977) *Analysing Jobs*. Gower Press, Aldershot.

[7] Sadler, P. J (1969). *Designing an Organization Structure. A Behavioural Science Approach.* Ashridge Management College, Berkhamstead.

[8] Von Bertalanffy, L (1966). The theory of open systems, reprinted in F. E. Emery (ed) *Systems Thinking*, Penguin Books, Harmondsworth.

[9] *loc.cit* ref 9.

[10] *ibid*

[11] There are no such organizations as education authorities in Ireland for primary and post-primary denominational schools (secondary). There are Vocational Education Committees that manage vocational schools. I am indebted to Róisín Gaynor and Aingeal Uí Mhaicín for information on marketing by primary schools in Ireland.

[12] Williamson, D. T. (1971). *Trade Balance in the 1970s. The Role of Mechanical Engineering.* National Economic Development Office, HMSO, London. Historians might take a less sanguine view of cottage industry. It was open to a great deal of exploitation. Nevertheless, the principle remains.

[13] ibid

[14] An internal document circulated by Volvo says that *"the possibility of having influence on his own work situation is of vital importance for the individual's job satisfaction and motivation. An increased participation also means a better utilization of the experience and initiative of the employee.. Participation is a right which conveys, simultaneously, an obligation of responsibility. The basis for increased participation is the willingness of each leader to utilize opportunities for delegating and joint consultation."*

[15] Emery, G and M. Emery (1975) Cuts and guidelines for raising the quality of working life in D. Ginzburg (ed). *Bringing Work to Life.* Productivity Council of Australia, Cheshire, Melbourne.

[16] see for example Heywood, J (1982). *Pitfalls and Planning in Student Teaching.* Kogan Page, London.

[17] Heywood, J (1994). *Enterprise Learning and its Assessment in Higher Education.* Report No 20. Learning Methods Branch, Employment Department, Sheffield.

[18] Murray, M (1986) Recent developments in the school curriculum in France in J. Heywood and P. Matthews (eds) *Technology, Society and the School Curriculum. Practice and Theory in Europe.* Roundthorn, Manchester.

[19] Heywood, J (2002). SCOOPE and other primary (elementary) school projects with a challenge for engineering education. *Proceedings Frontiers in Education Conference*, 2, F2C-6 to 10

[24] Murray, M (1991) An evaluation of an Introductory Programme in Management Stuides. Doctoral dissertation, University of Dublin, Dublin.

[20] MacMahon, J (1975). *The relationship between curricular innovation and organization structure in post-primary schools.* M. Ed Thesis. University of Dublin, Dublin.

[21] *ibid.* There is alternative evidence that this was the case. The non-innovative schools were "secondary" and committed to getting their students through the Intermediate and Leaving Certificate examinations. That was their *raison d'être*. The newer comprehensive and community schools had to deal with many students who were not suited to these traditional examinations. Moreover they had been exposed to alternative curricula for

such students that could be assessed by school based assessment. But these assessments were not recognised by the State even though the curricular were.

[22] Glover, D and D. Miller (2007) Leading changed classroom culture-the impact of interactive whiteboards *Management in Education*. 21, (3) 21 – 24.

[23] They distinguished between departments that had no coherent policies for their introduction where enthusiastic teachers with competence used the whiteboards. This approach was individualistic. At the other end of the spectrum were those departments who followed whole school policies, introduced whiteboards into all the classrooms and gave technical and pedagogic support to all the teachers. This approach they called *innovatory*. Between the individualistic and *innovatory* was an *incrementalist* approach that was characterized by the progressive introduction of the whiteboard. The teachers were at varying levels of competence and the speed with which they became competent depended on the support they received.

[26] Tse, K.K. (1995) *Marks and Spencer. Anatomy of Britain's Most Efficiently Managed Company*. Pergamon Press Oxford. Written before it fell from grace in the late nineteen nineties.

[27] Galbraith, J (1973). *Designing Complex Organizations*. Addison-Wesley, Reading, MA

[28] Diggins, P (2002) School Cultures that enable and School Cultures that inhibit staff development in J. Heywood and P. Taylor (eds). School Autonomy. *Bulletin of the EFEA* No 2. European Forum for Educational Administration

[29] *ibid* slightly adapted for contextual reasons.

[30] see for example Dorman, J. P (1996). Use of teacher perceptions in school environment research. *School Organisation*. 16, (2), 188 – 202.

[31] Peters, T and P. Waterman (1982). *In Search of Excellence. Lessons from America's Best Run Companies*. Harper and Row, New York

[32] Hoyle, E and M. Wallace (2005) *Educational Leadership. Ambiguity, Professionals and Managerialism*. Sage, London. they cite, Nias, J et al (1989) *Staff Relationships in a Primary School* where teachers spoke about the "Sedgefield Way" and Woods P et al (1997). *Restructuring Schools, Restructuring Teachers: Responding to Change in an Primary School*. Open University Press, Buckingham in which teachers referred to "Meadowfields Way."

[33] Miller, D (1990). *The Icarus Paradox. How Exceptional Companies Bring About Their own Downfall*. Harper, New York

[34] *loc.cit*

[35] Handy, C and R. Aitken (1990 printing). *Understanding Schools as Organizations*. Penguin, Harmondsworth. See also Handy, C *Gods of Management* which develops this thesis.

[36] Pring, R (2000) School culture and ethos towards an understanding in C. Furlong and L. Monahan (eds). *School Culture and Ethos. Cracking the Code*. Marino Institute of Education, Dublin.

[37] Handy, C. (1988). *Understanding Voluntary Organizations*. Penguin, Harmondsworth

[38] Handy takes a limited view of the proposition that organizations are made up of roles and assigns it to role culture. As is made clear in chapter 3 the general principles of role theory apply to any organization and the bureaucracy or hierarchical organisation is but one type. Everyone plays a role whatever the organization

[39] *loc.cit* p 91

[40] Furlong, C (2000) Comprehending Culture, school organisation a cultural perspective in C. Furlong and L. Monahan (eds) *School Culture and Ethos. Cracking the Code*. Marino Institute of Education, Dublin.

[41] See Mathew, R and S. Tong (1982). *The Role of the Deputy Head in the Comprehensive School*. Ward Lock, London. Handy's 1984 study was undertaken for the Schools Council

[42] *loc.cit* p 95

[43] Schein, E p22

[44] Swan, V (2008) Unpublished work for doctoral thesis. University of Dublin.

[45] Maehr, M and C. Midgely (1996). *Transforming School Cultures*. Westview Press, Boulder, Co.

[46] From a post-graduate case study.

[47] Distinguished social anthropologist who died in May 2007. One of her best known works was on *Symbols* (Penguin).

[48] Pavlič, G (2004). *Identity of Catholic Schools in the 21st Century Europe*. St Stanislav's Institution, Ljubljana

[49] Dorman see ref 29. Erickson, D. A (1981). The superior social climate of private schools. *Momentum* 12, (3) 5 – 8. Flynn, M (1985) *The Effectiveness of Catholic Schools*. St Paul Publ. Homebush, New South Wales. Rutter, M et al (1979) *Fifteen Thousand Hours. Secondary Schools and their Effects on Students*. Open Books. Dorman contrasted Government and Catholic Schools in Queensland using a teacher perceptions inventory of school environment. He found statistically significant differences on three scales- student support, empowerment and mission consensus.. Catholic non-order (religious) and girls schools had more positive environments than Government schools. In the catholic schools teachers of religion perceived their school environment to have higher empowerment and resource adequacy than science teachers. Catholic boys' schools were not found to besignificantly different to Government schools.

[50] Monahan, L (2000) School culture and ethos: towards understanding in C. Furlong and L. Monahan (eds) *School Culture and Ethos: Cracking the Code*. Marino Institute of Education, Dublin. They published school culture and ethos survey questionnaires. Scott Boldt, A Vantage point of values-findings from the school culture and ethos survey questionnaires, and D. McHugh and E. Charles A whole school approach to culture and ethos both in the same volume. See also McBeath, J (ed) *Effective School Leadership: Responding to Change.* Paul Chapman, London and McBeath, J (1999) *Schools Must Speak for Themselves,* Routledge, London for details of other instruments.

[51] Schein, E (1992). *Organizational Culture and Leadership*. 2nd edition. Jossey Bass, San Fransisco

[52] Argyris, C and D. Schön (1974) *Theory in Practice. Increasing Professional Effectiveness.* Jossey Bass, San Fransisco

[53] *loc.cit*

[54] McHugh, M and M. Ryle (1993). School merger: a stressful challenge. *School Organisation*, 13, (1), 11 – 26. They found among 76 teachers in Northern Ireland schools which had either merged or were under the threat of merger that those threatened with traumatic change exhibited the highest levels of stress. This finding has consequences for the management of amalgamations.

[55] O'Connor, R. B. V (2006). A Mixed Methodological Study of Amalgamation. Practice in Irish Primary Schools. MSt Thesis, University of Dublin, Dublin. See also Hoyle and Wallace ref 24.

[56] Hobby, R (2007). Two into one will go. *Managing Schools Today.* January/ February 18 - 21

[57] Pfeffer, J and R. I. Sutton (2006). *Hard Facts. Dangerous Half Truths and Total Nonsense. Profiting from Evidence based Management*. Harvard Business School Press, Boston, MA. See also Fidler, B (1998). How can a successful school avoid failure? Strategic management in schools. *School Leadership and Management*, 18, 497 – 509.

[58] *loc. cit* p 118. They cite the Nias research on primary teachers as an example of what could be achieved

[59] I recently completed an undergraduate course in the same building and can testify to that view.

[60] Beard, A (2007) Nice financing. Shame about the design *Managing Schools Today.* January/ February 66 - 72

[61] I had the experience of designing a science and technology building for a grammar school in the late 1950s that called for rooms to be custom designed for the teaching of technology. It included a room specifically designed for technology project work and an integrated workshop for all materials. Heywood, J (1963) Technical Subjects in Grammar Schools. FCP Thesis. College of Preceptors, London.

CHAPTER 6

LEARNING IN ORGANIZATIONS

Introduction

The purpose of this chapter is to consider organizations from the perspective of learning. While we commonly speak of an organizations learning curve the implications of this view are seldom examined in detail. The curve is a measure of success and failure. Organizations go through periods of success and failure. Some are able to overcome the failure while others die. Most organizations are in some form of competition and schools are no different in this respect. They are open to attack. Often the failure to learn, that is to remedy potential failure, presents a readily identifiable picture that gives an advantage to an attacker and extracting the organization from such attack can be difficult. To move to a new learning curve may be extremely difficulty and it may require drastic (second level) change rather than development of existing patterns (first level change). Success has to be continually earned and this requires that organizations (schools) continually learn. They have to continually evaluate their strengths weaknesses, opportunities and threats (SWOT). Whatever the problems associated with developing a school plan such planning, provided there is implementation and evaluation, gives an opportunity for learning.

Different dimensions of the learning organization are considered and Senge's five disciplines are summarised. His view of an organization is of a place where we are learning how to learn together. People in organizations have to learn to question the assumptions that drive them, and in so doing become inquiry-oriented. "Assumptional-dialogues" uncover pictures of the future. The development of an "inquiry oriented" institution requires a radical shift in thinking.

Organizations go through the same cycles of learning that individuals do when solving problems and making decisions As the demands for knowledge change so the requirements for particular types of personnel change. Different kinds of management style are required for different situations and sometimes managers are unable to adapt. This applies to schools as much as it does to business. The challenge for managers is to help themselves and their personnel to adapt.

An understanding of how we learn should facilitate adaptive behaviour. For this reason it is important that we should learn how to learn during schooling.

The basis of all learning is "conversation" whether it is with others or the media. Perkins argues that organizations are "conversations". Just as there is organizational learning so there is organizational intelligence.

One approach to the development of organizational learning is through the use of quality circles. Training is required if they are to be effective. It is argued that such training should begin in primary school. The importance of skill in self-assessment is noted.

Models of curriculum and instructional design and school planning are shown to belong to the same genre as management by objectives. The idea of school planning is considered and Tuohy's model for its implementation discussed. The danger is that such planning can become an end in its own right from which action does not emerge.

The chapter ends with a brief discussion of the role of Kaizen and Total Quality Management in education. Brief mention of a case study on TQM in a school shows that teacher professionalism was enhanced.

Learning Curves

Whatever the organisation it is driven by ideas. These ideas are driven by its mission whether expressed in a statement or not. Schools are no different in this respect to any other institution. When we undertake a new job we have to learn about that job and sometimes we speak of a steep learning curve because we have to assemble a lot of information very quickly in order to get the job done. Often those who talk of a person experiencing a deep learning curve do so because they see a person having to deal with problems and people they know to be difficult. So the phrase 'learning curve' is one that has every day parlance. There has even been a BBC programme about education with that title.

The diagram in figure 6.1 is a learning curve of a business.1 It is in the shape of an S (S curve) which describes the effort put in to improving a product or process and the results a company obtains from that investment. Foster shows that in the first phase of an innovation a great deal of money has to be invested for apparently little return. As knowledge is structured investment has to be increased substantially, and at the top more and more is put in for less return. As Foster puts it *"ships don't sail much faster, cash registers don't work much better, and clothes don't get much cleaner."* It is a measure of the value-added at different times in the life of the product or process. Two concepts are important in this theory. The first he called *"the attackers advantage."* If a company persists in investing in a product for little return it is at the mercy of an "attacker" who will look for alternatives using a different story. Schools can be the subject of attack. If a school has an identity crisis, for example where it is perceived wrongly to be the school for the disadvantaged and others with learning difficulties, other schools in the locality will seek to attract the supposedly able children of the upwardly mobile from that locality. The attackers can influence this process by telling parents who have a child with learning difficulties that their child would be better off in the other school. The demography of the school might be such that enrolments are falling thus causing the school to accept children that it would normally hope would go elsewhere. The position may be complicated by a requirement for a relatively open admissions policy.

The other concept is that of "discontinuity." This is the period of change from one group of products/processes to another with a new knowledge base. The new product/process starts a new S curve. To move to a new S curve companies have to recognise the limits of the existing technology. The function of science and technology is to predict the limits of a particular knowledge base and to help the company develop new know

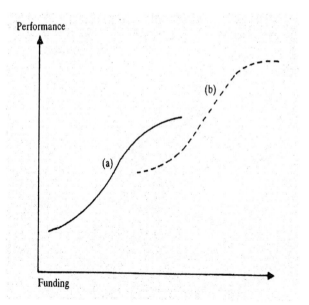

Figure 6.1 Foster's S curve of Innovation

-ledge bases. Currently schools embrace new technologies especially in ICT slowly. There is a reluctance to look at how a school should be reorganised and structured academically and physically to embrace the new technologies.[2] Schools are like companies they change often but in small incremental steps like the yearly changes that are made to a particular model of a motor vehicle. They are the next step in an accepted pattern. Such developments have been described as first level changes by Marzano, Waters and McNulty.[3] Schools can cope with this but not with major changes that involve dramatic changes from the expected both in defining the problem and finding the solution. These "second level" changes as Marzano, Waters and McNulty call them often falter in education because the procedures used to bring them about are inappropriate. The same can be said of innovation in business. Such changes are complex and often no single solution will suffice. An example of second level change relates to a report published by the government in England on teaching that calls for "hands-up" in response to questions to be limited because numerous children do not put their hands up.[4] This is a fact that has been understood by educational researchers for forty years. Among their recommendations have been to let children work in pairs and answer questions jointly. Another strategy is to give children more time to answer questions. There are other strategies that teachers use. But what about technology? Why not have every desk equipped with electronic devices connected to the teacher's desk so that the children who do not want to go public can go private, so to speak? Remember children like to compete.

A criticism of Peters and Waterman's *In Search of Excellence*,[5] which analysed the factors that contributed to excellence in industry, is that it did not consider what contributes to failure. Since then some of the largest American firms have either failed or gone through periods of apparent failure. A failure on the Foster's S curve would be marked by a downward trajectory. Miller, some time after the publication of *In Search of Excellence* published *The Icaurus Paradox*[6] in which he draws a paradox with the power of this mythical horse with wax wings. The horse's downfall came when he flew too near to the sun and his wings melted. The same thing can happen with an outstanding company. *"Their victories and their strengths often seduce them into excesses that cause their downfall. Success leads to specialization and exaggeration, to confidence and complacency, to dogma and ritual."*[7] Isn't this a description of the 2008 world-wide banking failure – indeed of any bubble? Schools are not free of this paradox. Fidler makes the same point. Also citing the Icaurus Paradox he points out that in successful organizations those who dissent have very little influence. Moreover the organization has little incentive to look outward so its picture of the environment can become distorted. Cognitive dissonance may make the perceptions fit existing preconceptions (see chapter 2). Such institutions tend to be insular and not adapt to the environment and restrict their information (intelligence) gathering.[8]

Success has to be continually earned and this requires that schools like industry must continually learn. One simple way of organizational learning is to carry out a SWOT analysis. An example is given in exhibit 6.1. An approach to this adopted by the principal of a Junior School in a rural town was to involve parents, past pupils and teaching staff in the analysis. They were asked to complete a questionnaire that simply consisted of four titled blank sections on a side of A4 paper. In the different sections they gave their views of the strengths, weaknesses, opportunities and threats that the school faced. *"No matter how well we thought we knew our school the results of the SWOT analysis brought surprises and a call to awakening [...] We now have to take on-going measures to ensure that we implement effective systems to determine customer requirements and demonstrate success in meeting these requirements."*[9] Some weaknesses were addressed immediately but others such as age profile of the teaching staff, gender imbalance and an overload of travellers and refugees could only be addressed in the long term.

The preparation of a whole school development plan[10] also supplies an opportunity for learning provided that it is implemented and evaluated.

Learning Organizations

Senge whose book *The Fifth Discipline* has done so much to popularise the concept of learning organisations argued that there are five component technologies that contribute to the development of a learning organization[11]. He argued that there was an ensemble of five dimensions that a learning organization must have. Prior to listing these dimensions he argued that the scholarly tradition that teaches us to analyse issues –*"break apart problems"* leads us to believe that complex tasks and subjects can be made more manageable. In truth however, such analyses make it difficult to see the consequences of our actions or to see the picture as a whole. *"We try to reassemble the fragments in our minds, to list and organize all the pieces. But, as the physicist David Bohm says, the task is futile- similar to trying to reassemble the fragments of a broken mirror to see a true reflection. Thus after a while we give up trying to see the whole altogether."*[12] Senge argues that we have to give up this idea and see the world and in particular organizations as a set of related forces *"where people are continually learning how to learn together."* A gestalt so to speak. A similar sort of argument has been made in discussions of the higher levels of *The Taxonomy of Educational Objectives.*[13] While academics and scholars are very good at developing the skill of analysis they are not terribly good at the higher order skill of synthesis. But such organizations are *"possible because, deep down, we are all learners."*[14] And this is the view that has been taken throughout this book beginning in the first chapter. In the future, Senge argues that the distinguishing mark of a learning organization will be the pursuit of five basic disciplines of which systems thinking is the most important. A discipline is a body of theory and technique through which skills and competencies are acquired.

The five disciplines are

- Systems thinking

- Personal mastery

- Mental models

- Building shared vision

- Team learning.

Strengths	Weaknesses
Enthusiastic staff and management Strong in technical subjects Strong parental support Excellent extra-curricular activities Good staff morale	Old buildings and lack of space Inadequate sports facilities A declining enrolment De-motivated students
Opportunities	Threats
Good community reputation in sport Good staff development programme Influx of new staff members Possibility of new facilities.	Risk of loosing experienced teachers Ethos of the town to send pupils –single sex schools Average exam results.

Exhibit 6. 1. A SWOT analysis of a vocational school in Ireland.

To obtain *personal mastery* we continually clarify and deepen our personal vision, the focus of our energies and try to see reality objectively. It is a commitment to learning

We need patience to achieve this end. It is *"the learning organizations spiritual foundation"*[15] And, there has to be a reciprocal agreement with the organization. If an individual is committed to learning so must the organization be. It is a reciprocal contract.

Mental models are very much like those models of Schein's that describe dimensions of peoples' motivation to work (chapter 4). They include stereotypes (chapter 2)). They can as we saw be very persuasive and affect our behaviour, not necessarily for the better. As we saw our mental models have to be continually challenged. We have to learn to question our assumptions. As I have argued elsewhere a school which is a learning organization or inquiry oriented has to continually question its assumptions in dialogues (assumptional-dialogues).[16] One area that is constantly in need of questioning is discipline, another is the extent to which the school teaches higher order thinking skills.

Senge also makes the point made earlier that mission statements tend to be just that and nothing more. They do not lead to action. In companies and educational institutions every one needs to be driven by a shared vision which in popular parlance "they own". Assumptional-dialogues are a vehicle for uncovering *"pictures of the future"* and for making mission statements a meaningful base on which to build a new reality. They are the basis of ownership. It is through dialogue that the available research is brought to the discussion and questioned. Such dialogues also form the basis of team learning. When teams think together their ability to solve problems is greatly enhanced. The intelligence of a team is often greater than that of the individuals in the team In reality teams work very well in the level 1 change situation but not so well in a level 2 change situation. *Systems thinking* is the most important of the disciplines because it integrates the other dimensions or disciplines it *"makes under-*

standable the subtlest aspect of the learning organization-the new way individuals perceive themselves and their world."[17] Learning of the kind that Senge seeks requires a fundamental shift in thinking. *"For a learning organization adaptive learning must be joined by a generative learning that enhances our capacity to create."*[18] As we have seen in earlier chapters structures can easily impede that capacity to create.

Senge also takes the view that is also a theme of this book that organizations are poor learners. They suffer the same disabilities as children and much of this is because organizations are poorly defined, jobs are not allocated to release potential, and *"most importantly, the way we have all been taught to think and interact (not only in organizations but more broadly) creates fundamental learning disabilities."*[19] Nevertheless. organizations do "think" so how can this be built upon and what implications does it have for education?

Organizational Learning

Figure 6.2 shows that from the acquisition of an idea a company goes through the same processes of learning as individuals, except that the phases take place over a long period of time.[20] Even so this happens with some of the strategic problems that individual's face. The steps in problem solving/critical thinking are shown in exhibit 6.2. Most models account for the problem solving process in this way although their terminology may differ. (See for example, figures 1.2). The steps require the utilisation of skills that are required by managers irrespective of the type of organization.

In the case of this company it has been shown elsewhere how the initial problem was formulated, and how the information collected by the purchase of a licence from the USA led to the quick structuring of knowledge. The progress of the cycle is from relatively unstructured knowledge to highly structured knowledge associated with the finished product. There is continuing feedback from the market, and the product is adapted to meet the needs of the market, which in turn is influenced by changing technology. We have also shown how the demand for particular kinds of knowledge, and therefore personnel, changed as the problem-solving cycle progressed. Those engineers capable of innovation were not necessarily effective in tasks related to care and maintenance of the product more generally in the market.

---

(1) Ability to recognize the existence of a problem

(2) Ability to define the problem

(3) Ability to select information pertinent to the problem

(4) Ability to recognize assumptions bearing on the problem

(5) Ability to make relevant hypotheses

(6) Ability to draw conclusions validly from assumptions, hypotheses and pertinent information.

(7) Ability to judge the validity of the processes leading to the conclusion.

(8) Ability to evaluate a conclusion in terms of its assessment.

Exhibit 6.2 Steps and abilities involved in critical thinking (after Saupé, 1961[21])

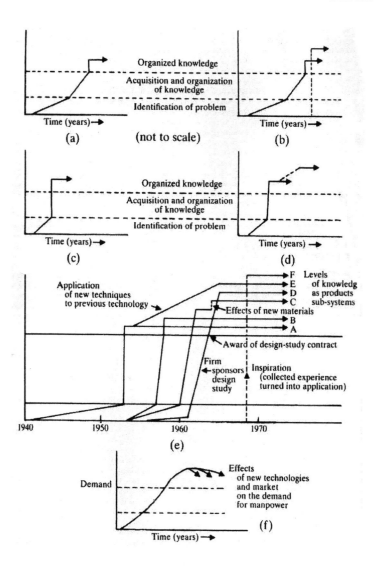

Figure 6.2 (a) curve of innovation (b) Effect of instantaneous application of organized knowledge; (c) Acquisition of knowledge by patent; (d) Application of new material devises or techniques to present knowledge; (e) The pattern of innovation in the compamny in this study (approximately to scale); (f) Illustration of the rate of change of demand for manpower as a function of the learning innovation curve (source *International Journal of Electrical Engineering Education* (1976) 12, p 229 and Youngman, M. B. et al (1978) Analysing Jobs. Gower, Aldershot.

The demand for particular types of manpower related to the particular stage of problem solving. The same is true of schools. Different situations may require different styles of management. However, unlike industrial organizations it is very difficult to change school managers (principals) and teachers to match the changing skill requirements of the school and this may make adaptation difficult. Adaptation involves among other things skills in the formulation of alternatives and the evaluation of their effectiveness. Relatively simple changes in design or hypotheses in research can bring about substantial changes in the system or plan of action for research. Adaptation to new knowledge demands substantial re-learning on the part of individual engineers as well as the groups with whom they work. The same is true of research students, teachers and their managers. Many people find adaptation difficult and sometimes change their management style not necessarily for the benefit of the organization.

For example a head teacher decided that she would have a career break. Up to that time she had been described as a charismatic leader. *"Her distinguishing personal qualities of vision, rhetorical skills, and the ability to build a particular kind of image in the minds and hearts of her staff afforded her this categorisation[...] Her rhetorical skills were not her forte but in her own repetitive way she succeeded in sharing her vision with the staff. The excitement in her own voice and her self trust in communicating her new plans and initiatives were sufficient to win the emotional and mental support of staff. "*[22] The person acting as her replacement also went on a career break after a short time and a new person was appointed who rather than accepting the status quo as his predecessor had looked for opportunities to initiate change. Duties were delegated and each teacher was made to feel central to the decision-making He displayed a capacity to tap people's commitment and capacity to learn at all levels of the organization. By now the environment had changed considerably and required of the head teacher returning from her career break considerable adaptation. She found it difficult to adapt to the more participatory environment that had been established and compensated for what must have been perceived to be a loss of control by a task-oriented leadership which in order to achieve her goals required that she took control of all the activities herself. This led her to distance herself from the staff and to lose their commitment.

It has been argued here and throughout the text that the more we understand how we learn and relate to others the more we are likely to be able to adapt, not necessarily without some pain and distress. It follows from research on adult learning that schools have an essential role to play in the development of attitudes associated with adaptability and flexibility. Adults who have some knowledge of learning how to learn, learn more easily than those who do not have this knowledge. This means that it is important that every individual should have knowledge of how they learn before they leave school. They should understand how learning influence's adaptability and is, in turn, influenced by the environment.

The teacher who commented on open and closed systems in chapter 5, also wrote that what most struck him *"was the extent to which the events bore out the details in the relevant literature and the extent to which an educated staff, including the author, seemed unaware of this. The necessity for a culture of collaboration based on supportive norms, beliefs, values and structures did not seem to be understood. Although learning was taking place there was no obvious awareness of the importance and the complexity of the learning process. Its central role in adaptation was not discussed and the school never moved towards accepting Kolb's contention that learning should be an explicit objective pursued...consciously and deliberately"*

How we learn remains one of the best kept secrets of the educational system, yet if we do not broach these problems how can individuals be expected to adapt? So it is that educators have to be as much concerned with the domain of action and emotion (affective) as they are with the cognitive as the outline taxonomy (exhibit 6.3) relating to adaptability and control shows. This is why there is so much interest in experiential learning and group work.

Learning, Conversation, Organizational Intelligence and Group Methods of Learning

What is learning? Answers to this question seem to be elusive. Look up the index of the Fifth Discipline and you will not find a reference to "definition of" learning. Come to think of it neither does the first edition of this book although there is quite a section on the organization as a learning system.

Of course there are many theories of learning but for the purpose of this text a general definition that is apposite for those who teach as well as their consumers is that learning is a process by which experience develops new and reorganizes old concepts. It is this process that the curves in figure 6.2 show. This definition is the basis that provides one of the arguments for a broad liberal education, for the broader the range of concepts we have, the more we are able to cope with new concepts. Such reorganization that we do is a form of problem solving and/or critical thinking. Primarily our activities in an organization are problem solving and thinking critically (reasoned thought) and that should be the case whoever we are or at whatever level we work. In such activities we use our intelligence, that is, as it was defined in chapter 1. We adapt to, select and shape those environments relevant to our lives.

Earlier in chapter 3 it was argued that whatever the organisation its basic unit was the role. We act out those roles. In some organizations we have more or less complete freedom to act out our scripts whereas in a bureaucracy the scripts have to be acted out precisely. All organizational activity is a form of theatre. The drama is made problematic because we all have different personalities and dispositions. To make the jobs we do possible we often have to enter into 'conversations' with others that apparently go beyond the role as defined. The enterprise we studied could not have functioned had this not been the case. While observers of people at work often note the large amount of gossip that occurs they do not take the step that David Perkins invites us to take and understand organizations as *"conversations."*[23] Even he had been forced to think about this concept by an Argentinian Ernesto Gore. *"Contemporary concepts such as knowledge management and communities of practice picture community and organizational life in terms of reservoirs of knowledge and expertise shared through conversations of various kinds via various media.[...] Of course, whether organizations are made of conversations depends on how broadly you construe conversations. The real topic here is distributed cognition, cognition shared across a collective, and its technical tools such as telephones and computers [...] feedback sessions, giving and taking orders, exchanging memo's, and issuing policies, some of it face to face and some of it by telephone, on paper, or by e mail".*[24] I would add reading because when we read we have a conversation with the text. I would also note that we often converse with ourselves when we try to determine a future action. We also have to remember that there are different kinds of dialogue. There is dialogue that is generative and strategic. There is dialogue that is social discourse: there is dialogue that is learning: There is dialogue that creates cultures and across these cultures are the dimensions of dialogue in which we think together, where conflict is transformed into cooperation, and which is evolutionary. All of these happen among people in organizations and the conglomerate can enhance or impede learning. With those additions it is easy to see the significance of conversations in learning for learning is a process of conversation that enables us to acquire new schema and reorganize old frames of reference. Thus in a very simple sense all organizations are learning systems although whether or not that learning is constructive is another matter. Some will be and some will not for organizations are just like any mixed class of students that is reasonably representative of the general population. Hence the argument on which this text is based is that if you can understand classroom behaviour, that is, what it is that makes students want to learn, you can understand what makes organizational groups behave in the way they do. And just as one can speak of organizational learning so one can speak of organizational intelligence. *"The intelligence of a collective, strong or not strong comes from individual contributions combined by a multitude of interactions of various kinds at various levels."*[26]

It is ironic that politicians who argue that student's should be prepared to work in industry as well as for life often condemn methods of learning most likely to prepare students for work in industry, especially in teams such as group learning, as fanciful theory. Rather they want students exposed to transmission methods of instruction that do not engage them with the skills of thinking and behaviour that they believe industry requires. They would presumably be appalled to learn that some educators advocate the use of some approaches to TQM (Total Quality Management) such as quality circles as a general teaching strategy. They are a useful technique for helping with the development of a learning organization.

Ability to adapt

The ability
- To perceive the organizational structure, its formal and informal relationships, its socio-technical systems, its value systems and languages
- To understand the technical, human and financial aspects of the system or situation.
- To perceive the different thought processes involved in the solution of human and technological problems.
- The ability to think laterally.
- The ability to stand aside from one's own situation.

Continues over

> **Ability to control**
>
> **The ability**
> - To know the key areas of management
> - To understand how skills should be organized for use.
> - To understand his or her own knowledge requirements in relation to his/her needs for communication, competence and excellence.
> - To understand a situation and know (1) what people ought to be doing, (2) whether they are doing it effectively, (3) what climate needs to be created to get the job done effectively.
> - To get action.
> - To discriminate between relevant and irrelevant information.

> **Ability to relate to people**
>
> **The ability**
> - To understand the rights, responsibilities and obligations of those involved in the activity.
> - To understand and predict the effect of his or her behaviour on a situation.
> - To evaluate his or her actions.
> - To understand the attitudes and values of people in all parts of the organization.
> - To create the feeling that the job is important; and so on

Exhibit 6. 3 **Partial derivation of a taxonomy of work behaviour derived from a typical industrial situation in which managers and workers were in confrontation due to W. Humble (source Heywood, J (1989)** *Assessment in Higher Education.* **Wiley, Chichester)**

Quality Circles

At the end of the second-world war (1945) and for a decade after the Japanese had a reputation for cheap and nasty copying which was depriving it of overseas markets. To remedy this defect a number of companies decided to promote quality and reliability throughout the workforce by involving the workers themselves in problem solving and decision making. To this end they made it possible for their workers to join together in small groups to solve the problems with which they were faced. These groups were called quality circles and they were one of the ideas imported from the United States and in particular William Deming to develop total quality management.[27] Of the principles underlying quality circles probably the most significant and most challenging was the idea that these work groups should be voluntary. Because they are voluntary there is a high probability they will build a shared vision for the completion of the task and perform Senge's 3rd discipline. There is necessarily team learning (4th discipline) and personal mastery and mental models are likely to be influenced). Overall the task ensures that there is systems thinking. In Senge's terms quality circles are organizations for learning. The other axioms were as follows

- Most people have the ability to solve a wide range of problems.
- Only a few of the abilities that people have are used at work.
- Given the opportunity, individuals will use their talents to solve problems.
- Given training, individuals will be able to organize their work.
- Work problems are best solved at the work place.

There is nothing novel about these axioms. As we have seen they are enshrined in McGregor's Theory Y and Maslow's self actualizing person. What was different was the technique for bringing it about on an almost national front.

As defined by Robson, a quality circle is a small group of volunteers who work with the same supervisor, who meet together once a week for an hour to identify, analyse and solve problems related to their own work.[28] It is not done in a haphazard way and training is provided in problem solving and problem finding. It follows the dictum that the learner will solve problems better or develop the skills of critical thinking better if he or she understands how problems are solved (see exhibit 6.2). Training is given in brainstorming to show the group how to generate ideas. The methods used for analysing problems are very similar to the techniques of lateral thinking advocated by de Bono and others. [29] There is an important training session on presentation to management, and other sessions on working together, and solving problems that the group create for themselves. Such training helps participants to learn to tolerate differences in perspective. During training the participants in the circle are encouraged to "win." Everyone is encouraged to win: there are no losers. Everyone is encouraged to enjoy the quality circle, and there is no obligation either to remain a member or for the group to persist.

The role of quality circles in schools should be self-evident. School planning meetings are often a source of problem identification that could be solved by a voluntary group. Indeed this often happens but not with the systematic approach of a quality circle. For example the school may understand on the basis of standardized test results that the level of literacy among the pupils needs to be improved *(problem identification)*. The next step is to set a realistic time limit for the completion of the task *(targets for improvement)*. Reasons for the current state of affairs are discussed and a problem solving team established *(analysis)*. The circle investigates the problem in order to determine an action plan for the school *(planning implementation of counter-measures)*. The task fails or continues at this stage for there has to be a school wide commitment to the solution and implementation. In this example the problem solving team *(quality circle)* recommended that the students should be tested regularly in addition to standardized testing *(evaluation)*. If successful the system would be incorporated into the time-table as an integral part of the school programme *(standardization)*. [30]

In the case reported to this writer the school did not have much difficulty in perceiving this to be part of its mission. The promotion of literacy was given high status by all as exemplified by a post of responsibility that would centre on the reorganization of the school library. This included the reorganization of children's authors and poets: a library module was introduced for second year classes. Other interesting features of the programme were- competitions based on reading throughout the year; the time tabling of English in the morning when children are thought to be more receptive; English to be the main component of homework; parents to be asked to participate in the reading programme at home; the establishment of a resource room; newly trained teachers to work with experienced teachers to familiarise them with the strategy; and participation in the *"writer in residence"* scheme; -and so on.

Each member of the team had particular tasks to achieve. There were regular reports to the staff and the final task of the team was to analyse test data and information from a questionnaire. These showed a general improvement in spelling and comprehension. Parents reported positive changes towards homework and reading and the local librarian commented on the large number of children using the library.

It was reported to this writer as follows *"The fact that membership of our problem solving team was voluntary was important, the leadership role was pivotal to our success and the support and commitment of the principal, other staff members and parents influenced us greatly. One area which I felt was neglected was that of training. As the first problem solving team set up in the school, we did not have any reference point and training would have made us more efficient in a shorter space of time."*

Training, Self-Assessment and Planning

There is nothing new about all this – education syllabuses are littered with statements of objectives that purport to meet the goals of higher order thinking. For example exhibit 6. 4 shows a set of skills we would expect undergraduates to acquire while in university, yet they were designed to meet the requirements of history, geography and environmental studies for pupils in the age group 8 – 13. Why isn't it that in these circumstances where much is done to foster these skills early on that employers continue to complain that graduates do not possess them? The Tipperary Leader group (see chapter 5) took the view that it was essential to develop them in primary schools because they would not be developed in post-primary education.[31] It has been argued that students in US colleges of higher education rarely reach higher levels of critical thought because they are not trained to do so: the lecture and tutorial methods are geared to giving and receiving knowledge.[32]

In England and Ireland it has been shown that unless there is direct link between the objective (outcome) to be obtained, the assessment procedure used and the instructional strategy, it is less likely that the objective will be obtained. Thus it is that many statements of objectives have no influence on teaching and learning since a systems approach is not used to bring them about (figure 6.3(a). The same can be said about the management by objectives approach which was commonplace in industry in the 1960s (figure 6.3 (b). The trouble with both these models is that the idea of objectives becomes trivialised. Instead of focusing on domains attention is directed to stating the many objectives that contribute to a domain.[33] The pursuit of the whole is sacrificed in pursuit of the parts that do not add up to the whole. Too much time is spent on working out these numerous parts at the expense of implementation.[34] School plans belong to the same category of heuristics (figure 6.4). They are mechanisms for learning, and they require the active participation of the learners for their success. This view is supported by

Kolb. From a different analysis of organizations he concluded that- *"learning should be an explicit objective pursued as consciously and deliberately as profit or productivity."*[35] Moreover he argued that managers should set aside time to critique and learn from important meetings and decisions. Self-assessment, evaluation if you prefer, is something managers, teachers and students are rarely trained to do, yet it could be argued that it is the most important of the higher order thinking skills. It is at the heart of strategic planning.

Self-assessment requires the development of the skill of self-reflection.[36] In this respect it is of more than passing interest to note that Heirs is of the opinion that the major factor that contributes to good management is the way in which managers think, not during decision making but before decisions are made.[37] From the perspective of learning this is not surprising for we now understand that behaviour is conditioned by the thinking process that goes before. Breadth of language can bring greater control over our actions. Managers must be thinkers not doers. They have the task of managing a 'thinking team' and, many of them fail to understand that this is their task. This is entirely consistent with the view that in participative organizations everyone is a learner, for learning and decision making are but different aspects of the same mental process. The power of reflection is illustrated in exhibit 6.4. What differentiates individuals one from another is their ability to act on that learning. And the same is true of institutions.

One of the reasons for grouping figures 6.3 and 6.4 together is to remind educators that many of the managerial ideas that prevail have their origins in business. The idea of whole school evaluation has its origins in the management by objectives and strategic or corporate planning movements that dominated managerial thinking in the 1960s and 1970s. Whether or not such planning affected performance for the better is a moot point. Much of the research that was done seems to have been of poor design and in any case the findings are inconsistent. Senge reports that he has *"witnessed few lasting shifts to longer term commitment and action. Personally, I have come to feel that our failure lies not in unpersuasiveness or lack of sufficiently compelling evidence. It may simply not be possible to convince human beings rationally to take a long-term view. People do not focus on the long term because they have to, but because they want to."*[38] Senge doubts that shared vision can emerge from the strategic planning process. He cited Hamel and Prahalad who wrote that *"Although strategic planning is billed as a way of becoming more future oriented, most managers, when pressed will admit that their strategic plans reveal more about today's problems than tomorrow's opportunities."*[39] Of course the former may lead to the latter. What has to happen, those authors say is to set *"a goal that is worthy of commitment."* Pfeffer and Sutton bring their review of the topic to a close with a quotation that ends *"so strategy is important. Figuring out what to do is important. Doing them and doing them well is equally important."*[40] It is in this light that school strategic (development) planning should be viewed.

Although the value of educational research is often questioned it does have one major advantage if it causes practitioners to question what they are doing and why. Thus both American and British research attempts to define what is meant by the terms used in whole school development planning and in particular "strategic planning."[41] For example, in the case of England what is meant by the term "strategic responsibility" in the framework for inspection has been the subject of detailed analysis and it is found that it is possible to have long term planning that is not strategic. For it to be strategic it has to question aims, and take into account current and future trends in the environment.[42] It does what would be expected of an open system (see chapter 5). In this conceptualisation strategic management is about asking fundamental questions about the aims of the organization. However, Bennett and his colleagues draw attention to an alternative definition of school development planning as the operationalisation of a strategic plan in the short and medium term.

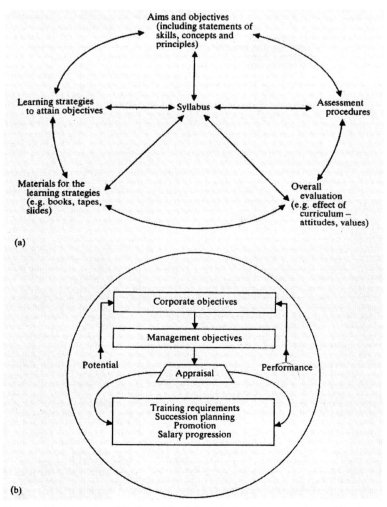

(a)

(b)

Figure 6.3. (a) A simplified model of the relation between aims, objectives, assessment, evaluation, learning strategies and syllabus to be compared with (b) a model for management by objectives based on Turner, B. T (1969). *Management Training for Engineers*, Business Books, London.. For a general text on this systematic procedure for planning the work of organizations which is characterized by collaboration between each manager and his/her superior in analysing the managers task's and establishing quantified objectives for their achievement se Humble, J (1972). *Management by Objectives*. Management Publications, London. the term is attributed to Peter Drucker.

They also point out that planning can be interpreted both narrowly and broadly. *"A narrow definition restricts planning to deliberate intentions of future action based on tight linkage between means and ends in situations of predictability and organisational control."*[43] Because it is unable to cope with unpredictable events it is likely to have a high level of implementation failure. In contrast broad planning relates to "flexible" school development planning *" a concept similar in some ways to Mintzberg's emergent strategy, but which blurs the distinction between planning and strategy."*[44] The American writer Mintzberg had distinguished between those strategies that are determined by existing plans and those that are determined by events as they unfold.

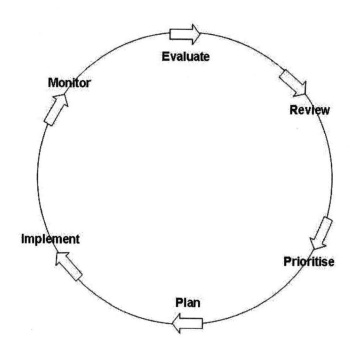

Figure 6.4. Outline scheme for school planning based on a diagram prepared for the School Development Planning Support Service, Drumcondra Education Centre, Dublin.

I am six on the Enneagram Personality test, my need for affiliation was high. I agree with the statement that "A person who has a strong need for affiliation is unlikely to adopt behaviours that would lead the group to exclude him or her from membership"

If I am honest enough with myself I realise that it is very true of me. I avoid embarrassing situations and to do this I use ego-defence mechanisms. These I have learned from experience. They are mental devices that help me to cope with the mental stress arising from conflicting needs. I think the ego-defence mechanism I use most frequently as principal is sublimation. It is the redirection of a motive from a relatively unacceptable goal to a more acceptable one. It helps me to control my behaviour. I over control myself and try to over control others because of my fear. I cannot cope with being out of control.

I realise that role analysis is a very important tool for examining an organisation. If I am to shape the school environment I need to understand how I perceive and develop and adapt my role as a Principal to meet the differing circumstances with which I am continually faced. My adaptability depends on my dispositions. I can be helped to develop this skill. To be able to adapt within a school I need to learn how my skills can contribute to the school and to understand how the skills of my staff will be utilised. Jobs need to be redesigned, to serve better both the individual staff member and the school.

Exhibit 6.4. Extract from a reflection at the end of a post-graduate assignment by a principal. Other parts of the reflection deal with Conflict, Power and Facing up to change. The list of ego-defence mechanisms too which reference is made is in Heywood, J. (1982) Ch on Motivation. *Pitfalls and Planning in Student Teaching*. Kogan Page, London.

What is clear from history is that school development planning has been seen on the one hand as bringing about change for the purposes of school improvement and on the other hand as a mechanism for quality assurance through the evaluation of an institutions resource management. In England *"Inspectors should consider how the governing body is fulfilling its strategic responsibility for planning the use of resources. The key to the judgement will be whether financial planning is based on good current data and sound projections, whether consideration has been given to alternative strategies for managing expenditure and handling contingencies [...]."*[45]

Tuohy[46] writing from an Irish perspective that almost dictates a curriculum oriented approach certainly at primary level,[47] points out that in schools planning may be used in one of two ways. The first is for the implementation of policy and the second is where a school develops in own policy in an autonomous way. An example of the latter would be where a school is in a competitive situation for students. A plan might be implemented for professional development. What a school chooses to do may involve the improvement or implementation of policy. In respect of the former schools are required to have policies for such things as admissions, discipline and child protection. Notice how such policies come within today's problems and not tomorrows opportunities. Notice also how such policies are often dealt with separately and in reaction to the requirements of policymakers.

Tuohy suggests there are seven stages in planning. The first he calls "stakeholder analysis" the purpose of which is to identify the people (groups) who should be involved. At first sight it might seem that in whole school evaluation only the teachers should be involved and may be that is right yet the SWOT analyses illustrated above showed that both parents and pupils could make a valuable input but in Touhy's model such analysis is the fifth stage. His model suggests that all of the stakeholders (teachers, parents, pupils and management) should be involved in someway from the beginning. Care needs to be taken in the selection of personnel for specific topics. For example, in one school where there was a problem of discipline a task force was set up to deal with the problem. Young members of staff were asked to join the group. *"They frequently displayed their levels of immaturity rather than maturity and argued among themselves and with year heads. They often insisted on radical sanctions like immediate suspension for minor offences like non-completion of homework over a period of time. They failed to consult the facts [...]"*[48] The commentator made the point that these young teachers might have been better employed in other groups where their high level of knowledge would be welcome. Equally they might have learnt more about discipline from working in a group with experienced teachers.

He calls his second stage "environmental scanning" which is to have an awareness of what is happening outside the school. The examples given above of the school in an open system have generally referred to competition for students and amalgamations. But Tuohy makes the point that the open system extends beyond the local through regional and national to international levels and he cites the awareness that schools should have in particular of EU (European Union) policies.

His third stage is the development of a *shared vision* one of Senge's five disciplines. However as Senge makes clear this is not an easy task for each of us has his/her own vision and a vision that is shared has to be built from those individual visions. *"Organizations intent on building shared visions continually encourage members to develop their personal visions. If people don't have their own vision, all they can do is "sign up" for someone else's. The result is compliance, never commitment."* (Or as we would say to day there is no sense of "ownership"). *"On the other hand, people with a strong sense of personal direction can join together to create a powerful synergy toward what I/we truly want."*[49] The leadership role in management is to bring people together to create such a synergy. That might be done by harnessing the vision of a member of the group, or by communicating their own vision for it to be shared. The importance of management at this stage cannot be overemphasised. Although exhibit 6.5 is intended to be self-explanatory and illustrate the importance of the leader/manager in the vision process the manager in the second school would also seem to illustrate Senge's discipline of *personal mastery*. Those who possess this discipline at a high level share several basic characteristics. They have a special sense of purpose that lies behind the vision and the goals. For such a person, a vision is a calling rather than simply a good idea. They see *"current reality" as an ally not an enemy. They have learned how to perceive and work with forces of change rather than resist those forces. They are deeply inquisitive, committed to continually seeing reality more and more accurately. They feel connected to others and to life itself. Yet they sacrifice none of their uniqueness. They feel as if they are part of a larger creative process, which they can influence but cannot unilaterally control."*[50] Unfortunately many managers feel that if they lose control they lose respect and status and that is one of the largest impediments to change.

Tuohy's fourth stage relates to *understanding the values of the different stakeholders.* Contradictions among them may impede the school in the attainment of a goal. He refers to a perennial problem in British and Irish education namely the reconciliation of the academic with the vocational. Thus parents and business may want the children to be prepared for the workplace while the mission statement proclaims that the school is for the development of the whole child. Some teachers would hold that the two are mutually contradictory because the development of the whole person demands a broad education whereas vocational education is too narrow. This was a very real problem for the Christian Brothers in Ireland when their education officers recommended that the secondary schools in their trusteeship should develop skills in enterprise learning and technology.[51]

The fifth stage is to review the *current situation* and Tuohy recommends a SWOT analysis of the kind described in earlier sections. The sixth stage is to prioritise. There are two points. First there are likely to be more things to do than are feasible in a reasonable period of time. For a single project that period could be up to eighteen months as for example the literacy project that was mentioned in an earlier section. If time is not allowed for projects they can become trivialised and this is the problem of trying to tackle everything at once. Even then some parts of the programme can be rushed. As a teacher reported: *"While we adapted and changed reasonably well, with limited resources at times, many of the changes envisaged were often rushed within a limited planning time frame. A one hour planning meeting in my view from 3pm-4pm is not sufficient to do the job properly and is not good for the psychological well being of staff."*[52]

Some schools have set about tackling their problems over a long period of time. One school, for example, as a result of a SWOT analysis decided to tackle its perceived problems over a five-year period. The problem areas were the future of the school; curriculum development; extra-school development; support structure , that is pastoral care and communications structures; discipline and staff development. Fidler noted that if a SWOT analysis was carried out that did not take into account the culture of the school the *status quo* could be perpetuated.[53]

The second point is that the relative importance of projects comes to be realised. Tuohy links the stages of implementation and review together. Since there is a tendency to implement and ignore review it might have been better to separate the two. There is no doubt that evaluation (review) is very difficult and often the techniques of evaluation that are used only get at part of the truth. For example, it is typical of many evaluations of student learning that they assess student attitudes toward learning or strategies for learning but do not establish exactly what has been learnt.

It will be seen that Tuohy's process of planning is very similar to the process outlined in figure 6. 4. There is little doubt that school planning can have a positive impact on schools. The five-year plan referred to in the previous paragraph yielded even after demographic changes are taken into account a substantial increase in the number of pupils attending the school but as other reports have shown in some schools its impact is not very great (See exhibit 6.5). But as one teacher enthusiast for school planning said there is always the danger that it will end up as an end in itself and this could happen if teachers are not encouraged and praised for the additional work they have to do. Much depends on the motivation and behaviour of management.

School 1
The school plan was not seen as a working document, it was seen as a mandatory document being produced to satisfy an outside body. The Principal had an unrealistic vision of the future of the school and a vision that was not shared by the rest of the staff. An input from the Board of management, parents, pupil or other stakeholders was not sought. [...] Whilst the principal maintained the status quo there was an inclination toward "crisis management."

School 2
This school apparently took a totally different approach to the planning process. The principal had good leadership qualities [...] He had a clear vision for the future of the school but he was also aware of "Starratt's "empowering covenant." He was therefore able to help the staff articulate their vision [...] He took on the "designated leadership role" and facilitated meetings and co-ordinated various working committees and a shared vision was created.

Fig 6.5 .Extracts from a case study of the planning process in two schools with particular reference to the role of the principals (The reference is to Starratt, R. J. (1995) *The Leaders Vision*. Corwen Press, Thousand Oaks, CA)

KAIZEN: Total Quality Management (TQM)

School planning came about because of political demands for accountability. As we have seen the ideas come from business and in this respect the Japanese have had considerable influence. Taking up the ideas of two Americans W. E. Deming and J. M. Juran they set about changing the image of their products from "cheap and nasty" to "high quality". The philosophy that arose was given the name "KAIZEN"[54] *"The essence of KAIZEN is simple and straightforward: KAIZEN means improvement. Moreover KAIZEN means ongoing improvement involving everyone, including both managers and workers. The KAIZEN philosophy assumes that our way of life-be it our working life, our social life, or our home life-deserves constantly to be improved."* It is a philosophy, a driving force, and one measure of the success of school development planning would be the extent to which it imbues a school with a way of life and a philosophical disposition. Imai believes that many who studied the Japanese miracle failed to understand the essence of Kaizen which is an umbrella concept that covers most of those *"uniquely Japanese practices that have received such world wide fame."* It is all about the pursuit of quality and Western approaches to this that embrace a range of techniques have been variously labelled Continuous Quality Improvement (CQI) and Total Quality Management (TQM).

Kaizen is not a grandiose approach to solving problems that is likely to fail for lack of resources.[55] Rather it is a series of small incremental steps. It might be translated as "Step by Step Improvement." One teacher contrasted it with her perception of the requirements of the Department of Education and Science (Ireland) for the school plan that she saw as requiring sweeping changes. She believed that while schools were creating many policies, her school in particular, that it would be better if it concentrated on one or two things. Citing Davies and West Burnham she said that *"successful action planning will only come about if schools are realistic about workload and do not try to achieve too much too soon."*[56] Just as was the case with the management by objectives movement in industry personnel spent too much time working out objectives, so to in school planning too much time can be spent in working out policies that are never followed up.

It would seem therefore that school planning could benefit from TQM and some schools have applied it to their practice. Murgatroyd and Morgan who commend it to schools list the five components of TQM as follows:

- Alignment and commitment to shared vision.
- An extended understanding of customer-driven process and strategy.
- Teams as the focus of organizational design
- "Outrageous" or challenging goals.
- Tools for systematic daily management.[57]

The parallels with Senge's five disciplines and quality circles will be apparent. As will be evident from what follows the quality circle approach adopted in the example above can lead to the same kinds of process and outcomes as TQM. The Principal of a rural single sex primary school was influenced in this way. Her story begins with the vision statement of the school that declared that an aim of the school was *"to provide a happy stress-free environment for all pupils."*[58] But it was inconsistent with fighting in the yard between different sub-cultures that seemed to be on the increase. Moreover, it was disrupting the normal flow of work within the school. She adapted the TQM approach found in Murgatroyd and Morgan[59] and decided to deal with the problem. She allowed the deputy principal to take charge of the problem and his first action was to see the staff and see if they could tackle the problem together as a team.

The general principles of TQM were explained. A key concept of TQM is that there are customers and she records that at first the teachers *"baulked at the notion of treating pupils and parents as customers."* But this was overcome and a meeting was held to work out which tools of measurement they should use from the list given by Murgatroyd and Morgan. She used a group thinking technique suggested by de Bono.[60] In the end *"we settled on a simple check list where we would record, the names of those fighting, the time and place, the outcome e.g. were parents involved, was anyone injured, did they have to stop class work, and finally the severity of fighting on a scale 1–5; 1 being for a few blows and 5 being a really serious fight with a few pupils involved."*[59] The process was managed by the deputy principal. Records were kept for a month during which time there were 15 serious fights. Five occurred during football because some one was not adhering to the rules. By instructing the children in the rules of Gaelic football and soccer and demanding that the children stick to the rule or risk suspension from playing the number of fights was drastically reduced.

Three of the fights took place in the yard and were the result of pupils colliding with each other. *"The remedy we tried here was role-play where we modelled the collision in the classroom and those involved were encouraged to get up, apologise and may be offer to help each other. Despite the pupils finding this behaviour peculiar and in their eyes and language "gay", in the beginning we persisted [...] with great success. On more than a few occasions we witnessed those involved dusting each other down and sometimes others not involved helping them."*[62]

Seven of the fights took place at the gates at 3 pm and these involved more than two boys. friends, cousins and siblings would join in to help. The problem was the *"adverse publicity the school received, as parents waiting for the children got involved to break them up or help a victim but sometimes, unfortunately parents became involved themselves."*[63]

TQM requires that data is collected and that data showed that three particular groups were involved. While anecdotal evidence might be true, parents cannot be faced unless there are facts.

The outrageous goal that they set themselves was to achieve a single month without a fight. And in order to achieve this the problem was tackled on three fronts, prevention, management and sanctions. Every fight continued to be recorded and Circle Time was used to allow the children to speak openly and report problems as well as to release tensions and frustrations. The idea of multiple-intelligences was used and this had a positive effect on discipline and self-concept. Another strategy used was that of a friendship week in each class where all the work done involves friendship, peacekeeping and resolving conflict. And sometimes lessons were done on *"old fashioned manners."* This is by no means the whole story because action was also taken to have a disciplined departure from the school at 3 pm.

There are three points that show the value of TQM. First the parents of the three families involved in the fighting at the gate would not accept responsibility for their children's behaviour. They also spread rumours about the school that caused some parents to enrol their children in other schools. The parents eventually asked me to meet with them. *"In this meeting the staff and I were, I think unfairly criticised. We were accused of not disciplining the children properly, of treating some children unfairly, of not correcting work, and a lot more. In this instance total quality management was my best ally. I set out all the data we had collated over 12 months. I showed the parents a map of the area on which I had marked the areas and some individual houses from which pupils were coming. 23 children out of 125 were passing schools to come to us. 50 lived closer to another school or schools. Only four children were leaving the area to attend an all-Irish school. Yes we were in some respects a business providing a service and doing well according to my data."*[64] When the next year began only 4 pupils had moved school. At the end of the year a questionnaire facilitated by the Parents Association revealed considerable parental satisfaction with the school.

The second point is that this exercise dominated the work of the school for a very long period of time. It was selected because it was a priority and all the resources of the staff were put into the exercise. There was a substantial spin-off that influenced the direction the school was taking. That is surely better than trying to plan for everything and not allowing sufficient time for any thing to be completed.

There is no quick fix as another case study illustrates. A post-primary suffering from falling enrolments brought in a facilitator to discuss the problem. In the way that is now common a SWOT analysis was undertaken and teams were formed to achieve specified goals during the year. The reporter participated in a team that aimed to improve the academic achievement of the school. The team decided to try and improve on the homework policy. Some changes were made to the homework policy but while the team worked hard at the policy other members of the staff were not impressed because they thought matters would return to where they were in a matter of time. The reporter felt they were right because the team had not used the five components of TQM. *"Our initial plan to brainstorm and then do a SWOT analysis of the staff was a good idea, but it lacked the first component of TQM. It lacked vision. We had broken our problems down into five or six areas into which we were to operate, but we took a short-term view. We wanted a quick fix to our academic problems and this can never happen under TQM. We should have concentrated our effort on our new first years. If we had made them aware of the value of doing homework, rather than the sanctions, we could have been more successful. By the time these first years had made it to sixth year, the new way of doing things would have been the norm in the school."*[65] The solution of problems takes time and sometimes it is of a span that is difficult to envisage.

The activities reported here were undertaken by principals and teachers without any formal training or understanding of schools as learning organizations. In the absence of any systematic school development toward this end it would seem essential that some preparation should be given in initial training.

But resources were not used. The team did not consult the customers- students and parents, and in respect of the whole school the teams did meet together so that sight was lost of the bigger picture. The teams *"were content to do their bit within the team but once they were finished they felt their work was done. We needed to bring the teams together in a unified manner in order to achieve our goals. Upon reflection, there were even cases where some teams were happy to put down the work of other teams in order to promote their own interests. In the end many staff members returned to their original way of doing things once they were back to the comfort zone of their classrooms."* [66]

Clearly there was little organizational learning. *"In terms of homework policy, we were content to look at what we had always been doing and then just try to modify it. There was no 'new learning.'"*[67] The reporter put this down to a failure to set outrageous goals. Our goal should have been *"every student does their homework every night, for every subject, to the best of their ability."* Finally no feedback was obtained on how the changes were working which is a reminder that information is a resource.

The third point arising from the discipline study is that this approach to TQM clearly changed the school into a learning organization. *"It got us working as a team and as we saw more and more success we continued working better as a team. With everyone thinking along the same lines we came up with a new, challenging strategy practically every other day. Teachers began to read books that previously lay on the shelves in the staff room and were given perhaps a few glances in the past. Discussions and the language of those discussions changed as people gradually began to pass on ideas and even admit and discuss mistakes with each other.*"[68] These are the hallmarks of "extended" professionalism about which more in chapter 8.

Notes and References

[1] Foster, R (1986). *Innovation: The Attacker's Advantage*. MacMillan, London.

[2] Beard, A (2007). Nice financing, shame about the design. *Managing Schools Today*. Jan/Feb, 66 – 72.

[3] Marzano, R. J., Waters, T., and B. A. McNulty (2005). *School Leadership that Works. From Research to Results*. Association for Supervision and Curriculum Development, Alexandria, VA.

[4] Blair, A (2007). An end to raising your arm in class? Hands up those who think that's a good idea. *The Times* p 3 June 1st.

[5] Peters, T and R. H. Waterman (1982). *In Search of Excellence. Lessons from America's Best Run Companies*. Harper and Row, New York

[6] Miller, D (1990). *The Icarus Paradox. How Exceptional Companies Bring about Their Own Downfall*. Harper Business, new York.

[7] The trajectory of a company that is failing will turn downwards on the S Curve. Miller describes 4 such trajectories (ibid pp 4/5) They are *"The focusing trajectory. It takes punctilious, quality driven Craftsmen, organizations with masterful engineers and airtight operations, and turns them into rigidly controlled, detail obsessed tinkerers, firms whose insular technocratic cultures alienate customers with perfect but irrelevant offerings". The venturing trajectory converts growth-driven entrepreneurial builders, companies managed by imaginative leaders and creative planning staffs , into impulsive greedy Imperialists, who severely overtax their resources by expanding helter-skelter into business they know nothing about. The inventing trajectory takes Pioneers with unexcelled R & D departments, flexible think-tank operations, and state-of-the-art products, and transforms them into utopian Escapists, run by cults of chaos-loving scientists who squander resources in the pursuit of hopelessly grandiose and futuristic inventions. The decoupling trajectory transforms Salesmen, organizations with unparalleled marketing skills, prominent brand names, and broad markets, into aimless, bureaucratic Drifters, whose sales fetish obscures design issues, and who produce a stale and disjointed line of 'me-too' offerings."*

[8] Fidler, B (1998). How can a successful school avoid failure? Strategic management in schools. *School Leadership and Management*, 18, 497 – 509.. Cites Miller see ref: 6

[9] (a) from a teacher assignment for a course in a management diploma. (b) for details of approaches to SWOT analysis see Murgatroyd, S and C. Morgan (1992). *Quality Management and the School*. Open University Press, Buckingham.

[10] (a) Diggins, P., Doyle, E., and D. Herron (1996) *Whole School Development*. Drumcondra and Dublin West Teacher centre, Dublin. (b) Department of Education and Science (1999). *School Development Planning: An Introduction for Second Level Schools*. Department of Education and Science, Dublin.

[11] Senge, P. M. (1990). *The Fifth Discipline. The Art and Practice of the Learning Organization*. Doubleday, New York.

[12] *ibid* p 3.

[13] Bloom, B et al.(1958/1964) *The Taxonomy of Educational Objectives. Vol 1. Cognitive Domain*. Longmans Green, New York/London.

[14] *loc.cit* ref 10 p 4.

[15] *ibid* p 7.

[16] This idea is taken from Cohn, M. M and R. B. Kottkamp (1995). *Teachers. The Missing voice in Education*. State University of new York Press, Albany, NY. They argue that the first step in the change process is to identify and question long established assumptions and structures. Arguing the case for inquiry oriented schools they continue *"Inquiry oriented schools could provide forums for what might be labelled "assumptional dialogues" – opportunities to raise awareness and examine largely unrecognized assumptions that*

currently underlie educational structures and practices and to generate alternatives to them. Such exchanges could in turn identify particular problems to be the foci of inquiry and change efforts". They suggest as one means of achieving this goal reflection seminars based on the work of Argyris and Schön. See Argyris, C. and D. A. Schön (1978) *Organizational Learning. A Theory-in –Action Perspective*. Addison-Wesley, reading MA. See Heywood, J (2008). *Curriculum and Instructional Leadership*. National Association of Principals and Deputies/Original Writing, Dublin- for examples of assumptional dialogues relating to the curriculum and instruction.

[17] *loc.cit* ref 4 p12

[18] *ibid* pp 14 - 143

[19] *ibid* p 18

[20] Youngman, M. B., Oxtoby, R., Monk, J. D and J. Heywood (1978). *Analysing Jobs*. Gower Press, Aldershot p 102.

[21] Saupé, J (1961) Learning in P. Dressel (ed). *Evaluation in Higher Education*. Houghton Mifflin, Boston, MA

[22] From a case study submitted to the author as part of a programme in management in education.

[23] Perkins, D (2003). *King Arthur's Round Table. How Collaborative Conversations Create Smart Organizations*. Wiley, New York.

[24] ibid see ch 2.

[25] These distinctions are due to Banathy, B. H (2008) Searching together. Approaches, methods and tools Ch 5 of Jenlink, P.M. and B. H. Banathy (eds) *Dialogue as a Collective means of Design Conversation*. Springer, New York

[26] *ibid*

[27] Robson, M (1982). *Quality Circles*. Gower, Aldershot. The Gower Press marketed a complete training course for quality circles.

[28] *ibid*

[29] de Bono, E (1971). *The Use of Lateral Thinking*. Penguin, Harmondsworth

[30] This paragraph and the three that follow are based on a case study reported to the author as part of a programme of study in management in education.

[31] Heywood, J (2002) SCOOPE and other primary (elementary) school projects with a challenge for engineering education *Proceedings Frontiers in Education Conference*, 2, F2C- 6 to 10.

[32] See Heywood, J. (2000) *Assessment in Higher Education. Student learning, Teaching, Programmes and Institutions*. Jessica Kingsley, London. See also Perry, W (1971). *Intellectual Development in the College Years*. Holt, Reinhart and Winston, New York.

[33] For a detailed examination of this argument in relation to curriculum objectives see ref 32

[34] *ibid*

[35] Kolb, D (1974) *Organizational Psychology. A Book of Readings* (2nd ed) Chapter on Management and the learning process. Prentice Hall, Englewood Cliffs, NJ.

[36] see for example (a). Brookfield, S. D (1995). *Becoming a Critically reflective Teacher*. Jossey Bass, San Fransisco. (b) Cowan, J (2006) *On Becoming an Innovative University Teacher. Reflection in Action* 2nd edition SRHE/Open University Press, Maidenhead.

[37] Heirs, B (1987). *The Professional Decision Thinker. Our New management Priority*. Sidgwick and Jackson (Grafton Books), London.

[38] *loc.cit* ref 10 p 210

[39] *ibid* p 214

[40] Pfeffer, J and R. I. Sutton (2006). *Hard facts. Dangerous Half Truths and Total Nonsense. Profiting from Edvidence-Based Management*. Harvard Business School Press, Boston, MA p 157.

[41] This paragraph is based on Bennett, N, Crawford, M., Levačič, R., Glover, D and P. Earley (2000). The reality of school development planning in the effective primary school: technicist or guiding plan? *School Leadership and Management*, 20, (3) 333 – 351.

[42] Fidler, B (1996) School development planning and strategic planning for school improvement in Earley, P., Fidler, B and J. Ouston (eds) *Improvement through Inspection? Complementary approaches to School Development*. David Fulton, London. cited by Bennet

et al ibid.

[43] *loc cit* ref 39

[44] cited by Bennett et al ibid. Mintzberg, H (1994). *The Rise and Fall of Strategic Planning*. Prentice Hall, Englewood Cliffs, NJ.

[45] cited by Bennet et al ibid. *Office for Standards in Education Guidance on the Inspection of Nursery and Primary Schools*. (1995) HMSO, London. They also cite national Audit Office (1994). *Value for Money at Grant Maintained Schools*. HMSO, London

[46] Tuohy, D (1997). *School Leadership and Strategic Planning*. Association of Secondary Teachers Ireland, Dublin.

[47] The financing of Irish primary schools is very different to that in England. Teachers salaries are paid directly by the Department of Education. Most of the schools are denominational but there are some "Educate Together" schools that are non-denominational. They are growing in number. Their management structure is somewhat different to the denominational schools. The denominational schools are managed by a Board of Managers. The Board must have a treasurer and all cheques must be signed by the Chairman of the Board who is appointed by the Patron usually the Bishop of a diocese. Until 2006 schools received a capitation grant from the government which was about sufficient to cover energy costs, insurance and some cleaning. The rest had to be raised by voluntary contributions and other fund raising activities. The Government also provides grants for specifically defined activities. Often Boards are distracted by the need to control expenditure and raise funds which distracts them from their role in school development planning. There have been two increases in the capitation since 2006 but schools will have to continue to raise funds.

[48] From a case study reported to the author as part of a programme of study in management in education.

[49] *loc.cit* ref 10 p 211

[50] *ibid p* 142

[51] The case was made in Heywood, J (1986) Toward technological literacy in Ireland. An opportunity for an inclusive approach. In J. Heywood and P. Matthews (eds) T*echnology and Society and the School Curriculum: Practice and Theory in Europe*. Roundthorn, Manchester.

[52] *loc cit* ref 38

[53] *loc.cit* ref 8

[54] Imai, M (1986). Kaizen (Ky'zen). *The Key to Japan's Competitive Success*. McGraw Hill, New York

[55] Sallis, E (2002). *Total Quality Management in Education*. Kogan Page, London.

[56] Davies, B and J. West Burnham (1997). *Re-engineering and Total Quality in Schools*. How to Reform and Restructure your School to meet the Challenge of the Future. Pitman, London.

[57] Murgatroyd, M and C. Morgan (1992). *Total Quality Management and the School*. Open University Press, Buckingham

[58] From a case study reported to the author as part of a programme of study in management in education

[59] *loc cit* ref 53. Murgatroyd and Morgan give a list of strategies

[60] de Bono, E (1978) is best known for his work on lateral thinking. See *Teaching Thinking*. Penguin, Harmondsworth

[61] *loc.cit* ref 54.

[62] *ibid*

[63] *ibid*

[64] From a case study reported to the author as part of a programme of study in management in education

[65] From a case study reported to the author as part of a programme of study in management in education

[66] *ibid*

[67] *ibid*.

[68] *ibid*.

CHAPTER 7

ADAPTIBILITY AND CHANGE

Introduction

Throughout the previous chapters the search has been for factors that inhibit and enhance adaptability, learning and motivation at work. It has been argued that these factors are the same as those that apply in the classroom and to student learning more generally. This chapter considers three more dimensions of change namely plausibility, readiness, power, learning style and identity. Some aspects of these, especially those relating to power have been touched on in earlier chapters. For example a distinction between 1st order and 2nd order change was made. The chapter begins by recording that we all live in a state of tension because of the need to change on the one hand and on the other hand the desire for security. All change involves us in a capacity to deal with ourselves as we construct and maintain our identity. We will drive for change if we believe it will help us find or develop our identity. All change involves changes, some small, some large in attitudes beliefs and values. All of this may be said of groups, for groups are but aggregates of individuals

Education systems throughout the world have been subjected to continuing change and at times in some countries this has been relentless. When it is it can breed resistance to change. On the whole it seems that teachers have found it easy to adjust to small incremental changes because our time span of accommodation goes unchallenged. Not so, big changes. Often we accommodate big change by adapting it to our own circumstances and in that situation there may on the surface seem to be change but in reality there has been little.

It has been argued that one of the reasons why it has been difficult if not impossible to produce lasting change in education, was that change-agents have often adopted the practices required for first-order change but not used practices that would have brought about second-order change. There follows a brief discussion of models of change. In respect of curriculum change it is found that centre-periphery approaches tend not to work because the development team is at the centre and as in hierarchical models of management edicts are issued and passed down the line. The recipient is then left to interpret them and interpretation is dependent on the individual's perceptions, values and beliefs.

Generally speaking proposed changes that lie outside the "plausibility structure" will be impossible to implement. Institutions have to be "ready" for change and this requires preparation and possibly training and undoubtedly leadership.

All change requires internalisation by the participant(s) if it is to be owned. Such internalisation takes long time and very often policy makers completely underestimate the time that is required.

The role of the leader in change and their response to the path that deviates from their own ideas are considered. The effectiveness with which change is implemented is dependent on the power of those who wish to implement change.

Whether at the institutional level or national level, innovations are very much subject to the values and beliefs of those in power if they are to be sustained. Thus in school based initiatives in the curriculum or otherwise those who are asked to organize them need to be continually sustained and be seen to be given the authority they need to process the development.
These ideas and principles are illustrated by two case studies. A third case study of school amalgamation is interwoven into the text.

Responding to Change

All of us to some degree or another live in a state of tension. On the one hand there is a strong desire for security, while on the other hand there is pressure for change. It does not matter which social system (work, family, club-) we currently inhabit change affects us in the same way. Teachers experience a number of tensions in relation to the effectiveness of their teaching. There is an inherent tension between collective responsibility and the need to work in teams and the individual autonomy they have in the classroom. At the post-primary level this tension is inherent because teachers come into post-primary education to teach a subject and that is what matters. Further tension may be created by the trade union they join if the policies that are designed to protect its members have the effect of preventing change that seems to be desirable. In some countries such as Ireland the unions are extremely powerful in other countries they are less so.

Some of us are change agents, others resist change and many stand passively by and do their best with what happens.. Many of us are afraid of change for no good reason other than the fear of being destabilised. For others there is a pressing desire for change. Their adrenaline rises as they press for change and they become prepared to risk the psychological insecurity that results.

Most of us lie somewhere in the middle of this continuum realising that whether we like it or not, we will have to respond to some change in our lives. We will view change as neutral until such time as it is demonstrated that it is harmful or beneficial. For the most part we are followers, easily led, and not truly worried. We leave the running of change to others. At another level we are quite happy to be driven to change by technological developments particularly those related to the governance of households viz: washing machines and the ubiquitous PC. While we expect advances in medical science to be made available to us at least cost we pay little attention to the moral problems which these and other scientific developments bring in their wake. We leave it to others to attempt the purposive control of these developments and no where is this better illustrated than by developments in fertility treatment and the watchfulness of investigations that organizations more often the churches conduct. Often we are guided by emotion and the "happiness for all" principle.

Change and Identity: Individuals and Groups

All change involves us in a capacity to deal with ourselves as we construct and maintain our identity.[1] As Hoare points out *"identity formation and development involve learning about work, and about oneself in work roles and functions [...] as a context for identity development, the work of one's mature years shapes many key psychosocial investments and learning opportunities. As a function of work, identity increases, learning (about content, contexts, others and self) shows marked development, self-reliance grows, and career salience deepens."*[2] If it is correct as was argued in a previous chapter that we inhabit a plurality of social systems then we will seek identities that are coherent with those systems and with our more general desire to be ourselves as we move forward. For this reason alone managers and leaders should focus not only on the aggregate needs of the employees for whom they are responsible but for the individuals themselves. Hence, the need for developmental programmes. I choose the term developmental rather than career development advisedly because career opportunities in teaching can be limited. If a term is required then "career renewal" may be more appropriate or "professional development"

Generally speaking we resist that which we think will shatter our identity. We go along with that which leaves our identity unaffected. That is why in post-primary education it is difficult to get teachers to participate in inter-disciplinary teams for teachers became post-primary teachers to become teachers of a subject. In the British Isles at least, they will have become socialized into that subject through three or four years of intensive study.[3] Moreover teachers of that subject will be intent on turning out more persons in their image and likeness, that is more historians, more physicists and so on. There is therefore, a tension between me as a 'historian' or whatever and me as a 'teacher' who can contribute more generally to the curriculum in the school. Some teachers want to escape into other avenues and there may be tension between them and the other teachers that teach their subject.

Nevertheless, we will drive for change if we believe it will help us find or develop our identity. All change involves changes, some small, some large in attitudes beliefs and values.

All of this may be said of groups, for groups are but aggregates of individuals. They form and re-form so as to retain the like minded and remove the difficult.[4] A group whose members strongly subscribe to the same norms and values is likely to be cohesive either in the face of or in the pursuit of change. Thus social identity is as important as individual identity in understanding the factors that influence change. Korte who has reviewed the implications of social identity theory for training writes that *"social identity is one lens through which individuals view their jobs, responsibilities, organizations and even the dynamics of work (eg.,causal attributions). Therefore social identity becomes an important lens through which people perceive new information, attribute causes, make meaning and choose to undertake new learning. Without addressing the identity factors stemming from group membership, the success of typical training efforts may fail to realize their promise of improving individual and organizational performance."[5]* Given the "isolation" of teachers in their classrooms this may seem of little significance. However the need to develop teams for interdisciplinary work gives it an importance that should not be underestimated. Any team will need to develop an identity if they are to be recognized and valued in the power structure of the organization and not as a peripheral activity in the life of the school.

The Failure of Major Curriculum Change to Persist

Generally in education change is very slow. It has been argued that there have been very few changes in the curriculum during the last 150 years that have been more than short lived.[6] An American reviewer of another work of mine on engineering education asked why it was that so many good ideas that had been reasonably well tested and shown to be of value were not generally adopted.[7] A report from the National Science Foundation threw some light on this because it showed that many instructional and curriculum innovations had not been disseminated in the fields for which it had responsibility.[8] But that cannot be the whole story. It does underline the importance of subject associations and the importance they play in developing and disseminating new ideas. But it is also a reminder that the number of teachers active in such associations is no different to other voluntary organizations. Somewhere I have seen the figure put at 10%!

Nevertheless during the last thirty years education systems throughout the world have been subjected to continuing change and at times this has been relentless in some countries. When it is it can breed resistance to change. On the whole it seems that teachers have found it easy to adjust to small incremental changes because our time span of accommodation (in the Piagetian sense[9]) goes unchallenged. Sometimes change is seen as necessary, as for example the updating of course content so as to be responsive to technological change. At other times change agents, often policy-makers face us with major problems as for example the pressure to change from teacher centred learning to so-called student centred teaching. Often such changes are ideologically based and not evidence based and this makes it all the more difficult for some of us to swallow. Often we accommodate big change by adapting it to our own circumstances and in that situation there may on the surface seem to be change when in reality there has been little.

Marzano, Waters and McNulty[10] have argued that one of the reasons why it has been difficult if not impossible to produce lasting change in education, was that change-agents have often adopted the practices required for first-order change but not used practices that would have brought about second-order change. First-order change was described as something incremental probably requiring only small adjustments. It is the next step, so to speak, in a chain of events. One study has shown that even when the curriculum is received[11] there is much experimentation at the micro-level of the lesson. No curriculum at this level can be totally received since that would imply authorised programmed instruction only, and allow for no intervention by the teacher. Such interventions are necessary if that educational aim of developing the potential of every person is to be allowed. The curriculum is continually being restructured at this level and this is part of the teacher's search for identity. Little changes as well as changing incrementally lead to changes in the content of syllabuses which have to be revised for this very reason every so often. It is for this reason as much as any other that great projects are soon forgotten, particularly in a world that bristles with new ideas.[12] Second-order change is altogether more dramatic requiring a change from the incremental both in defining the problem and in finding the solution. Such changes are complex and often no single solution will suffice. School amalgamations (mergers) are examples of second order change and they are not always successful. One of the reasons why some of large centrally directed curriculum projects failed was that information diffusion proved to be a major problem.[13]

Models of Change

Even when schools and teachers take collective responsibility for change the model of change they adopt may affect the outcome negatively. This applies in particular to changes that emanate from central authorities. Froyd, Penberthy and Watson[14] suggest that this is the case with current and espoused models of change. In higher education current change models are models based on the experience of individual teachers in the classroom who have attempted change within their classrooms. They often lack the rigour or clarity that would persuade colleagues to follow in their footsteps. These models apply in cases where curriculum and curriculum change are school based. Often external authorities follow an espoused model of change in which a curriculum is tested in a pilot project. If rigorous evaluation shows that the curriculum works it may be adopted, all other factors being equal. Sometimes its adoption may have to be forced by the external authorities if it is a matter of policy. The model has some limitations not least being that it is difficult to replicate educational experiments. Moreover, there are no guarantees that imposition will produce the desired outcomes. The model ignores motivation as do all proposals that are imposed and this might undermine attempts to change teacher values if to guarantee the success of an innovation they are required to change. Neither does it take account of the possibility that the intended outcomes may change as a result of the process. Change a method of instruction or learning and there will inevitably be a change in outcomes. Often inadequate support is given to faculty who are willing to support change. For example in Ireland when a new post-primary public examination curriculum was introduced in the nineteen nineties many teachers felt that the day of training that accompanied its introduction, (in each of the subjects), was inadequate. Thus Froyd and his colleagues argue that one of the reasons why change based on espoused models fails to create widespread improvement is that the human element is ignored.

Froyd and his colleagues who were working in higher education focused their work on *"changing peoples attitudes toward on going curriculum change and equipping them continually to change."*

They used an eight step business model of change based on work by Kotter.[15] It is of relevance to other sectors of education. The principles with Kotter's titles shown in brackets are

- "Establish need and energy for curricular change. *(Establishing a sense of urgency)*.

- Gather a leadership team to design and promote curricular change.*(Forming a powerful coalition)*

- Define and agree upon new learning objectives. *(Creating a vision)*

- Discuss the new objectives and environment within the [institution] and revise based on feedback. *(Communicating the vision)*

- Implement new curriculum using a pilot if possible. *(Empowering others to act on vision)*

- Conduct a formative evaluation of the programme investigating strengths and weaknesses of the current implementation, and indicators of short term gains. *(Planning for and creating short term wins)*.

- Decide how the new approach may be used for the entire [institution] and prepare implementation plan.(Consolidating improvements and producing still more change).

- Prepare [teachers] for the new implementation, implement and follow up with improvements." *(Institutionalizing new approaches)*

One of the reasons why centre-periphery approaches do not work is that the development team is at the centre and as in hierarchical models of management edicts are issued and passed down the line. The recipient is then left to interpret them and interpretation is dependent very much on the individual's perception, values and beliefs. Kotter's model as presented above leaves open issues related to the management (leadership) of the process and more especially the need to create a culture where change is an accepted part of the process of continuing development. That is they create a moral community in which one of the shared values that the community commits itself to is valid change.

A similar kind of model is due to Jenlink and Reigeluth[16] who propose a guidance system for designing new K – 12 educational systems. The phases of the discrete events (as distinguished from continuous human activity are Phase I –assess readiness and capacity. Phase II- prepare the initial core team. Phase III- prepare the extended team. Phase IV-design a new system and phase V implement and evolve the new system. They point out, which Froyd et al do not, that while the phases are being implemented there are a number of continuous activities in which the participants engage and these include the building and maintenance of political support, continuing support of the leadership, and the building of the community as a reflective body. These points are consistent with the arguments put forward in this paper although they derive from a particular approach to the design of systems.

That people matter in all kinds of change and that how the process is managed to achieve the goals of change is evident in school amalgamations. O'Connor who investigated amalgamations among primary schools in Ireland found that *"amalgamation is a people centred issue that requires careful and supportive scaffolding and sympathetic communication."* [17]

His findings show the importance of mangers (leaders) in handling the people involved in the merger. To quote from two principals whom O'Connor interviewed, the first on team building

"to pull the team members together if you like and to make sure no one person felt that they were not able to...and to form a team to constantly encourage and praise to be positive"

and

"People that are negative and have chips on their shoulders really are the most inhibiting factors [...]"

and

"The hardest part is keeping staff onside. Once you have the staff onside you are away."

That the garden is not always rosy is spelt out by O'Connor thus: *"Despite these efforts amalgamation poses insurmountable difficulties for some staff as this principal explains: 'there was an initial reaction, negative reaction towards it, and in fact that year I think a number of staff left because they felt that they couldn't face the amalgamation"*

By now it will be clear that management is a messy thing and it is further complicated by the fact that whereas first-order change might be thought to be accomplished with ease there may be a person who is pathologically averse to change. That is they resist any change. Fortunately that situation seems to be relatively rare. Moreover among any group there are likely to be those who like change and innovation and an equal number, if not more of persons who really don't want to change but of differing levels of persuasiveness. Such was case among the primary teachers facing amalgamation in O'Connor's study.

It is quite clear from the studies reported in previous chapters that the hallmark of managing change is employee involvement for at the heart of the change process is the need to change peoples' attitudes and values. So the first task is to establish a need for change. In parallel the change has to be seen as "plausible."

Being Plausible

All change involves changes in attitudes and values. When the demands are small we may well adapt with ease: but, what one perceives to be minor change another may perceive to be major. Therein lie the roots of conflict. Some kinds of large change may be accommodated without much forethought while some kinds of minor change may create cognitive dissonance. Generally speaking proposed changes that lie outside what Peter Berger[18] called the "plausibility structure" are unlikely to be adapted. Change has to appear to be plausible. One of the reasons why the recommendations of official committees and organizations of repute are ignored is because they are not perceived to be plausible. At the same time an idea can be plausible and run into entrenched interests from which there is no escape. Sometimes resistance to change is a combination of both. One of the reasons why teachers in some of the primary schools examined by O'Connor found amalgamation plausible was the fact it would merge two single sex schools to produce a co-ed school even though this was not the primary reason for the merger. It fitted the prevailing value system.

A Case study: Plausibility and the Development of Ideas

A good example that illustrates these issues is the response to the findings of the Irish Committee on the Form and Function of the Intermediate Examination. In their report (1974) they recommended an independent Measurement Evaluation and Assessment Service (MEAS) to become responsible for public examinations.19 The committee also recommended the use of standardised tests, a considerable amount of coursework, and much greater teacher involvement in the assessment of their pupils. At that time there were two public examinations for children in the age range 14 – 15. These were the "Group Certificate" and the "Intermediate Certificate." There is something, but only something in an analogy between the CSE and the GCE in England at the time. The "Group Certificate" was a vocational examination taken mainly by pupils in vocational schools whereas the "Intermediate Certificate" was taken mainly by pupils from secondary schools. They were at the time held to be generally of higher ability than those in pupils the vocational schools.[20] The secondary schools were perceived to have higher status than the vocational schools. At the time a network of community and comprehensive schools was just beginning to be built. The committee's proposals meant that the group and intermediate certificate examinations would be abolished and replaced by a single system of assessment. Although parents were being asked to move into the unknown and the school leaving age had only just been raised to 15 there was not a great hiatus in the press. The report was more of a damp squib than anything else which assisted those in the Department of Education who were determined to oppose it and this included both administrative and professional staff. These public examinations as well as the Leaving Certificate and other vocational examinations were the responsibility of those divisions of the inspectorate responsible for secondary and vocational education. The report showed that as much as eighty percent of an inspector's time could be devoted to examining (ie: setting papers, supervising marking). Members of the committee wanted the inspectorate to be released from this task so they could undertake duties more like those of their counterparts in the United Kingdom such as inspecting schools and preparing policy documents. The inspectorate were therefore being asked to change their identity and many were reluctant that this should happen. So as these things were managed, politically there was no official response to the report from the then Minister.

One of the things that one learns from *Newman's Essay on the Development of Christian Doctrine is that when the theological connotation is removed it becomes an essay on the development of ideas*.[21] And for change to take place if the idea is be kept alive over a period of time it may induce change although not necessarily in the form of the original idea. It so happened that the research unit of the Intermediate Certificate Committee had only begun work in the previous year and the Department allowed the unit (Public Examinations Evaluation Project-PEEP) to continue its work. It had been given the task of designing a system of examinations and assessment that would raise the standards. The Committee had in mind that the higher order skills of the Bloom Taxonomy should be tested. The unit believed that if there was to be a change in examining teachers would have to be trained to design new style examinations and test them on their pupils. This would hopefully demonstrate the validity of the new approaches and, if it did make them plausible to other teachers. So, based on a model of examining that had been developed for Engineering Science in the UK[22] the unit set out to train teachers in what were then called multiple objective examinations, that is a set of tests in each subject that would test knowledge and the higher order skills. A national programme of training, development and testing was put in place. It was found that the testing of some of the higher order skills could only be achieved by carefully designed coursework, in particular through project work. It was judged that the maximum amount of assessed coursework that a teacher could accomplish should contribute no more than 20% of the final mark to be awarded. It should be noted that the Association of Secondary Teachers of Ireland (ASTI) was opposed to the introduction of coursework but that they did not stop their teachers from participating in this experimental work. Neither did it stop them publishing an independent book on examining in second level education written by the project director.[23] The Association was in favour of an independent examining board and put its case strongly to several ministers. The idea was plausible to teachers even though the details of the techniques of assessment posed some difficulty. However, as indicated a strong argument exists for the view that the proposals were not plausible within the Department.

The programme was judged to have been successful and in the report[24] it was suggested that this mode of examining and assessment should be used. The organizational structure was modified and detailed costings were provided. At the heart of both reports was the idea that assessment was integral to the curriculum process and influenced the way in which subjects were taught and subjects were learnt. It followed from this that teachers should have a much greater involvement in the assess-ment/evaluation process. The ASTI took a traditional view and simply wanted an independent Board on which it had eight members with teachers on the sub-committees. [25]

At the time of the Committee's report it was argued by civ-il servants that its proposals would cost too much. This is a favourite mechanism for preventing innovation and the same technique was used to try and kill the research unit's report. However, The Chairman of the Committee and the Director of the Research Unit met succeeding Ministers in the hope of obtaining change. This happened in 1982 when the then Minis-ter set up an internal department enquiry into the matter. This resulted in the establishment of an interim Board for Curricu-lum and Examinations (CEB) in 1984. When that government was replaced the new government abandoned the CEB and created the National Council for Curriculum and Assessment (NCCA).

The CEB established a framework for a common examina-tion at the end of the junior cycle of post-primary education. Its successor the NCCA adapted and implemented the Junior Cer-tificate examination. It replaced the group and intermediate cer-tificate examinations. The separation of powers between those who set the examinations and those responsible for content con-tinued. One idea from the PEEP report that eventually found its way into the Junior Certificate was for three levels of assessment in mathematics and certain other subjects. In the Intermediate Certificate some subjects could be taken at ordinary an honours levels. The results of the PEEP evaluation in mathematics led to the proposal for a third and lower level so that the bottom end of aptitude grouping would have a chance of passing at a basic level of competency. This was a plausible idea and did not re-quire much selling. I am not here arguing that this was a direct consequence of the PEEP report but that it was an idea that it put into the system. There was no serious reaction against these developments from the public. The chief contestants in this bat-

tle for whom proposals had to be plausible were the inspectorate and the unions. In retrospect the implementation of the idea
of an independent curriculum board took place in a relatively
short period of time during which the idea was assimilated in
the system. The key idea of multiple strategy assessment has not
proved acceptable so far. The idea that the curriculum board
should be responsible for the organization and administration
of the examinations has not proved acceptable.

Readiness for Change

One controversial concept from educational psychology that can
seemingly be applied to organizational development and change
is that of "readiness." Typically associated with reading debate
has centred on the question of whether a pupil is ready to read
or can be taught readiness as Bruner believes.[26] More generally
without readiness a learning experience will be inefficient and
learning may not occur.[27] Substitute teacher or, even institution
for pupil. For example, O'Connor reported that readiness for
amalgamation is important. It can reduce anxieties.[27]

Either way it seems possible to apply the idea to institutions
and institutional behaviour. In terms of Vygotsky's zone of
proximal development (ZPD)[28] readiness is described by what
an institution can do now without any training and what it
might do with training. Institutions will differ in their zone
of proximal development in respect of any specified change.
Readiness of any kind requires a disposition toward changing
attitudes and values and this can only come from ideas likely
to promote change. Thus whether any change is first or second
order[29] will depend on prevailing attitudes and values and the
ZPD of the institution. Readiness depends on the provision of
a knowledge base that is understood and can be moved forward. Change arises from the release of energy bound in that
knowledge. These principles were understood by the PEEP unit
when they argued that it would be necessary to develop the
knowledge base of teachers about assessment and examining.

In order to do this training was supplied, the opportunity given to teachers to design their own assessment procedures, try them out and have them evaluated. In the case of an amalgamation between two schools it would seem that if they have different ZPDs there might be difficulties in creating a new common culture. Another case study is offered to illustrate these points.

Case study 2: Readiness and Prior Knowledge

In 1956 in England and Wales the government proposed to raise nine technical colleges to the status of Colleges of Advanced Technology (CATS).[30] The purpose was to provide graduate engineers and technologists for industry. Universities were to continue to prepare engineers for research. Central to this idea was the belief that these graduates would have to have experience of industry during their education. The idea was to beef up a system that depended on part-time study for the training of many engineers. Now instead of part-time study they would pursue sandwich courses (co-operative courses in the US). The students would study for six months in college and then do six months in industry followed by another six months in college throughout a four-year period. In this way they would receive a full time education that was more than equivalent to that obtained during a three-year university degree. The other differences between programmes offered by the universities were that students would have to follow courses in liberal/complementary/general studies, and in their final year they would complete a substantial technological project.

However, because it was held they would offer a different kind of education to a university the qualification they would award would be a diploma that would be equal to a degree. It would be validated by an independent organization for that purpose (National Council for Technological Awards).

In the highly selective British higher education system of the time this qualification created a dilemma for those colleges because they perceived themselves to be second class citizens a view that was supported by the level of qualifications of entrants when compared with entrants to universities. The colleges in London that had an association with and offered degrees of the University of London continued to offer degree programmes in direct competition with the sandwich offered by those colleges. One of these colleges offered only degree programmes which defeated the concept of a College of Advanced Technology. The CATs did not become the unique institutions' that was the intention. On the one hand some regional technical colleges were allowed to offer courses for the diploma and on the other hand some universities offered a form of sandwich course in which students went into industry on leaving school and did not take up their place until the following year. They were encouraged to do this because of grants from industry. Most of the engineering students on sandwich courses were sponsored by industry. Many of the students in the applied science courses had to find their own places in industry and support themselves as best they could. Some universities also encouraged project work.

From the beginning the seeds of destruction were sown into the idea that there could be an alternative technological qualification at degree level. Within the diploma technological courses there was a "curriculum drift" toward similarity with university programmes. There were some differences such as the nature and content of the mathematics that was taught. They were, therefore under pressure to seek status as universities. Their degree programmes were acknowledged to be comparable with degree level programmes in the universities by a committee on higher education in 1963. They received university status in 1967. However the same committee recommended that some 30 regional technical colleges be granted Polytechnic status with the right to offer validated degree programmes across the spectrum of subjects. So the NCTA was transformed into the Council for National Academic Awards (CNAA). In 1992 these Polytechnics also became universities and the CNAA was abolished. Variations of this model were to be found in Australia and Ireland where there were similar developments. Currently some members of the Irish Institutes of Technology wish these institutes to be given university status.[31]

But from the perspective of change neither the faculty in the colleges or their peers, mainly from the universities who validated them had any knowledge of educational theories that might have enabled them to change. To put it in another way no concept of an alternative other than those mentioned was available and as such they were not "ready." Also politicians put them in an untenable position where they had to compete not only with the regional colleges and universities, but among themselves. Their hands were tied behind their backs before they started.

The idea of "readiness" may also be illustrated by the idea of "integration." This concept arose from the theory that sandwich courses would better facilitate the "integration" of practice and theory. In reality if that happened then it happened by osmosis. Provided the students had a good experience of industry it seems they were satisfied with the programme. Exactly how it impacted on their learning is by no means clear. Potentially the concept of "integration" is a powerful idea but even at a superficial level of understanding it implies a substantial amount of planning by those responsible for the students' academic study and their industrial experience. Thus integration of this kind was never achieved except by accident because there was no theory of integration with which to understand the concept and its potential.

Yet ideas in Schools of Education that might have helped the development of integration and alternative curricular such as the two volumes of the *Taxonomy of Educational Objectives* were not then available. The volumes were published in England in 1964 some seven years after the CATS were established. The potential of the ideas in the Taxonomies was explored two years later for a British university but the ideas for an engineering curriculum that followed were too radical to be plausible. However, in so far as the integration of theory and practice was concerned one or two institutions began to assess the industrial experience and a study in the nineteen eighties of a course in environmental education and public health revealed the value of assessment in creating integration.[32] But by this time the idea and support for sandwich courses had been lost and now students were being encouraged to take a year out between ending school and joining university to pursue their own thing. It is now known as the "Gap" year.

Internalisation

All change requires internalisation if it is to be owned. Some kinds of change require very little effort such as the change to College of Advanced Technology from technical college and later from CAT to university. These changes have been sought and there is a collective will that demands them. They are first order changes. But there are other changes at the institutional level that are second order as for example the amalgamation (merger) of two schools or whether to retain an internationally recognised department for research when its student numbers fall away. At the operational level change may be second order that is much more difficult. For example the change from teacher to so-called student centred learning or even in the change of a teacher's professional attitudes (see chapter 8).

Changes in curriculum and instruction are first order or second order as a function of the knowledge, experience, attitudes and values of the individual(s) concerned. Teaching about instructional activities and curriculum design is a rather superficial exercise unless a student teacher is able to participate in such activities although it does provide the essential language and frame of reference. But unless the culture of the school encourages the student to experiment the student is soon drawn into the culture of the school and the teaching that prevails. In an examination culture such as that that has prevailed in Ireland there has been much teaching designed to help students memorise information in order to pass examinations. Such "rote" teaching defeats the objective of teaching higher order thinking skills. The case study described above showed that the move to teaching and assessing by objectives (outcomes) seemed to require a change in cognitive structure and individuals have to be motivated to make the change to reduce the discrepancy that exists between the new and old structures. A person has to assimilate and then accommodate so as to adapt to the new environment.

Work with school teachers to train them to design public examinations in history and mathematics (case study 1) and elsewhere to implement the assessment of coursework in engineering science showed that internalisation does not come readily. In the case of mathematics and history in the PEEP project the teachers were given prior training. They designed examinations and assessments that were piloted among their own pupils. The evaluation showed them that there was a need to revise their approaches and to try again. One round was insufficient to arrive at a product where the teachers had internalised the processes of both assessment and instructional techniques required to obtain the objectives they themselves had set. An independent evaluation by D. E. Murphy concluded that a cycle of between eighteen months to two years was required for such internalisation.[33]

In the case of engineering science from which the PEEP model was developed the teachers had a commitment to getting their students through the examination because it contributed to the admission process for university.[34] But the examination was in a new format and set to test specific domains of cognitive skill (objectives, outcomes). The teachers were required to assess their students' practical work (laboratory investigations) and a project, and prepare them for the new style examinations. The coursework would be assessed by new style semi-criterion referenced rubrics. Feedback on the general performance of pupils in the examination(s) was given to the teachers by the moderators. The moderators who visited the schools for the purpose of moderating coursework were also involved in the design of the examinations. Both the teachers and moderators were in a process of continuous learning through discussion. Even so the teachers also required time to internalise the processes.

A teacher who participated in the Christian Brothers Transition Year Project[35] found that planning for change takes time. *"It is a slow and complicated process."* She cited Everard and Morris to the effect that *"one of the biggest traps is the failure of organisational leaders to resist the temptation to rush through the planning stage to get to the action stage."*[36] But it is more than planning for internalisation results from doing and she also cited Bridges who said that *"even though the external new beginning may happen quite quickly once it becomes evident, the internal identification and engagement occur more slowly."*[37] In her concluding remarks she related the process of change to the Perry model of development. She wrote *"This paper clearly demonstrates that managing change within an organisation amounts to supporting the personnel within that organization. Therefore those managing change must facilitate the cognitive growth of individuals operating within same. They must realise as Perry puts it, "each of the upheavals of cognitive growth threatens the balance between vitality and depression hope and despair. It may be that great joy to discover a new and more complex way of thinking and seeing,"*[38] but it *"appears that it takes a little time for the guts to catch up with such leaps of mind." [...] adjusting to change clearly requires that cognitive growth take place. With this in mind, it is clear that no attempt should be made to speed up the process of change. Managing change is above all else a slow process."* Evidently organizational learning implies growth.

The same applies to organizational change. O'Connor in his study of primary school amalgamations found that the time available for preparation varied greatly.[39] Some schools received as much as years notice of amalgamation while others received as little as four months. This seems to show a disregard by the authorities for those involved in the amalgamation. It would seem to be the attitude of the authorities that since a command has been given it will be effected. Time to attend to whole school review, creation of organizational policies, creation of common curricular plans, planning a new school crest/uniform, evaluating/monitoring amalgamation process and planning the amalgamation timetable is evidently necessary. But some of the Principals in O'Connor's survey found such time to be a luxury.

The lessons of these case studies are that for second order change to be successful the participants have to be adequately prepared so that they are "ready" for the change. Further such change cannot be accomplished "overnight." Time has to be allowed for it to be internalised. It seems that policy makers are unaware of the impediments to change. Often they push through change too quickly. When that happens, then it is quite likely that change will only be superficial because it is not internalised and assent (which is assumed) is not given.

Change and Leadership

O'Connor found that a major concern in his study of amalgamation was the late appointment of the principal who was to run the combined school and the fact that the in-school management teams were not appointed until after the amalgamation date. Early appointments can lead to planning contact between school staffs. There was some evidence that in some amalgamations there was little planning contact between the schools.

Once a change agent has become involved with a group then the group must be prepared for the fact that in the surge of opinion that is likely to arise, the direction of the "ship" is likely to change. For a time no one may be sure where it is going. Newman wrote *"there will be a general agitation of thought, an action of mind both of itself and other minds. There will be a time of confusion, when conceptions and misconceptions are in conflict, and it is uncertain whether anything will come of the idea at all."*[40] The point is that the progenitors of an idea, because of the nature of human thought, expect their idea to emerge from such agitation unscathed. It won't. It bears on leadership for by definition leadership involves change. So leaders require skill in what, for want of a better term, might be called "positive agitation." But they also need to have emotional constructs that will enable them within broad parameters to follow the idea as it develops and changes without being too upset if their original idea has changed.

In the discussion about why innovations in teaching and learning that have a proven track record often fail it has been argued that they are impeded by the lack of a "natural" innovator. Such persons are analogous to the engineer in an industrial research and development laboratory. They would in the school system be curriculum and instructional leaders, about which more in chapter 10. But that person would also have to have a "product champion."

Power

The idea of a product champion is one of the most useful to come from industry. The development and continuation of the engineering science project with the Joint Matriculation Board depended on a product champion.[41] Within the Examination Board he was able to argue that engineering science involved a different mode of thinking to that in physics and that from an engineering perspective that was a better entrance examination for engineering departments than physics. At a time when there was a shortage of highly qualified entrants to engineering departments he believed that the provision of engineering science studies (including design) would be attractive to students in schools. However he never got the support of the engineering professors of whom he was one to encourage students to take this subject for admission to universities. They remained wedded to physics.

Similarly in Ireland attempts to pilot and evaluate a school technology programme that had been developed on the basis of research and practical experiments in the classroom were not acceptable to the then Minister for Education. She was persuaded to follow other developments that would suit woodwork and metalwork teachers who would have to be found places in teaching the new curriculum. In the UK the engineering science examination had to give way to technology on the one hand and on the other hand physics. Whether at the institutional level or national level, innovations are very much subject to the values and beliefs of the culture if they are to be sustained. Thus in school based initiatives in the curriculum or otherwise those who are asked to organize them need to be continually sustained and be seen to be given the authority they need to process the development.

Small projects

The projects described in the previous paragraphs have been relatively large scale although it is apparent that the principles relate to schools and the specific problems that schools have. One of the case studies reported to me suggested that Schein's approach to change (see page 114) could be used to solve problems that schools had. This case study dealt with a problem that is common to many schools namely the punctuality of staff. The reporter wrote *"Good time keeping is essential if an organization is to function effectively and tolerance of consistent lateness in teachers and students alike results in classes being disrupted and/or unsupervised and could lead to accidents and large insurance claims. It also saps morale of those who make the effort to be punctual and results in a mismatch between stated policy and reality. An approach which could be used to address the specific problem of the lack of punctuality of a very small number of staff would be to unfreeze the current culture by addressing staff as to the reality of actual incidents witnessed in other schools arising from the late arrival of teachers. This could also include information on the liability of the individual teacher should an accident occur. To provide the psychological safety spoken of by Schein, the information could be given in a non-threatening way by being general in nature and not singling out individual teachers and could be couched in terms of the unfair burden being carried by the rest of the staff who must cover for late colleagues. Having unfrozen the culture, the cognitive redefinition could be to promote punctuality as a whole school policy with definite targets for the school to meet and which would be rewarded in some concrete way. The refreezing of the new cognition could come when learning outcomes improve due to the longer time on task and when discipline improves due to the punctuality habit being formed."*

In practice the unfreezing was done by the Chairman of the Board of Management using the same formula but with the introduction that the matter to be raised was a concern of the Board of Management.

In Conclusion

Walkington[42] in Australia drew the following conclusions about change
"Change is a journey, not a blue print. It is non-linear loaded with uncertainty"
Consider the journey a school takes in the space of a week.

"Both individualism and collectivism have a place within the process."
Consider how in new curriculum areas that demand for the integration of widely different content a school is dependent on the one had on individual teachers doing their best and on the other hand a group willing to plan and implement. Consider how they might have to share work that they would otherwise have done by themselves in the past.

"Every person involved is a change agent with a variety of contributions to make."
Consider the change in attitudes, values and beliefs necessary to bring this about.

"Curriculum changes require contextual change for them to be accepted and sustained"
Consider how this axiom also applies to any major change that is to be brought about in a school.

"Evaluation is a necessary component of change."
Consider how in the absence of evaluation a development might have gone astray. Consider also how easy it is to neglect valuable spin-offs.

We should add to these that generally speaking proposed changes that lie outside the "plausibility structure" are likely to be difficult, if not impossible to implement. Institutions have to be "ready" for change and this requires preparation and possibly training and undoubtedly leadership. All change requires internalisation if it is to be owned. Such internalisation takes long time and very often policy makers completely underestimate the time that is required.

Whether at the institutional level or national level, innovations are very much subject to the values and beliefs of those in power if they are to be sustained. Thus in school based initiatives in the curriculum or otherwise those who are asked to organize them need to be continually sustained and be seen to be given the authority they need to process the development.

Notes and References

[1] Identity is used here in the sense that it was originally defined by Eriksen. Hoare (2006) following Erikson writes *"Identity [...] is personal coherence, and a sense of agency and authenticity. In this coherence, the person feels like an actively engaged 'insider' in the vocational-social domain of his or her choice, an engagement that carries commitment without pretence."* P348 C. Hoare (ed) *Handbook of Adult Development and Learning.* Oxford UP. Ch 16. Work as the catalyst of reciprocal Adult Development and Learning identity and Personality by C. Hoare. Erikson's basic theory is in Erikson, E. H. (1950). *Childhood and Society.* Norton New York but Hoare points to Erikson, E. H. (1956) The problem of ego identity. *Journal of the American Psychoanalytic Association* 4, 56 – 121- which shows that the problem of identity is complex and should not be delineated, as for example, into operational terms suitable for testing.
[2] *ibid* p353
[3] for a detailed explanation of teacher socialization see Cohn, M. M and R. B. Kottkamp

(1993) *Teachers. The Missing Voice of Education*. State University of New York Press, Albany, NY. Although an American study the picture is very similar to that obtaining in other countries.

[4] see for example Mant, A (1978). *The Rise and Fall of the British Manager*. Pan, London on Bion's theories of group behaviour.

[5] Korte, R. F (2007) A review of social identity theory with implications for training and development. *Journal of European Industrial Training*, 31, (3), 166 – 180.

[6] Cuban, L (1992). Curriculum stability and change in P. W. Jackson (ed) *Handbook of Research on Curriculum*. AERA/Macmillan, New York p 237. With reference to the situation in Britain see Jenkins, S (1995) *Accountable to None: The Tory Nationalisation of Britain*. Hamish Hamilton, London.

[7] Heywood, J (2005) *Engineering Education. Research and Development in Curriculum and Instruction*. IEEE/Wiley, New York.

[8] Eisman, J and J. Fairweather (1996). *Evaluation of the National Science Foundation's Undergraduate and Curriculum Development Program*. National Science Foundation Washington DC. Cited in Fisher, P. D. Fairweather, J and M. Amey (2001). Systemic reform in undergraduate education. The role of collective responsibility. *Proceedings of the 31st ASEEE/IEEE Frontiers in Education Conference*. T1A – 1 to 6.

[9] Piaget suggests that there are schemes or structures which enable the child to *assimilate* the external environment. But the *assimilation* of new information also requires that there should be change in existing structures so that there is a congruence between external reality and the child's mental structures. This process is called *accommodation*. *Equilibration* is the adjustive process required for assimilation and accommodation. But these processes surely apply throughout life See Dawson-Tunik, T. L (2006) The meaning and measurement of conceptual development in adulthood in C. Hoare (ed) *Handbook of Adult Development and Learning*. Oxford University Press, New York.

[10] Marzano, R. J, Waters, T and B. A. McNulty (2005) *School Leadership that Works. From Research to Results*. Association for Supervision and Curriculum Development, Alexandria, VA

[11] The received perspective arises from the belief that there is a fixed body of knowledge that has to be handed down from generation to generation. It is structured by disciplines which we call subjects. It is the *raison d'être* for public examinations of the kind set in the British Isles. It is also the basis for a common core curriculum. See Eggleston, S. J (1977). *The Sociology of the School Curriculum*. Routledge and Kegan Paul, London.

[12] Heywood, J (1984). *Considering the Curriculum during Student Teaching*. Kogan Page, London.

[13] *ibid* p 41 and pp 142 – 148. See also Munro, R. G (1977) *Innovation. Success or Failure?* Hodder and Stoughton, Sevenoaks

[14] Froyd, J. E., Penberthy, D and K. Watson (2000) Good educational experiments are not necessarily change processes. *ASEE/IEEE Proceedings Frontiers in Education Conference* F1G-1

[15] Kotter, J (1996) *Leading Change*. Harvard Business School Press, Boston, MA See also Kotter, J. P (1998) Leading change. Why transformation efforts fail Ch 1 *Harvard Business Review of Change*. Harvard Business School Press, Boston, MA. Cited by Horn, R.A. A Post-Formal intervention strategy. Ch 18 of Jenlink, P. M. and B. H. Banathy (2008) (eds) *Dialogue as a Collective Means of Design Conversation*. Springer, New York.

[16] Jenlink, P. M. and C. Reigeluth (2000 July) A Guidance System for Designing new K-12 educational systems. Paper presented at the meeting of the International Society of Systems Science, Toronto, Canada.

[17] O'Connor, R. Mst. Thesis. School of Education, University of Dublin, Dublin.

[18] Berger, P (1970) *A Rumour of Angels. Modern Society and the Rediscovery of the Supernatural*. Penguin Press Harmondsworth.

[19] Committee on the Form and Function of the Intermediate Certificate Examination. Final report. Government Publications, Dublin (1974)

[20] In the nineteen sixties somewhat analogous with the difference between grammar

Schools and modern Schools in England except that secondary schools were denominational and the range of aptitude in them somewhat broader than the grammar schools

[21] Newman, J. H (1845). *An Essay on the Development of Christian Doctrine*. Penguin, Harmondsworth.

[22] Carter, G., Heywood, J and D. T. Kelly (1986) *Case Study in Curriculum Assessment. GCE Engineering Science (Advanced)*. Roundthorn, Manchester.

[23] Heywood, J (1978) *Examining in Second Level Education*. Association of Secondary Teachers Ireland, Dublin. For a detailed analysis of the ASTI attitudes to public examinations see Coolahan, J (1984) *The ASTI and Post-Primary Education in Ireland 1909 – 1984*.Association of Secondary Teachers Ireland, Dublin pp 329 – 337 and 384 – 285.

[24] Heywood, J., McGuinness, S and D. E. Murphy (1980) *Final report of the Public Examinations Evaluation Project*. School of Education University of Dublin, Dublin. See also note 12 pp 147 – 149 for a summary evaluation.

[25] *loc.cit.* Coolahan ref 23.

[26] Reading readiness is a controversial topic and not in general discussion at the present time. The idea of readiness is however useful. It relates to both prior-knowledge and the predisposition to learn which is one of Bruner's characteristics of a theory of instruction. A theory of instruction, he argues must be concerned with the experiences and contexts that will tend to make the child willing and able to learn when he/she enters school. From this supposition he is able to argue that readiness can be taught. see Bruner, J (1966). *Toward a Theory of Instruction*. Harvard University Press, Camb. Mass.

[27] Saupé, J. L (1961) in P. Dressel (ed) *Evaluation in Higher Education*. Jossey Bass, San Fransisco.
loc.cit ref 17

[28] Vygotsky, L. S. (1978). *Mind in Society. The Development of Higher Psychological Processes*. Harvard University Press, Boston, MA

[29] *loc.cit* ref 9

[30] For a detailed study and history of the Colleges of Advanced Technology (CATs) see Heywood, J (1969) An Evaluation of Certain Post-war Developments in Higher Technological Education. Thesis 2 volumes. University of Lancaster, Lancaster.

[31] Reported in *The Sunday Times* (review section) February 10th 2008.

[32] Ford, N and D. Renney (2000) The development of an authentic assessment scheme for the professional placement period of a sandwich course in Heywood, J, Sharp, J and M. Hides (eds) *Improving the Quality of Teaching in Higher Education*. University of Salford. Salford, UK

[33] Murphy, D. E. (1976) *Problems associated with the development of a new national scheme of assessment in Ireland*. MEd Thesis. School of Education, University of Dublin.

[34] For a complete study of the examination see Carter, G, Heywood, J., and D. T. Kelly (1986) *A Case Study in Curriculum Assessment. GCE Engineering Science (Advanced)*. Roundthorn, Manchester.

[35] Heywood, J and M. Murray (20050 Curriculum-Led Staff Development. Towards Curriculum and Instructional Leadership in Ireland. *Bulletins of the European Forum on Educational Administration* No 4, pp 3 - 97.

[36] Everard, B and G. Morris (1990) *Effective School Management*. 2nd Edition. Paul Chapman, London.

[37] Bridges, W (1993). *Transitions* Addison Wesley.

[38] Perry, W (1985). Cognitive and ethical growth. The making of meaning in Chickering A. W. and assocites (eds). *The Modern American College*. Jossey Bass, San Fransisco.

[39] *loc cit* ref 24

[40] *loc.cit*

[41] *loc.cit* ref 29. The product champion was Professor H. Edels , Dean of the Faculty of Engineering Science, University of Liverpool

[42] Walkington, J (2002) Curriculum change in engineering education. *European Journal of Engineering Education* 27, (2), 133 – 148.

CHAPTER 8

FROM RESTRICTED PRACTICE TO PROFESSIONALISM: FROM ACCOUNTABILITY TO RENEWAL

Introduction

The chapter begins with a brief summary of historical approaches to the study of the professions in order to determine if teaching is a profession. In those terms teaching is considered to be a sub-profession. The professions have sought to be self-regulatory and State recognized bodies have been established for this purpose although recently the effectiveness of self-regulation has come under scrutiny. In the British Isles teachers have sought status through the creation of Teaching Councils that control behaviour and the intake by means of educational requirements. However, through the control of the curriculum and even directions about the methods of instruction some governments have severely curtailed the freedom of teachers to teach in ways that they see fit. In consequence such professionalism as they have is severely limited. It is argued that teachers have allowed this to happen and that this is a consequence of the way they are socialized into the profession and what they perceive the teaching role to be.

Following Hoyle a distinction is drawn between being a restricted professional and being an extended professional. It is argued that teachers are by and large restricted professionals. Their training does not prepare them to be extended professionals and they lack a common agreed technical pedagogy.

The remainder of the chapter is concerned with how teachers can become extended professionals.

Extended professionalism will begin if teachers begin to exercise reflective practice and engage in self-accountability (assessment) for self-accountability is a requisite of more general accountability to the school and society. Accountability is the evaluation of whether agreed goals are met and if not why not. Its purpose is to maintain and improve teacher competence where necessary. A person who becomes skilled in self-assessment is likely to be willing to allow colleagues in their classroom to seek advice.

For self-accountability to be successful there needs to be a "critical friend" who can assist the teacher plot his/her future activities. "Positive appraisal" is the task of the principal for it is the principal who should have access to resources that may help the teacher achieve the agreed goals. Self-assessment given the primary role of the teacher is about classroom assessment. This can be conducted at several levels and a technical pedagogy is created within a school when teachers share their experiences and are encouraged to undertake research in their classrooms. Principals have to create a climate in which this can happen. An Appendix to this chapter shows the possibilities that can arise when a teacher has the support of the principal.

One model for creating a culture is the inquiry oriented school referred to in previous chapters in which all participate in looking to the future through the questioning of existing assumptions and practices. The case study in the appendix is an example inquiry oriented practice.

Is Teaching a Profession?

Surprisingly, given the many studies that were made of the professions in the middle of the last century.[1] *The Oxford Dictionary's* definition of a profession makes no reference to the characteristics that define a profession. It assumes that a profes-

sion is *"one requiring knowledge in some branch of learning."*
On the one hand this definition enables it to embrace a wide
range of occupations that call themselves professions, and on
the other hand, it enables it to ignore the characteristics that so-
ciologists have used to define a profession. There is no mention
for example of the semi-profession suggested by Carr-Saunders
and Wilson as long ago as 1933.

I am aware of an alternative approach taken to understand
the professional culture of teaching by Helsby[2] and others (sum-
marized in Knight and Saunders, 1999). However, in English
speaking cultures the characteristics derived from normative
trait theories of the profession help to locate teaching in a spectrum of professional characteristics defined by relative status. In
this respect teaching fails miserably. Teaching, like social work
and nursing, would be classified as a semi-profession.[3] Marshall
has explained how many of these *"new semi-professions are really subordinate grades placed in the middle of the hierarchy of
modern business organization."* We might substitute education
system for business organization. Nevertheless the occupations
that concern us here are ones based on extensive knowledge
and/or social skills in virtue of which they generate a special
mystique of their own. The clients of these occupations constitute a varied and heterogeneous population who offer considerable potential for exploitation by members of the occupations
as defined. Clarke has pointed out that little attention has been
paid to the students who are the chief clients of teachers, and in
this context poor teaching is exploitation.[4]

Professionals tend to establish formal associations to create
and protect a monopoly and to control entry. They build up a
system of education and training and define standards of acceptance; and these may be beyond or at a level higher than is
really necessary for the task. In order to establish a position as
responsible guarantors of the public interest they adopt a code
of practice or professional ethic.[5] However, it has been pointed
out that in some professional organizations, such as those as-

sociated with engineering, a code of conduct for their members meant little more than what was required of them as employees. The threat of dismissal was more real than the threat of expulsion from their professional organization.[6] It seemed to one authority *"…that ultimate conduct was largely determined by the employer, and that if engineers in subordinate positions always accepted the values of their employer, then their power was always given authority. As private individuals they might also have other attitudes, but might have to operate dual standards of conduct with dual morality."*[7] In the United States where engineering undergraduates commonly take courses in engineering ethics as part of their programme much attention has been given to the problems arising from "whistle blowing," that is the making public of unethical practices. In one case a "whistle blower" given a public award by President Regan for his actions found himself, out in the cold without a job![8] Nevertheless, the profession considered it important to publish a code of conduct. The Royal Academy of Engineering in the UK has recently published such a code[9] and there is a continuing debate about ethics and engineering.

We might in the situation where individuals are subject to their employers justifiably question whether those persons can be professional in circumstances where ethical/moral judgements cannot be made without fear of retribution. We might cite the example of teachers who are told to teach in a certain way in spite of their better judgement. This raises the question of the autonomy that teachers have in their classrooms in different cultures and at different levels (ie primary, post-primary, post-secondary) within those cultures.

Taken together, all this serves to provide the professional person with status, and society clearly acquiesces in the hierarchy that has evolved. For example most 'doctors' in the British Isles don't possess a doctorate. Nevertheless we all accept that they should be called 'doctor.' In Ireland dentists without a doctor qualification are now calling themselves doctor which seems to be con trick. In contrast in the British Isles the public does not generally call those who posses a doctorate in philosophy doctor whereas those who have that qualification on the European continent are called doctor. There are cultural differences in the attitudes that different peoples have toward professionals and the status they occupy. Interestingly enough doctors working in the British health service are employees. They do not enjoy self-employed status.

The selection process also enables a profession to restrict entry and so create a scarcity value for the services that it offers. Education and training are used as the prime means of selection. This discriminatory role would seem to be important for it seems, as indicated above, that sometimes an education is provided that is not necessarily suited to the work task. A high scarcity value usually enhances the prestige of a profession. It should be noted that scarcity and shortage are not the same thing. A shortage of teachers may be due to the status with which the profession is perceived in particular cultures.[10] Even so there is hardly a scarcity of teachers for the overall numbers of persons employed as teachers at any one time is generally relatively large.

It is against this background that the relative position of teaching on the spectrum of professions should be considered, and it is clear that it does not come out of such an analysis favourably. In many countries teachers have low status although this has not been the case in Ireland. Although the teacher unions believe the status of teaching is declining all the available places for training can be filled.[11]

It should be noted that we are not discussing the issue of whether or not teaching should be a profession but whether or not it is.

The professions operate restrictive practices in the same way that unions do and it is debatable whether these are always in the public interest[12] as has been shown by recent debates about the effectiveness of the General Medical Councils in Britain and Ireland. It is questioned whether they and other regulatory bodies such as the Law Society are capable of self-regulation.[13] Self regulation implies that each member of a profession is self-accountable for his her activities.

In spite of these criticisms Registration Councils for Teachers have been established in Scotland and subsequently in England and Ireland. While such councils obtain some powers in respect of the training required for entry to the profession they are no guarantee of status. In the case of Ireland the Minister could refuse to implement its recommendations but the Minister would have to say why. Moreover, the Council could only advise the Minister on the minimum standards for entry to the profession and the minimum standards of educational attainment required for entry into initial teacher education programmes. In the past it has been very difficult to prove malpractice and in consequence dismissal is rare. In any case the actual practice of teaching in the classroom apart from malpractice continues to be constrained by factors not in the control of the Council but in the direct or indirect control of the Department of Education.

An important characteristic of a profession is that its members should be responsible for the training of new entrants. They should enable new entrants to have an effective apprenticeship.

Common usage means that it is no longer possible to confine discussion of the professions to the Church, the Army and the Law. The term is widely used and possibly the most useful definition is that from the Oxford Dictionary which began this section *"one requiring advanced knowledge in some branch of learning."* But even that can be queried given the widespread use of the term professional. Thus actors speak of the 'acting profession', engineers the engineering profession, nurses of the nursing profession and so on. We also speak of professional civil servants. A professional is a member of a profession and professional behaviour is the behaviour expected of a professional person. It is clear that through their professional associations and/or unions that they can and do operate restrictive practices to the extent of withdrawal of labour.

The term has also been abused as for example in soccer where the a deliberate foul on a player to prevent them scoring a goal is called a "professional foul!" If it is accepted that teaching is a profession then it is possible to argue that in some countries teaching has been deprofessionalized in the sense that teachers are not allowed to behave in a professional manner toward their clients because of the restraints placed upon them by government. In pursuing this theme it will be argued that teachers play into the hands of government and that this is due in no small part to the way in which they are socialized into teaching. This has the effect of orienting them toward a restricted professionalism.

Governments and the deprofessionalization of teaching

Governments exert control over teachers and entry to the profession in numerous ways. Not least among these is the rate of remuneration. But they also exert control over the curriculum and this they do in a variety of ways. In Ireland in post-primary education this is exerted through the system of public examinations. Many teachers believe they place a premium on the recall of facts. Teaching has become limited to one or two styles and attempts to introduce variety and experiment by young teachers are often greeted by their more experienced and older colleagues with scorn. At the same time there is no rubric that states that teachers should teach in these preferred ways, or for that matter public and publicised pressure on them to do so. Neither is there a target oriented post-primary curriculum. The situation in Ireland is in marked contrast to that in the United Kingdom. In the UK at primary level it is teacher centred whereas in Ireland at the primary level the curriculum is child-centred and there are no 'literacy' and 'numeracy' hours in which teachers are given precise instructions on what to teach and when. While the unions have representatives on the Council and the committees of the National Council for Curriculum and Assessment which advises the ministers on the curriculum overall teachers have little say in the structure of the curriculum or its content, and many do not think this matters. Such attitudes contribute to the deprofessionalisation of teaching. Moreover, it seems that trainee teachers are already socialised into this view. That is, they take the curriculum as given,

It is evident that trainee teachers are far more concerned with the 'nuts and bolts' of practice in the classroom than any theorising about the curriculum or how it should be constructed. Weaknesses of this kind enable governments to take control and reduce teaching to little more than a rote activity that implements without too much thought the implementations of the controllers. In these circumstances autonomy in the classroom becomes restricted to behavioural management. Otherwise the teacher is a conduit or mediator of the curriculum and sometimes instruction. This 'restricted' professionalism is deeply ingrained. Within that framework the majority of teachers do their best but in these circumstances do they merit the term 'professional?'

'Restricted' professionalism

As used here the term 'restricted' professionalism originates with a British educational sociologist Eric Hoyle.[14] He contrasted it with "extended" professionalism. The differences between the two are shown in exhibit 8.1. Hoyle argued that one of the reasons why it was so difficult to change the curriculum was because of the restricted professionality of teachers.

We would probably want to make some changes to the categories because of an increased understanding about extended professionalism. In the first place we would want to assert the ethical dimension of responsibility as it relates to performance and accountability. If there is to be sensible accountability in schools then it has to begin with professional accountability. That is, with the accountability that a teacher owes their identity as a professional. Such accountability arises from what is currently termed "reflective practice" or "educational connoisseurship."[15] The "value" of whole school evaluation depends on such practice.

The origins of these attitudes lie as much in the way individuals become socialized into teaching as they do in anything else.

Learning to teach begins at a very young age. Three-year olds try to direct the activities of their one year old siblings. They are very authoritarian. Some children set up a classroom with their dolls. I taught my Teddy Bear. In those days teachers in grammar and public schools in Britain and Ireland still wore gowns. Somehow I knew this, so I wore my dressing gown over my shoulders. Again it was very authoritarian, all about control, all about not being naughty. The curriculum was "received" by the Teddy Bear; his mind was a *tabula rasa*. Only occasionally was he told that he was good. And all this could happen in spite of attendance at a play-group. The next step is primary school, then post-primary school and then if we don't gamble some form of appropriate third level education. All the time we are learning about teaching but I doubt if we are learning much about learning. We are socialised into attitudes and beliefs about teaching from a very early age and it has a profound effect on the assumptions we make about teaching and learning and, apparently they differ little between cultures.

Restricted Professionality	Extended Professionality
Skills derived from experience.	Skills derived from a mediation between experience and theory.
Perspective limited to the Immediate time and place.	Perspective embracing the broader social context of education.
Classroom events perceived in isolation.	Classroom events perceived in relation to institution policies and goals.
Introspective with regard to methods.	Methods compared with those of colleagues and with reports of practice.
Value placed on autonomy.	Value placed on professional collaboration.
Limited involvement in non-teaching professional activities.	High involvement in non-teaching professional activities (e.g. subject associations)
Infrequent reading of professional literature.	Regular reading of professional literature.
Involvement in in-service work limited and confined to practical courses.	Involvement in in-service work considerable and includes courses of a theoretical nature.
Teaching seen as an intuitive activity.	Teaching seen as a rational activity.

Exhibit 8.1. Hoyle's characterisation of the dimensions of restricted and extended professionalism among teachers. (The term institution is a substitute for school in the original since the argument applies equally to third level education. See Warren Piper, 1994).

Nowhere has this problem been more examined than in the United States. Cohn and Kottkamp[16] repeated with some adaptation a study of teachers that had been undertaken twenty years earlier by Lortie.[17] They found a remarkable degree of consistency between his results and theirs. Lortie had argued that teaching reflects its institutionalised origin in the urban schools of the nineteenth century where teaching became 'womens work' lacking any type of pay equity. Lortie argued that the ways teachers are recruited and socialised into the profession leads to persons who value the status quo. *"Those who enter because they like school or a flexible schedule that is conducive to child care are unlikely to invest time to change the organization."* Today in the British Isles there is a good proportion of males in teaching especially in post-primary education and certainly in Ireland there are a number of males in primary education. Cohn and Kottkamp affirm Lortie's view that stability, and thus a reluctance to change stems in part from the way that teachers are *"recruited, and socialized into the occupation and rewarded for their efforts."*

"In the domain of socialization, Lortie maintained that although prospective teachers are required to have a certain amount of formal preparation, they are not expected to complete a highly demanding program. All teachers must have at least a college degree, and their formal schooling includes both general special schooling. One unique feature of the general schooling of teachers is that it actually functions in Lortie's terms as an "apprenticeship of observation", in that those who become teachers have as students, already had at least sixteen years of contact with teachers. This apprenticeship encourages the observers to internalize traditional patterns and leads to a widely accepted belief that "we teach as we were taught." The special schooling, moreover, is relatively short and citing Lortie is "neither intellectually nor organizationally as complex as that found in the established professions". It includes a mini-apprenticeship in the form of student teaching, which can be as short as six to eight weeks, and which is highly dependent

for its quality on the skill of the supervising classroom teacher. Once hired, a beginning teacher is given the same full load of responsibilities that experienced teachers have and is expected to "learn by doing". The novice typically seeks advice from more experienced colleagues but is disposed to accept or reject suggestions largely on personal grounds. The criteria for acceptance appear to be those that fit one's situation or style that they "work".[18]

This process of socialization leads, in Lortie's words to an *"emergence and reinforcement of idiosyncratic experience and personal synthesis" and to the absence of "a common technical culture". The inability to draw on an accepted body of knowledge in turn affects status and contributes to the individualistic and conservative outlooks of the occupation".[19]*

Since everyone is taught then every one is socialized into the same set of attitudes and beliefs, everyone knows how to teach. And in these circumstances whether they are politicians, civil servants, inspectors or parents they are entitled to an equal opinion. Moreover, it is not in their interests to admit the possibility of a technical pedagogy. Teachers are there to act as purveyors of knowledge in ways determined by others. The implications of this state of affairs for management are profound.

In the absence of a 'technical pedagogy' it is no wonder that *"teachers do not feel confident to speak as a group or to respond to the demands of others from an authoritative knowledge base."[20]* As Cohn and Kottkamp write, *"the overall weakness and brevity of the formal socialization simply cannot counteract the tendencies to absorb and use the ideas and approaches of one's prior personal experience."[21]* Teachers do not have learned or professional societies (as distinct from unions and teaching councils) such as the Royal College of General Practitioners or the engineering societies in Britain and the US through which they can be renewed, develop a technical pedagogy or take evidence based public stands. The College of

Preceptors (now College of Teachers) founded in the nineteenth century never achieved this role in Britain in spite of the fact that its Royal Charter gave it the power to award qualifications. So teacher pedagogy continues to be based on experience and as we have seen it is well documented that over reliance on experience inhibits change and innovation and encourages professional autism[22] (see Chapter 2).

The situation is exacerbated by the fact that they have to teach to a prescribed curriculum (*a received curriculum* as Eggleston, describes this paradigm[23]). This means that they and many teacher trainers do not see the need to study the curriculum as defined here, per se. They soon find when they are dissatisfied with the curriculum that the authorities are not prepared to consult them on curriculum matters. However they are not in a position, except in a naive way, to argue about the curriculum because they have rejected access to the knowledge base on which they could build their criticism. In any event many of them see no reason why the curriculum should change. So they affirm the divorce between the curriculum and teaching that was created in the nineteenth century. Clandinin and Connelly who charted the history of the curriculum reported that the term "teacher" did not feature early in the curriculum literature. *"The development of an association of "teacher" with "curriculum" appears to have been mostly a consequence of a working distinction between ends and means, which presumed that teachers and teaching mediate between the curriculum and its object, students." [...][24]* The teacher acts as a conduit. Later they write, *"it is we think fair to say that the conceptual histories of the teacher and the curriculum as seen in the research literature have been more or less independent."[25]* It is contended here that this has been detrimental to the development of teaching as a profession. This is because teachers are treated as ciphers whose job is to transmit the intentions of the curriculum authorities to the students without any consideration of what they are asked to teach. Clandinin and Connelly cite studies from many countries to show that this divorce (they call it *"functional split"*), is alive and well. One might argue that often there is also a functional split between teaching and learning.

Referring to the many curriculum projects reported in the international literature[26] they note that even when teachers are involved in project development an underlying purpose of their participation is conversion to the values of the reform. Moreover they believe this to be the case that this applies to school-based staff and curriculum development.[27]

They also conclude that the *"view of curriculum development as a form of imposed teacher development [...] if teacher development did not occur, student development in the direction specified by the reformers would not follow. Teachers in this view are as much the target of reform as are students."*[28] Thus reform projects typically develop materials for teachers and some reformers try *"to limit the teacher's role either by constructing materials in such a way that teachers' screening influence between materials and students was minimized or by devising implementation strategies to ensure materials were used as intended."*[29] Teachers reinforce this philosophy because they neither have the wish or the knowledge to develop their own materials or curriculum. Thus they are happy for the authorities to change curriculum content (which is what is normally meant by curriculum reform) provided that they are given training and some would demand it in school-time. In this they concede their authority, they confirm an idea prevalent among politicians and journalists that if reforms fail it is due to the teacher. They allow themselves to be put in the position where they are told how to teach and recently in the UK how to examine. In a nutshell they are not allowed or encouraged to be very professional. The vast majority of teachers are "restricted" in their professionalism. Clearly Cohn and Kottkamp are seeking the attitudes among teachers of the extended professional. However, they also argue, and Hoyle would not disagree, that if meaningful learning is to be made the norm that *"the system itself as well as the teachers in it must undergo substan-*

tial change, and that such change must be grounded in a more meaningful conception of learning."[30] To which I would add *"and curriculum."* We might expect the extended professional to have developed defensible theories of learning and instruction and defensible positions in the philosophy and sociology of education and to embrace school based curriculum development. We would expect those teachers who find security in prescribed syllabuses to resist school based curriculum development and to demonstrate the characteristics of a restricted professional.

For such change to take place new knowledge is required. That knowledge is contained, perhaps not satisfactorily in knowledge areas in teacher education that are commonly rejected by student teachers whether graduate or undergraduate. Given that this is the case then change will not come about unless those entrusted with educational leadership see it as a primary function of their task to develop a common technical culture and make use of it in their schools. So how can change be brought about? As has been argued in other chapters change is of two kinds. There is that which is incremental and linear and there is that which is radical. Incremental change is more likely to be acceptable than radical change so any programme for change needs to begin with first order changes and lead to the ideal that demands a radical re-think. The sections that follow adopt that approach.

The Principal and Change

One of the findings of the task analysis of engineers mentioned in an earlier chapter was that the term engineer was used in a very loose fashion. It could imply a very highly qualified person acting in a senior capacity or it could imply someone working in what might be described as a clerical task. When the investigators attempted to describe a taxonomy of engineering objectives they found that nearly everyone in the firm, however high, however lowly performed some kind of managerial task. Everyone exerted some form of direction and control over themselves and their job and sometimes over others. As was pointed out at the time there is nothing very new in this finding.[31] After all we have to manage ourselves from the time we get up in the morning to the time we go to bed. What was different was the assertion that every person was a manager and that this had implications for organisational behaviour as well as the organisational structure of the firm.

As we have seen in earlier chapters one of the investigators subsequently developed this point in respect of education. Teachers want to have a greater say in the running of their schools. In so far as teachers are concerned they want the schools to be democratic and they want principals to respond to that democracy. But many of them want consensus and it takes but one teacher to exert her/himself to bring change to a halt. Neither do they necessarily want to engage in public accountability. At some stage it becomes an act of management by the teachers to allow the principal to act on their behalf. We have explored this route elsewhere. Suffice it to say that once we wish to exert direction and control on proceedings we are managing, and suffice it to say that in this respect the management of a classroom is no different to that of management anywhere else.

The same is true of leadership. Much to much time is spent trying to make distinctions between management and leadership. Just as every one is a manager so everyone is a leader. Leading implies following. To the extent that we set ourselves goals, and to the extent that we set about obtaining those goals, we both lead and follow. In this sense every individual is a leader. Because this is the case, each individual has within him or herself the attributes of leadership. What distinguishes one person from another as a leader is the use to which they put the attributes of leadership in the varying situations in which they find themselves. To acknowledge the findings of educational research and not to do anything about them is a neglect of professional responsibility. It is also a denial of the professional's responsibility to lead. It prevents the development of an agreed technical pedagogy and if professionalism is to be extended an agreed pedagogy is necessary.

Evaluations of teacher expectations of principals show teachers expect principals to be leaders even if they find it difficult to say what they mean by leadership. Quite simply on the one hand this might be about leading the school toward a vision or on the other hand in the "way" a teacher is asked or empowered to do a particular task. Suffice it to say that once we wish to lead proceedings we are leading, and suffice it to say that in this respect leadership in the classroom is no different to leadership anywhere else.

We deduce from this that the development of a culture that will support extended professionalism will depend not only on the managerial and leadership qualities of the principal but on those of his/her colleagues as well. As we have seen opportunities for such exercises in the context of the curriculum differ as between one educational system and another.

Thinking about the Profession

A beginning can be made if teachers are asked to consider what it means to be a professional. While teachers think of themselves as professionals I doubt if put to it they could explain in any depth what there understanding of a profession is. They, need therefore to explore how they perceive themselves in terms of restricted and extended professionalism. From traditional analyses of the professions teachers can ask themselves whether or not they are truly accountable. They should also ask whether or not they take the obligation to train new entrants to the profession seriously. In the light of recent thinking about professional behaviour they can ask themselves if they are truly reflective practitioners for good reflective practice equates with self-accountability. They will almost inevitably find themselves limited by the lack of a technical pedagogy upon which they all agree. There is therefore a need to develop a technical pedagogy. Attempts have been made to begin the development of such a pedagogy elsewhere.

Accountability and Reflective Practice

Elliott has argued that developing skills of self-accountability is a necessary preparation for more general accountability to the school and society.

" *If teacher education is to prepare students or experienced teachers for accountability then it must be concerned with developing their ability to reflect on classroom situations. By "practical reflections" I mean reflection with a view to action. This involves identifying and identifying those practical problems which exist for the teacher in his situation and deciding on strategies for resolving them. The view of accountability which I have outlined, with its emphasis on the right of the teacher to evaluate his own moral agency, assumes that teachers are capable of identifying and diagnosing their practical problems with some degree of objectivity. It implies that the teacher is able to identify a discrepancy between what he in fact brings about in the classroom and his responsibilities to foster and prevent certain consequences. If he cannot do this he is unable to assess whether or not he is obliged to. I believe that being plunged into a context where outsiders evaluated their moral agency without this kind of developmental preparation would be self-defeating since the anxiety generated would render the achievement of an objective attitude at any of these levels extremely difficult.* "[32]

While outside inspections that take a look at the teacher in one or two classes cannot give a true picture of a teacher it is surely right that they should be made because society needs to know that its schools are run by competent teachers. In any event the prospect of inspections might cause among teachers who don't normally reflect such reflection.[33] They have an obligation to defend their practices and this means that they "*need not only understand that something is so; the teacher must further understand why it is so, on what grounds its warrant can be asserted, and under what circumstance our belief in its justification can be weakened or even denied."* [34] This quotation is from Shulman cited by La Boskey[35] who went on to point-out that while this applied to subject content it also applied to pedagogy. Shulman writes that teachers have to continually ask, *"How do I know what I know? How do I know the reasons for what I do? Why do I ask my students to perform or think in different ways?"* [36] Add to these Cowan's What if.......?[37] and other questions that prompt reflection. It is instructive to note LaBoskey's comment that reflective teachers ask "why" questions whereas non-reflective teachers seldom do. Of such are the questions of accountability, and the answers may be uncomfortable because they must question epistemology as well as accountability. The answers may be uncomfortable to policy makers as well as teachers because they must question educational practices and assumptions that may be dearly held even by those who expect them to be accountable.

Clearly the intention of self-accountability is to maintain and improve where necessary teacher competence. Equally clearly when such questions begin to be asked the more one explores ones own situation and tests it against what is written as well as the views of others.

Extended professionalism begins with self-accountability and it gains confidence when a colleague is invited to contribute to that self-assessment. A person who is comfortable in a classroom room with a colleague observer is likely to be we prepared for subject review by an inspector. That person is also more likely to make an informed contribution to whole school planning and evaluation. But those who fear being found out are unlikely to benefit. As Brookfield shows they may put on a performance that is at odds with what they normally do. He gives the example of a performance put on by a teacher that was spotted by the students who seemed to feel it was not for their benefit.

Training with these points in mind should also foster a willingness to go beyond this level of understanding. It should enable the teacher to *"see his (her) work in the wider context of the community and society, ensuring that his work is informed by theory, research and current exemplars of good practice, being willing to collaborate with other teachers in teaching, curriculum development and the formation of school policy, and having a commitment to keep himself professionally informed.*[38]

Positive appraisal: Encouraging Renewal

Self-accountability cannot be conducted in isolation. Both Society as represented through a government department of education and schools have goals that have to be achieved. Nevertheless the central role of the teacher, one that is often forgotten, is to help pupils learn. Everything else is subordinate and intended to support that role and accountability has to be seen in that light. A person who wants to be self-accountable has to be open to that system and it is in this respect that the principal occupies a key role for it is with the principal that the teacher has to share his/her aspirations, achievements and failures. It is for the principal acting as a "critical friend" to see how the teacher might be encouraged, helped or whatever the case may be. Appraisal it might be but it should be for the purpose of personal growth not for the purpose of criticism and this applies equally in the first instance to teachers who are said to be "failing." It has to be positive. Accountability is the evaluation of whether agreed goals are met and if not why not. This does not imply that goals must be met for it may be obvious that some goals should be changed. It may also be obvious that resources are required if some goals are to be met and this may be a matter for the governance of the school. In some cases the provision of rewards will in effect be rewards for good performance. Of course there will be occasions when extreme sanctions must be applied and this is something that stakeholders in many countries prefer to avoid.

For self-assessment to be successful it has be known among the teachers that the principal also self-assesses him or herself and does it in consultation with another, perhaps a senior teacher in the school, perhaps another principal or perhaps the chair person of the managing (governing) body. It will be readily appreciated that self-assessment is a form of managing and leading ones self. Self-assessment requires that I understand how to manage myself, that in asking what my strengths and weaknesses are I also come to a real understanding of my values and what I can contribute to the organization. It invites me to understand my relationships and responsibilities. It also asks me to consider how I manage the second half of my life in an age when the working life is likely to extend to fifty years. It invites a "critical friend" to help me explore these issues, and given that friend is the principal to help me handle the tensions in the plurality of social systems that I occupy, recognising that his task is to inspire my teaching. Of course the same questions apply to the principal and the leadership he/she offers the school.

The Assessment of Teaching

Since instruction for learning is the central task of teaching self-accountably implies the evaluation of teaching. A simplistic view of this that is all to often held, is that so long as one's students perform relatively well in tests every thing in the garden is rosy. But there is more to it than that, for test results describe the overall performance of a group. They do not say whether the high and average performers could do better or indicate if measures have been taken to help those who are behind. A teacher has to be able to make realistic comments on all the pupils he/she teaches and to judge their performance in the light of their teaching. One question teachers will have to answer is the extent to which the test material they use is valid and reliable. There are many other issues related to instruction. For example, one important issue for every teacher is whether the knowledge about students in their possession is the best available knowledge. Should, for example, the learning styles of the students be derived at regular intervals the corollary of which is should teaching and learning styles be matched?

It is not the purpose of this text to dwell on the theory and practice of instruction or the theory and practice of assessment. It is important however to point out that there is an extensive literature on instruction and assessment with which a teacher intent on self-assessment should be aware. Moreover there are a range of techniques available for classroom assessment as Angelo and Cross have shown in their book of that title.[39] (The reader, on completion of this chapter, may like to turn to the last chapter where this view of classroom assessment is explored in more detail).

A principal who wishes to encourage a teacher who has conducted classroom assessment may suggest that the teacher should engage in classroom research of one kind or another. In so doing he/she will be encouraging more rigorous inquiry and reflection. But personal inquiries of this kind only affect individual teachers. They can, of course, ask other teachers to visit their classrooms, something that is seldom done, and they could become the catalyst for the engagement of the whole school in solving some of its problems. A case study of a teacher stimulated school activity of this kind is given in the appendix.

These are models of teaching as research and a principal who encourages teachers to systematically evaluate their work is promoting a different culture, a culture in which reflection on action for action is valued. One way to change a culture is to generate a spirit of inquiry.

Renewal: Developing an Inquiry Oriented School

But initial training will be worthless unless it is continually reinforced. Some call this professional development. I prefer the term renewal but the issue of terminology is neither here nor there. As we have seen this will often require a change in the culture of the school. Several models might be used for this purpose. For example total quality management requires a whole school approach. In this final section the radical proposal for inquiry oriented schools suggested by Cohn and Kottkamp and mentioned in earlier chapters is discussed.

Making the Future: Toward Inquiry Oriented Schools

The American management guru Peter Drucker wrote in 1999 *"one thing is certain for developed countries-and probably for the entire world: We face long years of profound changes. They are not even primarily technological changes. They are changes in demographics, in politics, in society, in philosophy and, above all, in world view [...] there is no social theory for such a period. [...] It is futile, for instance, to try to ignore the changes and to pretend that tomorrow will be like yesterday, only more so.[...] "* Nowhere, is this more likely to be true than in educational institutions. It is he says a delusion to think things will remain the same. The current leaders will not be around in thirty years time and in any event it is not possible to predict the changes. Therefore *"the only policy likely to succeed is to try to make the future."* This has to happen within the restraints imposed by present certainties but Drucker believes that the *"future is still malleable. It can still be created."* And, all of this applies to the curriculum and instruction.

It is a bold aim to seek such change. A step that can be taken toward this end that also creates the culture in which self-assessment is seen not as an imposition but as a contribution to personal and institutional renewal is the development of inquiry-oriented schools. Cohn and Kottkamp credit R. J. Schaefer with the idea. They cite a statement of his that is reminiscent of Drucker. *"We can no longer,"* he wrote, *"afford to conceive of the schools simply as distribution centers for dispensing cultural orientations, information, and knowledge developed by other social units. The complexities of teaching and learning in formal classrooms have become so formidable and the intellectual demands upon the system so enormous that the*

*school must be much more than a place of instruction. It must
also be a center of inquiry-a producer as well as a transmitter
of knowledge. One basic fact is our ignorance of teaching. We
simply do not know how to master the abstract knowledge and
the analytical skills modern society demands. It seems necessary to transform at least some schools into centers for the production of knowledge about how to carry out the job."* [41]

Cohn and Kottkamp recognise that our understanding of
the teaching process has greatly improved but student teachers and indeed teachers would affirm that theories of instruction are largely unemployed. There is a gulf between theory and
practice and as has been argued experience is valued more than
theory and because this view is embedded it is difficult to bring
about change. Cohn and Kottkamp suggest that because of the
frustration that teachers have with externally prescribed curricular an inquiry-oriented school would contribute to the intellectual health of the teachers because of the intellectual challenges provided. They are critical of Schaefer because his model
is concentrated on pedagogy and the training of teachers to be
behavioural scientists rather than agents of change. The same
criticism can be made of the teacher as research model that is
limited to instruction. Cohn and Kottkamp argue that *"transformation in learning into meaningful interaction requires a
systemic approach, inquiry must examine not only individual
behaviours but also assumptions, structure, and culture that
permit or inhibit behavioral change."* [42] This is an altogether
bigger challenge that may not be unpalatable to policy makers
for implicit in it is the hypothesis that structures will inevitably have to change. But the idea can be applied to institutions
working within the restraints imposed by the present system
because self-assessment by teachers should be a strong basis for
inquiry.

Cohn and Kottkamp suggest that an inquiry oriented school
is one *"where teachers and other stakeholders might (1) col-
laboratively identify problems or questions that are critical for*

today and tomorrows concerns, (2) study past efforts of others to solve school problems and bring about structural change, (3) create and study new approaches and structure toward the end of successful reform."[43]

There are some similarities with the approach of TQM and school planning, but it is school planning with a difference.

Principles such as these can be thought of as the mechanisms for either bringing about radical change or for dealing with the substantial problems that exist within the restraints imposed by the policy makers. In the case of the latter they could lead to radical change if the authorities take note of what is happening in the school.

As has been argued in previous chapters by far the most important issue is the unravelling of the problems that a school has. One way of achieving this is through an assumptional-dialogue. *"Assumptional dialogues"* provide *"opportunities to raise awareness and examine largely unrecognized assumptions that currently underlie [the] educational structures and practices [in a school, institution or system] and to generate alternatives to them."*[44] Assumption digging suggest Cohn and Kottkamp often provides the potential to motivate teachers. The idea is to bring to the surface the assumptions and structures that underlie the processes of education in an institution and to subject them to question. One problem is to release or make explicit the tacit knowledge that is embedded in our thinking and is difficult to explicate. We know, argues Polyani, more than we can say: our "theories-in use" derive from that knowledge. Assumption digging helps us articulate that knowledge.[45] One method developed by Argyris and Schön is the reflective seminar.[46] A reflective seminar is a voluntary group that is committed to learning and understanding about a particular issue (e.g of discipline). Its membership should comprise different role occupants so that different perspectives merge. One of them would agree to summarise the research and general literature on the issue. It also ensures that all the stakeholders have some say in what happens and that the members gain a better understanding of each others positions. Through such reflection they also obtain a better understanding of their own position. In such groups power differentials have to be exorcised so that everyone can speak freely and the effects of power and control in the structures on the performance of the institution revealed. Cohn and Kottkamp provide illustrations of this and other approaches that provide the base for action research. They may of course lead to the solution of problems without the need for research. There is a strong similarity between this approach and that of quality circles.

Thus it is that Cohn and Kottkamp envision *"schools as communities of scholar- teachers, where everyone including principals collaborate on action research projects that have the capacity to change the very structure of schools or significant elements within them."*[47] Inquiry-oriented schools will of necessity extend the professionalism of the teachers within them and those teachers will take responsibility for beginning teachers.

None of this should be read to have said that there are no extended professionals in teaching. There are many as is evidenced by those who pursue professional development courses at their own expense. But like any other society the active numbers are but a fraction of the whole.

Appendix: A Case Study

Example of action research initiated by a teacher with the support of his Principal.

Pat Prior set out to establish the validity of Elliott's model of action research in an Irish primary school. He did this with the support of his Principal and his colleagues on the staff.[48] As defined by Elliott action research is *"the study of a social situation with a view to improving the quality of action within it."*[49]

The start of any research is to clarify the problem and this is often by no means easy. In the first place Prior used, as did Elliott the Nominal Group Technique.[50] This is an extension of brainstorming. It has 6 stages 1. Question setting; 2. Reflection; 3, Pooling; 4.Clarification; 5. Evaluation; and 6. Review. It is quite an extensive procedure[55] and Prior found that in order to clarify the problem he required more than one session.

One effect is that it requires teachers to publicly declare problems they have and in so doing they have to try and separate self-esteem from classroom activity. Elliott had found that teachers find this difficult to do. Exercises like this also demonstrate that the problems that teachers face in isolation are likely to be the case in other classrooms. Prior's study found that his school was no exception.

Prior circulated a summary of the first meeting. Before the next meeting he also circulated a document that set down the aims and guidelines for future meetings. At this stage the purpose was seen to be *"to make a largely academic curriculum more meaningful for the development of the whole student."*[51]

At this stage the investigator also recorded the inability of the project to alter the academic emphasis of the curriculum. The principal said that nothing could be done about it. *"Efforts should be made to make the academic curriculum more attractive to academically less able students."*[52] Nevertheless, Prior reported that the variety of issues that had been raised offered scope for classroom research. The teachers had to learn to focus. To get this focusing Prior decided to intervene during the third meeting with the teachers through means of a statement and a question. Comparison between the records of the earlier meetings and this meeting suggested to Prior that at last the teachers had begun to focus.

The next stage in the Elliott model is reconnaissance. It has two components -description and explanation of the problem. The problem now became that (1) some pupils were not fully occupied in the class, and (2) how could this situation be improved? The first would be for research the second would be for discussion meetings. Prior now asked his colleagues to observe and record what happened in their classrooms. The questions to guide observation are shown in exhibit 8.2. The written results ranged from the diary type listing of events to reflection. The general conclusion was that teachers' lessons aimed at the average group and that those above or below this range were neglected.

At this stage Prior asked the teachers to shadow study a single pupil and to invite observers into their rooms (triangulation). Tape recorders were also provided. The principal assisted by supervising the class of a teacher who was observing. But at this stage Prior records that a crisis occurred (in so far as the investigation was concerned) because what was happening was not leading to change. He, therefore, decided to continue at a lower level and to concentrate on change in classrooms rather than at school/staff level.

Ten hypotheses had emerged as a result of classroom observation. It was accepted that there was a serious problem that centred on teacher's problems in dealing with students of all ability levels. It was proposed that there should be an in-service but for a number of reasons including the failure of the university (this writer) to come up with a facilitator it never ran. There were now only 5 weeks left. So Prior decided to ask teachers to become researchers in their own classrooms and to devise, implement and evaluate a lesson that took into account the earlier findings and the hypotheses they generated. The results were of some interest. One teacher whose study is fully recorded was very successful but found the exercise exhausting.

Teachers were also asked to submit any aspect of learning that interested them, and an interview with the principal was also conducted.

Prior points out that while many teachers said that change was not possible because of class size one teacher had actually achieved such change.

This is by no means all but that is not for this text. While the project met with many vicissitudes there is no way that it can be regarded as a failure. It may not have achieved its goals but like any action research it achieved many things en-route. First, it showed that many teachers find it difficult to reflect and have to be helped if they want to achieve a new level of thinking. Second, the whole process is lengthy. Prior felt that if he were to do it again he would shorten the process of finding the problem. Perhaps, however, teachers should go through that lengthy process. Third, at the time he wrote he did not see a direct connection with the whole school plan. When he undertook the project whole school planning was in its infancy. Similarly research on TQM (Total Quality Management) in educational institutions was only beginning to appear in books and journals. It seems clear from this research that a school that concentrates on a project like this over a year is likely to achieve much more than the engagement of different small groups in small projects. Here the whole school was involved in a problem of teaching mixed-ability groups, a problem that is still with many teachers. It is in this sense that we begin to understand the concept of teamwork in schools. Fourth, the project indicates, as does the recently published project on the Transition Year53 that there is much more to the design of instruction than is currently thought to be the case. Fifth, the conduct of the project provided a *chocs des opinions* and began to get the teachers thinking outside of their normal frames of reference.54 Instructional leaders will find the maintenance of such attitudes difficult unless agreed changes are built into the curriculum. Sixth, although teachers believed they were constrained by a *received* curriculum and large class sizes they nevertheless, were able to undertake developments within these constraints. In all, during this period the school was of the kind described by Cohn and Kottkamp - inquiry-oriented and the teachers were acting as extended professionals.

Aim

To gather evidence from classrooms which is relevant to the following problem; There are some pupils who are not fully occupied in class. How can this situation be improved?

Guidelines

Teachers are asked to observe and describe the fact of the situation, using the following suggestions:

Which pupils are not adequately occupied in class?

What are such pupils doing when they should be working?

Do pupils so behave during a particular type of class or teaching or at certain times of the day?

Any other instance and circumstances of time-wasting noticed.

Exhibit 8.2. Prior's Guidelines for his colleagues for observation of their classes.

Notes and references

[1] See for example Carr-Saunders, A and P. A. Wilson (1933) *The Professions*. Frank Cass, London.
Johnson, T (1971) *The Professions and Power*. Macmillan, London.
Lees, D. S. (1966). *The Economic Consequences of the Professions*. Institute of Economic Affairs, London.
Marshall, T. H (1939). The recent history of professionalism in relation to social structure and social policy reprinted in T. H. Marshall *Sociology at the Crossroads*. Heinemann, London (1966).
Moon, J. A. (1992) *The Evolution of an Ethical Code for Professional Mechanical Engineers*. Ph. D. Thesis, University of Brighton.
Prandy, K (1965). *Professional Employees. A Study of Engineers and Scientists*. Faber and Faber, London.
For more recent work see Abbot, A (1988). *The System of the Professions*. Chicago University Press, Chicago.
Burrage, M and R. Torstendahl (eds) (1990) *Professions in Theory and History*. Sage, London.
[2] Helsby, G (2000) *Changing Teachers' Work*. Open University Press cited by Knight, P. T and M. Saunders (1999) Understanding teachers' professional culture through interview: a constructivist approach. *Evaluation and Research in Education* 13, (3), 144 – 156.
[3] Heywood, J (1983) Professional studies and validation in C. H. Church (ed). *Practice and Perspective in Validation*. Society for Research into Higher Education, London.
[4] Clarke, P (2000) "The autonomous school" in special issue of Proceedings for the Society for Management in Education Ireland. Subsequently published as "Informed Discretion: Redefining the Autonomous School" in Heywood, J and P. Taylor (eds) School Autonomy. *Bulletins of the European Forum on Educational Administration* No 2 pp 47 – 60.
[5] *loc cit* Johnson 1971, Moon, 1992 ref 1, and Houle, C. O (1980). *Continuing Learning in the Professions*. Jossey Bass, San Fransisco.
[6] *loc cit* Prandy (1965) and Moon (1992) ref 1.
[7] Moon, J (1968). *The Ethical Attitudes of Chartered Mechanical Engineers and their Relationship to Formal Education*. Mlitt Thesis. University of Lancaster, Lancaster.
[8] Brown, F. K (1983) Technical ethics. *Engineering Education* 73, (4), 298 – 300.
[9] The Royal Academy of Engineering (2005). *Proceedings of a Conference on Ethics and the Engineer*. Royal Academy of Engineering, London.
[10] Clements, I and I. Roberts (1980) Practitioner views of industrial needs and course content in J. Heywood (ed) *The New Technician Education*. Society for Research into Higher Education, London. Newspaper reports in 1999 suggested that the British Government was not enamoured with the nursing degrees that had been introduced during the eighties and nineties, which were not thought to be sufficiently practical.
[11] Oliver, E (2000) Accountability in the classroom: a key issue in talks on teacher pay. *Irish Times*, p 14. 24th January.
[12] See chapter 8 of Heywood, J (1989). *Learning, Adaptability and Change*. Paul Chapman, London. See Lord David Lipsey in *The Times*, January 20th 2000 on the reason for opposing in the House of Lords in Britain a bill to reduce the right to trial by jury in certain circumstances.
[13] *Sunday Independent* (Ireland) 11th November 2007. Report of the Competition Commissioner on the ability of the Law Society in Ireland to regulate itself.
[14] Hoyle, E and A MacMahon (1976) in Hoyle, E (1984) The Professionalism of Teachers. A paradox in P. Gordon (ed) *Is Teaching a Profession ?* Bedford Way Papers No 15. University of London Institute of Education, London. See also Hoyle, E (1973) Strategies for curriculum change in Watkins, R (ed) *Inservice Training Structure and Context*. Ward Lock, London. also cited in Heywood (1984) p 160
[15] A term coined by Eisner. He argued against the scientific approach to curriculum study. He argued that there was a need for educators to develop a technique of evaluation

similar to the kind of criticism used in art which he calls educational connoisseurship. *"The consequence of using educational criticism to perceive educational objects and events is the development of educational connoisseurship. As one learns how to look at educational phenomena, as one ceases using stock responses to educational situations and develops habits of perceptual exploration, the ability to experience qualities and their relationships increases..."* Eisner, E (1979) *The Educational Imagination: On the Design and Evaluation of Educational Programs.* Collier Macmillan, New York.

[16] Cohn, M. M and R. B. Kottkamp (1993) *Teachers. The Missing Voice in Education.* State University of New York Press, Albany.

[17] Lortie, D. C (1975). *Schoolteacher: A Sociological Study.* Chicago University Press, Chicago.

[18] *loc.cit* ref 16 p21

[19] *ibid*

[20] *ibid*

[21] *ibid*

[22] see Hesseling, P (1966) *A Strategy for Evaluation Research.* Van Gorcum, Aassen.

[23] Eggleston, J (1977) *The Sociology of the School Curriculum.* Routledge, Kegan and Paul, London. The *received* paradigm arises from the belief that there is a fixed body of knowledge which has to be handed down from generation to generation. It is structured by disciplines and while the disciplines tend to persist, although differently arranged in different countries, (as for example the UK and the US where social studies incorporates history and geography). The content in the disciplines is subject to change and is often the subject of heated public debate as for example what should be taught in history and what should be taught in English in both the UK and US. The philosophical studies of Paul Hirst lend support to a *received* view of the curriculum, as does the psychology of Jerome Bruner. An opposite paradigm stems from the view that knowledge is relative to the person and that the curriculum can be negotiated. Eggleston calls the paradigm of a curriculum based on this kind of epistemology *reflexive*. He sees value in each and suggests a *restructuring* paradigm that involves elements of both. See also Heywood, J (1984) *Considering the Curriculum during Student Teaching.* Kogan Page, London.

[24] Clandinin, D. J and F. M. Connelly (1992) The teacher as curriculum maker in P. W. Jackson (ed). *Handbook of Research on Curriculum.* Macmillan, New York.

[25] *ibid.*

[26] *ibid.* They refer to large reform oriented projects in the US and UK. They note that Canada, America and Israel adopted previously developed projects and that the OECD carried out curriculum adaptation projects in Ireland and Scotland. Projects conducted in Austria, Germany and Sweden are also discussed. In their discussion of the UK they detail the Humanities project to illustrate some of their points. They do not, however refer to evaluation of some of the mainstream examination syllabus projects eg Waring, M (1979) *Social Pressures and Curriculum Innovation. A Study of the Nuffield Foundation Science Teaching Project.* Methuen, London

[27] *ibid* p 377 *"The literature suggests an alliance between reformers and researchers with policy makers and school administrators-that somehow if these groups work together more closely, they would be able to force reforms through the conduit of the classrooms."*

[28] ibid p 373. Anyone who is asked to participate in a project is "involved" in the project but the degree of involvement may be peripheral. There is in these conditions no guarantee that the teacher will do what the centre expects. See Munro, R. G (1977) *Innovation: Success and Failure.* Hodder and Stoughton, London. Clandinin and Connelly suggest that the UK Geography 14-18 Project,The Australian Learning Objectives for Vocational Schools Projects and the German Mathematics projects represent a continuum, as ordered, in the degree of teacher responsibility for the ideas and materials developed citing Gary, R., Connelly, F. M and E. Ditman (1975). Interpretative Case- Study of Selected Projects in P. Dalin (ed) *Handbook of Curriculum Development,* OECD, Paris p 105

[29] *ibid* p 374

[30] *loc.cit* Ref 16

[31] Youngman, M. B., Oxtoby, R., Monk, J. D and J. Heywood (1978). *Analysing Jobs*. Gower Press, Aldershot.
[32] Elliot, J (1976) Preparing teachers for classroom accountability. *Education for Teaching* 100. Pp49 - 71 cited by Heywood, J (1984). *Considering the Curriculum during Student Teaching*. Kogan Page, London.
[33] Tobin, K (2007) Mst Thesis. University of Dublin, School of Education.
[34] Shulman, L. S (1986) Paradigms and research programs in the study of teaching. A Contemporary perspective in M. C. Wittrock (ed) *Handbook of Research on Teaching*. 3rd edition Macmillan, New York.
[35] La Boskey, V. K (1994) *Development of Reflective Practice. A Study of Pre-Service Teachers*. Teachers College Press, Columbia University Press, New York.
[36] also cited by LaBosky *ibid*.. Shulman, L. S (1988). The dangers of dichotomous thinking in education in P. P. Grimmett and G. L. Erickson (eds) *Reflection on Teacher Education*. Teachers College Press, Columbia University, New York.
[37] Cowan, J (2006). *On Becoming an Innovative University Teacher. Reflection in Action*. SRHE/Open University Press, Maidenhead.
[38] Brookfield, D (1995). *Becoming a Critically Reflective Teacher*. Jossey Bass, San Fransisco p 42. This view of the reflective teacher is taken by MacKernan, J (1996). *Curriculum Action Research. A Handbook of Methods and Resources for the Reflective Practitioner*. Kogan Page, London.
[39] Angelo, T and K. P. Cross (1993). *Classroom Assessment*. Jossey Bass, San Fransisco
[40] Drucker, P (1999) *Management Challenges for the 21st Century*. Harper Collins, New York.
[41] *loc.cit* Ref 16 p 263. Schaefer, R. J. (1967) *The School as a Center of Inquiry*. Harper and Row, New York.
[42] *ibid* p 265
[43] *ibid* p 264
[44] *ibid*. Cohn and Kottkamp p 266
[45] *ibid* p267 and Polyani, M (1967). *The Tacit Dimension*. Doubleday, Garden City NY
[46] *ibid* and Argyris, C and D. A. Schön. *Theory in Practice. Increasing Professional Effectiveness*. Jossey Bass, San Fransisco.
[47] *ibid* p 283
[48] Prior, P (1985) *Teacher self-evaluation using classroom action-research. A Case study*. M.Ed Thesis. University of Dublin, Dublin
[49] *loc.cit* and Elliott, J (1981). *Action-research: a framework for self-evaluation in schools*. Mimeo. Cambridge. For more recent comments Elliott, J (1991) *Action Research for Educational Change*. Open University Press, Milton Keynes. (reprinted 2001)
[50] *Loc.cit*. George, J and J. Cowan ref 2 p 93 and 94. Also O'Neil, M. J. and L. Jackson (1983). Nominal Group Technique; a technique for initiating curriculum development in higher education. *Studies in Higher Education*, 8, (2), 129 – 138.
[51] *loc cit*
[52] 1 *ibid*
[53] Heywood, J and M. Murray (2005) Curriculum Led Staff Development. Towards Curriculum and Instructional Leadership in Ireland *Bulletins of the EFEA* No 4 pp 3 – 97. (European Forum on Educational Administration)
[54] see ch 2 Hesseling

CHAPTER 9

LEADERSHIP

Introduction

Most organizations depend for their functioning on the performance of a variety of roles. In many schools principals (head teachers) combine administrative, managerial and leadership roles if it is thought necessary to persist with a sharp differentiation between management and leadership. Just as it was argued, firstly in chapter 1 that every person is to a greater or lesser extent a manager so it is argued here that each person is to a greater or lesser extent a leader. In both cases the extent of the exercise of management and leadership is how the person interacts with the organisational culture in which the person finds himself or herself. The focus of this chapter is on the leadership dimension in schooling.

Volumes have been written about leadership in the past fifty years. One consistent finding is that many people report that the worst most stressful aspect of their job is their immediate supervisor. Pfeffer and Sutton did not have their tongue in their cheek when they suggested that the most important part of selection is to avoid bad leaders rather to search for great ones.

To a large extent this chapter is complementary to the preceding chapter but it hopes to add to the insights already given and seeks to further examine what it is we want from the persons we call leaders (managers). One approach to finding an answer to this question is trait theory. We try to describe from empirical studies the kind of traits that are representative of good and poor leadership. We describe them in pictures, profiles if you will. Clearly traits relate to management style. Since this book is about learning the discussion on styles begins with one derived from Kolb's theory of learning. His Learning Styles Inventory has been widely use among managers. Murray in his proposal for a self renewing school show how the Kolb model can be applied to the curriculum, design, evaluation process as strategic planning exercise for the shole organization.

Numerous styles and inventories to assess them have been proposed and some are considered here including the Blake Mouton grid. Perkins has classified these styles of leadership within four categories. These are- Answer- centred, Vision-Centred, Inquiry-Centred, and Leadership by Leaving Alone. In theory a school is an ideal organization for inquiry centred leadership and the focus of this text has been on the school as a learning organization. In this context learning and renewing have the same objective even if they are not perceived to be the same activity An example of an inquiry oriented project is given. Perkins places the "servant leader model" with which the section ends within the inquiry-centred category.

Leading and Following

It is now twenty years since I drafted the lectures on leadership that became the chapter on that topic in *Learning, Adaptability and Change.* One would have supposed that in the eighteen years that followed publication much would have changed. In some ways it did but not to the extent that it changes the original argument. There were changes to be sure, not least among them the huge growth in the number of business books published. According to the Stanford management academics Pfeffer and Sutton writing in 2006 there were 30,000 business books in print and 3,500 new titles are published each year. Add to that the increase in the number of journals devoted to management and the consequent growth in the number of articles, then anyone investigating the field is faced with a daunting task. In respect of the subject of leadership, they found some 15,000 peer-reviewed articles had been published since 1975. Amazon.com gave 110,000 listings.[1] In one way, this number makes for an impossible task, but the task is simplified for the reader because the number of books on the shelves of shops is limited. Unfortunately, however, they often try to sell a particular idea and between the books there are many inconsistencies and contradictions. For every thesis that is published there is a contradictory argument in another book. Pfeffer and Sutton provided a short but telling tabulation of books that said one thing with books that said the opposite.[2] In this text in an earlier chapter *"In Search of Excellence"* which is still marketed was contrasted with *"The Icaurus Project"* that asked a somewhat different question about why excellent organizations failed. The view that I have taken is that useful ideas were found in both books that could contribute to the theme(s) I wished to develop. We should not be bound by the axioms in one or the other book: Rather we should use them to reflect on ourselves, and the actions we would like to take in the contexts in which we live and act. This is what Perkins calls reflective intelligence. It is why I defined management as intelligent behaviour in Chapter 1. It is *"the contribution of general strategies, disposition, and mental management to intelligent behaviour."*[3]

These articles and books contain a wealth of argument, information and polemic on leadership. One might be forgiven for thinking that there are almost as many definitions of leadership as there are articles. Be that as it may these twenty years have seen the growth of educational management as a formidable subject. Fifty years ago in the UK it used to be thought of as educational administration, then the term management was introduced and now leadership. At the risk of offending many friends and colleagues the British Educational Management and Administration Society felt it necessary a few years ago to become the British Educational Leadership, Management and

Administration Society. I do not think it fanciful, perhaps cynical, to suppose that some of those involved in the change were concerned with the status of the society and in British culture felt that the inclusion of leadership added status. After all were not those in charge of the vegetable stands, meat counters, and grocery shelves in the supermarkets now called managers. The search for world-wide status led the British Institute of Management to drop the British from its title and then to seek a Royal Charter. Another way of looking at this in cultural terms is to see that change as the coming of age of a middle class profession, one more professional than that of teaching, for in the future managers will in a sense be self-employed. In 1999 before the Institute obtained its Royal Charter Handy considered the implications of the changing role of managers for their careers. *"The emergence of managers as would be professionals has meant that individuals now believe in transferable skills and resent patronage or paternalism. The obverse of this, of course, is that the organization has no obligation to hire the professional when his or her services are no longer required [...] managers will have to become proactive in the development of their careers."*[4] Teachers in state-provided systems of education are largely protected from such change but they are not protected from the need to search for status and that has led to unreal distinctions between management and leadership. It may be argued that in the job of the Principal it is practically impossible to distinguish between the two because however badly done, a Principal is expected to occupy a number of roles. Borrowing from Minzberg, Handy summarizes these roles as leading, administering and fixing. *"The mix of roles varies from job to job. Top jobs have a larger element of "leading" roles, first line supervisory jobs more "fixing" while middle layer jobs are inevitably landed with administering and informational roles – but every job has some of each."*[5] Handy said that one of the reasons for using these colloquial categories was *"partly because they are easy to remember and partly to emphasize that 'managing' includes leading, administering and fixing."*[7] Handy points out that the mix of roles is to some extent dependent on the size of the organization and this is no different for schools. Moreover the nature of the problems faced by a school at a particular time may affect the relative importance of the different roles. Missing from Handy's discussion is any comment on responsibility as it relates both to the 'actuality' and the 'feeling' of management. However, in relation to the previous point on professionalism he suggests that in professional organizations such as civil service and the law professional leadership is separated from administration and fixing, moreover they have eschewed such titles as manager. Thus the finance person in a private school or university college is often known as the Bursar. But managerialism of this kind has made serious inroads into schools and colleges. My own university has recently appointed a chief operating officer! He also suggests that it is only in business that the term management is used to embrace all three roles. Yet principals (head teachers) have to combine all three roles especially in small schools but the current focus of much recent writing and research is about the leader aspect of the role. So do they make a big difference? Do Leaders make a difference?

For many people the notion of leadership derives from their knowledge of what have sometimes been called "hero" leaders, for example individuals such as Winston Churchill and Martin Luther King jnr. Such leaders are considered to have had very positive effects but as Pfeffer and Sutton point out leaders like Hitler and Stalin had profoundly negative effects.[8] They go on to cite research which shows that organizational leaders at all levels of scale, small and large can make a difference for better or worse. This is as true for schools as it is for any other organization. A review of investigations on school effectiveness showed that there is a core of consistency to be found across the studies conducted in different settings in different countries.[9] The reviewers concluded that there were eleven key characteristics that contributed to an effective school. These are shown in exhibit 9.1. The first is professional leadership.

Within the research on leadership a block of fifty years of research into organizational climate consistently shows that 60% to 75% of the employees in any organization irrespective of occupational group *"report that the worst most stressful aspect of their job was their immediate supervisor."* [...] *"abusive and incompetent management create billions of dollars of lost productivity each year."*[10] Yet in spite of all the research that has been done there are still bad leaders *"who destroy the health, happiness, loyalty and productivity of their subordinates."*[11] It happens all the way down the chain and even persons of minor significance in the organization have leadership roles that effect the climate of the organization. The morality of the *"every person a leader (manager) approach"* is that everyone has responsibility for organizational climate and the direction the organization takes however the performance of an organization is measured, the effects of top leadership on that performance are likely to be modest in most organizations. So while many factors intervene to influence performance the contribution of each person to the organizations performance remains significant when aggregated. Pfeffer and Sutton suggest that perhaps the most important goal of selection is to avoid bad leaders rather than to search for great ones.[12]

---

1. Professional leadership
2. Shared vision and goals.
3. A learning environment.
4. Concentration on teaching and learning.
5. Purposeful teaching.
6. High expectations.
7. Positive reinforcement.
8. Monitoring progress.
9. Students rights and responsibilities.
10. Home-school partnership.
11. School based development.

Exhibit 9.1. The Eleven Characteristics that contribute to an effective school.[13]
Mortimore defined an effective school as one in which students' progress further than might be expected from its intake of students. An effective school thus adds value to its students' outcomes in comparison with other schools serving similar intakes.

Ultimately, effective management depends on people, and we have expectations of those persons. More often than not, we become disappointed with the performance of people in top posts and their charisma fades. This is a problem for principals who have been in post for a long time and from which there is little escape. Most of the people regarded as leaders in very top jobs who have been asked to discuss the qualities of leadership can be shown to have made many mistakes in their careers. The popular management journals and business columns of the newspapers are full of the success stories of companies that, a year or so later, are found to be wanting. We all know of schools that have reputations that decline and make a comeback, perhaps under new management. It would seem almost as if leadership is a short-lived quality. The most important art in leadership might be to know when to give up and hand on to someone else. But that is fairy-eyed if there is nowhere else to go. Change may not be important if there is sustained growth (however growth might be defined in terms of a school), but come a time of stagnation or renewal different qualities may be required. It is not surprising, therefore, to find that writers and researchers often classify leaders into 'types' for the purpose of establishing what makes a leader and as a by-product answering questions about the nature of leading and leadership. The same can be said of management.

Leading implies following. To the extent that we set ourselves goals , and to the extent we set about obtaining those goals, we both lead and follow. Just as every individual is a manager so, too, is every individual a leader. Because, this is the case, each individual has with him or herself the attributes of leadership. What distinguishes one person from another as a leader is the use to which they put their attributes of leadership in the varying situations they find themselves. In some situations they may find they can lead well while in other situations they may find they are disaster. Leadership is, therefore, partly a function of personal disposition, personality if you like, and partly a function of the situation that embraces an individual at a particular time. This is as true of the individual who seeks a goal that is largely independent of others, as it is of the individual who has to direct and control a group of persons in pursuit of a common goal. Thus it is that leadership almost inevitably involves management and vice versa. Just reflect on the duties a principal has to carry out on a daily basis. Very often they have to 'fire fight' and if they do not put the fire out it can have consequences not merely for a class of pupils but for the school as a whole. Apart from that there are a whole lot of routine duties that need to be done to keep the ship afloat. If the staff do not think the principal makes a good job of everyday management it is hardly likely to inspire them to pursue a strategic vision. But that is not all there is to leadership because some people, like the prophets, cause people to follow whatever it is they are called upon to follow, without actively involving themselves in the organization. Others do the management for the leader. But in schools to quote the authors of a best selling text on educational management, *"leadership is an indispensable part of management,"* and for this reason they did not *"think it helpful to create an impermeable boundary"* between the two.[14] This is also my position for principals are expected both to manage and lead. But, as we have seen, exactly what this means depends on the expectations that others have and how they might conflict with the managerial and leadership ideas and actions actually offered. Evidently, as is clear from the previous chapters leadership (management) is a complex activity and this makes its study complex. To a large extent this chapter is complementary to the preceding chapters but it hopes to add to the insights already given. So what is it we want (look for) in the person whom we call a leader (manager)?

Factors contributing to leadership

Many attempts have been made to understand the factors contributing to leadership in organizations.[15] There have been studies of leaders in the military, political and industrial fields that have contributed to our understanding of the many facets of leadership, and to the development of leadership training programmes. Among the approaches to the study of leadership that have been taken are trait theory, style theory, situational theory and path-goal theory.

(a)   Trait theory

Adair calls qualities such as 'initiative', 'perseverance', 'integrity', 'humour', 'tact' 'compassion' etc., traits.[16] There are many more. These particular examples are taken from Adair because he uses them in pairs to show how they relate to three areas that embrace an organization and its goals. These are the 'task', the 'team' and the 'individual.' For example 'initiative' and 'perseverance' have functional value in respect of the task: 'integrity' and 'humour' in respect of the team: and 'tact' and 'compassion' in respect of the individual. In the early trait research, no account was taken of the needs of the employee – neither was their relative importance specified. In Adair's framework the use of qualities takes care of these objections. He developed a programme of training that was designed to help individuals to understand the characteristics of leadership, if they possess them, and if they don't, and to perceive whether they could develop themselves through such training. Adair's readers are invited to rate, for their importance to leadership 25 items such as enterprise (13), astuteness (15), capacity to speak lucidly (14), willingness to take risks(12), ability to meet unpleasant situations (10), and analytical ability (7). The numbers in brackets showed how they were rated by a cross-section of managers. The first five from the 25 in order of significance were the ability to take decisions, leadership, integrity, enthusiasm, and imagination. I would suggest that this is what any group (students, family, sports people, industrialists, members of the church, politicians) expect of their leaders. The other qualities are important but not as important so it seems. It seems self evident that positive (good) leaders require self-confidence, justice, moral courage, and consistency. Handy's analysis of trait theory suggests that intelligence (but not overwhelmingly so), initiative and self-assurance are important.[17] (See below).

We respond to trait analysis. Writing in *The Sunday Independent* (21:12: 2008) Kenny reported a study by the University of California and the Irish Management Institute of more innovative Irish leaders and found that they were productive. They *"got things done, they have levels of aspiration; high intellectual capacity, fluency in expressing ideas and quickly got to the heart of the problem; they are responsible and dependable; behave in an ethically consistent way; are candid and forthright with others; value their autonomy and behave assertively. The traits least characteristic of them are withdrawal in the face of frustration; self-pity, negative and obstructive attitudes; disorganization under stress; submissiveness; unpredictability in behaviour or attitudes, and a lack of personal meaning to life."* A quite a serious question is what is new for why should it be necessary to repeat such profiles? The same story is told in the literature on managers. Would it be to cynical to suggest that public service encourages rather more negative traits than it does positive?

Pfeffer and Sutton argue that irrespective of the situation leaders have to talk and act as if they are in control, hence the importance of self-assurance or confidence. *"They have to believe that their words and deeds actually shape organizational action and performance (although wise leaders don't believe in their own powers and superiority too much)."*[18] This is because say Pfeffer and Sutton *"everyone expects leaders to matter a lot, even if they have limited actual impact. Leaders need to act as if they are in control, project confidence, and talk about the future, even while recognizing and acknowledging the organizational realities and their own limitations."*[19] No where is this more important than in schools where the attempt by the controlling bureaucracy is to micro-manage.

It seems that it is very difficult to maintain a strict definition of traits. Handy for example includes helicoptering.[20] That is, *"the ability to rise above the situation and perceive it in its relations to the general environment."* This is surely a combination of the skills of synthesis and reflection and they lead to the definition of leadership offered by Pfeffer and Sutton. This is to the effect that *"leaders often have the most positive impact when they help build systems where the actions of a few powerful and magnificently skilled people matter least. Perhaps the best way to view leadership is as the task of architecting organizational systems, teams, and cultures – establishing the conditions and preconditions for others to succeed."*[21] One might ask, "what is the difference between those activities and management?"

Examination of programmes for social and life skill development that have been offered over the years among older students in schools suggests that some of them are programmes in leadership although they do not often use the term.[22] Perhaps they should. It is not, therefore, without significance that apart from intelligence differences in achievement are often accounted for in terms of traits. For example, the low-achieving student is often said to lack confidence and motivation. There is nothing worse than a manager who is perceived by his or her workers to lack motivation and worse, to allow others to provide that motivation. The British Government when it supported the Enterprise in Higher Education Initiative clearly thought new graduates, as a general species, lacked the personal transferable skills that would enable them to perform well in industry. Or, that if they possessed the traits with which these skills could be associated they were insufficiently developed.[23] It may be objected that I am creating confusion between stable personality traits and skills but some of the qualities cited as traits are clearly skills. The Government could find support for the Initiative in a substantial body of literature that considers that interpersonal abilities have considerable generality and substantively contribute to general competence[24] and I would add, confidence.

Trait theory will always have some importance if only because it employs terms commonly used to describe leaders. Ask experienced teachers on management courses to discuss the role of the principal, the chances are that they will produce a long list of traits or expectations. The trouble with such lists is that they require paragons of virtue rather than human beings to inhabit the office of principal. We like leaders to demonstrate initiative, self-assurance and decisiveness but as Handy has pointed out there are too many exceptions for some successful leaders do not possess all the traits.[25] He argues that good leaders are likely to have intelligence, initiative and self-assurance. However, while possession of these traits may be a necessary condition of success it is not a sufficient condition for it is an observed fact of life that some people with these traits are 'bad' leaders.

Nevertheless training schemes and selection procedures are often based on traits although they may not be specified. The best selection procedures are more likely to be based on the assessment of competencies and use relatively expensive methods of selection such as assessment centres although they are not designed to measure stable personality traits but situation specific skills.[26] Alverno College which has a strong management school, uses them as a learning device in their ability based curriculum.[27] One of the ideas that is given considerable attention in that College's curriculum is idea that learning and teaching styles are important. So to as management theory developed, more attention was paid to management styles and their effect on performance.

(b) *Leadership (Management) Styles*

There is some confusion about the term style in the literature. Although in earlier chapters theories X and Y have been associated with management styles, in this section I shall for the most part follow Perkins categories since they embrace various approaches to leadership that have been much discussed in recent years. Since this book is about learning this section will begin with a brief introduction to the idea of learning styles as generated in the work of Kolb.[28]

Among the talents that students bring with them to learning are dispositions to the way they organize, remember, and think about new knowledge. These are called cognitive or learning styles. They are to be distinguished from the strategies which students use when they are called on to learn something or another. Strategies are the ways students adapt to meet the rules of the game as for example those of assessment. Cognitive/learning styles are thought to play an important part in learning and study and in consequence have implications for the management of learning and therefore teaching.[29] Many styles such as convergent and divergent thinking have been isolated. It is commonly argued that teachers prefer convergent to divergent thinkers and because of that use approaches to teaching that favour convergent learning. It is not part of the purpose of this book to engage in a lengthy discussion of the many styles that have been suggested or the instruments for their measurement but rather to develop the idea of style in behaviour. For this purpose two inventories will be discussed. They are those due to Kolb, and Honey and Mumford. Kolb's theory of experiential learning is a derivative of Piagetian theory. Kolb proposes that the learning of concepts takes place in cycles that involve four processes. These are concrete experience (feeling) reflective observation (watching), abstract conceptualization (thinking), and active experimentation (doing). The process in the first quadrant is characterised by divergent thinking, in the second quadrant by assimilation, in the third quadrant by convergent thinking, and in the fourth quadrant by accommodation.

Divergent thinkers ask "why?" questions. Divergence relates to that part of the problem-solving process that identifies differences (problems) and compares goals with reality. Divergers are the opposite of convergers. Divergers are best in the situations of concrete experience and reflective observation. They like to "imagine" and generate ideas. They are emotional and relate well to people, but do not perform well in tests that demand single solutions. They like teaching strategies such as brainstorming and group work.

Assimilators ask "what?" questions. They are not so much concerned with people as they are with abstract concepts. They are interested in the precise and logical development of theory than its application. Kolb described them as pure rather than applied scientists. They tend to like problem solving by the instructor.

Convergers ask "How?" questions. Convergence relates to that part of problem solving that is related to the selection of a solution and the evaluation of the consequences of the solution. The dominant styles of convergers are abstract conceptualization and active experimentation. It is a mode of learning often associated with traditional learning (teaching) and assessment. They like tests with single solutions. They are not very emotional and tend to prefer things to people.

The accommodators ask "what if? questions. Accommodation is related to the selection of goals and the execution of solutions in the problem solving process. Their dominant strengths are concrete experience and active experimentation. They like doing things and want to devise and implement experiments. They are risk takers compared with those with the other learning styles. They are at ease with people although they are relatively impatient. They are creative problem solvers but rely on others for technical analysis.

In relation to the renewing school (see below) Murray has argued that any proposal towards the development of the "Renewing School" rests on the principle that the development of the teacher is central to the issue. Figure 9.1 shows how he applied the preferential learning style theory of Kolb to each stage of the curriculum design and evaluation process. He argues that when teachers have mastered the skills associated with the inventory in their day to day activities they *are able to participate effectively in the Analysis-Design-Implementation-Evaluation Cycle as a strategic planning exercise for the whole organization.*"[30] It is easy to see how this approach can be built into a model of an inquiry oriented school.

(c)   Other inventories and styles

There are other similar inventories. One due to Honey and Mumford distinguishes between activists, reflectors, theorists and pragmatists.[31] Their inventory is a derivative in the tradition of the Kolb theory. Here is their description of the activist. *"Activists involve themselves fully and without bias in new experiences. They enjoy the here and now and are happy to be dominated by immediate experiences. They are open-minded, not sceptical, and this tends to make them enthusiasts about anything new. Their philosophy is 'I'll try anything once'. Their days are filled with activity. They tackle problems by brainstorming. As soon as the excitement of one activity dies down they are busy looking for the next. They tend to thrive on the challenge of new experiences but are bored with implementation and longer-term consolidation. They are gregarious people constantly involving themselves with others but, in so doing, they seek to centre all activities around themselves."* The implications for leadership (management) should be self-evident as should be the reasons for giving learning style inventories in selection procedures. In this respect the Myers-Briggs Indicator (MBTI) is very popular.[32]

Clearly there is a relationship between learning and teaching styles and the question has been asked whether teaching styles should be matched to learning styles? Research at school level suggests that when an appropriate inventory is administered to pupils that the results are indicative of different dispositions in the class. This suggests that a teacher should teach a concept using the strategies appropriate to each of the styles of learning. There is some evidence that such an approach can be successful but the more important finding seems to be that when teachers know and accept their own styles they appreciate that sometimes they neglect the needs of some of their pupils. The evidence suggests that if teachers understand the learning dispositions of their pupils they can develop their understanding of the needs of those pupils. Applied directly to organizations as learning systems it suggests that workers will have different dispositions to learning and that this may account for some of their behaviour in the work place.

The same applies in leadership (management). Sixty or more years ago, as we have seen, distinctions were made between authoritarian and democratic styles of management. Theory X and Theory Y if you like. It will be noted that these styles have some affinity with teacher-centred and child-centred teaching. Tannenbaum plots the styles against 'concern for results' at one end of the spectrum and 'concern for relationships' at the opposite end.[33] Questions were asked about whether it was possible for a manager to change from authoritarian to democratic styles with success.. Such changes were not always successful. The former is autocratic and the latter democratic. In between are paternalistic and consultative styles.

One of the most used typologies is the Blake-Mouton Grid that relates the degree of concern for people in a 9-position matrix.[34] The Y axis of the grid plots from low to *'high concern for relationships:'* the X axis plots from low to high *'concern for results'*. The 1,1 style describes a person who makes minimum effort to get the work done required to sustain membership of the organization. At the other end of the diagonal the 9.9 style obtains work from persons highly committed in both directions, and creates interdependence throughout the organization through a common purpose. A 9.9 leader creates relationships of trust and respect and focuses on the team. 9.1 leaders focus exclusively on the task. 1.1 leaders are neither concerned with the task or people. 1.9 leaders avoid conflict at all costs and encourage people so long as they are doing their best. The 5.5 style in the middle of the matrix represents middle of the road leadership. A description of a principal in a secondary school offered by a post-graduate student said that- *"Overall staff have great confidence in his leadership of the school and his support for them in trying times. His ability to get post-holders to undertake duties for their renumeration as well as involving many*

other staff members places him in the 5.5 tending toward 9.9"
A principal placed in the 1.9 dimension was described as *"being
very much in the laissez-faire mode. An unwillingness to act
decisively when called on to do so and an avoidance of decision
making did not endear him to the staff."*

From his inventory Kolb argued that the different subjects of
the curriculum tended to attract students of particular dispositions. For example, business management requires accommoda-
tive thinking although as Whitfield[35] has shown for engineering,
(it is unlikely to be different in other subjects), that at sometime
in the process from research through design to manufacture
there is a demand for the use of all styles.

It will be evident that there is a link between style and trait.
This may be illustrated by the English *Leadership Programme
for Serving Head Teachers* which distinguishes between six
styles. The traits are shown in the brackets. They are- *Coer-
cieve (The do it the way I tell you style)*, *Authoritative (The
firm but fair style); Affiliative (People first, task second style);
Democratic (Participative style): Pacesetting (The do it myself
style)*, and *Coaching (The developmental style)*.

Perkins Classification of Styles

There is a general, if not explicit assumption in the foregoing
that leadership (management) style influences performance and
over the years, as has been shown, various styles have been advocated. Perkins has provided a useful classification and analysis.[36]
He has four categories. These are *Answer Centred Leadership,
Vision Centred Leadership, Inquiry Centred Leadership and
Leadership by Leaving Alone*. He defines these in relation to
what he calls the 'deal.' By 'deal' he means the commitment you
make to the achievement of certain goals in return for specified
rewards. It is easy to see how this relates to industrial situations
but teachers also enact a 'deal' to teach pupils in a school as
directed. Unlike workers in industry many teachers are not in

situations where they can receive bonuses. Their 'deal' is related to a fixed salary. There is a sense in which teachers have 'deals' with their pupils and also with the Principal. The 'deal' *can certainly get a good deal done in the world.*" Perkins argues that when the solution to a problem requires extra commitment it also leads to the *"whither and why questions of leadership: What can I do when people don't see the way forward, despite the 'deal' (the whither question)? What can I do when people aren't motivated enough to take the way forward, despite the 'deal' (the why question)?"* Some will say these are also the whither and why questions of management. Perkins four categories (he calls them 'forms) of management are:

Answer-centred leadership. *Declares what's to be done, how and why (This gives people the whither they need, leaving it mostly to the Deal to provide the why).* Perkins does not see this as theory X even though it is command and control leadership. It is also called transactional leadership because the deal is the transaction. He points out that it can lead to micro-management and authoritarianism that in some situations breeds fear. Like theory X it assumes that motivation occurs because of the deal: similarly there is no need to attend to the 'growth' needs of individuals or the groups in which they work. In such situations workers can become dependent on the leader and problems arise if the leader does not have answers to the question posed. (I have qualified this comment in chapter 10)

The second form of leadership is vision centred. *"It offers a strong energizing vision about the direction, along with great personal commitment. (The overall vision provides a broad whither, as well as an inspiring why)."* I associate vision and mission with Christianity and in particular the religious orders and congregations although its use in leadership arises from studies of leaders by Bennis and Nanus in the United States.[36] They had found that four strategies were important in leadership. One of these was vision. The others were communication, trust and self-knowledge. As Handy points out it is little use having a dream if you cannot communicate that dream or as I have found out provide a trigger that is sufficiently understandable for other people to work out the details. Engineers will often do this with drawings/sketches. For people to follow you they have to trust you, and to be trusted you have to know your strengths and weaknesses and be able to build on the strengths hence the need for self-assessment. Perkins points out that answer centred and vision centred leadership have something in common in that that they both offer answers even though the vision is the big answer and *"and gives overall direction and informs immediate plans."* One of the problems with visionaries is that some charismatics can be overzealous to the point of irrationality. Perkins cites the case of religious leaders who lead their followers to mass suicide or politicians who build their success on the hatred of other ethnic groups as is sometimes the case in Africa.

Perkins considers that the concepts of transformational leadership, visionary leadership and charismatic leadership are strongly related to his idea of vision centred leadership.

At a practical level Everard and Morris place vision in the perspective of having to describe the future. *"It pays,"* they say, *" to think operationally, so as to build a self-consistent picture that has a ring of reality about it, rather than to fantasize about a dream world in which unlimited resources are available and the laws of logic and arithmetic repealed."*[38] They cite Fullan[39] to the effect that vision building should be more of a corporate effort taking into account the personal visions of the staff and we might add parents.

An experienced teacher on a post graduate development course compared the work of two principals. On vision she wrote of one that[40]
- *"Y's vision is the effective school which is basic to school life*
- *The effective school illuminates the ordinary.*

- *Y articulates the vision of our school being an effective school in such compelling ways that it becomes a shared vision of the staff and, it illuminates their ordinary activities with dramatic significance.*
- *Y implants the effective school" in the structures and processes of the school so that people experience the vision of the effective school in the various patterned activities of the school.*
- *Y and the staff make day to day decisions in the areas of curriculum and instruction in a manner which reflects the values of the effective school.*
- *The staff and pupils celebrate in ritual ceremonies and art forms the effective school model."*

She associated the leadership of this school with this particular principal as "transformational."[41] He had replaced a leader whose style she rated as transactional but she did not come down on one side or the other. *"The ten years which have been the focus of this study have been an incredible experience for me. The transition from transactional to transformational leadership has sparked my own interest in management. The complexity of both individuals and their respective management styles is incredible. I feel a blend of traditional and modern is the best way forward. It is important not to lose the human touch in adopting the more formalised management approach. We all need to remember we are dealing with people, each of whom deserves our respect while also realising the possibilities that management theory open for any learning institution. In short, I want to reach for the stars while keeping my feet firmly planted on the ground."*

In Ireland some of the Religious Congregations have wanted to leave a legacy so that the schools for whom they are trustees carry on the mission they began. That is that their school should continue to transmit their values in the future. For this reason they have been concerned that schools as a corporate body develop mission statements that enshrine those values. Of course they are reliant on future generations of teachers ascribing to those values and this means that even if they do not teach in the schools now, under their trusteeship the schools are inspired to maintain that value system. A lay teacher in a denominational school links marketing and the need for a strategic plan to its mission. He wrote *"that schools are being forced into developing market strategies which should transform the school mission from an obsolete plaque on the wall to a vision for the future. The organization with clear purpose encourages the people who work in that organization to be committed and motivated [...] All marketing begins with an evaluation of how effectively a service is meeting with expecatations of the community and what the organization's strengths and weaknesses are in providing this service. An organization cannot carry out a successful marketing campaign unless the product being promoted is of an intrinsically high quality. According to Pfeiffer and Dunlap[42] 'if a school system is to be described in glowing terms, the school has to glow.'"*

Some years ago one of the leaders of the Christian Brothers Michael Murray evaluated an experimental programme (an introduction to management studies) in the Irish Transition year.[43] He was a participant observer. Later he developed a theory of whole school development based on his study of this move away, if only for a year, from the subject-based curriculum.[44] He presented a model of the ideal (renewing) school. His starting point was with the aims that the teachers set themselves. These required them to move from an academic subject-centred curriculum to a more needs-based approach sensitive to the changing demands of the individual, society, and the economy. They had to change from being traditional teachers to, facilitators and evaluators. Murray argued that this experience of change within a classroom and a subject would provide the insights and skills necessary for school renewal. In the previous section it was shown how Murray applied preferential learning theory to the involvement of all the teachers in the school. His model of the renewing school used terminology of which was based on that used by religious institutions for their own renewal.

The first part of any renewal process, (which follows the Kolb process of analysis-design-implementation-evaluation) is to return to the founding vision. This has to take into account the wider community in which the institution resides. In the language of the models of this text it is a return to the educational and social aims of the school. They have to be interpreted in terms of the curriculum and its implementation. Any renewal is an emotional exercise that involves the affective domain. The renewing school has to respond to needs for affiliation (N-Aff), power (N-Pow), and achievement (N- ach). *"As in the case of the ideal business, the corporate goal of the ideal school community it to provide each member within it, with a sense of belonging, power and achievement."*[45] Murray points out that at the cognitive level questions about the identity of the institution have to be answered. *"What business are we in? Whom do we serve? What service do we offer?"* He argues *"that the mutuality between the individual and corporate goals helps the individual to internalise goals and become engaged in the learning experiences which affect character change".* Thus Murray would understand a school to be a learning organization which is open and organic.[46] Organizations *"in which individuals understand their role in terms of the general aims of the organisation so that everyone contributes to the common goal and the head is not omnipresent."*[47] By identifying the learning styles of the school the leader can direct them to the appropriate phases of the innovation cycle and by repeated involvement in the cycle the school community is more able to participate in the innovation (renewal) cycle. The models are expressed in figures (9.1 showing the learning styles, 9.2 showing the Needs for achievement, affiliation and power and 9.3 showing the integrated relationships.

The programme that Murray had investigated was found to have emphasised the development of people in the belief that it is their creativity that makes a difference to organisational effectiveness. While a certain minimal level of resources were required- *"Freed from the constraints of externally imposed courses, the teachers were able to internalise goals. By anal-*

*ogy, it pointed to the possibility that a whole school staff could
exercise greater autonomy in the curriculum they offered. They
could adopt a set of corporate goals more compatible with the
goals of individual teachers than those dictated by a national
education authority. Because the internalisation of goals is better facilitated in such circumstances, the probability of organisational renewal is enhanced."*[48] That is some challenge to the
general community, policy makers, parents and peers.

It has to be appreciated that the teachers in this small project
acquired substantial training both formally and informally
at their own expense and initiative. This training, the details
of which have been given elsewhere, catered for the achievement, affiliation and power needs of the individuals involved.
This is in contrast to many training schemes that on functional
performance. These teachers were provided with a systematic
programme of study in the curriculum process. At the same
time they had to engage in that process. The teachers from the
participating schools including two principals, working in two
networks, were asked to design, implement, assess and evaluate courses in *learning how to learn* and *management studies*
for the Transition year programmes in their schools. They were
asked to design and implement a common method of assessment
to be used in all the schools in the network. They were asked to
run the networks themselves and to report back to the project at
regular intervals. The Transition Year Opportunity gave teachers the freedom and responsibility to develop their own curriculum within some very broad goals that it was expected would be
obtained. In this way the need for power was met. The problem
was that few teachers had any in depth knowledge of the curriculum process and it was the purpose of this project to provide
this knowledge and then see what the teachers, so trained, could
achieve. In this way their needs for achievement were met. They
could assess what their students had learnt, they could use other
evaluation tools if they wished and they could of course talk
with their students. Working particularly in the networks and
also with their students met their needs for affiliation. For these

networks to function the teachers had to be personally effective. Overall as Murray points out the process encouraged intrinsic motivation and personal development whereas the tendency in all the other years of post-primary schooling was for the system of public examinations to encourage extrinsic motivation. This is not say that dedicated teacher do not find intrinsic motivation in teaching it is to suggest that organizational constraints make it much more difficult. It is also to argue that an inquiry oriented school will encourage intrinsic motivation.

Murray's primary point is that experience of micro-projects of this kind provide the experience necessary for whole school renewal, and can provide the motivation and encouragement for the larger activity. All this is to suggest that schools should engage in micro-projects and this they will not be able to do unless they have the knowledge based resource of curriculum and instructional leaders. Clearly the organization that Murray envisages would have to be inquiry oriented for it to succeed and would require some form of inquiry centred leadership. I say some because Perkins argues that there are number of concepts in the literature that have the same spirit of inquiry as his inquiry centred leadership. He cites adaptive leadership, facilitative leadership, and servant leadership.

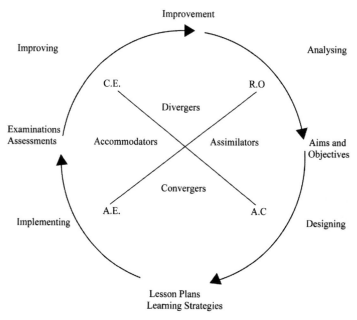

Improvement

Improving

Analysing

C.E.

R.O

Divergers

Examinations
Assessments

Accommodators

Assimilators

Aims and
Objectives

Convergers

A.E.

A.C

Implementing

Designing

Lesson Plans
Learning Strategies

Key to Diagram

C.E. Concrete Experience
R.O Reflective Observation
A.C. Abstract Conceptualisation
A.E. Active Experimentation

Figure 9.1 The experiential learning cycle and school renewal (Murray, 1994). *"The sets in the development of the renewing school are modelled in terms of Kolb's theory of learning. From the variety of individual learning styles, the skills associated with each of the stages in the Analysis-Design-Implementation-Evaluation innovation cycle are mastered, through participation in the school based innovations labelled respectively 1,2,3,4. The individual learning developed from involvement in school innovations, no matter how small, are directed toward the renewing school concept through repeated involvement in the experiential learning cycle."* Inquiry centred leadership *"fosters inquiry at various levels through questions, facilitation and establishing community and organizational structures supportive of inquiry."*[46]

Inquiry centred leadership *"fosters inquiry at various levels through questions, facilitation and establishing community and organizational structures supportive of inquiry.*"[49] In theory a school is an ideal organization for inquiry. It is hoped that in such an organization people will find *"their own particular whither within the overall agenda,"* and thus *"will develop more individual and collective ability and a sense of why. Besides, the leader may need the group's help to find a good direction."*[50]

Perkins takes an idea from Kanter that is very apt to schools. Kanter had distinguished between compartmentalization and segmentalism. Organizations need and schools necessarily have compartmentalized structures (classrooms and subject departments at post primary level) but Kanter argued that these need to be supplemented by participative structures. *"Parallel participative organization that deliberately mixes people from different levels and divisions"*[51] in the service of inquiry. It would seem to be a form of matrix organization. Inquiry oriented organizations rely on the intrinsic motivation of individuals and the leader helps them to figure out the whither and why questions. Perkins considers that fostering inquiry is difficult and that if a leader is not careful there can be underfacilitation in which case the organization can drift. Similarly the leader can appear to be open whereas in truth he already has his own answers. In genuine inquiry the leader has to follow the results wherever they lead. An example of inquiry oriented leadership is the approach used in the Public Examinations Evaluation Project in Ireland. As indicated in an earlier chapter this project was asked to develop and evaluate systems of assessment that would raise the level of cognitive skill assessed in public examinations. It was argued by the project team that the only way to do this was to train teachers in examinations and assessment design and then let them design and administer assessments on their students that would be evaluated. This would give an idea of what was possible in schools and ensure its plausibility. The teacher groups were assisted by project officers who offered advice as required. They also maintained the momentum of the project and evaluated the results.

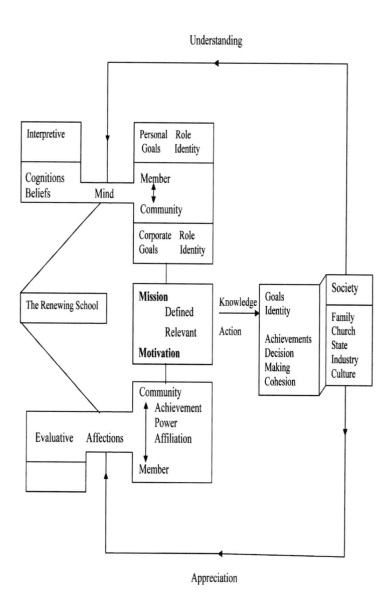

Figure 9.2. The Cycle of renewal in the renewing school (Murray, 1994)

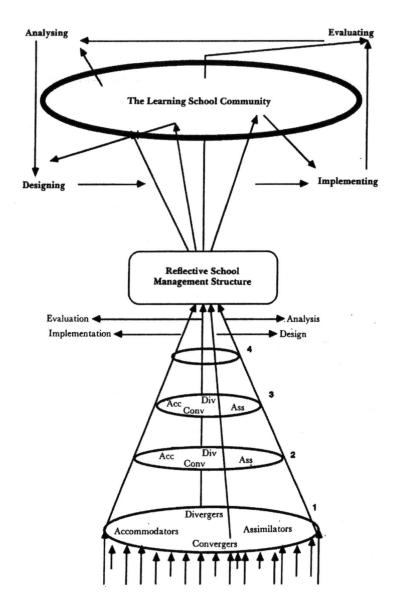

Figure 9.3. The individual learning styles are harnessed by the initiative and are directed by school management toward the development of a learning/problem solving school (Murray, 1990)

Perkins points out that this approach risks underutilising the knowledge of some people in the group who know much more than others, a problem that will be taken up in the next chapter. He also notes that a leader can be perceived to be weak or lacking in knowledge if it is not well done.

The final concept is of leadership by leaving alone. As Perkins points out it is or has been the norm in some groups, as for example academic departments in universities. *"Leaving alone does not speak directly to the whither and why questions. It declines to provide direction beyond whatever broad assignments are part of the picture. It does nothing specific to motivate people beyond the deal."*[52] There are individual's who need more structure who would find this approach to be psychologically insecure. Perkins rated the four forms for "leadership for intelligence" against the parameters of knowledge processing and the perception of the leader's behaviour –'symbolic content'. His interpretation is that on balance the preferred form is inquiry-centred leadership *"with [...], an appropriate mix of the others-that generates progressive interactions and spreads them throughout the group, creating a more intelligent collective."*[53] Servant leadership is a special case of inquiry-centred leadership.

The Servant Leader

The idea of servant as leader is to be found in a small pamphlet by Greenleaf.[54] He argued that in the early 1960s there was a crisis of leadership, and that this was in part due to the fact that individuals allowed the problems of our times to be dealt with wholly in terms of systems, ideologies and movements. Put in this way, we can see at once how pressure groups have arisen, and how the tendency of many people in all social classes to let others get on with the job is self-imposed alienation. In Greenleaf's dictum, individuals often deny themselves wholeness and creative fulfilment by failing to lead when they could. However, I have argued that most individuals do not perceive leadership to be a possibility. Nevertheless, with appropriately chosen learning strategies throughout their formal education, they can be brought to a greater understanding of leadership and the dependency factor in leadership. Like Greenleaf, one of the themes of this book is founded on the premise that the total process of education is indifferent *"to the individual as servant and leader, as a person in society."*[55]

Greenleaf holds the view that there are prophetic voices of wisdom and clarity speaking all the time. There are times when they are not heard, and these occur, as now, when the level of seeking and the responsiveness of hearers is low. The prophet grows in stature as the people respond to his message. Thus it is the seekers who make the prophet and the led who make the leaders. Both, by the action of choice, have obligations to each other. *"We listen to as wide a range of contemporary thought as we can attend to. Then we choose those we elect as prophets – with old and new- and mould their advice with our own leadings. This we test in real life experiences to establish our own position."*[56]

We do the same with the small things of life, the family, the local community and the job or the new job. Greenleaf puts his argument thus:
"A fresh critical look is being taken at the issues of power and authority, and people are beginning to learn, however haltingly, to relate to one another in less coercive and more creatively supporting ways. A new moral principle is emerging which holds that the only authority deserving one's allegiance is that which is freely and knowingly granted by the led to the leader in response to, and in proportion to, the clearly evident servant stature of the leader. Those who choose to follow this principle will not casually accept the authority of existing institutions. Rather, they will freely respond only to individuals who are chosen as leaders because they are proven and trusted as servants. To the extent that this principle prevails in the future, the only truly viable institutions will be those which are servant led."[57]

One of the problems Greenleaf sees, and it has been one of the several themes in this book, is that education is far too occupied with criticism and analysis. This is at the expense of those skills essential to creative leadership, which is to help everyone to grow as a person. It is leadership of community, of listening and understanding, of language and imagination, of acceptance and empathy, of awareness and perception, of healing and serving, of conceptualization, and of action. It is very optimistic, but as Collinson points out such leadership has to be tempered by realism.[58] Effective planning, for example, can cause human problems. Friendship does not mean that everyone should like each other. It does contain the ability to express honest hostilities while maintaining co-operation. One incongruity, irony if you prefer, is that much of what is proposed and enacted in programmes for low achievers contains all the ingredients of leadership training!

The concept of leadership put forward by Greenleaf, who was a Quaker will be understood by Christians, who may see it as modelled by Christ. But the notion of servant in the Gospel is somewhat different, and Christ is careful to point this out:

"A man can have no greater love that he lay down his life for his friends. You are my friends, if you do what I command you. I shall not call you servants any more, because a servant does not know his master's business: I call you friends because I have made known to everything I have learnt from my father."[59]

Modern education and the media, especially the media, have made us know and want to know our master's business but they have not made us friends. Therein lies the challenge to leaders and led, managers and managed. How then should the individual respond?

Every Individual a Leader

In previous chapters the view has been put that to all intent and purpose the processes of learning and decision making are the same. In all our everyday activities we show skill in management. The same applies to leadership. We all take on leadership roles in one way or another- mostly I suspect to get our own way but sometimes to help a group or a family to cohere and develop. We may even intervene in the role-set at work. In some work situations, such as school and college where there is a high level of democracy, we might even want to wield power through the group or committee, and that power might not be wielded with a positive purpose in mind.

Participation has been the 'in' thing for many years. This is as it should be, for are we not now better educated and better equipped to participate? But for many organizations this is far from the reality of the actual situation. We have to start at where we are. Collinson calls this "reality-centred" leadership, in which we all have a leadership role to play.[60]

One of the reasons conflict emerges particularly in democratic situations such as schools, and colleges is that we don't really want anyone to lead because management and leadership imply that we will not be left alone to pursue our own devices. Leadership implies change and many of us do not want to change. Peters and Waterman cite Ernest Becker who in *Denial of Death* wrote of the paradox in individuals that:

"Man thus has the absolute tension of dualism. Individuation means that the human creature has to oppose itself to the rest of nature (stick out). Yet it creates precisely the isolation that one can't stand- and yet needs, in order to develop distinctively. It creates the difference that becomes such a burden: it seems the smallness of oneself and the stickoutness at the same time."[61]

Our play when in a group is in no small measure a reaction to our perceptions of ourselves. We make judgements about our own capabilities and decide whether we can or would wish to lead. If we are deprived of leadership or do not enter the stakes, the tendency is to 'let the other chap get on with it[...]" We are no longer responsible.

It follows from the view that every person is a manager that everyone is a leader. Each role requires leadership, for each role requires the exercise of responsibility: each role requires that the individual understands the contribution he or she can make to the group leader's task. It is the philosophy (principle) that is missing from so many institutions and among so many people. That managers and leaders should have a defensible philosophy is essential for the first task of leaders of large and small groups is to build a value system acceptable to all, the pursuit of which engulfs the energy of the group.

If organizations have personality, so they also have culture and values. Systems or organizations are viewed as sets of ideas or conversations, *"the meaning of which has to be managed."*[62] Leaders give culture shape through the creation of language, ideology, myth, and ritual.[63] Peters and Waterman contend that the successful organizations they studied were rich in legend and parable, whereas unsuccessful companies were not. They go on to argue that where the culture was very dominant, the highest levels of true autonomy were to be found. It is within the culture that meaning is found and needs thereby satisfied and goals achieved. In the school system in England, for example, the defining differences between public (independent fee paying and for the most part boarding) schools and state schools are their cultures. The former, appear to be able to create a culture for learning more easily than some state schools. Possibly, in the same country, the success of faith schools within the state sector is a function of the culture they create.

This brings us full circle to role theory and the fact that culture is a conversation between roles. Just as we are likely to develop better skills of critical thinking, so we will perform better in groups the more we understand our roles and the way we interact with others. Belbin brings the idea of roles as presented in chapter 3 into sharp relief in terms of leadership and the management of groups[65](see page 54). He argued that each member in a team (group) has a functional role as well as team role. The teacher's functional role is clear, that is to teach. While presenting the functional aspect, the individual does this within a predetermined disposition, and this may be related to the way they choose (albeit unconsciously) act out team roles. Belbin argues that the team roles individuals adopt are limited to eight. Others have different ideas and types but the general principle is the same. That is, the way roles are played out can enhance or impede the work of the team.

It will be recalled from page ?? that these roles were the 'chairman' who is concerned with the attainment of objectives. The 'shaper' is the person who, in a group, always wants to bring everything together so that the project can be initiated and completed. Shapers are bundles of nervous energy able to challenge and respond to challenge. Evidently they need skill in synthesis. The 'plant' is the person with imagination who, when the team is bogged down, looks for new ideas. Together with the 'monitor-evaluator, he or she is highly intelligent. The monitor-evaluator brings dispassionate critical analysis to the problem. Tse calls him or her, a 'cold fish'.[66] The 'company worker' is the individual concerned with practical implementation. His or hers is a disciplined approach that requires plenty of character. The 'resource investigator' looks outside for ideas and brings them back to the group while the 'team-worker' is the one who understands the emotional needs of the group. The team-worker tries to promote unity and harmony. The 'finisher' is the anxious one; the individual who worries about detail; who wants to get things done properly. Of course some individuals in groups may take on more than one role.

Similar types to these will be found in any group and teachers in departmental or staff meetings are no exception. They will be found in gangs of children. Each type has its strengths and weaknesses, which Belbin has documented. While it would appear that individuals have a natural predisposition to some roles and always behave in a way associated with the role, it is possible in training exercises to develop them in these roles. They can also be located in the organisation in such a way that its structure demands that they play the role. Each of the roles has a managerial or leadership function that contributes to the success of the group and its overall leadership. Just as there is a time in management when the senior manager (ment) must be allowed to manage, so to an act of leadership is to allow a leader to lead. Taken together with the servant led model of leadership the concept of the every person a leader presented here is consistent with a concept currently in vogue --distributed leadership.[67]

A teacher in a post-graduate assignment discussed the role of the principal from two different perspectives that she had observed in schools. Put simplistically, like other participants before her she compared a democratic style with an authoritarian style of management. Her conclusion is somewhat different to what might have been expected and provides a suitable ending to this chapter.

"How", she asked, *"has this assignment changed my attitudes and how will it influence my behaviour in the future? Rather than seeing myself professionally as an individual independent wheel, I am now much more inclined to view myself professionally as one of many cogs ensuring the operation of a larger wheel. I have developed an awareness of the need to check every so often that I am in harmony and synchronization with all the other cogs. The concept of the school as an integrated whole of many different elements has come to the fore, rather than it merely being my place of work where I go and work largely in isolation and independently for five and a half*

hours a day. The multiplicity of relationships the complexity of the organization and the vast array of skills required by the leader of that organization have come very sharply into focus. I feel now that far more than having a right to contribute to policy formulation and input into the running of the school I have a duty to do so."

" " Each role requires leadership, for each role requires the exercise of responsibility: each role requires that the individual understands the contribution he or she can make to the group leaders task." "[68]

" It is against the backdrop of this altered perception of my professional position that I shall approach my job for the fore-seeable future."

Notes and references

[1] Pfeffer, J. and R. I. Sutton (2006). *Hard Facts. Dangerous Half-Truths & Total Nonsense. Profiting from Evidence-Based Management.* Harvard Business School Press, Boston, MA. p33

[2] *ibid* p34.

[3] Perkins, D (2003). *King Arthur's Round Table. How Collaborative Conversations Create Smart Organizations.* Wiley, New York p73.

[4] Handy, C (1999). *Understanding Organizations* 4th edition. Penguin, London. P339

[5] *ibid* p 322. Minzberg Interpersonal roles (Handy's leading), Figurehead-leader-liaison. Informational roles (Handy's administrating)- Monitor-disseminator-spokesman. Decisional roles (Handy's fixing) –Entrepreneur-disturbance handler-resource allocator-negotiator. Minzberg, H (1979) *The Structuring of Organizations.* Prentice Hall. Englewood Cliffs, NJ

[7] *ibid.*

[8] *loc.cit* p 189.

[9] Sammons, P (1994). Findings from school effectiveness research. Some applications for improving the quality of schools in P. Ribbins and E. Burridge (eds). *Improving Education. The Issue of Quality.* Cassell, London.

[10] *loc.cit.* p191. They cite Hogan, R., Murphy, G. J and J. Hogan (1994)What we know about leadership: effectiveness and personality. *American Psychologist,* 49, 493.

[11] *ibid*

[12] *ibid* p 194.

[13] Beginning some thirty years ago the school effectiveness movement spawned numerous research studies in the UK (a), and the US(b). These studies sought to establish the influence of schools, teachers and the education they provide on student achievement. They arose in response to studies in the United States that schools had a relatively small effect on performance (c). Since then the majority of studies in the UK and the US, although sometimes with different goals have been on inner city schools (d). It is only recently that studies have been undertaken that control (statistically) for the intake of students (e). This is important when, as in the UK, performance tables of schools are published in the national press.

It needs to be understood that definitions of effectiveness are dependent on a number of factors including the sample of schools evaluated, the choice of outcome measures, and control for the differences between institutions, methodology, and time scale i.e. i.e. longitudinal versus snapshots (f) [...]

The critical review of school effectiveness research already referred to pointed out that there were problems (not withstanding the above) in relation to its definition. There were also problems in relation to the type of evidence collected, methodology of analysis, and the transferability of data. It was concluded that there is a core consistency to be found across a variety of studies conducted in different settings in different countries (g)

(a) Rutter, M., Maughan, P., and J. Ouston (1979). *Fifteen Thousand Hours: Secondary Schools and their Effects on Children*. London, Open Books

(b) Goodlad, J (1984). *A Place Called School. Prospects for the Future*. New York, McGraw Hill.

Coleman, J. S. et al (1966). *Equality of Educational Achievement*. Washington, DC. US Government Printing Office.

Jencks, C. et al (1972). *Inequality: A Reassessment of the Effects of Family and Schooling in America*. New York. Basic Books.

(d) Sammons, P., Hillman, J., and P. Mortimore (1995) *Key Characteristics of Effective Schools. A Review of School Effectiveness Research*. London. Institute of Education, University of London.

(e) Mortimore, P., Sammons, P and S. Thomas (1995). School effectiveness. Assessment in Education. *Principles, Policy and Practice*, 1, (3), 315-352.

(f) Sammons, P (1994). Findings from school effectiveness research. Some applications for improving the Quality of Schools in P. Ribbins and E. Burridge (eds). *Improving Education. The Issue of Quality*. London., Cassell.

(g) *ibid* (d)

[14] Everard, K. B, Morris, G., and I, Wilson (2004) *Effective School Management*. Paul Chapman Publishing, London. P 22. For those who wish to make a differentiation they suggest that West Burnham (1977) *Managing Quality in Schools*. Falmer Press, London) sums it up thus *"Leading is concerned with vision, strategic issues, transformation, ends, people, doing the right things. Management is concerned with implementation, operational issues, transactions, means systems, doing things right."* This definition really highlights the fallibility of such distinctions for managers are clearly involved with people.

[15] see for example Dessler G. (1976) *Organization and Management* Prentice hall, Englewood Cliffs, NJ. Hunt, J. W. (1979). *Managing People at Work* McGraw hill, Maidenhead.

[16] Adair, J (1983). *Effective leadership. A Self-Development Manual*. Gower, Aldershot

[17] *loc.cit* ref 4 pp 98-100

[18] *loc.cit* ref 1 p 202

[19] *ibid* p 202

[20] *loc cit* ref 4 pp 98 - 100

[21] *loc.cit* ref 1 p 200

[22] See for example *Planning, Introducing and Developing Transition Year Programmes. Guidelines for Schools* (1986). Curriculum and Examinations Board, Dublin. In the UK Hopson, B and M. Scally (1981). *Life-Skills Teaching*. McGraw Hill, Maidenhead UK

[23] See for example Heywood, J (2005). *Engineering Education. Research and Development in Curriculum and Instruction* IEEE/Wiley, New York pp 38 to 47

[24] See for example Mentkowski, M and Associates (2000) *Learning that Lasts*. Jossey Bass, San Fransico. P 148

[25] *loc.cit* ref 4 p 99

[26] For a brief summary of Assessment Centre Technique see Heywood, J (2000) *Assessment in Higher Education. Student Learning, Teaching, Programmes and Institutions*. Jessica Kingsley, London. pp 323 and 324. The Assessment Centre is a multiple strategy approach to the assessment of performance in specified situations based on job/task analysis. It uses simulations to assess leadership; oral communication and presentation skills; written communication; planning and organizing; information gathering and problem analysis; decision making; delegation and control; self objectivity and disposition to lead.

[27] see ref 24 which is an evaluation of the unique curriculum offered by Alverno College in the liberal arts. For a brief summary see Heywood, J (1989) *Assessment in Higher Education* 2nd edition. Wiley, Chichester. 338 to 340

[28] Kolb, D. A (1984) *Experiential Learning. Experience as a Source of Learning.* Prentice Hall, Englewood Cliffs, NJ

[29] for definitions of cognitive style see Messick, S and associates (1976) *Individuality in Learning. Implications of Cognitive Styles and Creativity for Human Development.* Jossey Bass, San Fransisco.

[30] Murray, M (1994). From subject based curriculum development to whole school improvement. *Educational Management and Administration* 22, (3), 160 - 167

[31] Honey, P and A. Mumford (1992). *The Manual of Learning Styles.* Peter Honey, Maidenhead.

[32] Kiersey, D and M. Bates (1984). *Please Understand Me: An Essay in Temperament Styles.* Oxford Psychologists Press, Oxford. See also Kline, P (1993) *The Handbook of Psychological Testing.* Routledge, London.

[33] Tannenbaum, A. S (1966) *Social Psychology of the Work Organization.* Wadsworth, Belmot, CA

[34] For its application education see p 16 and 151 of Everard, K. B., Morris, G., and I. Wilson (2004) *Effective School Management* 4th edition. Paul Chapman, London. Original text Blake, R and J. Mouton (1964). The Managerial Grid. Gulf Publishing

[35] Whitfield, P. R (1975). *Creativity in Industry.* Penguin, Harmondsworth.

[36] Perkins, D (2003) *King Arthur's Round Table. How Collaborative Conversations Create Smart Organizations.* Wiley New York.

[36] Bennis, W and B. Nanus (1985). Leaders. *The Strategies for Taking Charge.* Harper and Row, New York.

[38] *loc.cit* ref 14 p 260

[39] Fullan, M (1993). *Change Forces.* Routledge/Falmer, London.

[40] She based this on a scheme by Starratt (1986) which she found in Beare, H., Caldwell, B and R. Millikan (1993). Leadership in M. Preedy (ed). *Managing the Effective School.* Open University Press, Buckingham.

[41] Transactional leadership. One in which there is an exchange of rewards for compliance. Transformational leadership influences followers by raising strong emotions and identification with the leader. See Yukl, G (1994). *Leadership in Organizations.* 3rd edition. Prentice Hall, Englewood Cliffs, NJ. Pp 352 –353.

[42] cited by Hanson, E. M. and W. Henry (19940 Strategic marketing for educational systems. *School Organization* , 12, (3) 255 – 265.

[43] Murray, M (1992). *An Evaluation of an Introductory Programme in Management Studies in Schools.* Doctoral dissertation. University of Dublin, Dublin. Murray participated in two studies of the transition year for details of the srecond see Heywood, J and M. Murray (2005) Curriculum-Led Staff Development. Towards Curriculum and Instructional Leadership in Ireland. *Bulletins of the EFEA (European Foundation on Educational Administration)* No 4 pp 3 – 97 for a history of the Transition year.

[44] *loc.cit* ref 30.

[45] *loc.cit* ref 30

[46] He cites Burns, T and G. Stalker (1961). *The Management of Innovation*, Tavistock, London.

[47] *loc cit* ref 38. He also cites Heywood, J (1989). *Learning Adaptability and Change.* Paul Chapman, London.

[48] *loc.cit* ref 30

[49] *loc.cit.* ref 36

[50] *ibid*

[51] *ibid* p 100. See Kanter, R. M (1983) *The Change Masters.* Simon &Schuster, New York.

[52] *ibid* p 103

[53] *ibid* p 106.

[54] Greenleaf, R. K (1973). *The Servant as Leader.* Windy Row Press, Peterborough, NH

[55] *ibid.*

[56] *ibid*

[57] *ibid*

[58] Collinson, L (1985). How to plan for people. *Management Today* June pp 94 – 98.

[59] John 15: 13 – 15.

[60] *loc.cit* ref55.

[61] quoted by Peters, T and R. H. Waterman (1982). *In Search of Excellence. Lessons from America's Best Run Companies.* Harper and Row, New York.

[62] Martin, J (1980) Stories, scripts and organization settings. Research report 543. Graduate School of Business Study, Stanford University. Stanford, CA. On the personality of organizations see Mant's comment on the work of Bion. Mant, A. (1979) *The Rise and Fall of the British Manager.* Pan Books.

[63] Pettigre, A. M. (1976) the creation of organizational culture. Joint EIASM/DANSK Management Seminar. For more recent work see ch 6 and work by Schein.

[65] Belbin, R. M. (1981) *Management Teams. Why they succeed or Fail.* Heinemann, London.

[66] Tse, K. K. (1985). *Marks and Spencer. Anatomy of Britain's Most Efficiently Managed Company.* Pergamon, Oxford.

[67] There are a number of articles that provide an introduction to distributed leadership as it is advocated in North America and Britain. Central to all discussions of leadership types, styles and organizations is whether this or that leadership leads to an improvement in outcomes. Harris, A (2004) Distributed leadership and School Improvement. *Educational Management, Administration and Leadership* 32, (10, 11 –24. In her exploration of the concept she draws attention to the view that distributed leadership is a *"way of thinking about leadership rather than as another technique or practice."* Taken in that sense it is consistent with the view of every person a leader put forward in this text. Harris writes *" in understanding leadership in this way it inevitably challenges assumptions about the nature and scope of leadership activity as it reconceptualizes leadership in terms of the leadership of the 'many rather than the few"* This of course cuts across hierarchies and pay structures. In the Irish context principal's have sometimes had to go outside the posts of responsibility structure to get co-ordinators for activities like the Transition Year. That is they have had to find expertise wherever it exists in the organization. That seems to be at the heart of distributed leadership ie. to engage expertise wherever it exists. In another work (Harris 2005) it is made clear that distributed leadership is not delegation but collective leadership rather than top-down authority. (Leading or misleading? Distibuted leadership and school improvement. *Journal of Curriculum Studies* 37, 255 – 265.That said there still appear to be difficulties in establishing exactly what distributed leadership is See Arrowsmith, T (2007) Distributed leadership in secondary schools in England: the impact of the role of the head teacher and other issues. *Management in Education.* 21, (2) 21 –27. Woods considers that there is some force in the criticism that distributed leadership is about sharing responsibility but concentrating power. He notes that concepts of distributed leadership and professional learning communities are bedfellows in the search for school improvement. (Woods, P. A (2007) Within you and without you: leading towards democratic communities. *Management in Education* 21, (4), 38 – 43).

[68] citing Heywood, J (1989) *Learning, Adaptabilty and Change.* Paul Chapman, London.

359

CHAPTER 10

EDUCATIONAL, CURRICULUM AND INSTRUCTIONAL LEADERSHIP

Introduction

The purposes of this short chapter are to discuss the role of the principal in curriculum and instructional leadership and to consider the role of curriculum and instructional leaders in distributed or delegated leadership systems. The concept of the curriculum is defined and from this the idea of curriculum leadership is derived. It is a sub-set of educational leadership and instructional leadership is a sub-set of curriculum leadership. From a typical analysis of the tasks that principals undertake, it is argued that while a principal should have the knowledge base that curriculum and instructional leaders have, the principal's function is to promote and support curriculum and instructional leadership within the framework of an inquiry oriented school.

The abilities required by curriculum and instructional leaders are described. The view is taken that instructional leadership does not begin with the principal but with individual teachers and this is the basis of accountability. The principal has the function of creating a culture in which instructional leadership can thrive at all levels within the organization. An important role that all teachers have is in the mentoring of beginning teachers and to help them on the path to instructional leadership.

Levels of instructional and curriculum leadership are defined and the skills associated with each discussed. How they relate to the inquiry oriented school and the need to assumption dig is considered. Level 1 is personal instructional leadership when the teacher regularly uses classroom assessment techniques to evaluate his/her own work. Level 2 is when the teacher is conversant with the research literature and conducts research into their own teaching. Level 3 is when, given they have the appropriate interpersonal skills and knowledge they are used to advise on matters of curriculum and instruction. Level 4 is when, given they have the appropriate knowledge and communication skills they participate in public debate from an evidence based perspective.

Beyond educational leadership.

The view contained in the Irish White Paper is far from American idea of the principal as instructional leader that expects principals to help failing teachers. This would not have been the intention of the White Paper since the irony is that there has been in post-primary education an unwritten convention that principals administrate and teachers teach. Principals do not enter a classroom for the purpose of observing instruction. Although teaching is for the exam the only sanction that a principal has for a permanent teacher who is failing is to keep him or her away from classes in the years that students take examinations. Four years ago (2005) the National Association of Principals and Deputies made a submission to the Minister that principals should be enabled to carry out their instructional leadership role and be relieved of some of the chores that caused them to be full time administrators. However, it seemed that neither the principals or the Minister had a clear understanding of what was meant by instructional leadership. The remaining pages of this short chapter attempt to clarify the concepts of curriculum an instructional leadership.

Curriculum and Instructional leadership

In order to define the roles of curriculum and instructional leaders it is necessary to define curriculum.[1]

Here, it is defined as the *formal mechanism through which educational aims are intended to be achieved, and as such, it embraces all the factors that contribute to content, assessment and evaluation, instruction and learning.*

Instructional leadership is a sub-set of curriculum leadership. It focuses on assessment, evaluation and learning specifically within the context of teaching in the classroom.[2] Clearly curriculum leadership is a sub-set of educational leadership which is an overarching concept that embraces a concern to ensure that the aims of the school are met. It is, therefore, the responsibility of the principal, but given all the things that a principal is expected to do they could hardly undertake the leadership at the shop floor level necessary to introduce a new curriculum such as the transition year. Clearly it requires what is now called distributed management or leadership (see below). At the same time, it is clear that the responsibility for the task is the principal's. Thus the principal has to have a knowledge first of "change" models (i.e how to bring about and maintain change – see chapter 7) and second of the technical pedagogy required to bring about change. If that technical pedagogy does not exist the principal is obligated to facilitate its acquisition among those whose task is curriculum change and/or development. Neither can the principal escape responsibility for the instruction given in the school and in the event of weaknesses being detected to take appropriate action even to the extent of helping teachers in instructional difficulty.

Recent research in Ireland and the United States shows that the task of the principal is so multi-faceted that the principal would necessarily have to delegate the task of curriculum and instructional leadership to others. Exhibit 10.1 summarizes the results of a meta-analysis of research on leadership in the United States that found that Principals' had 21 responsibilities that could influence student performance. Clearly the items could be clustered in different ways. However, teachers in Ireland would have expectations that principals would take responsibilities in all of the areas except items 11, 12, 13 and 14. The NAPD (National Association of Principals and Deputies) in Ireland, however, has clearly come to a view that they should be part of the principal's role. While the practice of 12 and 13 may be delegated, the practice of 15, (inspire and lead new and challenging innovations), in the curriculum area would remain essential. For this the principal would have to have a "technical pedagogy" since its understanding is imperative if curriculum leadership is to function within the schools at all levels. It would require principals to have a defensible theory of learning as well as defensible epistemology. In any case, without that, how could the principal practice item 11-(intellectual stimulation). So what should curriculum and instructional leaders do?

Responsibility	Extent to which Principal
1 Affirmation	Recognises and celebrates accomplishments and acknowledges failures
2 Change Agent	Is willing to challenge and actively challenges status quo
3 Contingent Rewards	Recognizes and rewards individual accomplishments
4 Communication	Establishes strong lines of communication with and among students
5 Culture	Fosters shared beliefs and a sense of community and cooperation

6 Discipline	Protects teachers from issues and influences that would detract from their teaching time or focus
7 Flexibility	Adapts his or her leadership behaviour to the needs of the current situation and is comfortable with dissent
8 Focus	Establishes clear goals and keeps those goals in the forefront of the school's attention.
9 Ideals/Beliefs	Communicates and operates from strong ideals and beliefs about schooling
10 Input	Involves teachers in the design and implementation of important decisions and policies
11 Intellectual stimulation	Ensure faculty and staff are aware of the most current theories and practices and makes the discussion of these a regular aspect of school culture.
12 Involvement in curriculum , instruction and assessment	Is directly involved in the design and implementation of curriculum, instruction and assessment practices
13 Knowledge of curriculum, instruction, and assessment	Is knowledgeable about current curriculum and instruction, and assessment practices.

14 Monitoring/evaluating	Monitors the effectiveness of school practices and their impact on student learning.
15 Optimizer	Inspires and leads new and challenging innovations
16 Order	Establishes a set of standard operating procedures and routines.
17 Outreach	Is an advocate and spokesperson for the school and to all stakeholders
18 Relationships	Demonstrates an awareness of the personal aspects of teachers and staff
19 Resources	Provides teachers with materials and professional development necessary for the successful execution of their jobs.
20 Situational awareness	Is aware of the details and undercurrents in the running of the school and uses this information to address current and potential problems.
21 Visibility	Has quality contact and interactions with teachers and students.

Exhibit 10.1. 21 Responsibilities of Principals derived from a meta-analysis of researches on principal leadership in schools in the United States. Marzano, J., Waters, T and B. A. McNulty (2005). *School Leadership that Works. From Research to Results.* Association for Supervision and Curriculum Development (ASCD), Alexandria, VA. And Mid-Continent Research for Education and Learning, Co. ASCD, Alexandria Va

One answer to this question has been provided by Fitzmaurice who as part of a research for a higher degree investigated his own role as an instructional leader in a four teacher rural primary (elementary) school. At the time when he undertook the study (circa 1995) the term curriculum leader had hardly entered the vocabulary but the term instructional leader had. Its worth noting that in the same year that he published his thesis a book was published in America with the title *"A Handbook for Teacher Leaders.*[3] Fitzmaurice did not have access to that book but he examined a considerable volume of material on educational and instructional leadership, mostly from the United States and found that the terms were very confused. It was moreover, voluminous.[4] From this review he deduced an operational description of the instructional leader. Fitzmaurice's sevenfold profile reads as follows

1. The instructional leader leads others in the process of change through school planning which involves
-Identification of instructional or curriculum areas that need change/improvement/innovation
-Preparation of and planning processes that prepare the ground by pooling resources, selection through consensus, and designing a plan.
-the implementation of change in the classroom.
-Review and assessment.

2 The instructional leader energises and encourages others to focus on the two main concerns of schools- teaching and learning. This is used as the bottom line reference whenever there is controversy or indecision.

3 The instructional leader uses reports, test results, feedback from parents, management, inspectors and pupils to identify areas for instructional improvement.

4. The instructional leader provides resources from a variety of sources to support, maintain or initiate change, improvement and reflection. This may include reports, studies articles, advice, teacher-centres, fellow professionals, support groups, in-service courses and new technology.

5. The instructional leader speaks to and questions teachers about children, teaching, subject areas, problems, projects, concerns and difficulties in their teaching and classrooms. This can be done both formally and informally.

6. The instructional leader supports teachers in their efforts in classrooms by being available to offer advice, opinion, praise, judgement and encouragement to their work and the efforts of children. He/she might encourage the display of projects and provide a public area for this. He/she might check copies or essays on classroom visits.

7. The instructional leader is a reflective practitioner who continually seeks to improve the teaching/learning process in his/her class and throughout the school by constantly asking- what and how can we improve? He she must also lead and train others in this process of reflection so that it becomes school-wide and automatic.

Pellicer and Anderson considered that teacher leaders should help teachers plan instruction, teach effectively and learn from their students. They also suggested that teacher leaders should help teachers to grow professionally, and help teachers develop a system of peer coaching. [5]

Fitzmaurice who was a teaching principal in a four teacher national (elementary) school in rural Ireland wanted to find out if it was possible to carry out the duties of a principal who had to teach through the day, and at the same time, be an instructional leader. The occasion was a good report from an inspection that carried with it a recommendation that the school should do much more science in its curriculum. He described how he persuaded his colleagues over a period of months to design a new curriculum, and found that up to that stage it had been possible for him to be an instructional leader. He was clearly providing curriculum leadership rather than instructional leadership, and that accords with the more precise definitions given here. It is not too difficult to read the same into Pellicer and Anderson's definition of instructional leadership, that is *"the initiation and implementation of planned change in a school's instructional program, supported by various constituencies in the school, that results in substantial and sustained improvement in student learning"*.[6]

Guidance about the abilities required of curriculum/instructional leaders may be obtained from Joseph Schwab who believed that the university-based curriculum specialist should be an educator of school-based curriculum specialists.[7] This was the purpose of the course for which Fitzmaurice undertook his assignment. His view of the abilities required by a curriculum specialist in schools differed little from that of Schwab as Philip Jackson's summary of outcomes shows.[8] The apparent differences between Schwab's thesis and the intentions of the course are shown in italics.

-Skilful use of the rhetoric of persuasion (which includes knowing how to elicit participation in small group settings and person to person encounters). *(A knowledge of the factors influencing change in educational organisations)*.

-Experience in deliberation *(and causing people to deliberate at greater levels than they have before)*.

-Ability to read learned journals and the habit of doing so.

-Ability to guide colleagues in the use of the journals, *and to encourage them to believe that their classrooms are laboratories for valid research.*

-Knowledge of curricular practices *(their design and improvement, including instruction and assessment).*

-Knowledge of the behavioural sciences which contribute to the guidance of educational policy and practice *e.g. branches of psychology and sociology.*

-*Knowledge of the humanities which contribute to the guidance of educational policy and practice e.g. philosophy, and history.*

-*Defensible theories of learning and instruction*

-*Defensible positions in respect of the philosophy and sociology of education.*

-"nodding" acquaintance with the academic fields from which school curricula are drawn.

-*Assist teachers preparing for accountability.*

There are difficulties with this list as my additions show. The first item would pre-suppose that the person is a propagandist for a particular model of the curriculum or instruction. In the case of the latter there may well be empirical evidence to back up the argument. In the case of the former the advocate should be prepared to summarise research in terms of the advantages and disadvantages of particular curriculum and instructional models, as for example when a department is considering change to a problem-based programme. It presupposes a desire to promote a professional pedagogy as a professional activity, and it takes into account the need to have an understanding of the factors that enhance or impede change.

To summarise, both curriculum and instructional leaders require to function in a common technical culture with an accepted body of knowledge (pedagogy) as is the case in other professions like medicine. There are levels of knowledge and practice that distinguish curriculum from instructional leadership. It follows from the definitions given above that instructional leadership relates to the performance of individual teachers in delivering the programmes for which they are responsible. Curriculum leadership relates to the total curriculum of the school and the design, implementation and evaluation of new programmes. Like Pellicer and Anderson the view is taken that *"instructional (/curriculum) leadership does not necessarily begin and end with the principal. Rather, instructional (/curriculum) leadership must come from teachers if schools are to improve and if teaching is to achieve professional status"*.[9] But the principal has overall responsibility for instructional and curriculum leadership, the professional development of teachers, and facilitation of a culture in which such leadership can flower at different levels throughout the school. The questions that arise from curriculum and instructional leadership are questions for assumptional-dialogues.

Levels of Curriculum andInstructional expertise: The School as a Learning Organisation.

Teachers are accountable for what they do to numerous stakeholders of whom the pupil is the most important. Because pupils do not have the knowledge to judge the merits of teachers, the profession has probably a more important role in this respect than do, say the professional organisations that represent medical practitioners. The profession has to act on behalf of pupils. Although it is disputed teachers claim to be professionals (see chapter 8). Therefore, like any other expert profession they have obligation to ensure that beginning teachers have an adequate training that projects them on to the road of curriculum leadership. They also have an obligation to be aware of the pedagogical knowledge that is available to inform the curriculum process in which they are partners.

Given that this is the case it is surprising that the notion that teaching and learning should be informed by research is not high in the minds of teachers. Mostly pedagogical knowledge, if it is perceived to be pedagogical knowledge, is gained from the vagaries of experience. Even then there is little reflective practice. K. Patricia Cross has argued in respect of university teaching, that such teaching will not become a respectable activity until teachers treat their classrooms as laboratories for research,[10] and this applies as much to school teachers as it does to university teachers.

To encourage the development of this idea Tom Angelo and Patricia Cross worked with teachers to develop and evaluate fifty techniques of classroom assessment. They are intended to help *"individual teachers obtain useful feedback on what, how much and how well their students are learning. Faculty* (teachers) *can then use this information to refocus their teaching to help students make their learning more efficient and more effective"*[11] Many of these assessment tasks can be used in post primary education, as for example, the minute paper and concept mapping. The minute paper with its half sheet response *"provides a quick and extremely simple way to collect written feedback on student learning. To use the minute paper, an instructor stops the class two or three minutes early and asks students to respond briefly to some variation on the following two questions: what was the most important thing you learned during the class? And what important question remains unanswered?"* Answers are written on half a sheet of paper.[12] Twenty-four similar, (not all of them identical), techniques for formative evaluation have been described by George and Cowan. [13]

This is a first level of instructional/curriculum expertise it is a level at which the teacher exercises self-accountability. It assumes that a teacher is relatively "effective" and that the purpose of these exercises is to check that effectiveness. It is a level of self-leadership.[14] As such it is level when the ability required is to reflect on ones performance and educational beliefs. A major step is taken if the teacher asks a colleague into his classroom to observe him at work with a view to helping his development. In short it is not too much to ask that teachers who consider themselves to be professional function at this level. Culver (private communication) considers that most teachers operate at a level 0- a point that is self-explanatory.

A second level is reached when a teacher tries to learn through more formal research into her/his classroom practices, and even more generally into other dimensions of the curriculum process. Patricia Cross and Mimi Steadman followed up the earlier Angelo and Cross study to show how this might be done.[15] In Ireland this writer required his post-graduate students to investigate and evaluate their own teaching using a semi-scientific approach. He had two purposes in mind. The first was that the students should purposefully evaluate the theories they learnt about in lectures and texts. The second was that they would learn some kills that would lead them to treat their classrooms as laboratories of research for the improvement of their teaching through better understanding student learning. As with level 1 a major step is taken when two or more teachers agree to undertake such research.

Classroom assessment and classroom research require different levels of expertise. Classroom research requires more knowledge before one can begin. This might be related to a specialist topic (e.g. cooperative learning, teaching mixed-ability classes), concept learning, motivation, and other instructional theories) or, it may be of a more general kind (e.g. the redesign of a curriculum).

Teachers who, in an ethos that values experience above research, spend time on classroom assessment strategies are leading themselves, and by example others. If they try to persuade others that such activities are worthwhile and lead to better practice, they are leading in the traditional understanding of leadership. The same is true of classroom research, the second level of expertise.

More generally part of the role of the professional teacher is to lead beginning teachers into the pedagogy of education. In

Ralph Tyler's words, they have the goal of *"helping practitioners who want to improve the curriculum of the schools in which they work."* [16]

There will be those who have acquired the capability to do this at the first level of expertise. There will be others who can do it at the second level of expertise. Those who take on these leadership roles can help create a climate of cultural change from the bottom up. By themselves such activities cannot be expected to maintain cultural change since they are often due to the initiatives of individuals. In any event those individuals also need support from the top, and this means that those at the top will have to have an understanding of the professional pedagogy. While they may wish to act as curriculum leaders themselves, given the scope of the knowledge required there would seem to be the need to recognise the need for curriculum leaders and leadership in schools who have a third level of expertise. That is the ability to use knowledge at the second level to persuade others to improve their instruction and engage in curriculum activities. Such persuasion requires that change is *"perceived to be intelligible, beneficial, plausible and feasible."* [17] Such expertise involves a developed skill in curriculum making over and above the micro making that takes place during instruction.

At the same time there is other testimony to the fact that while principals may sanction "experiments" if they do not give the teacher(s) continuing support such "experiments" may come to grief. Northfield points out, that principals not only have to sanction an "experiment" but they have to continually support it through the provision of resources, reinforcement and encouragement. They also have to push and nudge.[18] *"For the principal, as for any educative leader, the key features are the leader (as a learner) providing opportunities for participants to develop personal understanding and encouraging the conditions for reflection and practice."*[19]

A key role for the principal is the selection of persons to undertake curriculum responsibilities at this level. For example the coordinators for the Transition year and Leaving Certificate

Applied in Ireland.[20] High level skills in the so-called affective domain will be required for such work by both principal and those appointed. A principal might through curriculum leaders initiate school wide curriculum and instructional policies and evaluations for it is clear that all teachers need to extend their professionality.

The implications of this view are quite profound because teaching (and the teachers' role) should be viewed from the perspective of a learning organisation. Extended professionalism begins with a commitment to learning. This entails the acquisition of a technical pedagogy. The leaders first task is to assist teachers acquire that pedagogy within the framework of a commitment to the school as a learning organization. All professionals have a responsibility for the mentoring of new comers to the profession.As we have seen Cohn and Kottkamp argued that if learning is to be made more meaningful then the assumptions and structures of the prevailing educational system will have to be changed. There is no reason to believe that the performance of educational systems has changed for the better in the period since their book was written. To provide this challenge they proposed that a certain number of schools be established as centres of inquiry into the teaching learning process and the structures that support it in a contemporary context. As we have seen they found a rationale for this in the writings of Schaefer who in 1967 wrote *"we can no longer afford to conceive of schools simply as distribution centers for dispensing cultural orientations, information, and knowledge developed by other social units. The complexities of teaching and learning in formal classrooms have become so formidable and the intellectual demands upon the system so enormous that the school must be much more than a place of instruction. It must be also a center of inquiry-a producer as well as a transmitter of knowledge. One basic fact is our ignorance of teaching. We simply do not know how to master the abstract knowledge and the analytical skills modern society demands. It seems necessary to transform at least some schools into centers for the production of knowledge about how to carry out the job."*[21]

While I do not disagree with these sentiments realism dictates that change has to begin within systems that are publicly controlled by those who have little regard for pedagogy and where teachers and controllers collude to produce systems that are primarily information giving. Some will see that as an impossible task as they did of the Public Examinations Evaluation Project in Ireland.[22] But they were shown through involvement in "experiments" that teacher involvement in the design of public examinations was feasible. This continues to be an issue. It will also be argued that very much more is known about instruction and learning and that much more can be learnt about learning and instruction than teachers have cared to accept.

In the United States one of the few substantial investigations into inquiry based learning funded by the Wallace Foundation provided evidence and illustrations that support this view although the procedures used differ from those discussed in this text. They affirm that it is a *"step toward reclaiming a degree of professionalism and responsibility that is lacking in far too many schools."* [23] In the three approaches they describe the issues of accountability loom large, and those involved including a single classroom teacher engaged themselves in trying to answer the questions "Why do we do what we do? Why do we do it in the way that we do it? How might we do it better? It is with these questions that this text is concerned.

Their view of teachers and teaching at a time when there is a lack *"of respect for both students and teachers, for the subject matter, and for the processes of learning and teaching"* is no different to the view taken here. They write (p 155) that a *"central premise of this [work] and of the inclination to establish collaborative inquiry among teachers in schools is that teachers are fully capable and, in many ways, uniquely situated to achieve these new understandings and invent more effective teaching practices. They need all the help they can get of course. But they don't need someone else to do all of the work for them. In the end, no one can do the work of understanding and invention for anyone else, though we all benefit from the insights of others and can, through collaboration, often solve problems and design new practices that we could barely approach on our own.*" It is argued here that the development of a culture of collaboration is a major task for the educational leader who will require the support of one or more curriculum and instructional leaders.

Relatively simple inquiries in the classroom can have major implications for the curriculum and the way that it is assessed, and for the "theory-in-use" that teachers have.[24] It has been shown that much can be done to improve instruction and facilitate learning even within the constraints of a public examination system. The argument is that teacher "theories-in –use" can only be changed through the acquisition of new knowledge. This may, for example, may be achieved through action research that evaluates the explicit theories and practice made available in the literature and/or *"assumptional dialogues"* that provide *"opportunities to raise awareness and examine largely unrecognized assumptions that currently underlie [the] educational structures and practices [in a school, institution or system] and to generate alternatives to them."*[25] Assumption digging suggest Cohn and Kottkamp often provides the potential to motivate teachers. Thus it is that Cohn and Kottkamp envisioned *"schools as communities of scholar- teachers, where everyone including principals collaborate on action research projects that have the capacity to change the very structure of schools or significant elements within them."*[26] Such schools will of necessity extend the professionalism of the teachers within them and these teachers will take responsibility for beginning teachers.

Leadership skills will also be required for a fourth level of curriculum leadership that requires engagement with the "authorities" responsible for the curriculum and structures, that is, with the external debate that goes on in public outside the school, as for example, the education and training of teachers. Such an engagement would challenge existing assumptions on the basis of research. This view has implications for the type of person selected by organisations such as managerial bodies and trade unions to represent them on organisations that control the curriculum and structures.

At levels three and four those who would seek to implement change need to have knowledge of the factors that inhibit or enhance change.[27]

In this approach technical pedagogy is obtained through increased expertise in research, development and design in curriculum and instruction. It is evidence based leadership skills are acquired from increasing advice and advocacy among ones colleagues and in the outside world.

Notes and references

[1] I am conscious of the fact that there is no escape from the colloquial usage of the term curriculum. Outside of this text the term is used as a function of the context in which it is employed. At one level it is used to describe all subjects (contents) that comprise a course (programme) of studies that an individual pursues. Thus, we speak of the school curriculum. Sometimes the term programme is used instead of curriculum. In the case of degree courses in the British Isles we speak of the subject (or subjects when it is a two subject degree) studied. In this sense subject is being used instead oc curriculum. But within these subjects numerous other subjects may be taken that are often called courses. Sometimes teachers use the term curriculum for the subject they teach. A list of content for such subjects is often called a syllabus. Thus each school subject will have a syllabus. The point is that we know what we mean when we are talking to colleagues. In this paper the term applies to the total process of curriculum design, implementation, assessment and evaluation for either the school curriculum as a whole or a subject within it.

[2] In the British Isles the term 'instruction' is often associated with training, and is not used as an alternative to 'teaching'

[3] Pellicer, L. O. and L. W. Anderson (1995). *A Handbook for Teacher Leaders*. Thousand Oaks, CA. Corwin Press.

[4] FitzMaurice, J. MSt Thesis. School of Education, University of Dublin. See also the July 2001 issue (Volume 29 No 3) of *Educational Management and Administration* which is devoted to leadership although it is focused on problems in Britain. It was published at a time when the National College for School Leadership established by the British government was getting under way.

[5] *loc.cit.*

[6] *ibid*

[7] Schwab, J. J. (1978) *Science, Curriculum and Liberal Education. Selected Essays, Joseph J. Schwab*. Ed by I, Westbury and N. J. Wilkof. Chicago. Chicago University Press

[8] Schwab, J. J. (1983). The Practical 4. Something for curriculum professors to do. *Curriculum Inquiry*, 13, (3), 239-265

[9] *loc.cit*

[10] Cross, K. P. (1986). A proposal to improve teaching or "what taking teaching seriously should mean. *AAHE Bulletin*, September pp 9-14.

[11] Angelo, T and P. Cross (1993) *Classroom Assessment Techniques*. 2nd edition. Jossey Bass, San Fransisco.

[12] *ibid* p 148.

[13] George, J and J. Cowan (1999). *A Handbook of Techniques for Formative Evaluation.* Kogan Page, London.

[14] In many ways this is a combination of what Gardener calls intra-personal and inter-personal intelligence. The first relates to understanding of one's self and the second to the reading of the intentions and desires of the student's' in the teacher's class. Gardener, H (1985) *Frames of Mind. The Theory of Multiple Intelligences.* Basic Books, New York. P 239.

[15] Cross, K. P. and M. Steadman (1996). *Classroom Research.* San Fransisco, Jossey Bass.

[16] Tyler, R. W. (1949). *Basic Principles of Curriculum and Instruction.* Chicago. Chicago University Press.

[17] Northfield, J (1992) Leadership to Promote Quality in Learning in P. Duignan and R. J. S. McPherson (eds) *Educative Leadership. A Practical Theory for New Administrators and Managers.* Falmer Pre, London, p 90

[18] *ibid* pp 99 –100. Northfield lists the activities required under each of these headings.

[19] *ibid* p 100.

[20] This is a year between the formal ending of compulsory post primary education at 15+ years (or thereabouts) and the beginning of senior cycle education in post-primary schools to the age of 18 or thereabouts. The students are expected to pursue a programme designed by the school that will enable them to learn life skills. They continue with about 20% or so of the time devoted to traditional studies. The ending of compulsory education is accompanied by a public examination set by the State called the Junior Certificate. Separate examinations are set for each subject of the curriculum. The students may take as many subjects as they wish (i.e. perceived to be capable of). Some subjects (eg mathematics) are set at three levels so as to cater for the whole population. A similar examination is set at the end of the senior cycle called the Leaving Certificate. This is set at two levels Honours and Ordinary. Points are awarded according to the level taken and the grade awarded at that level in each subject. The aggregate of the points taken for all subjects is the basis of selection to university. In order to encourage students from the whole range of ability to continue their education in senior cycle a Leaving Certificate Applied Examination was introduced with a somewhat different content and subject basis and with grades determined from a considerable component of coursework assessment. Teachers were given much more responsibility in this course.

[21] *loc. cit* Cohn and Kottkamp pp 363-364 citing Schaefer, R. J. (1967). *The School as a Center of Inquiry.* Harper and Row, New York. p 2.

[22] Heywood, J., McGuinness, S., and D. E. Murphy (1980). *Final Report of the Public Examinations Evaluation Project.* University of Dublin, Dublin.

[23] Weinbaum, A et al (2004) *Teaching as Inquiry. Asking hard Questions to Improve Practice and Achievement.* Teachers College, Columbia University, New York and National Staff Development Council, Oxford, Ohio.

[24] Cohn and Kottkamp draw on work by Argyris and Schon on organizational learning who point out that it is the "theory in use" that determines the behaviour of individual or organizational action. In this case it relates to teachers theories of discipline, learning, knowledge and the curriculum. Cohn and Kottkamp point out that these theories –in-use are deeply embedded and the assumptions on which they are based are not easily articulated. What matters in this text is that it is understood that many teachers reject the theories of curriculum, instruction and learning taught in their education courses in favour of modules that fit the prevailing climate of instruction in schools.

[25] *ibid.* Cohn and Kottkamp p 266

[26] *ibid* p 283.

[27] A point that is both illustrated and supported by Cohn and Kottkamp as well as in many other studies.

CHAPTER 11

RETROSPECT AND PROSPECT

Retrospect

After the second-world war a major dimension of research in behaviour in organizations was its focus on what motivated people to work. At the same time there were some major studies of what motivated students to learn. Some studies like those on achievement motivation spanned both industry and learning in schools and higher education. These investigations followed in the wake of pre-second world war studies of behaviour at work commonly known as the "Hawthorne" studies or investigations. Among other things those investigations had highlighted the importance of social relationships at work. Thus began the development of alternative ways to the managerialism of Fayol and Taylor[1] to the understanding the nature of work and the meaning that work had for individuals. Attention focused on the worker as a person a feature that was consistent with the work of humanistic psychologists such as Carl Rogers[2] and Abraham Maslow[3] whose work continues to be influential.

The major text that set the tone for the nineteen-sixties was the *"Human Side of Enterprise"*. In that work McGregor described two theories of worker motivation which he labelled "Theory X" and "Theory Y."[4] Schein described a model of the "rational-economic man" that corresponds with theory X and is consistent with the tenets of managerialism.[5] He pointed out that what we believe about how people are motivated or how they learn will inform our behaviour toward them and condition the arrangements we make for their learning and motivation. A Theory X style of management or learning will lead to structures that have a high degree of control over what is done, sometimes to the point of coercion. A classroom will have its desks organised so that they all face a dais behind which is a blackboard (whiteboard) and on which is the teacher's desk. It is designed for chalk-and-talk or rote teaching. It is designed to ensure that the class is highly disciplined. In contrast a Theory Y classroom is more likely to have tables and chairs that can be organised either for chalk and talk teaching or for co-operative learning where the teacher is a facilitator rather than a controller. Theory X is in the lineage of Taylorism and theory Y is in the lineage of self-actualization.

Of course Schein recognised that the model of the self-actualising man that comes from Maslow's theory does not give an adequate explanation of why people are motivated to work and taking account of the various models that he had described he proposed a model of the complex individual. The same model is easily translated to show the complexity of reasons that make a person want to learn. In Britain Daniel and McIntosh concluded that the critical question was not the one that was frequently posed of -*"what are people really interested in or most interested in job satisfaction and intrinsic rewards than money and extrinsic rewards,* (which is the essential dichotomy between Theory X and Theory Y), *but rather when they are interested in intrinsic rewards and when they are interested in extrinsic rewards."*[6] It was argued that this applies to learning as much as it does to work. To put it in the way of another British research sometimes people are prepared to have an instrumental attitude to work for the monetary rewards that it brings. The meaning that life has for them is obtained outside their work.

Following in the tradition of Maslow, Herzberg[7] and his colleagues found that the factors that satisfied professional people at work related to such things as achievement and recognition whereas the factors that diminished job satisfaction, (they called them hygiene factors), were such things as company policy and administration, and salary.

These studies continue to be of interest. In the last decade there has been research that has sought to understand teacher attrition and retention in terms of these two factors. The role of principals (head teachers) has also been investigated in these terms. Experienced teachers on post-graduate courses who have chosen to examine the management style of the principals with whom they have worked have often used Theory X and Theory Y to describe their pictures of these principals. And some have related them to the authoritarian and democratic personalities that were much discussed at the time.

During the nineteen fifties The Tavistock Institute of Human Relations[8] described a theory of social-technical systems. They had found that technology created social systems that were sometimes an impediment to work and sometimes enhanced work. In this respect the organization of a classroom is a social-technical system.

In the same period there was also considerable interest in the factors that assisted and impeded innovation in firms. A Scottish study found that when companies were more hierarchically organized like a bureaucracy they were less likely to innovate than companies that were less bound by hierarchical structures and more, to quote, "organistically" organized.[9] A similar conclusion was reached from a Harvard Business School inquiry that found (following Von Bertallanfy) that organizations that were relatively open systems were likely to be more productive than those that were relatively closed systems.[10] The two studies complemented each other in that the closed system was hierarchically organized and the open system enabled both vertical and lateral communication. Moreover, its engineers followed the jobs that became available and were not confined to their specialisms as were the engineers in the hierarchically organised operation.

Again, in Ireland at least one study of a limited number of schools with different organizational structures lent support to the findings of the Scottish study. Also, In Ireland where there is competition for students among schools the concept of open and closed systems has been found to be of value. Case studies show that marketing should not simply be the preparation of a glossy brochure but like the cell that has to change because it is open to its environment so to do schools have to look at their internal working to see if they need to change.

In the long run neither schools or industrial organizations can survive if they remain closed and in so far as schools are concerned, even when they are relatively open, there are factors, such as demography, that can lead to their closure. Even so all schools like industrial organizations are the subject of a continuing flow of minor changes to which they adapt without much trouble. It is big changes that cause dissension: changes that lie outside the plausibility structure and challenge the identity of those involved. Big changes in the curriculum often do not survive and as writers on both sides of the Atlantic affirm the curriculum in its broad outline if not in the precise details of content persists and has persisted for a hundred or more years.

If we are to accommodate the demands of change that will be made on us, and at the same time, retain our commitment to the goals of the organization in which we work, we need to understand the factors that contribute to or impede the organization achieving its goals. This is sometimes called organizational learning. So the focus of *Learning, Adaptability and Change* was on the factors that impede and enhance change in education and industry. This revision has focussed solely on educational institutions, in particular schools.

The questions that were asked were

1. Why are some individuals more able to adapt to changing circumstances in the home and at work than others, and what are the circumstances that encourage or inhibit adaptation?

2. Why do some individuals work well in some systems of organization and not in others, and what are the characteristics of organizations that make for effective work?

3. Why are some individuals better able to provide leadership and management than others?

The first principle was that the factors that impede change and innovation in an organization are the same as those that impede and enhance learning in a classroom. We need, therefore, to understand how we learn, and it is incumbent on policy makers, managers, and leaders to create environments in organizations that are conducive to learning.

If we are to teach ourselves to change (to be adaptable) then we have to understand how we interact with people and that begins with how we perceive and respond to the world - this to embrace how we acquire knowledge and how that is shaped by our environment. Among the many factors that shape our perceptions are the ambiguities we find. In schools they often relate to roles and that is one of the reasons that management theorists argue that tasks have to be clearly defined. Even then there may be ambiguity and as our study of engineers at work showed ambiguity helped the firm to function for if the tasks had been specifically other than generally defined the engineers might have been prevented from communicating with others.[11] The essential points are to prevent role conflict through overlapping roles and in tasks that receive the same reward to ensure that they are roughly comparable. One of the problems for principals in the Irish context is how do you get important tasks done when there are no rewards available for their performance.

Such understanding has to take into account learning and personality, and already in the nineteen sixties Argyris and Schön had begun to talk about the mental health of organizations, and organizations as learning systems.[12] And during the nineteen sixties and seventies some engineering educators and their professional societies began to argue that engineers required some tuition in these areas and a few degree programmes offered engineering with management in which the study of behaviour in organizations was incorporated. It was not until the late nineteen eighties that the British Department of Employment tried to persuade universities that all graduates required the personal skills and knowledge necessary for them to work in industry and commerce.[13] And that proposal included teachers.

During the early nineteen seventies we undertook an analysis of engineers in an innovative firm in order to determine objectives for the training of technologists and technicians. The personnel whose tasks were analysed were all called engineers and they ranged from persons dealing with contracts and stores with relatively low levels of qualification to those engaged in research and development with relatively high level qualifications. We found that given our understanding of management and the skills required for direction and control that almost everyone was engaged in management. We did not find any single manager work-type. We found that even at the lower levels individuals had needed to widen the scope of their initial brief through skills of communication and liaison in order to take some action. We found that communication is a complex skill the nature of which varied with the type of activity undertaken. People had to change their roles in order to communicate and we considered that the organization was best considered as a system of persons in relation rather than a set of people in a hierarchy. Had Perkins idea of organizations as conversations between participants been available that analogy would undoubtedly have contributed to our understanding of what was happening, as would the recent work by Jenlink and colleagues on 'design conversation.'[14] All of the tasks required the use of some or another management skill for which action training (within company) could have been given. Take this picture to any other organization, as for example a supermarket, and it will be evident that there is a similar picture: All of which is to suggest that we have the potential to be trained in management skills but not necessarily to manage. Management would seem to be a contingent activity dependent on context. We may find it easier to manage others than ourselves and vice versa.

So when *Learning, Adaptability and Change* came to be drafted the starting point was how from the beginning of life we learn to manage ourselves and sometimes others. Following developments in theories of intelligence such as Sternberg's view of intelligence as the purposive adaptation and selection and shaping of real world environments we could define management as practical intelligence or intelligent behaviour.

Since intelligence is the ability to select and shape the real world in which we live, we too have a responsibility to help those whom we allow to lead and to manage to create that environment. It follows from this that, if this is to come about that a much greater participation in the management of educational institutions will be required if there is to be a creative response to continuing economic and social change. That will require a communality of understanding among management and the managed, in which the principles to be understood relate to adaptability, and thus to learning how to learn in a changing environment.

The present

The case studies reported by experienced teachers who have studied with me over the years show that the principles enunciated in *Learning, Adaptability and Change* continue to have relevance to the understanding of behaviour in schools. They relate especially in the way that teachers and pupils interact with the organizational structures that are in place. But they also provide new insights that merit consideration sufficient to cause the re-ordering of the book so that it only focused on educational issues while taking into account some recent work in general management.

From the perspective of theory, the immediate development, a year or so after the publication of *Learning, Adaptability and Change* was the publication of the *Fifth Discipline; The Art and Practice of Learning Organizations by Senge*. This book continues to have an impact.[15] As is shown in chapter 6 Senge views learning in a somewhat different way to this text. A field book of practical ideas was later published. Together they served to cement the ideas of learning organizations and organizational learning. Educators have developed the idea of professional learning communities.

Second there was a huge growth in the literature on management and leadership in educational institutions and currently the focus is very much on leadership. During that time leadership studies departed from trait and personality theories and began to look at style. Perkins grouped the approaches into four different categories- Answer Centred leadership, Vision Centred Leadership, Inquiry Centred Leadership and Leadership by Leaving Alone, which if a university department is anything to go by is a recipé for anarchy. Included in vision centred leadership are transformational leadership and charismatic leadership. While it seems that transformational leadership has proved to be very attractive Perkins favours inquiry centred leadership, a category that includes servant leadership. It fosters inquiry at various levels through questions, facilitation and establishing community and organizational structures supportive of inquiry. In theory a school is an ideal organization for inquiry and this is the key difference between the twenty- year old book and this text, that is the promotion of the concept of the inquiry-oriented school, and therefore, servant or inquiry oriented leadership. The inquiry-oriented school is seen as a means of extending the professionalism of teaching. So what stands in its way?

Third, and as answer to the question during the last twenty years governments have asserted considerable control over the education system. It was ever thus in Ireland, except in so far as the religious dimension was concerned. But compared with what has happened in Britain it was loosely controlled. In Britain by contrast managerialism of the Taylor type has taken control and there is a desire to micro-manage even to the extent of dictating teaching methods. This reinforces the restricted professionalism that pervades teaching. The assault on professionalism in England is well summarised by another Taylor. He points out that it is supported by skills based teacher training that emphasises the practical and that principle is extended to the training of head teachers. It is very much a nineteenth century model of the training of artisans which was thought to be best done through experience and watching persons judged to be good practitioners. Taylor notes that *"if a major role for head teachers is to manage this technocratic skills-based process, then teachers will have even less discretion to decide what to teach and when to teach it."*[16] Taylor notes that others suggest that the ideal of teacher autonomy before the 1988 act was frequently belied by reality. It was a professional myth. This is consistent with the view of restricted professionalism put in other chapters. Certainly the opportunities were there but they were not taken. He found from a survey of teachers that that some believed their discretion had been radically affected whereas others thought that there was *"always scope for discretion because change creates new situations which demand imaginative responses."* That some teachers find this to be the case should be cause for hope, as does the fact that one primary school challenged prevailing assumptions and dictates to develop its own programme that it thought would improve the school.

Common between the two Governments and indeed in many jurisdictions in the western world has been an emphasis on leadership. In a Green Paper the Irish Government wrote that the *"recent research on the characteristics of effective schools confirms the importance of leadership, teamwork and sound management structures."* And in a White paper that followed *"effective management and leadership at all levels within the school are essential if the school's goals are to be met. The achievement of school effectiveness depends crucially on the leadership offered by experienced and skilled principals, sup-*

ported by vice-principals and post holders."[17] In England and
Wales in 1997 a White Paper stated that *"The vision of learning
set out in this White Paper will demand the highest qualities of
leadership and management from head teachers. The quality of
the head often makes the difference between success or failure
of the school.*"[18] While this acknowledges indirectly the findings of the school effectiveness and improvement movements in
respect of the centrality of the head ' (principal's) role it leaves
open the definitions of leadership and management in this context. Wright has argued that it is a 'bastard' leadership that is
not leadership at all even though the rhetoric and discourse are
similar.[19] It is managerialist. He quotes Glatter to the effect that
leaders are seen as *"conduits of government policy and the content of the field is beginning to be defined by government agencies rather than within the field itself."* Thus in both England
and Ireland agencies have been set up for the training of head
teachers that have to take into account the policy requirements
of government. In this case it is convenient for policy makers to
allow leadership and management to be elusive constructs.

It is true that in Ireland government reports on the primary
curriculum recommend guided discovery learning and compared with the UK the system remains relatively open. There
are no staged assessments, secondary schools are forced to select because of demand but any tests they use are their own.
There are no national tests at 7 and 11. In post-primary education there is relatively little coursework assessment and national
examinations governed by the State are set at the end of the Junior and Senior Cycles. Myths about the best way to get through
these examinations dictate teaching methods to a large extent.
In many respects it is reminiscent of the British system before
the advent of the national curriculum and assessments in 1989.
The really interesting feature that no one has investigated is
why no comparison has been made between the two systems. If
that were to be done much would be revealed about the relative
effectiveness of different political approaches to management.
It is interesting to note that teacher training for post-primary

teaching in Ireland retains the foundation courses of philosophy, sociology and psychology as applied to education.

The problem for governments is that they think they know best, and this is not a prerogative of left or right. Moreover, they cannot guarantee that their policies will be carried out effectively or without unintended consequences. One of the most valuable contributions to the literature on management in education to have been published in recent years comes from Hoyle and Wallace in *Educational Leadership, Ambiguity, Professionals and Managerialism.*[20] Much of what they say is consistent with this commentary. They raise four main areas of contention, and they relate the ironies associated with each. (I am conscious that there is a fifth but it is of a different dimension to the others). The first issue of concern is that too little notice is taken of the fact that all organizations are *"characterized by ambiguities, dilemmas and incommensurable values."* They would argue that I have not made as much of the issue of ambiguity that I should have for my emphasis was on ruling out some ambiguities that were unnecessary in organizations and in my view made them less effective. I make no apologies for this although in the brief reference to our studies of engineers at work I made the point that the existence of ambiguities was sometimes beneficial to the functioning of the operation. Indeed in my own experience as a progress chaser of the manufacture of prototypes in an a small batch assembly line I was dependent on the good will of the employers for there were no rules for such production. Later in a research unit craftsmen in a model shop would suggest how a design could be developed. In both cases, I and many others who were in functional tasks that required line assistance were in ambiguous positions where interpersonal skills were at a premium. My concern in the sections on ambiguity was primarily for its potential to create conflict.

If I have one regret it is that I have made to little of the view of the idea that there is a perfect organization, be it in industry or education is nonsense! It follows that management/leadership is messy and sometimes very messy.

Hoyle and Wallace argue that a rational approach to policy making demands that ambiguities be removed. The purpose of the educational reforms in Britain has been to remove ambiguity through *"tightly specifying the work of head teachers and teachers, coupled with equally tight surveillance and punitive measures for failure to meet specification."* This is of course belief in the model of the rational-economic person or Theory X. It assumes that head teachers (principals) and teachers are not rational and need to be controlled.

Their second concern is with the view, some might say fallacy, that a continuing flow of legislated reform will produce the responses that are required. They give examples of how failed reforms are followed by other reforms that seek to remedy the defects of previous reforms and so it goes on. But strangely and this echoes the findings of Cuban and Jenkins on the curriculum *"the educational enterprise- learning and teaching-has remained relatively untouched."*

The third area of contention is that school staff are encouraged to make radical change in circumstances were the constraints imposed by the same policy makers are such as to make radical change nigh impossible. And in this context they single out the idea of transformational leadership. In an echo of Wright's 'bastard leadership they say *"transformation at the school level means in practice, finding more efficient ways of implementing government policy."* But that should not ignore the possibility that a principal can inspire teachers in the educational dimensions of their job. There is evidence in the case studies that they do.

Fourthly they suggest that head teachers in Britain rather than rejecting educational reforms have acted as mediators to make the reforms congruent with needs of their schools. They call this stance one of principled infidelity. One of their examples is of particular interest. *"A widespread manifestation of the ironic response of principled infidelity occurred in relation to the Technical Vocational Education Initiative (TVEI) which ran from 1983 to the introduction of the National Curriculum in 1988. It gave rise to what Helsby (1988) termed the 'paradox of TVEI.' Essentially the irony resided in the subversive use of government funds by head teachers and teachers to reintroduce some of the very aspects of the curriculum and pedagogy, such as interdisciplinary studies and discovery methods, which had been the target of reform."*[21] Whether or not this is an irony, it is certainly a paradox. On the one hand the policy of the Department of Education was to concentrate on standards which it, and many newspapers thought were best achieved by 'traditional' teaching methods. During this period the idea of a tightly controlled national curriculum was developed. Yet, because of complaints by industry and commerce and the need to provide a trained workforce the government asked the Manpower Services Commission, (which might be regarded as an arm of the Department for Employment), to implement a voluntary initiative to better prepare 14 to 18 year olds for work. These TVEI programmes would have to emphasise initiative, motivation, enterprise and problem solving skills. The carrots for those who volunteered were the large monetary rewards that were made available.[22] Head teachers were clearly attracted by these rewards which could be utilised throughout the school, and for many teachers the only way to pursue these goals was through non-traditional methods of teaching that many would regard as more liberal than those being promoted by the 'traditional teaching movement' in the media. How subversive this was is a moot point. A similar sort of paradox is to be found in 1989 when the same government introduced the Enterprise in Higher Education Initiative in higher education on a voluntary basis for universities. It was argued that the requirements led to a better liberal education than was previously the case.[23] The universities happily took the money.

Not withstanding Hoyle and Wallace's point we are reminded again of the major problem faced by all educators that everyone thinks they know how to teach. The paradox is that in the absence of evidence that is either disregarded or not sought policy makers propose laudable aims such as the view that students should be taught to think critically while at the same time encouraging teaching methods that will not bring it about. Schools are left to pick up the pieces.

Hoyle and Wallace do not pretend to have written a detached account of their argument. Nevertheless it is compulsory and at times compulsive reading. They have certainly illustrated all the games that people play as they navigate themselves through life's particular circumstances. They attach no blame to anyone. They believe that policy makers, principals (head Teachers) and teachers act in good faith and have the moral purpose of improving education but their sympathies lie with the *"head teachers and teachers who persist, despite the power of external forces, in doing their best for their students."* They invite discussion about the model that resulted from their thinking.

In response to that question let me take up some points. It seems to me that there is considerable confusion between managerialism and good management just as there seems to be an irrational fear of all things to do with industry and commerce. Few teachers have experience of either. In *Learning, Adaptability and Change* I incorporated a chapter on wealth creation and the need for achievement to try and demonstrate the importance of industry and commerce. Without the wealth they create there would be no education system, and that is why one of the goals of education has to be preparation for working life with the object of producing people who will want to improve that dimension of their lives.

During my working life it is the business schools that have been seeking to understand what makes good management. There is, as I hope I have shown, and a recent paper by Hallinger and Snidvongs[23] lends support to the view that educators have much to learn from good management practices in industry. For example, there is no more useful monograph for introducing concepts of teamwork than Smith's book on team work and project management.[24]

In chapter 9 when discussing Perkins view of answer-led or transactional leadership I took a somewhat cynical view that it could be aligned with theory X. If, however it is taken to mean effective management or administration then it becomes important. In the introduction I pointed out that Leithwood had deduced that transformational management fails unless it is supported by good management which he called transactional.[25] If a distinction is made between management and leadership as many are won't to do then good management makes leadership possible. The opposite makes leadership impossible. The implication for training programmes is profound for as Hallinger and Snidvongs argue like MBA's they have to focus on both management and leadership.[26] That has been the intention of this book. It is based on the theory that there is nothing great or wonderful about management or leadership. They are things we all do all of the time and it is evident that the skills we posses for these activities can be developed. Our success will be very much dependent on the context in which we have to deploy them. What it can give us, and what we can give it will depend on many factors. Management education should give us the opportunity to explore what they might be.

Prospect

In all walks of life there are swings and roundabouts. It is quite likely that there will be a reaction against the micro-management of educational systems, but when is anyone's guess. It might be brought about when it is realised that the large sums of money that are being put into reforms are having very little effect, in Hoyle and Wallace's terms "marginal." They do not deny that some reforms have been beneficial but they argue that "perpetual revolution" alienates rather than motivates and that is the message of organizational theory as represented in this text. One of the problems of perpetual revolution is that some good initiatives are stopped. The TVEI referred to by Hoyle and Wallace would seem to this writer to be a case in point.

The trouble is that it suffered from problems of recognition. It is a problem for the Leaving Certificate Applied in Ireland, a programme that bears many similarities with TVEI. There is insufficient recognition of the powerful social pressures specific to particular cultures, in particular those related to the selection of students for university places when making curriculum reforms.

As we have seen Hoyle and Wallace conclude that all organizations are characterized by endemic ambiguity and we have to learn to live with it. But that is life! While much of life is spent trying to remove ambiguity equally there are times when we create ambiguity in order to move on, or prevent others from finding us out! Those of us who take Rokeach's[27] position that generally we want to know the truth will tend not to hide behind ambiguity for open-mindedness demands that this should be the case. In the area of examinations and assessment there can only be a limited tolerance of ambiguity unless it is cleared in the rubrics. Students' perceptions of a question have to be similar if their answers are to be judged. Unfortunately this can all too easily lead to the demand for objective type tests only. Assessment systems necessarily have to be multi-strategy if they are to test a wide-range of student capability. Today, the BBC tells us that oral language tests in the national school exams are too difficult and will be replaced with continuous assessment with all the ambiguities that that involves.

But the removal of ambiguities from an assessment system should not mean the declaration and death by a thousand outcomes (or standards as they are called in the US). It does mean clarity not mystery about what is meant by such domains as creativity and critical thinking.

Neither does the fact that we live in situations of ambiguity absolve us from personal and professional accountability. In teaching that means first of all self-appraisal. It is a continuing act of management and leadership on the individual's part. It also means that an act of management and leadership is to allow someone else to participate in the process at some stage. That is, for a peer or a superior to conduct a 'positive appraisal.' That is the action of a professional person. But 'positive appraisal' has to be undertaken for the purpose of renewal not for the purpose of judgement. 'Positive appraisal' implies that we set ourselves an objective or a limited number of objectives to be achieved in a given time; say a school year. If they are not achieved we need to understand why, and sometimes they may have to be changed. A 'positive appraisal' that does not evaluate the objectives is senseless. Equally senseless is the demand that objectives for which the resources are not available should be achieved. The purpose of 'positive appraisal' should be to encourage the development of professionalism through reflective practice, this to mean the participation in practices that extend professionalism.

As indicated above Hoyle and Wallace argue that there may well be a deceleration in the reform movement in the UK because it will be found that the cost-benefits are marginal, especially the costs of surveillance. There is an equally powerful analogy that is, if you tighten the strings of musical instruments too much they snap. Too much stress on a system or a person causes a breakdown and the systems pendulum swings in the opposite direction. The trouble is that the pendulum can swing hard in the opposite direction and all sense of control is lost and this causes the cycle to start all over again. Once again the merits of comparing the situation in Britain to that in Ireland come to the fore. The other extreme is where 'positive appraisal' is thought to be impossible and accountability unnecessary. This has been the position of the teacher unions in Ireland. For example the Department of Education and Science is not required in law to publish league tables. Slowly matters are changing and it is to be hoped that there is not a violent swing to the extremes of the British reforms.

The *modus vivendi* that Hoyle and Wallace seek is in what they call "Temperate management." It means a *"temperate approach to leadership and management, fostering teacher's freedom to teach within broad consensual established limits"*. (p 198). In their summary paper they write that temperate management would be *"characterized by a reduction in managerial activity by making the primary focus of leaders the support of teachers-taking the strain and absorbing the stress, and by an emphasis on incremental, local improvement. Our appeal for temperance is far less likely to stir the blood than the intemperate rhetoric of transformation connoting a radical and ambitious change in educational goals and the means of achieving them, a rhetoric that currently dominates educational management discourse. But temperate leadership and management are far better attuned to the ironies of practice and policy with which teachers must deal in endeavouring to improve pupil's learning in the contingent circumstances of their individual classrooms."*[28]

This is what the case studies I have examined and my conversations with teachers would lead me to believe that Irish teachers would want their principals to be. But I suspect that that is really a statement that in so far as what I do is concerned, the principal should leave me alone. There are differences between the expectations of teachers of their principals in the primary, secondary and vocational sectors.

The key function of temperate leadership in the British system is to absorb so that the non-teaching duties that have been imposed on teachers are reduced. This is somewhat different to Ireland where the impositions on teachers are somewhat less. Indeed Irish teachers who have experience of the English system remark on the amount of paperwork that teachers in that country have to do. It is true that Irish teachers do expect principal's to take the stress but this does not show that there is no need for positions of responsibility to do particular tasks. There is a danger, at least this is my observation of primary school principals that they become overburdened and stressed with the executive (as opposed to strategic) tasks they have to perform. It is my observation that many principals want the time that will help them and their teachers to improve their practices and many seem to achieve this goal. For example *"[...] An appraisal of the role of the Principal of X primary school must make reference to his strong belief in the theory of learning by experiment and discovery. Experiment and discovery are the twin axis of his teaching methodology. This twin axis is to the forefront of his teaching at all times. I use the word 'teaching' in its widest context. I am not just referring to his class teaching but I am also referring to the manner he has taught, not only his fellow teachers but also the various educational partners."*

And later

"X primary school prides itself on being progressive and proactive. Its clear and distinct vision is forever to the fore. It boasts of a wide ranging, inclusive, child-centred curriculum where the needs of the child, in his or her environment, are of paramount importance. The key to the success of the school lies in the centrality of concept sharing – sharing of vision, sharing of management and sharing of responsibility. All of this stems from the fact that the Principal is progressive and proactive." [...] *"He adheres to, and is a strong advocate of, shared management. One of his many fortes is his ability to recognise, foster and encourage the talents of others and to use those talents for the betterment of the school as a whole. He acknowledges that we all have something to contribute to the task of management and encourages his staff to do so. He believes that for the school to achieve maximum effectiveness all the educational partners must partake in the task of management. Being a firm advocate of innovation he is forever conscious of factors that may impede this and when they arise he is prompt, in a spirit of collegiality, to eliminate or neutralise them. During a period of rapid and radical change he has proven adept at adapting himself to the ever changing needs of the modern primary school."*
29

Is this transformational or visionary leadership or is it inquiry-oriented leadership? Some may believe that it is a bit of each. It would certainly seem to be balanced, especially since we are told that this principal shared with his staff his difficulties in developing the RSE programme. He had personal reservations about the programme. He found it difficult to talk about the ideas in the programme that he put down to the generation from which he came. Moreover he had some moral reservations about some of the content of the programme. Yet we are told that he took responsibility for the lack of progress which caused him concern. Is this temperate leadership? It is certainly balanced and a reminder that we are likely to demand too much of principals as the tasks listed in exhibit 10.1 would suggest.

Hoyle and Wallace also take the view that there is room for those who try to make big moves. This is supported by those case studies that have described the progress of schools under different principals. At times different styles of leadership are required. The problem is that whether or not the right person is in the right place at the right time is luck. Often the problem is that management style and teacher expectations diverge. Principals have to able to change styles to fit the situation. It is clear that no principal can ever be perfect. They have to live with the same ambiguities as their colleagues. The problem for the 'many' is finding the time to join with their colleagues in improvement when they are bound up solving the continuous flow of unexpected problems. For others there is a question of having the appropriate knowledge to pursue the task.

Hoyle and Wallace do not use the terms restricted and extended professionalism but they regard the principal (head teacher) as ensuring that the teachers in their care behave and act professionally. While they may be able to provide for the external professional development of members of their staff in the UK the funds for this do not exist in Ireland so the problem becomes how do they promote professional learning among their colleagues within the institution. A temperate leader will *"convey a general expectation of learning without over-spec-ification."* A teacher said that he had had a wish to introduce shared reading. To put his "vision" into practice the first step on the journey *"was to sell my concept to my Principal. While I anticipated at the time that this task would not prove difficult I had not envisaged the extent to which he would put flesh and bones of my vision [...] I am now on the way to seeing my vision brought to fruition [...] What I had hoped would be a shared vision is fast becoming a shared reality [...]"* In 'management speak' this is job enrichment. They both display the characteristics of instructional leadership, and it is in the area of classroom practice that there is the possibility of job enrichment.

In that context the Irish White Paper drew attention to the need for instructional leadership. It said, *"The Principal is central in shaping the aims of the school and to creating the supporting structures, which promote the achievement of those aims. This underlines the crucial importance of principal's instructional leadership role. She or he facilitates the creation of a high-quality learning environment and mobilises staff, individually and collectively, to establish educational objectives, to support their continuous achievement and to evaluate and learn from experience."*[30]

Two concepts have been put forward in this text to accomplish such goals: the self-renewing school and the inquiry oriented school. The one complements the other. These it was argued would create the conditions for the development of extended professionalism. But for that they will require curriculum and instructional leadership and that cannot be the function of the principal alone. The personnel in such schools would necessarily consider organization to be a process rather than a structure written in stone and imposed top-down so temperate leadership would be open to other forms of organization and Hoyle and Wallace cite distributed leadership, and communities of practice as examples. An inquiry-oriented school would surely be a community of practice. And so the ambiguities of terminology continue! But so to does the need for temperate management and leadership that embraces not only the generalities of school life but curriculum and instruction as well.

Notes and references

[1] Taylor, F. W. (1911) *The Principles of Scientific Management*. Harper, New York.

[2] Rogers, C (1961). *On Becoming a Person*. Houghton Mifflin, Boston.

[3] Maslow, A (1964) *Motivation and Personality*. Harper and Row, New York.

[4] McGregor, D. M. (1960). *The Human Side of Enterprise*. McGraw Hill, New York.

[5] Schein E. H (1965)(1975). *Organizational Psychology*. Prentice hall, Englewood Cliffs, NJ.

[6] Daniel, W.W. and N. McIntosh (1972). *The Right to Manage*. Macdonald and Janes, London.

[7] Herzberg, F., Mausner, B., and B Synderman (1959). *The Motivation to Work*. Wiley, New York.

[8] See articles by Emery, F. E and E. L. Trist in F. E. Emery (ed). *Systems Thinking*. Penguin, Harmondsworth.

[9] Burns T and G. Salker (1961) *The Management of Innovation*. Tavistock, London.

[10] Barnes, L. B (1960) *Organizational Systems and Engineering Groups*. Harvard School of Business Administration, Cambridge MA. Von Bertalanffy, L (1966) The theory of open systems in F.E. Emery (ed) *Systems Thinking*. Penguin, Harmondsworth.

[11] Youngman, M. B., Oxtoby, R., Monk, J. D and J. Heywood (1978). *Analysing Jobs*. Gower, Aldershot.

[12] Argyris, C (1965) *Organization and Innovation*. Dorsey, New York.

[13] *Enterprise in Higher Education Initiative*. (1989) Employment Department, Sheffield. Brochure.

[14] Perkins, D (2003). *King Arthur's Round Table. How Collaborative Organizations create Smart Organizations*. Wiley New York. See also Jenlink, P.M and B. H. Banathy (2008) *Dialogue as a Collective Means of Design Conversation*. Sprimger, New York. Is of particular interest because it analyses different kinds of dialogue and shows their relevance in different kinds of discourse. Clearly in an organization there are many kinds of discourse. Some will impede and some enhance learning.

[15] Senge, P. M (1990) *The Fifth Discipline. The Art and Practice of the Learning Organization*. Doubleday, New York.

[16] Taylor, I (2007). Discretion and control in education. The teacher as street-level Bureaucrat. *Educational Management, Administration and Leadership* 35, (4), 555 – 572.

[17] Department of Education (1992). *Education for a Changing World*. Green Paper. Government Publications, Dublin.

[18] Department of Education and Employment (1997) *Excellence in Schools*. Cmnd 3681. HMSO, London.

[19] Wright, N (2001) Leadership 'bastard' leadership and managerialism. *Educational Management and Administration* 29 (3), 275 – 290. The term bastard leadership comes from an analogy with a term used by historians to describe a change in Feudalism

[20] Hoyle, E and M. Wallace (2005) *Educational Leadership. Ambiguity, Professionals and Managerialism*. Sage, London.

[21] Hoyle, E and M. Wallace (2007) Educational Reform. An Ironic Perspective. *Educational, Management, Administration and Leadership*.35, (1), 9 – 25.

[22] See for an example the use of TVEI funds in the development of technology studies that clearly had a beneficial effect on teaching and learning. Hill, G (1986) An electronics course established under the Technical Vocational Education Initiative in Heywood, J and P. Matthews (eds) *Technology, Society and the School Curriculum. Practice and Theory in Europe*. Roundthorn, Manchester pp 125 –146.

[23] Heywood, J (1994). *Enterprise Learning and its Assessment in Higher Education*. Technical Report No 20. Learning Methods Branch, Employment Department, Sheffield.

[23] Hallinger, P and K Snidvongs (2008). Educating Leaders. Is there anything to learn from business management. *Educational management, Administration and Leadership*, 36, (1), 9 – 32.

[24] Smith, K. A (2004) *Teamwork and Project Management*. 2nd edition. McGraw Hill, New York.

[25] See endnote 4 of the introduction.

[26] *loc cit*. They consider that modern business management courses will include sections on functional knowledge, problem solving, global perspectives, leadership, ethical judgement and decision making, adaptability, self-reflection and personal development, communication, managing information and technologies and management competency.

[27] Rokeach, M (1960) *The Open and Closed Mind*. Basic Books, New York.

[28] *ibid*

[29] From a case study

[30] Green paper

Name Index

Subject Index